# Microsoft® SQL Server™ 2000 Performance Optimization and Tuning Handbook

# Microsoft® SQL Server™ 2000 Performance Optimization and Tuning Handbook

Ken England

**Digital Press**
An imprint of Butterworth-Heinemann

Boston • Oxford • Auckland • Johannesburg • Melbourne • New Delhi

**Library of Congress Cataloging-in-Publication Data**

England, Ken, 1955–
    Microsoft SQL server 2000 performance optimization and tuning handbook / Ken England.
        p. cm.
    Includes index.
        ISBN 1-55558-241-9 (pbk. : alk. paper)
        1. Client/server computing. 2. SQL server. 3. Relational databases. I. Title.

    QA76.9.C55 E635 2001
    005.75'85—dc21

                                    2001017498

**British Library Cataloging-in-Publication Data**

A catalogue record for this book is available from the British Library.

The publisher offers special discounts on bulk orders of this book.
For information, please contact:

Manager of Special Sales
Butterworth–Heinemann
225 Wildwood Avenue
Woburn, MA 01801-2041
Tel: 781-904-2500
Fax: 781-904-2620

For information on all Butterworth–Heinemann publications available, contact our World Wide Web home page at: http://www.bh.com.

10  9  8  7  6  5  4  3  2  1

Printed in the United States of America

To Margaret, Michael, and Katy

# Contents

# 3    Indexing                                                                51

# 4    The Query Optimizer                                                       119

# 5    SQL Server 2000 and Windows 2000                                          227

# 6    Transactions and Locking                                                  275

# 7    Monitoring Performance                                                    329

# *Preface*

My last SQL Server performance book was aimed at SQL Server 6.5. When Microsoft released SQL Server 7.0 it was almost as if it were a new product. Although it was backward compatible in many areas with SQL Server 6.5, the architecture was very different. For starters, the on-disk structure was completely changed. The usage of files was much improved over SQL Server 6.5, and SQL Server 7.0 now had an 8 Kb database page size. The query optimizer was greatly enhanced with many new query plans possible, in particular in the use of multiple indexes and table joins. The query processor could also now execute complex queries in parallel. As well as all these changes and many more, Windows 2000 was beginning to slowly appear on the horizon.

For these reasons, I decided that upgrading a SQL Server 6.5 performance and tuning book to SQL Server 7.0 was not going to be a trivial task and would be much more than an editing exercise. I decided that my goal would be to work with SQL Server 7.0 through its lifetime in my usual performance-tuning-consultancy capacity and not rewrite the book until I felt confident with the way the new architecture behaved. Of course, nothing stays still for long with software, especially Microsoft software, and so the actual book-writing goal was to write a SQL Server 2000 version.

SQL Server 2000 has added many useful enhancements to SQL Server 7.0, but it is still the SQL Server 7.0 architecture and, therefore, behaves pretty much in the same way. I say to my students that if you know SQL Server 7.0, you pretty much know SQL Server 2000.

So here goes—the follow-up to the SQL Server 6.5 performance and tuning book. I hope you like this updated SQL Server 2000 version.

The chapters are written to follow one another in a logical fashion, building on some of the topics introduced in previous chapters. The structure of the chapters is as follows:

- Chapter 1 introduces the goals of performance tuning and the elements of the physical database design process including data volume analysis and transaction analysis. It also introduces the example BankingDB database.

- Chapter 2 describes the SQL Server storage structures including database files, databases, database pages, and extents.

- Chapter 3 introduces clustered indexes and nonclustered indexes. How data is inserted and retrieved and choosing the appropriate index for a given situation are discussed.

- Chapter 4 introduces the query optimizer and steps in the query optimization process. This chapter also discusses the special approach to query optimization used by stored procedures.

- Chapter 5 looks at the interaction between SQL Server and Windows 2000 in the areas of CPU, memory, and disk I/O. How to track down and remove bottlenecks is explored.

- Chapter 6 introduces SQL Server locking mechanisms and strategies and the methods and tools available for monitoring locks.

- Chapter 7 looks at performance monitoring and the tools available to assist the database administrator.

- Chapter 8 provides a performance tuning aide-mémoire.

I really enjoy tuning databases and making them run fast. Even more, I really enjoy taking an elusive performance problem, tracking it down, and fixing it. I hope you, too, find the same level of enjoyment that I do and that this book kick-starts your interest in performance tuning SQL Server.

# *Acknowledgments*

Most of all, I would like to thank Margaret, Michael, and Katy England for their long suffering while I was locked in my study writing this text. Writing about databases is, unfortunately, not an activity in which most of the family can join in. Because of this, writing and being sociable are usually mutually exclusive!

Margaret had to spend many a weekend anchored to the house. Michael missed out on computer game time, kicking a ball around, and tinkering with our old Series II Land Rover. He was very patient while his dad kept disappearing in front of a PC for protracted periods of time. Katy missed out on company while she watched cartoons.

Also an apology to Holly, my German Shepherd, who missed out on many walks. It's best not to annoy German Shepherds too much!

As well as the friends and colleagues who encouraged me with the book, I would like to give an extra special thanks to the following people.

A very special thank you to Keith Burns, who always has a bubbling enthusiasm for SQL Server; Nigel Stanley and the folk at ICS Solutions for helping to put SQL Server on the map; Dave Gay from Microsoft (UK), an old friend, who stimulates my grey matter through many deep discussions; Chris Atkinson from Microsoft, another old friend, who has helped me out on many occasions and has also stimulated my grey matter; and also, Doctor Lilian Hobbs, a database comrade-in-arms, and Doctor Jeff Middleton for debating many SQL Server and related topics while on 20 mile hikes!

I would also like to thank Karl Dehmer, Lori Oviatt, and Adam Shapiro from Microsoft Training Development, who came all the way over to the United Kingdom to teach an absolutely superb SQL Server 6.5 performance tuning and optimization course a few years ago. Their enthusiasm then for SQL Server performance tuning rubbed off on me and gave me a much-needed boost to complete the SQL Server 6.5 book and now this one. Another special thanks goes to friends at Butterworth–Heinemann. Many thanks to our other friends in Microsoft, without whose skill and hard work SQL Server 2000 would not be the excellent product it is today.

Ken England
January 2001

# Introducing Performance Tuning and Physical Database Design

## 1.1    What is performance tuning?

What is the goal of tuning a SQL Server database? The goal is to improve performance until acceptable levels are reached. Acceptable levels can be defined in a number of ways. For a large online transaction processing (OLTP) application the performance goal might be to provide subsecond response time for critical transactions and to provide a response time of less than two seconds for 95 percent of the other main transactions. For some systems, typically batch systems, acceptable performance might be measured in throughput. For example, a settlement system may define acceptable performance in terms of the number of trades settled per hour. For an overnight batch suite acceptable performance might be that it must finish before the business day starts.

Whatever the system, designing for performance should start early in the design process and continue after the application has gone live. Performance tuning is not a one-off process but an iterative process during which response time is measured, tuning performed, and response time measured again.

There is no right way to design a database; there are a number of possible approaches and all these may be perfectly valid. It is sometimes said that performance tuning is an art, not a science. This may be true, but it is important to undertake performance tuning experiments with the same kind of rigorous, controlled conditions under which scientific experiments are performed. Measurements should be taken before and after any modification, and these should be made one at a time so it can be established which modification, if any, resulted in an improvement or degradation.

What areas should the database designer concentrate on? The simple answer to this question is that the database designer should concentrate on those areas that will return the most benefit. In my experience, for most database designs I have worked with, large gains are typically made in the area of query and index design. As we shall see later in this book, inappropriate indexes and badly written queries, as well as some other contributing factors, can negatively influence the query optimizer such that it chooses an inefficient strategy.

To give you some idea of the gains to be made in this area I once was asked to look at a query that joined a number of large tables together. The query was abandoned after it had not completed within 12 hours. The addition of an index in conjunction with a modification to the query meant the query now completed in less than eight minutes! This magnitude of gain cannot be achieved just by purchasing more hardware or by twiddling with some arcane SQL Server configuration option. A database designer or administrator's time is always limited, so make the best use of it! The other main area where gains can be dramatic is lock contention. Removing lock bottlenecks in a system with a large number of users can have a huge impact on response times.

Now, some words of caution when chasing performance problems. If users phone up to tell you that they are getting poor response times, do not immediately jump to conclusions about what is causing the problem. Circle at a high altitude first. Having made sure that you are about to monitor the correct server use the System Monitor to look at the CPU, disk subsystem, and memory use. Are there any obvious bottlenecks? If there are, then look for the culprit. Everyone blames the database, but it could just as easily be someone running his or her favorite game! If there are no obvious bottlenecks, and the CPU, disk, and memory counters in the System Monitor are lower than usual, then that might tell you something. Perhaps the network is sluggish or there is lock contention. Also be aware of the fact that some bottlenecks hide others. A memory bottleneck often manifests itself as a disk bottleneck.

There is no substitute for knowing your own server and knowing the normal range of System Monitor counters. Establish trends. Measure a set of counters regularly, and then, when someone comments that the system is slow, you can wave a graph in front of him or her showing that it isn't!

So, when do we start to worry about performance? As soon as possible, of course! We want to take the logical design and start to look at how we should transform it into an efficient physical design.

# 1.2    The physical database design process

Once the database logical design has been satisfactorily completed, it can be turned into a database physical design. In the physical design process the database designer will be considering such issues as the placement of data and the choice of indexes and, as such, the resulting physical design will be crucial to good database performance. The following two important points should be made here:

1.  A bad logical design means that a good physical design cannot be performed. Good logical design is crucial to good database performance, and a bad logical design will result in a physical design that attempts to cover up the weaknesses in it. A bad logical design is hard to change, and once the system is implemented it will be almost impossible to do so.

2.  The physical design process is a key phase in the overall design process. It is too often ignored until the last minute in the vain hope that performance will be satisfactory. Without a good physical design, performance is rarely satisfactory and throwing hardware at the problem is rarely completely effective. There is no substitute for a good physical design, and the time and effort spent in the physical design process will be rewarded with an efficient and well-tuned database, not to mention happy users!

Before embarking on the physical design of the database, it is worth stepping back and considering a number of points, as follows:

■  What kind of system are we trying to design? Is it a fast online transaction processing (OLTP) system comprised of perhaps hundreds of users with a throughput of hundreds of transactions per second (TPS) and an average transaction response time that must not exceed two seconds? Is it a multigigabyte data warehouse, which must support few online users but must be able to process very complex ad hoc queries in a reasonable time, or is it a combination of the two?

The type of system will strongly influence the physical database design decisions that must be made. If the system is to support OLTP and complex decision support, then maybe more than one database should be considered—one for the operational OLTP system and one, fed by extracts from the operational OLTP system, to support complex decision support.

- What are our hardware and budget constraints? The most efficient physical database design will still have a maximum performance capability on any given hardware platform. It is no use spending weeks trying to squeeze the last few CPU cycles out of a CPU bound database when, for a small outlay, another processor can be purchased. Similarly, there is little point purchasing another CPU for a system that is disk I/O bound.

- Has the database design been approached from a textbook normalization standpoint? Normalizing the database design is the correct approach and has many benefits, but there may be areas where some denormalization might be a good idea. This might upset a few purists, but if a very short response time is needed for a specific query it might be the best approach. This is not an excuse for not creating a normalized design. A normalized design should be the starting point for any effort made at denormalization.

- How important is data consistency? For example, is it important that if a query rereads a piece of data within a transaction it is guaranteed that it will not have changed? Data consistency and performance are enemies of one another, and, therefore, if consistency requirements can be relaxed, performance may be increased.

How does a database designer move from the logical design phase to a good physical database design? There is no single correct method; however, certain information should be captured and used as input to the physical design process. Such information includes data volumes, data growth, and transaction profiles.

## 1.2.1    Data volume analysis

It is very important to capture information on current data volumes and expected data volumes. Without this information it is not even possible to estimate the number and size of the disk drives that will be required by the database. Recording the information is often a case of using a simple spreadsheet, as shown in Table 1.1.

This may appear to be a trivial operation, but it is surprising how few database designers do it. It is also interesting to find the different views from business users on what the figures should be! Another column that could be added might represent how volatile the data is in a particular table. The percentage annual growth of a table might be zero, but this may be because a large amount of data is continually being removed as well as being added.

**Table 1.1**     *Capturing Simple Data Volume Information*

| Table Name | # of Rows | Row Size | Space Needed | % Annual Growth | Space Needed in 12 Months |
|---|---|---|---|---|---|
| Accounts | 25,000 | 100 | 2,500,000 | 10 | 2,750,000 |
| Branches | 100 | 200 | 20,000 | 5 | 21,000 |
| Customers | 10,000 | 200 | 2,000,000 | 20 | 2,400,000 |
| Transactions | 400,000 | 50 | 20,000,000 | 25 | 25,000,000 |

Simple addition of these figures gives the data size requirements, but this is only part of the calculation. The database designer must take into account the space required by indexes, the transaction log, and the backup devices; no experienced database designers would ask for the disk space that came out of the sum in Table 1.1. They would, of course, add on a percentage for safety. Users typically do not phone you to complain that you oversized the database by 20 percent; however, they do phone you to complain that the system just stopped because the database was full!

So how are the size of indexes calculated? The *Creating and Maintaining Databases* online book gives sample calculations to assist in the sizing of tables, as well as clustered and nonclustered indexes with both fixed, and variable-length columns. It is highly recommended that these calculations are performed, and it is worth using a spreadsheet such as Microsoft Excel to perform the calculations in order to save time and effort. Watch the newsgroups for stored procedures in circulation that do these calculations. Also check out the SQL Server resource kits. At the time of writing the Microsoft BackOffice 4.5 Resource Kit contains a tool named data sizer, which will assist in the sizing of databases.

A rule of thumb is to double the size of the user data to estimate the size of the database. Crude though this appears, by the time indexes and some space for expansion have been added, double the size is not far off!

What about the size of the transaction log? This is difficult to size, since it depends on the write activity to the database, frequency of transaction backups, and transaction profiles. Microsoft suggests that about 10 percent to 25 percent of the database size should be chosen. This is not a bad start, but once the system testing phase of the development has started the database designer can start monitoring the space use in the transaction log with dbcc sqlperf (logspace). The transaction log space is a critical resource and running out of it should be avoided.

Unfortunately, many factors contribute to transaction log growth. These include the rate per second of transactions that change database data and the amount of data these transactions change. Remember that in an operational system, if a transaction log backup fails for some reason, the transaction log will continue to fill until the next successful transaction log backup. It may be desirable to have a transaction log large enough so that it can accommodate the failure of one transaction log backup. Replication failures will impact the effectiveness of transaction log backups, and, of course, there is always the user who runs a job that updates a million-row table without warning you.

For all these reasons, do not be tight with transaction log space. With the price of disk space as it is, a transaction log can be created with a large amount of contingency space.

Finally, do not forget that as a database designer/administrator, you will need lots of disk space to hold at least one copy of the production database for performance tuning testing. Not having a copy of the production database can really hinder you.

So, we now have documented information on data volumes and growth. This in itself will determine a minimum disk configuration; however, it is only a minimum, since transaction analysis may determine that the minimum disk configuration will not provide enough disk I/O bandwidth.

If data volume analysis is concerned with the amount of data in the database and the space it needs, transaction analysis is concerned with the way in which data is manipulated and at what frequency.

## 1.2.2   Transaction analysis

Data in the database may be manipulated by code, such as Visual Basic, or a tool such as Microsoft Access, or a third-party product accessing SQL Server. Whichever way the data is accessed, it will presumably be as a result of a business transaction of some kind. Transaction analysis is about capturing information on these business transactions and investigating how they access data in the database and in which mode. Table 1.2 shows some attributes of a business transaction it might be useful to record.

Clearly, by their very nature, it is not possible to capture the information shown in Table 1.2 for ad hoc transactions nor is it practical to capture this information for every business transaction in anything other than a very simple system. However, this information should be captured for at least the most important business transactions. By most important we mean those

**Table 1.2**    *Capturing Transaction Attributes*

| Attribute | Explanation |
| --- | --- |
| Name | A name assigned to the transaction |
| Average frequency | Average number of times executed per hour |
| Peak frequency | Peak number of times executed per hour |
| Priority | A relative priority assigned to each transaction |
| Mode | Whether the transaction only reads the database or writes to it also |
| Tables accessed | Tables accessed by the transaction and in which mode |
| Table keys | Keys used to access the table |

transactions that must provide the fastest response times and/or are frequently executed. A business transaction that runs every three months and can be run during a weekend is unlikely to appear on the list of most important transactions!

It is important to prioritize transactions, since it is virtually impossible to be able to optimize every transaction in the system. Indexes that will speed up queries will almost certainly slow down inserts.

An example of the attributes captured for a transaction are shown in Table 1.3.

**Table 1.3**    *Example Transaction Attributes*

| Attribute | Value |
| --- | --- |
| Name | Order Creation |
| Average frequency | 10,000 per hour |
| Peak frequency | 15,000 per hour |
| Priority | 1 (high) |
| Mode | Write |
| Tables accessed | Orders (w), Order Items (w), Customers (r), Parts (r) |
| Table keys | Orders (order_number), Order Items (order_number), Customers (cust_number), Parts (parts_number) |

**Table 1.4**    *Capturing Simple Transaction Analysis Information*

| Transactions/Tables | Orders | Order_items | Parts | Customers |
|---|---|---|---|---|
| Customer inquiry | | | | R |
| Order inquiry | R | R | | |
| Order entry | I | I | R | R |
| Customer inquiry | | | | cust_number |
| Order inquiry | order_number | order_number | | |
| Order entry | order_number | order_number | parts_number | cust_number |

There are various ways to document the transaction analysis process and some modeling tools will automate part of this documentation. The secret is to document the important transactions and their attributes so that the database designer can decide which indexes should be defined on which tables.

Again, it is often a case of using simple spreadsheets, as shown in Table 1.4.

The first spreadsheet maps the transactions to the mode in which they access tables; the modes are I for insert, R for read, U for update, and D for delete. The second spreadsheet maps the transactions to the key with which they access tables. Again, there is nothing complex about this but it really pays to do it. Depending on how the system has been implemented, a business transaction may be modeled as a number of stored procedures, and, if desired, one may wish to use these instead of transaction names.

It is also important when considering the key business transactions not to forget triggers. The trigger accesses tables in various modes, just as the application code does.

Data integrity enforcement using declarative referential integrity should also be included. Foreign key constraints will access other tables in the database and there is nothing magical about them. If an appropriate index is not present, they will scan the whole table like any other query.

Once the transaction analysis has been performed, the database designer should have a good understanding of the tables that are accessed frequently, in which mode, and with which key. From this information one can begin to derive the following:

- Which tables are accessed the most and therefore experience the most disk I/O?

- Which tables are written to frequently by many transactions and therefore might experience the most lock contention?

- For a given table, which columns are used to access the required rows; that is, which common column combinations form the search arguments in the queries?

In other words where are the hot spots in the database?

The database designer, armed with this information, should now be able to make informed decisions about the estimated disk I/O rates to tables, the type of indexes required on those tables, and the columns used in the indexes.

Relational databases, and SQL Server is no exception, are reasonably easy to prototype, so there is no excuse for not testing the physical design you are considering. Load data into your tables, add your indexes, and stress your database with some representative Transact-SQL. See how many transactions a second you can perform on a given server or, to look at it another way, how much disk I/O does a named transaction generate? Which resource—CPU or disk—do you run out of first?

Start stress testing with simple experiments. Jumping in at the deep end with many users testing complex functionality is likely just to confuse the issue. Begin with simple transactions issued by one user and then try more complex transactions.

Do not forget multiuser testing! Lock contention cannot be tested unless some kind of multiuser testing is performed. In its simplest form this might involve persuading a number of potential users to use the test system concurrently by following set scripts while performance statistics are monitored. In its more sophisticated form this might involve the use of a multiuser testing product, which can simulate many users while running automated scripts.

Transaction analysis and performance testing can be approached in a much more sophisticated way than has been described above. The important point, however, is that it should be done—the level of sophistication being determined by the available resource, be it time or money.

Again, note that physical design and performance testing are ongoing activities. Systems are usually in a constant state of flux, because business requirements are usually in a constant state of flux. Therefore, performance should be regularly monitored and, if necessary, the database tuned.

### 1.2.3   Hardware environment considerations

The previous section described preproduction performance testing. This should have given the database designer a feel for the hardware requirements of the production system. Obviously, there is a hardware budget for any project, but it is clearly critical to have sufficient hardware to support the workload of the system. It is also critical to have the correct balance and correct type of hardware.

For example, there is no point in spending a small fortune on CPU power if only a small amount of money is spent on the disk subsystem. Similarly, there is no point in spending a small fortune on the disk subsystem if only a small amount of money is spent on memory. Would the application benefit from a multiprocessor configuration or a single powerful processor?

If the application's main component is a single report that runs through the night but must be finished before 9:00 A.M., a single powerful processor might be a better choice. On the other hand, if the application consists of a large number of users in an OLTP system, a more cost-effective solution would probably be a multiprocessor configuration.

Take a step back and look at the application and its hardware as a whole. Make sure the system resource is not unbalanced and do not forget the network!

## 1.3   Where to next?

Once we have performed our data volume and transaction analysis we can start to consider our physical design. We will need to decide what transactions need to be supported by indexes and what type of index we should use. Chapter 3 discusses indexes in detail, but before we look at indexes we need a more general view of the storage structures used in SQL Server, and these are covered in the next chapter.

# SQL Server Storage Structures

## 2.1 Introduction

A developer of application code is probably quite content to consider a SQL Server as a collection of databases containing tables, indexes, triggers, stored procedures, and views. As a database designer and a person who will be responsible for the performance of those databases, it is useful to be able to look a little deeper at the storage structures in SQL Server. A lot of the internals of SQL Server are hidden and undocumented, but we can still learn a fair amount about the way the product works. This chapter investigates the storage structures that SQL Server uses and the methods available to view them.

## 2.2 Databases and files

A database contains all the tables, views, indexes, triggers, stored procedures, and user data that make up an application. A SQL Server will typically host many databases. Usually individual databases are backed up, restored, and integrity checked, so a database can also be thought of as a unit of administration. Because a database is the container for our objects, we will need to spend some time here looking at how databases are structured and managed. We will then drill down into the database files and investigate database pages and other structures.

A database resides in one or more operating system files, which may reside on FAT, FAT32, or NTFS partitions depending on the operating system. These operating system files are known in SQL Server terminology as database files. These database files may be used to hold user and system tables (data files) or track changes made to these tables (transaction log files). There can be as many as 32,767 files per database and 32,767 databases hosted by a SQL Server. A database can be as large as 1,048,516 terabytes (TB). A data file in a database can be as large as 32 TB and a transaction log file as large as 4 TB. Of course, most sites will never come remotely close to these numbers, but it is nice to know that there is plenty of headroom!

The files used by a SQL Server 2000 database belong exclusively to that database. In other words, a file cannot be shared by databases. Also, a file cannot be used to hold both data and transaction log information. This means that a database must consist of a minimum of two files. This is a much cleaner model that used in previous versions (prior to SQL Server 7.0).

There are three file types associated with a SQL Server 2000 database, as follows:

1.    The primary data file is the starting point of the database and contains the pointers to the other files in the database. All databases have a single primary data file. The recommended file extension for a primary data file is an .mdf extension.

2.    Secondary data files hold data that does not fit on the primary data file. Some databases may not have any secondary data files, while others have multiple secondary data files. The recommended file extension for secondary data files is an .ndf extension.

3.    Log files hold all of the log information used to recover the database. There is at least one log file for each database. The recommended file extension for log files is an .ldf extension.

The primary data file will hold the system tables and may hold user tables. For most users, placing all their database tables in this file and placing the file on a suitable RAID configuration will be sufficient. For some users, their user tables may be too large to place in a single file, since this would mean that the file would be too large to place on one of the storage devices. In this case, multiple data files—a primary and multiple secondary files—may be used. User tables would then be created and populated. SQL Server would allocate space from each file to each table so that the tables were effectively spread across the files and, consequently, the physical storage devices.

Figure 2.1 shows a simple database topology using a single file to hold the system tables and user tables and a single file for the transaction log. The files reside on separate physical storage devices, which may be single disks or RAID configurations. RAID configurations are discussed in Chapter 5.

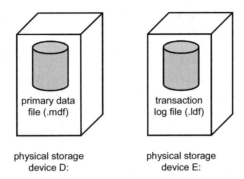

**Figure 2.1**
*A simple database topology*

Figure 2.2 shows a more complex database topology using multiple files to hold the system tables and user tables and multiple files for the transaction log. The files reside on separate physical storage devices, which may be single disks or RAID configurations.

For those users with even greater database performance and size requirements, filegroups may be used. The role of a filegroup is to gather data files together into collections of files into which database tables, indexes, and

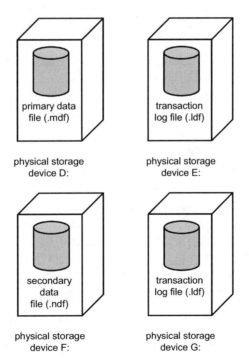

**Figure 2.2**
*A more complex database topology*

text/image data can be explicitly placed. This gives the database administrator great control over the placement of these database objects. Perhaps two database tables that are very heavily accessed can be separated into two filegroups consisting of two sets of data files residing on two sets of physical storage devices. The tables could also be separated from their nonclustered indexes in a similar fashion. Nonclustered indexes are described in Chapter 3. From an administration perspective, individual filegroups can be backed up allowing a large database to be backed up in parts.

Some rules govern the use of filegroups. Transaction logs are never members of filegroups—only data files are. Also, data files can only be a member of one filegroup.

For most users, though, the use of filegroups and multiple data and transaction log files will not be necessary to support their performance and administration requirements. They will use one data file and one transaction log file. Though they will not use user-defined filegroups, even in this simple case the database will contain a filegroup known as the primary filegroup. This will contain the system tables and user tables. It will also be the default filegroup. The default filegroup is the filegroup into which tables, indexes, and text/image data is placed when no filegroup is specified as part of their definition. Any filegroup can be made the default filegroup, and there is a school of thought that advocates always creating a single user-defined filegroup and making this the default filegroup when the database is first created. This ensures that the system tables alone reside in the primary filegroup and all user data resides in the user-defined filegroup in a separate, secondary data file.

## 2.3   Creating databases

Databases can be created by means of the Create Database Wizard, the SQL Server Enterprise Manager, or the Transact-SQL CREATE DATABASE statement. Since the Create Database Wizard is merely a wrapper around the SQL Server Enterprise Manager database creation dialog boxes, it will not be discussed further here. A database may also be created with the SQL-DMO (Distributed Management Objects). Creating a database with the SQL Server Enterprise Manager is accomplished as follows:

1.   Expand the server group and expand the server.

2.   Right-click Databases, then click New Database.

3.   Enter the name of the database and collation on the General tab.

4.    Enter the name, file, size, and attribute information for each data file on the Data Files tab.

5.    Enter the name, file, size, and attribute information for each transaction log file on the Log Files tab.

6.    Click OK.

Depending on how large the database will be, this may take a considerable length of time. In this case using a Transact-SQL script running in the background may be a better bet. The SQL Server Enterprise Manager Database Properties dialog box with the Data Files tab selected is shown in Figure 2.3.

As can be seen in Figure 2.3, various properties can be set for each data and transaction log file. The Filename of the file is the name by which it is referred to within SQL Server—for example, by various system stored procedures such as sp_helpfile. The location is the physical storage location where the file will reside. A filegroup may also be entered for data files other than the primary at this point, in which case the secondary data file will be

**Figure 2.3**
*The Database
Properties dialog
box*

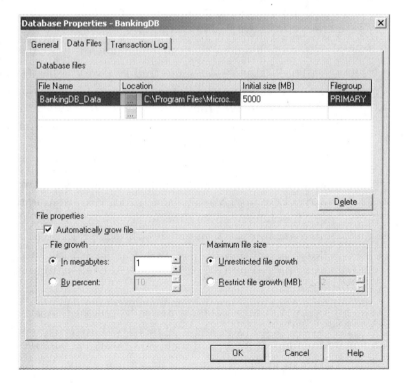

placed in that filegroup. Other attributes of the file relate to size and growth, which will be discussed shortly.

An example of creating a database using the Transact-SQL CREATE DATABASE statement is as follows:

```
CREATE DATABASE BankingDB
ON PRIMARY
(   NAME = BankingData,
    FILENAME = 'd:\data\BankingData.mdf',
    SIZE = 200MB,
    MAXSIZE = 800MB,
    FILEGROWTH = 40MB )
LOG ON
(   NAME = 'BankingLog',
    FILENAME = 'e:\data\BankingLog.ldf',
    SIZE = 100MB,
    MAXSIZE = 500MB,
    FILEGROWTH = 50MB )
```

As with SQL Server Enterprise Manager, a name is specified for the file—this time with the NAME option—and a physical location is specified with the FILENAME option. The ON keyword introduces a list containing one or more data file definitions, and the LOG ON keyword introduces a list containing one or more transaction log file definitions.

The PRIMARY keyword identifies the list of files following it as files that belong to the primary filegroup. The first file definition in the primary filegroup becomes the primary file, which is the file containing the database system tables. The PRIMARY keyword can be omitted, in which case the first file specified in the CREATE DATABASE statement is the primary file.

Regardless of the mechanism by which a database is created, size and growth information may be specified. The *Initial size (MB)* in the SQL Server Enterprise Manager and the SIZE keyword in the CREATE DATABASE statement specify the initial size of the file. In Transact-SQL, the units are, by default, megabytes, although this can be specified explicitly by using the suffix MB. If desired, the file size can be specified in kilobytes using the KB suffix, gigabytes using the GB suffix, and terabytes using the TB suffix.

In SQL Server 2000, when a data file or transaction log file fills it can automatically grow. In the SQL Server Enterprise Manager, a file is allowed to automatically grow by checking the *Automatically grow file* check box. This is, in fact, checked by default. In Transact-SQL, the file, by default, will be allowed to grow unless the FILEGROWTH keyword is set to 0. When a file grows, the size of the growth increment is controlled by the *File growth* property in the SQL Server Enterprise Manager and the FILE-GROWTH keyword in Transact-SQL. The growth increment can be specified as a fixed value, such as 10 megabytes, or as a percentage. This is the percentage of the size of the file at the time the increment takes place. Therefore, the size increment will increase over time. In Transact-SQL, the FILEGROWTH value can be specified using the suffix MB, KB, GB, TB, or %, with MB being the default. If the FILEGROWTH keyword is not specified in Transact-SQL, the default is 10 percent.

The file may be allowed to grow until it takes up all the available space in the physical storage device on which it resides, at which point an error will be returned when it tries to grow again. Alternatively, a limit can be set using the *Restrict filegrowth (MB)* text box in the SQL Server Enterprise Manager or the MAXSIZE keyword in Transact-SQL. The MAXSIZE value can be specified using the suffix MB, which is the default, KB, GB, or TB. The keyword UNLIMITED can also be specified—this is the default.

---

**Note:** Every time a file extends, the applications using the database during the file extension operation may experience performance degradation. Also, extending a file multiple times may result in fragmented disk space. It is advisable, therefore, to try to create the file with an initial size estimated to be close to the size that will ultimately be required by the file.

---

The following example shows a CREATE DATABASE statement, which will create a database consisting of multiple data and transaction log files:

```
CREATE DATABASE BankingDB
ON PRIMARY
( NAME = BankingData1,
  FILENAME = 'd:\data\BankingData1.mdf',
  SIZE = 50MB,
  MAXSIZE = 200MB,
  FILEGROWTH = 25MB),
( NAME = BankingData2,
  FILENAME = 'e:\data\BankingData2.ndf',
  SIZE = 50MB,
  MAXSIZE = 200MB,
  FILEGROWTH = 25MB)
LOG ON
( NAME = BankingLog1,
  FILENAME = 'f:\data\BankingLog1.ldf',
  SIZE = 50MB,
  MAXSIZE = 200MB,
  FILEGROWTH = 25MB),
```

```
( NAME = BankingLog2,
  FILENAME = 'g:\data\BankingLog2.ldf',
  SIZE = 50MB,
  MAXSIZE = 200MB,
  FILEGROWTH = 25MB)
```

The following example re-creates the multiple file BankingDB database created in the previous example, but this time a user-defined filegroup, Filegroup1, is created. Since the file named BankingData2 follows the filegroup definition, it is placed in this filegroup. This means that tables, indexes, and text/image data can be explicitly placed in this filegroup if required. If no filegroup is specified on the object definition, the object will be created in the DEFAULT filegroup, which, unless it is changed, is the primary filegroup.

```
CREATE DATABASE BankingDB
ON PRIMARY
( NAME = BankingData1,
  FILENAME = 'd:\data\BankingData1.mdf',
  SIZE = 50MB,
  MAXSIZE = 200MB,
  FILEGROWTH = 25MB),
FILEGROUP Filegroup1
( NAME = BankingData2,
  FILENAME = 'e:\data\BankingData2.ndf',
  SIZE = 50MB,
  MAXSIZE = 200MB,
  FILEGROWTH = 25MB)
LOG ON
( NAME = BankingLog1,
  FILENAME = 'f:\data\BankingLog1.ldf',
  SIZE = 50MB,
  MAXSIZE = 200MB,
  FILEGROWTH = 25MB),
( NAME = BankingLog2,
  FILENAME = 'g:\data\BankingLog2.ldf',
  SIZE = 50MB,
  MAXSIZE = 200MB,
  FILEGROWTH = 25MB)
```

Various attributes of a database can be modified after it has been created. These include increasing and reducing the size of data and transaction log files, adding and removing database and transaction log files, creating filegroups, changing the DEFAULT filegroup, and changing database options.

These operations are achieved by using the ALTER DATABASE statement, DBCC SHRINKFILE, and DBCC SHRINKDATABASE. These operations can also be changed through the SQL Server Enterprise Manager. Let us first look at increasing the size of a database.

## 2.4   Increasing the size of a database

To increase the size of a database, data and transaction log files may be expanded by using the SQL Server Enterprise Manager or the Transact-SQL ALTER DATABASE statement. Increasing the size of a file in the SQL Server Enterprise Manager is merely a case of entering a new value in the *Space allocated (MB)* text box, as shown in Figure 2.4.

In Transact-SQL, the ALTER DATABASE statement is used, as follows:

```
ALTER DATABASE BankingDB
  MODIFY FILE
   (NAME = BankingData2,
    SIZE = 100MB)
```

Note that file attributes such as MAXSIZE and FILEGROWTH may also be modified with an ALTER DATABASE statement.

**Figure 2.4**
*Increasing the size of a database file*

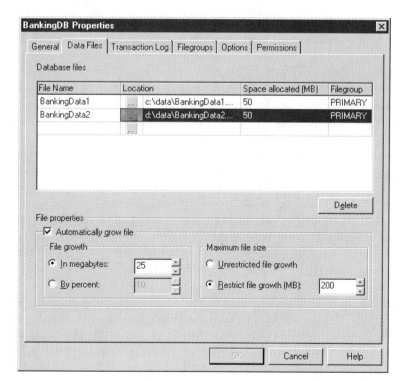

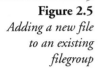

**Figure 2.5**
*Adding a new file
to an existing
filegroup*

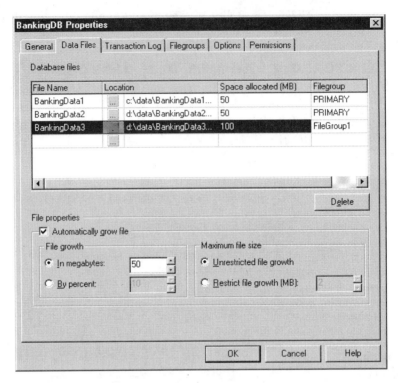

Another way of increasing the size of a database is to add data and transaction log files, as follows:

```
ALTER DATABASE BankingDB
   ADD FILE
   (NAME = BankingData3,
    FILENAME = 'h:\data\BankingData3.ndf',
    SIZE = 50MB,
    MAXSIZE = 200MB,
    FILEGROWTH = 25MB)
```

Note that to add a transaction log file the ADD LOG clause is used.

To add a file to an existing user-defined filegroup, the ADD FILE ... TO FILEGROUP syntax is used, as follows:

```
ALTER DATABASE BankingDB
   ADD FILE
   (NAME = BankingData3,
    FILENAME = 'd:\data\BankingData3.ndf',
    SIZE = 50MB,
    MAXSIZE = 200MB,
    FILEGROWTH = 25MB)
    TO FILEGROUP FileGroup1
```

In the SQL Server Enterprise Manager, adding a new file to an existing filegroup is achieved by selecting the appropriate filegroup from the drop-down *File group* list, as shown in Figure 2.5.

---

**Note:** A file that already exists in the database cannot be subsequently added to another filegroup.

---

## 2.5   Decreasing the size of a database

There are a number of mechanisms that can be used to decrease the size of a database. On one hand, a database can be flagged to allow automatic database shrinkage to occur at periodic intervals. This requires no effort on the part of the database administrator, but it also allows no control. On the other hand, DBCC statements can be used to manually shrink a database or individual database files. These DBCC statements provide the database administrator with the greatest control over how the shrinkage takes place. The SQL Server Enterprise Manager also provides a means to shrink a database or file, and this operation can be scheduled under the control of the database administrator.

Before we look at shrinking a database, it is worth considering why we might want to do so. Obviously, shrinking a database in a way that physically releases space back to the operating system is an attractive proposition if space is limited on the server and disk space must be shared among applications. However, if space is taken away from a database and used by another application, it is no longer available for use by that database. If the database is likely to grow and need the space in the short term, it is pointless releasing the space. Also, the process of expanding the database files in increments, as previously discussed, is not necessarily efficient, since the act of extending the file may impact the performance of applications, and the file extents may end up being fragmented around the disk drive.

However, if a database has grown in an uncharacteristic fashion because a large amount of data has been added and then removed, it makes sense to release the space that is not likely to be needed again. With these thoughts in mind, let us look at how a database and its files can be shrunk.

### 2.5.1   The autoshrink database option

A database option can be set that makes a database a candidate for automatically being shrunk. Database options and how to set them will be discussed shortly. At periodic intervals a database with this option set may be shrunk if there is sufficient free space in the database to warrant it. Note that the database administrator has no control over exactly what happens and when.

### 2.5.2 Shrinking a database in the SQL Server Enterprise Manager

A database can be shrunk using the SQL Server Enterprise Manager, as follows:

1.  Expand the server group and expand the server.

2.  Expand Databases, then right-click the database to be shrunk.

3.  Select All Tasks and Shrink Database.

4.  Select the desired options.

5.  Click OK.

The SQL Server Enterprise Manager Shrink Database dialog box is shown in Figure 2.6.

The dialog box offers the database administrator some options concerning database shrinkage. By choosing to move the pages to the beginning of the file before shrinking, SQL Server will reorganize the data in the database files by relocating pages at the end of the file to the beginning of the file.

**Figure 2.6**
*Shrinking a database using the SQL Server Enterprise Manager*

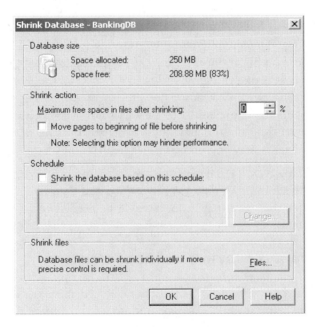

This will typically result in empty pages at the end of the file. Whether this option is chosen or not, SQL Server will truncate the files, releasing the free space at the end of the files back to the operating system. How much free space is not released but kept at the end of the file can be controlled by the option to specify the maximum free space after shrinking. The option to shrink the database on a scheduled basis is also provided.

This dialog box pretty much maps onto the DBCC SHRINKDATA-BASE statement, which will be described shortly. There are two restrictions to bear in mind when using a shrink database operation. First, a database cannot be shrunk in such a way that user data is lost. Second, the files that comprise the database cannot be shrunk past their initial size—that is, the size at which they were initially created. For greater control, the Files button may be mouse-clicked. The Shrink File dialog box is displayed in Figure 2.7.

When a file is shrunk using this dialog box, it can be shrunk below its initial creation size as long as user data would not be lost. Various options allow a finer level of control. The file can be reorganized (compressed) and the free space truncated from the end or the free space truncated from the end without the compression taking place first. The target file size can be set—this option will compress and truncate. There is also an option to migrate data from the file to other files in its filegroup so it can be emptied

**Figure 2.7**
*Shrinking a database file using the SQL Server Enterprise Manager*

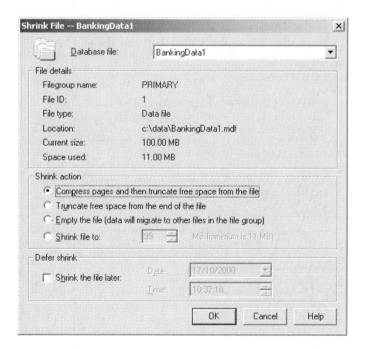

and then removed from the database. The option to shrink the database file on a scheduled basis is also provided. This dialog box pretty much maps onto the DBCC SHRINKFILE statement described in the following section.

### 2.5.3   Shrinking a database Using DBCC statements

The greatest control over database shrinkage is provided by two DBCC statements—DBCC SHRINKDATABASE and DBCC SHRINKFILE. The first statement considers all the files in the database when attempting to shrink it. The second statement only considers the named file.

The SQL Server Enterprise Manager actually executes a DBCC SHRINKDATABASE statement when it is used to shrink a database and a DBCC SHRINKFILE statement when it is used to shrink a database file.

Let us first consider DBCC SHRINKDATABASE. The syntax diagram for this statement is as follows:

```
DBCC SHRINKDATABASE
( database_name [, target_percent]
[, {NOTRUNCATE | TRUNCATEONLY}]
)
```

The target percent parameter is the desired percentage of free space left in the database file after the database has been shrunk. If this parameter is omitted, SQL Server will attempt to shrink the database as much as possible.

The NOTRUNCATE option ensures that any free file space produced by relocating data is kept within the database files and not given back to the operating system. If the database files were examined with Windows Explorer before and after the shrink operation, no change in file size would be observed.

The TRUNCATEONLY option ensures that any free space at the end of the data files is returned to the operating system but no data is relocated within the files. If the database files were examined with Windows Explorer before and after the shrink operation, a change in file size may be observed. The target_percent parameter is disregarded when the TRUNCATEONLY option is used.

If neither of these is specified, data is relocated in the files, and the free space at the end of the files is released to the operating system.

The operation of shrinking a database is not quite as straightforward as it first appears. Various restrictions come into play, and you may not always see shrinkage as large as you may expect. For example, as we have said, a database file cannot be shrunk, using DBCC SHRINKDATABASE, smaller than the size at which it was first created. Also, a database cannot be shrunk smaller than the model database (a DBCC SHRINKFILE can shrink a file smaller than its initial size). Data files and transaction log files are also treated differently. In the case of data files, each file is considered individually. In the case of transaction log files, all the files are treated as if they were one contiguous lump of transaction log.

Of course, a database can never be shrunk smaller than the amount of data it currently holds.

Let us now consider DBCC SHRINKFILE. The syntax diagram for this statement is as follows:

```
DBCC SHRINKFILE
( {file_name | file_id }
{ [, target_size]
| [, {EMPTYFILE | NOTRUNCATE | TRUNCATEONLY}]
}
)
```

The target size parameter is the desired size to which the database file should be shrunk. If this parameter is omitted, SQL Server will attempt to shrink the file as much as possible.

The NOTRUNCATE and TRUNCATEONLY options have the same meaning as DBCC SHRINKDATABASE. The EMPTYFILE option moves the data contained in the file to other files that reside in the same filegroup and stops the file being used to hold new data. This option is most often used to prepare a file for removal from the database. It could not otherwise be removed if it contained data.

### 2.5.4    Removing database files

Files can be removed from the database by using the ALTER DATBASE statement. Neither data files nor transaction log files can be removed from a database if they contain data or transaction log records. In the case of data files, the DBCC SHRINKFILE statement with the EMPTYFILE option can be used to move data out of the file that is to be removed to other files in the same filegroup. This is not possible in the case of transaction log files. The transaction log will have to be truncated to remove transaction log records before the removal of a transaction log file is possible.

**Figure 2.8**
*Removing a file*
*with the SQL*
*Server Enterprise*
*Manager*

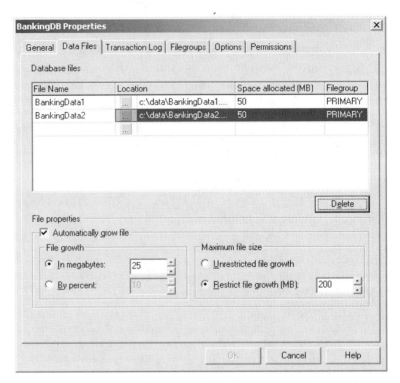

The following example removes a file from the BankingDB database created earlier:

```
ALTER DATABASE BankingDB
   REMOVE FILE BankingData2
```

Remove a file using the SQL Server Enterprise Manager is merely a case of selecting the file to remove and mouse-clicking the Delete button, as shown in Figure 2.8.

A filegroup can also be removed, as follows:

```
ALTER DATABASE BankingDB
   REMOVE FILEGROUP FileGroup1
```

However, a filegroup cannot be removed if it contains files.

## 2.6   **Modifying filegroup properties**

The properties of a filegroup can be changed. Filegroup properties can be READWRITE, READONLY, and DEFAULT. The READWRITE property is typically the property that is set for most filegroups. This means that objects such as tables and indexes in the filegroup can be both retrieved and changed. The READONLY property is the opposite of the READWRITE property in that those objects in a filegroup with the READONLY property set cannot be changed; they can only be retrieved. The primary filegroup cannot have this property set.

The DEFAULT property is by default set on the primary filegroup. A filegroup with this property set is used to store objects whose definition does not include a target filegroup specification. The DEFAULT property can be set on a filegroup other than the primary filegroup, but only one filegroup in a database can have this property set. The following example sets the READONLY attribute on the filegroup FileGroup1:

```
ALTER DATABASE BankingDB
   MODIFY FILEGROUP FileGroup1 READONLY
```

**Note:** Setting the properties READONLY or READWRITE requires exclusive use of the database.

## 2.7  Setting database options

Database options are the attributes of a database and control the way it behaves and its capabilities. The database options are listed in Table 2.1.

To set a database option the SQL Server Enterprise Manager or the ALTER DATABASE statement can be used. The system stored procedure sp_dboption is supported for backward compatibility.

To use the SQL Server Enterprise Manager, do the following:

1.   Expand the server group and expand the server.

2.   Expand Databases, then right-click the database whose options are to be set.

3.   Select Properties.

4.   Select the Options tab and the required options.

5.   Click OK.

The SQL Server Enterprise Manager Options tab is shown in Figure 2.9.

**Table 2.1**   *Database Options*

| Settable Database Options | Meaning |
| --- | --- |
| ANSI null default | This option controls the database default nullability. If a table column is created without specifying NULL or NOT NULL, the default behavior is to create the column with NOT NULL. However, the ANSI standard specifies that the column should be created with NULL. Set this option to follow the ANSI standard. It is recommended that NULL or NOT NULL always be explicitly specified to avoid confusion. |
| ANSI nulls | This option controls the result of comparing NULL values. If it is set, comparisons with a NULL value evaluate to NULL, not TRUE or FALSE. When not set, comparisons of non-Unicode values with a NULL value evaluate to TRUE if both values are NULL. |
| ANSI padding | If ON, strings are padded to the same length before comparison or insert. If OFF, strings are not padded. |
| ANSI warnings | This option controls whether warnings are issued if, for example, NULL values appear in aggregate functions. |
| arithabort | If ON, a query is terminated when an overflow or divide-by-zero error occurs during the execution of the query. |
| auto create statistics | This option controls whether statistics are automatically created on columns used in the search conditions in WHERE clauses. |
| auto update statistics | This option controls whether existing statistics are automatically updated when the statistics become inaccurate because the data in the tables have changed. |
| autoclose | This option controls whether a database is shut down and its resources released when the last user finishes using it. |
| autoshrink | This option controls whether a database is a candidate for automatic shrinking. |
| concat null yields null | This option controls whether NULL is the result of a concatenation if either operand is NULL. |
| cursor close on commit | This option controls whether cursors are closed when a transaction commits. |
| dbo use only | This option controls whether access to a database is limited to members of the db_owner fixed database role only. |
| default to local cursor | This option controls whether cursors are created locally or globally when this is not explicitly specified. |
| merge publish | This option controls whether the database can be used for merge replication publications. |
| numeric roundabort | If ON, an error is generated when loss of precision occurs in an expression. |
| offline | This option ensures that the database is closed and shut down cleanly and marked offline. |

**Table 2.1**   *Database Options (continued)*

| Settable Database Options | Meaning |
| --- | --- |
| published | This option allows the database to be published for replication. |
| quoted identifier | This option controls whether identifiers can be delimited by double quotation marks. |
| read only | This option controls whether a database can be modified. |
| recursive triggers | This option controls whether triggers can fire recursively. |
| select into/bulkcopy | This option allows nonlogged operations to be performed against a database. |
| single user | This option limits database access to a single user connection. |
| subscribed | This option allows the database to be subscribed for publication. |
| torn page detection | This option allows incomplete I/O operations to be detected. |
| trunc. log on chkpt. | This option allows the inactive portion of the transaction log to be truncated every time the CHECKPOINT process activates. |

**Figure 2.9**
*Setting database
options*

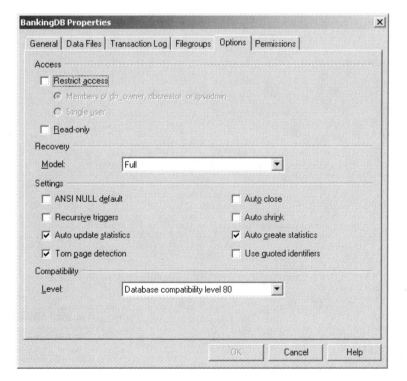

Because some options—for example, replication options—are set by other parts of the SQL Server Enterprise Manager, the options displayed in the Options tab are a subset of the available database options.

The following example sets a database option using Transact-SQL:

```
ALTER DATABASE BankingDB
    SET AUTO_SHRINK ON
```

# 2.8    Displaying information about databases

Information about databases can be obtained through the SQL Server Enterprise Manager or various Transact-SQL statements. We have already seen the properties page that is displayed when a database is right-clicked and Properties selected. This shows us quite a lot of information, including

**Figure 2.10**
*Viewing the details of a database*

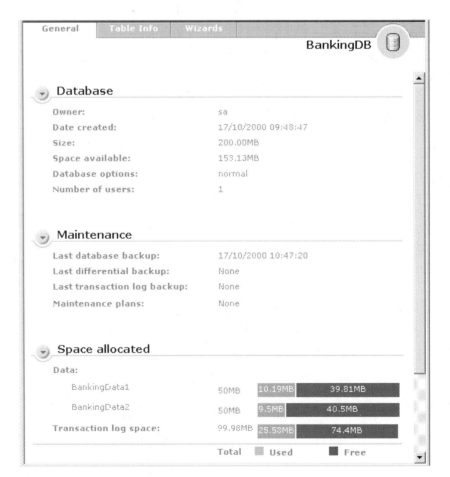

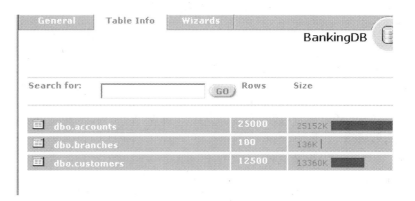

**Figure 2.11**
*Displaying space
allocation
information*

the files that comprise the database. An example of this is shown in Figure 2.4. If a database is mouse-clicked, a taskpad is displayed in the SQL Server Enterprise Manager, as shown in Figure 2.10.

A database administrator can drill down by clicking on, for example, Table Info. The resultant output is shown in Figure 2.11.

In Transact-SQL, the sp_helpdb system stored procedure is very useful. This is as follows:

```
EXEC sp_helpdb

name         db_size      owner   dbid       created       status
----         -------      -----   ----       -------       --------------
BankingDB    1500.00 MB     sa       6    Oct 23 2000    Status=ONLINE…
Derivatives    25.00 MB     sa       8    Oct 18 2000    Status=ONLINE…
master         17.00 MB     sa       1    Oct 12 2000    Status=ONLINE…
model           1.00 MB     sa       3    Oct 12 2000    Status=ONLINE…
msdb            8.00 MB     sa       5    Oct 12 2000    Status=ONLINE…
pubs            3.00 MB     sa       4    Oct 12 2000    Status=ONLINE…
tempdb          2.00 MB     sa       2    Oct 19 2000    Status=ONLINE…
```

This outputs one row for each database on the server. The db_size column is the total size of all the files in the database.

A database name can be specified as a parameter, as follows:

```
EXEC sp_helpdb BankingDB

name         db_size      owner   dbid       created       status
----         -------      -----   ----       -------       --------------
BankingDB    1500.00 MB     sa       6    Oct 23 2000    Status=ONLINE…


Name          fileid   filename                   filegroup   size         maxsize     growth    usage
----          ------   --------                   ---------   ----         -------     ------    -----
bankingdata   1        d:\data\bankingdata.mdf    PRIMARY     1024000 KB   Unlimited   1024 KB   data only
bankinglog    2        d:\data\bankinglog.ldf     NULL         512000 KB   Unlimited   1024 KB   log only
```

This displays information about the files in the database. Other useful system-stored procedures, which can be used to obtain information about files and filegroups, are sp_helpfile and sp_helpfilegroup. Another useful system-stored procedure is sp_spaceused, which returns space use information.

## 2.9    System tables used in database configuration

The configuration of a database is reflected in various system tables held in the master database and the user database. The master database contains a system table, SYSDATABASES, which contains one row for every database resident on the SQL Server. The structure of this system table is shown in Table 2.2.

**Table 2.2**    *The SYSDATABASES System Table*

| Column | Datatype | Description |
|--------|----------|-------------|
| name | sysname | The database name |
| dbid | smallint | The unique ID of the database |
| sid | varbinary(85) | The Windows NT system ID of the database creator |
| mode | smallint | Internal lock mechanism used in database creation |
| status | integer | Database status bits (O = set by sp_dboption):<br>1 = autoclose (O)<br>4 = select into/bulkcopy (O)<br>8 = trunc. log on chkpt (O)<br>16 = torn page detection (O)<br>32 = loading<br>64 = prerecovery<br>128 = recovering<br>256 = not recovered<br>512 = offline (O)<br>1,024 = read only (O)<br>2,048 = dbo use only (O)<br>4,096 = single user (O)<br>32,768 = emergency mode<br>4,194,304 = autoshrink<br>1,073,741,824 = cleanly shut down |

**Table 2.2**     *The SYSDATABASES System Table (continued)*

| Column | Datatype | Description |
|---|---|---|
| status2 | integer | 16,384 = ANSI null default (O) <br> 2,048 = numeric roundabort (O) <br> 4,096 = arithabort (O) <br> 8,192 = ANSI padding (O) <br> 65,536 = concat null yields null (O) <br> 131,072 = recursive triggers(O) <br> 1,048,576 = default to local cursor (O) <br> 8,388,608 = quoted identifier (O) <br> 33,554,432 = cursor close on commit (O) <br> 67,108,864 = ANSI nulls (O) <br> 268,435,456 = ANSI warnings (O) <br> 536,870,912 = full text enabled |
| crdate | datetime | Date when database was created |
| reserved | datetime | Reserved by Microsoft |
| category | integer | Contains a bitmap used for replication: <br> 1 = Published <br> 2 = Subscribed <br> 4 = Merge Published <br> 8 = Merge Subscribed |
| cmptlevel | tinyint | Set by sp_dbcmptlevel—specifies the database compatibility level |
| filename | nvarchar(260) | Location of the primary data file for this database |
| version | smallint | SQL Server internal code version that created the database |

As can be seen, the SYSDATABASES system table contains a column, filename, which points to the primary data file (.MDF) of a database on the server. This is the pointer from the master database to each user database. Once the primary data file of a database has been located, the SYSFILES system table, which resides in every database, can be located. This has one row representing each file—data or log—found in the database.

The SYSFILES system table is shown in Table 2.3.

One other system table found in each database is worthy of note at this point: the SYSFILEGROUPS system table, which contains one row for every filegroup in the database.

The SYSFILEGROUPS system table is shown in Table 2.4.

**Table 2.3**    *The SYSFILES System Table*

| Column | Datatype | Description |
| --- | --- | --- |
| fileid | smallint | Unique identifier for the file within the database |
| groupid | smallint | Identifier of the filegroup to which the file belongs |
| size | integer | File size in (8 KB) database pages |
| maxsize | integer | Maximum file size in (8 KB) database pages. 0 = no growth and -1 = unlimited growth. |
| growth | integer | Growth increment of the file. 0 = no growth. This is in units of 8 KB pages or a percentage, depending on the status column. If the status column contains 0x100,000, then growth is in percentage, not pages. |
| status | integer | Status bits for the growth value in either megabytes (MB) or kilobytes (K):<br>0x1 = Default device<br>0x2 = Disk file<br>0x40 = Log device<br>0x80 = File has been written to since last backup<br>0x4000 = Device created implicitly by the CREATE DATABASE statement<br>0x8000 = Device created during database creation<br>0x100000 = Growth is in percentage, not pages |
| perf | integer | Reserved by Microsoft |
| name | nchar(128) | Logical name of the file |
| filename | nchar(260) | Full path of filename |

**Table 2.4**    *The SYSFILEGROUPS System Table*

| Column | Datatype | Description |
| --- | --- | --- |
| groupid | smallint | Unique identifier for the filegroup within the database |
| allocpolicy | smallint | Reserved by Microsoft |
| status | int | 0x8 = READ ONLY<br>0x10 = DEFAULT |
| groupname | sysname | Filegroup name |

All of these tables can be queried with SELECT statements, but it is easier to use the system stored procedures provided, namely sp_helpdb, sp_helpfile, and sp_helpfilegroup. We have already seen an example of sp_helpdb. Examples of sp_helpfile and sp_helpfilegroup are as follows:

```
EXEC sp_helpfile

Name          fileid  filename                 filegroup   size        maxsize     growth    usage
------------  ------  -----------------------  ----------  ----------  ----------  --------  ---------
bankingdata   1       d:\data\bankingdata.mdf  PRIMARY     1024000 KB  Unlimited   1024 KB   data only
bankinglog    2       d:\data\bankinglog.ldf   NULL         512000 KB  Unlimited   1024 KB   log only

EXEC sp_helpfilegroup

groupname                                                               groupid filecount
----------------------------------------------------------------------  ------- ---------
PRIMARY                                                                     1        1
```

## 2.10   Units of storage

A database is a collection of logical pages, each 8 KB in size. Database pages are always this size and cannot be adjusted by the database designer. The 8 KB page is the fundamental unit of storage and it is also a unit of I/O and a unit of locking (there are other units of I/O and locking).

Tables and indexes consist of database pages. The way that database pages are allocated to tables and indexes is through extents.

An extent is a structure that contains eight database pages (64 KB). Extents are of two types—uniform and mixed. A uniform extent devotes its eight pages completely to one object, for example, a particular table in the database. A mixed extent allows its pages to be used by up to eight different objects. Although each page can only be used for one object, all eight pages in a mixed extent can be used by different objects. For example, a mixed extent can provide space for eight tables. A uniform extent is shown in Figure 2.12, and a mixed extent is shown in Figure 2.13.

**Figure 2.12**
*A uniform extent*

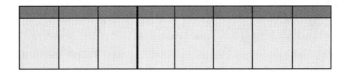

**Figure 2.13**
*A mixed extent*

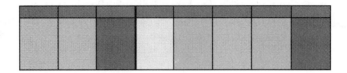

The reason that SQL Server 2000 uses mixed extents is to ensure that a whole eight page (64 KB) extent is not used for a small table. Instead, single pages are allocated to the table one at a time as the number of rows it contains grows. When eight pages have been allocated and more pages are needed, uniform extents are used to allocate eight pages at a time.

To observe the allocation of space to a table, try the following:

1.    Create a table, T1, with a single column of data type CHAR(8000). A single row only can fit onto a database page.

2.    Insert eight rows, one at a time, checking the space allocated to the table with the sp_spaceused system stored procedure after each insert (e.g., EXEC sp_spaceused T1).

3.    Insert another row, checking the space reserved.

What you will find is that after each row is inserted, the data column (the amount of space used by data in the table) is incremented by 8 KB— that is, a single page from a mixed extent. The reserved column (the amount of total reserved space for the table) is also incremented by 8 KB.

**Note:** The reserved column displays 8 KB more than the data column, since a page is used in the table's page allocation to hold a special structure called an Index Allocation Map (IAM), which we will discuss later. This is the 8 KB that is displayed in the Index_Size column. There is no index space actually used, since there is no index on this table.

After eight rows have been inserted, the data column will display 64 KB and the reserved column will display 72 KB. After row 9 is inserted, however, the data column will display 72 KB but the reserved column will display 136 KB. This is because a whole eight page uniform extent has now been allocated to the table, causing the reserved value to jump by 64 KB.

Let us have a quick look at the sp_spaceused system stored procedure.

To see the space allocated to a table use the system stored procedure sp_spaceused, as follows:

```
sp_spaceused branches

name       rows    reserved    data    index_size    unused
-----      ----    --------    ----    ----------    ------
branches   100     72 KB       64 KB   8 KB          0 KB
```

In the above example, sp_spaceused reports that there are 100 rows in the Branches table and that 72 KB or 9 database pages of space have been reserved for it. Out of the 9 pages, 8 pages have been used by the table to store rows and another 1 page has been used for index space which, as mentioned above, is actually used by a IAM page. Note that the system stored procedure sp_spaceused gets its information from the sysindexes system table, which only holds estimates. It does this to avoid becoming a bottleneck at run time, but it can become inaccurate. To synchronize the sysindexes system table with the real space used, execute a DBCC CHECKTABLE or a DBCC UPDATEUSAGE statement, which will scan the table and indexes.

# 2.11 Database pages

Database pages are used for a variety of tasks. Database pages that are used to hold table rows and index entries are known as data pages and index pages, respectively. If the table contains columns of the data type TEXT or IMAGE, then these columns are usually implemented as structures of Text/Image pages (unless the TEXT/IMAGE data is stored in the row). There are other types of pages also, namely Global Allocation Map (GAM) pages, Page Free Space (PFS), and Index Allocation Map (IAM) pages. We will discuss these types of pages shortly.

First, though, let us take out the magnifying glass and take a closer look at a typical page structure. The most common database page we are likely to meet is a data page, so we will use a data page as an example.

The basic structure of all types of database pages is shown in Figure 2.14.

There is a fixed 96-byte page header, which contains information such as the page number, pointers to the previous and next page (if used), and the object ID of the object to which the page belongs. The pointers are needed, because pages are linked together, as shown in Figure 2.15. However, this only happens in certain circumstances, as we shall see in Chapter 3.

What does a data page look like inside? The internal structure of a data page is shown in Figure 2.16. We can see the data rows, but there is also

**Figure 2.14**
*The basic structure
of a database page*

Page 23

**Figure 2.15**
*Pages linked in a
chain*

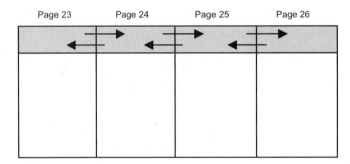

Page 23          Page 24          Page 25          Page 26

**Figure 2.16**
*The internals of a
data page*

Page 23

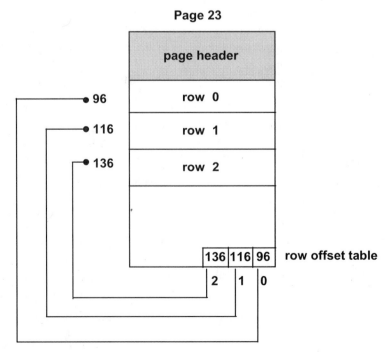

another structure called a row offset table. The row offset table contains two byte entries consisting of the row number and the offset byte address of the row in the page. The first row in our page is at byte offset 96, because of the 96-byte page header. Our row (plus overhead) is 20 bytes in length, so the next row is at byte offset 116 and so on. The row offset table basically gives us a level of indirection when addressing a row. This is important because, as we shall see in Chapter 3, nonclustered indexes may contain pointers to data rows in their leaf-level index pages. Such a pointer is known as a Row ID and is made up of a File ID, database page number, and a row number. The File ID and database page number (a Page ID) take SQL Server to an individual page in a file and the row number and then takes SQL Server to an entry in the row offset table. In our example, the Row ID of the row nearest the fixed page header would consist of the page number, 23, and the row number, 0.

Entry 0 in the row offset table contains byte offset address 96. SQL Server can then use this offset to retrieve the row. Because the Row ID is implemented this way, we can see that a row can change position in the table without the Row ID having to change. All that has to change is the offset address in the row offset table entry. Why would a row change position in a page? In Figure 2.16, if row 1 were deleted, row 2 may move up to row 0 in order to keep the free space in the page contiguous if a new row needed to be inserted. The Row ID for row 2 would not change.

**Note:** SQL Server 2000 will not shuffle rows like this for the sake of it. It will only do so to accommodate new inserts on the page.

What does a data row look like inside? Data rows contain columns of data, as you would expect, but they also contain overhead. The amount of overhead depends on whether the row contains all fixed-length columns or whether there are also variable-length columns. In Figure 2.17 we have the structure of the Accounts table row in our BankingDB database. The Accounts table has five fixed-length columns. The first three columns are of type integer, the fourth column is of type money, and the last column is of type char(400).

The first two bytes are used for status bits. The first status byte holds information that tells SQL Server, for example, whether the row is a primary data row or a forwarded row (described in Chapter 3). A status bit in

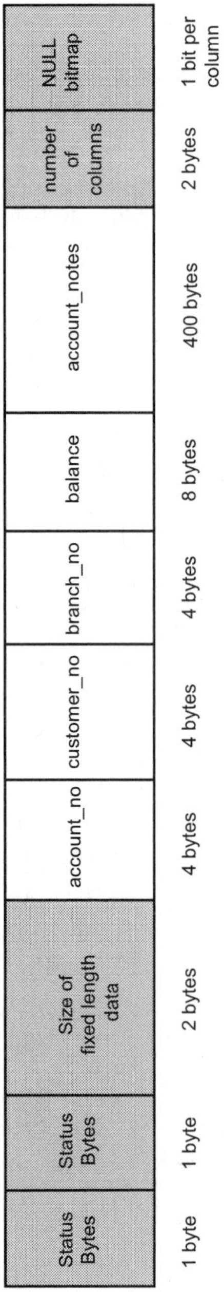
Status Bytes
Status Bytes
Size of fixed length data
account_no
customer_no
branch_no
balance
account_notes
number of columns
NULL bitmap
1 byte
1 byte
2 bytes
4 bytes
4 bytes
4 bytes
8 bytes
400 bytes
2 bytes
1 bit per column

**Figure 2.17** *A row containing only fixed-length columns*

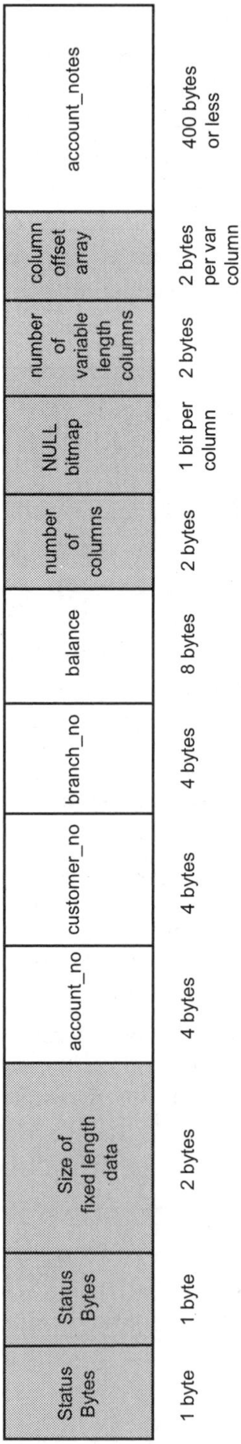
Status Bytes
Status Bytes
Size of fixed length data
account_no
customer_no
branch_no
balance
number of columns
NULL bitmap
number of variable length columns
column offset array
account_notes
1 byte
1 byte
2 bytes
4 bytes
4 bytes
4 bytes
8 bytes
2 bytes
1 bit per column
2 bytes
2 bytes per var column
400 bytes or less

**Figure 2.18** *A row containing fixed- and variable-length columns* this byte also specifies whether there is variable-length data in the row. In our example there are no variable-length data.

The next two bytes hold a number representing the length of the fixed data in the row. This number is the number of bytes of data plus the two status bytes and these two bytes themselves.

The fixed-length data now follow. Finally, there are two bytes holding a number that represents the number of columns in the row and a variable number of bytes holding a NULL bitmap. This contains one bit for every column with a bit set to show whether the column contains a NULL value. (See Figure 2.17.)

The shaded area represents the overhead. Our Account row, which we expected to be 420 bytes in length, has turned out to be 424 bytes in length—and that does not include the fields holding the number of columns and the NULL bitmap.

Suppose the last column in our Accounts table was not a char(400) data type but a varchar(400). The structure of our row containing variable length data is shown in Figure 2.18.

The structure shown in Figure 2.18 assumes that the account_notes column does indeed contain 400 characters. If it contains less, then less bytes will be used to hold the account notes. We can immediately see two differences between the structure of a row containing only fixed-length columns and a row that also contains variable-length columns. First, the fixed-length columns are grouped together separate from the variable-length columns, which are also grouped together. Second, there are more overhead bytes.

Looking at the structure, the first status byte will now have a bit set to specify that variable-length columns are present in the row. After the two status bytes the next two bytes hold a number representing the length of the fixed data in the row followed by the fixed data, the two-byte field holding the number of columns, and the NULL bitmap. Now we find extra fields. A two-byte field holds the number of variable-length columns followed by a field known as the column offset array, which contains a two-byte cell for each variable-length column used to hold information that SQL Server uses to find the position of the variable-length data.

We can see that the order of the columns in a row that contains variable-length columns is not the same order as the table definition.

## 2.12 Looking into database pages

I often find it useful and educational to be able to burrow into the contents of a database page. A useful DBCC statement that will allow you to do this is DBCC PAGE. This DBCC statement is not documented as an option of the DBCC statement in the Microsoft SQL Server documentation; however, some references to it can be found on TechNet and various other sources.

The most useful form of the syntax of this statement is:

```
DBCC PAGE (dbid  | dbname, file id, page number)
```

or:

```
DBCC PAGE (dbid  | dbname, file id, page number, 1)
```

The first form of the syntax displays the page header; the second form also displays the contents of the page—that is, data in the form of rows and the row offset table.

How do you know which page number to display? One of the columns in the sysindexes system table, described in Chapter 3, contains a column first. This contains the Page ID (File ID plus page number) of the first data page in the table if the sysindexes entry is a table or clustered index (indid = 0 or 1). Also, if the sysindexes entry is a table, the root column holds the Page ID of the last data page in the table.

To find the relevant entry in the sysindexes table you need to convert the table name to an Object ID because the sysindexes table holds the Object ID rather than the table name. The Object_ID function can be used to translate the table name to its Object ID. For example, suppose we want to look at pages in the Accounts table. To get the start Page ID from the sysindexes table, use the following example:

```
SELECT first FROM sysindexes WHERE
  id = OBJECT_ID ('accounts')
  AND
  indid IN (0,1)
```

```
first
--------------
0x1E0000000100
```

Unfortunately, the Page ID is represented in hexadecimal and a swapped byte order, so some manipulation will be needed to arrive at the page number.

First of all, take away the 0x symbol and separate the number into one-byte (two-digit) values:

```
1E   00   00   00   01   00
```

Now you must reverse the order of the bytes:

```
00   01   00   00   00   1E
```

The first two bytes hold the File ID number, and the last four bytes hold the page number:

```
00   01   |   00   00   00   1E
```

Therefore, in our example, the File ID number is 1 and the page number is 30 (the decimal equivalent of hexadecimal 1E).

To get information out of DBCC PAGE we must initiate tracing to the client:

```
DBCC TRACEON (3604)
```

We are now ready to display the contents of a page, but first of all let us just display the page header so we can see what is in it:

```
DBCC PAGE ('BankingDB',1,30)


PAGE: (1:30)
------------

BUFFER:
-------

BUF @0x18F0BF80
--------------
bpage = 0x1B14C000   bhash = 0x00000000   bpageno = (1:30)
bdbid =              breferences = 1      bstat = 0x9
bspin = 0            bnext = 0x00000000

PAGE HEADER:
------------
```

```
Page @0x1B14C000
----------------
m_pageId = (1:30)          m_headerVersion = 1    m_type = 1
m_typeFlagBits = 0x0       m_level = 0            m_flagBits = 0x8000
m_objId = 199305813        m_indexId = 0          m_prevPage = (0:0)
m_nextPage = (0:0)         pminlen = 424          m_slotCnt = 16
m_freeCnt = 1232           m_freeData = 6928      m_reservedCnt = 0
m_lsn = (5:84:25)          m_xactReserved = 0     m_xdesId = (0:0)
m_ghostRecCnt = 0          m_tornBits = 1

Allocation Status
-----------------
GAM (1:2) = ALLOCATED        SGAM (1:3) = NOT ALLOCATED
PFS (1:1) = 0x63 MIXED_EXT ALLOCATED   95_PCT_FULL    DIFF (1:6) = CHANGED
ML (1:7) = NOT MIN_LOGGED
```

We can see the entry m_pageId = (1:30) telling us that this is page 30 in File ID 1. The entry m_objId = 199305813 tells us what Object ID the page belongs to. OK, we know this but there are occasions when error messages contain page numbers and in that situation the Object ID is very useful.

The m_level and m_indexid fields are meaningful if this page is an index page. The level is the index level where this page resides, and indid tells us the ID of the index to which this page belongs. The field m_freeData is the offset of the start of the free space on the page, and the pminlen field tells us the smallest value a row can be. The entry m_slotCnt tells us how many slots (entries) there are in the row offset table.

Let us now look at the contents of the page. I will omit the page header from the example for clarity:

```
DBCC PAGE ('BankingDB',1,30,1)

DATA:
-----


Slot 0, Offset 0x60
-------------------
Record Type = PRIMARY_RECORD
Record Attributes =  NULL_BITMAP
1b14c060:   01a80010  00000001  00000001  000003e9  ...............
1b14c070:   057e8dbc  00000000  6576654e  766f2072  ..~.....Never ov
1b14c080:   72647265  206e7761  20202020  20202020  erdrawn
1b14c090:   20202020  20202020  20202020  20202020
  :
1b14c1f0:   20202020  20202020  20202020  20202020
1b14c200:   20202020  20202020   000005                      ...
  :
```

```
Slot 1, Offset 0x20b
--------------------
Record Type = PRIMARY_RECORD
Record Attributes =   NULL_BITMAP
1b14c20b:   01a80010   000186a1   00000001   000003e9 ...............
1b14c21b:   03ee6580   00000000   6576654e   766f2072 .e......Never ov
1b14c22b:   72647265   206e7761   20202020   20202020 erdrawn
1b14c23b:   20202020   20202020   20202020   20202020
1b14c24b:   20202020   20202020   20202020   20202020
   :
OFFSET TABLE:
-------------
Row - Offset
15 (0xf) - 6501 (0x1965)
14 (0xe) - 6074 (0x17ba)
13 (0xd) - 5647 (0x160f)
   :
3 (0x3) - 1377 (0x561)
2 (0x2) - 950 (0x3b6)
1 (0x1) - 523 (0x20b)
0 (0x0) - 96 (0x60)
```

We can see, in the DATA section, each row and the offset of the row. We can see, in the OFFSET TABLE section, each entry in the row offset table. Each entry contains a slot number and an offset—for example, the row referenced by slot 0 is at offset 96 (straight after the page header), and the row referenced by slot 15 is at offset 6,501.

## 2.13   Pages for space management

There are a number of pages resident in a primary or secondary database file that are used to manage space in the file. These special pages are as follows:

- Global Allocation Map (GAM) pages
- Secondary Global Allocation Map (SGAM) pages
- Index Allocation Map (IAM) pages
- Page Free Space (PFS) pages

To understand how GAM and SGAM pages fit into the picture we need to remind ourselves that there are two types of extent in SQL Server 2000. Uniform extents are eight pages in length and are allocated exclusively to one object when it requires space. For example, if a uniform extent is allocated to the Accounts table in the BankingDB database, then only rows from that table can use space on the eight pages.

Mixed extents are eight pages in length also but are allocated one page at a time to many objects when they require space. For example, a mixed extent may provide space for the Accounts table in the BankingDB database plus another seven tables. As we discussed earlier, mixed extents exist to save space, and, as such, the first eight pages of a table (or index) are allocated from mixed extents.

GAM pages hold information concerning which extents are currently allocated—that is, are not free. A single GAM page can manage 64,000 extents, which equates to nearly 4 GB of space. If more than 64,000 extents are present in the file, additional GAM pages are used. A GAM page uses a single bit to represent each extent out of the 64,000 extent range. If the bit is set (1), the extent is free; if it is not set (0), it is allocated.

SGAM pages hold information concerning which extents are currently being used as mixed extents and have one or more unused page—that is, have space that can still be allocated to objects. A single SGAM page can also manage 64,000 extents. If more than 64,000 extents are present in the file, additional SGAM pages are used. An SGAM page uses a single bit to represent each extent out of the 64,000 extent range. If the bit is set (1), the extent is being used as a mixed extent and has at least one unused page; if it is not set (0), it is not being used as a mixed extent, or, alternatively, it is a mixed extent but all the pages are in use. These settings are shown in Table 2.5.

To find a free extent to allocate as a uniform extent, the GAM is scanned for a bit that is set (1)—that is, an extent not currently in use. The bit is then set to 0 (allocated). To find a mixed extent having at least one free page that can be allocated, SQL Server searches the SGAM for a bit that is set (1). To find a free extent to allocate as a mixed extent, the GAM is scanned for a bit that is set (1)—that is, an extent that is not currently in use. The bit is then set to 0 (allocated). The equivalent bit in the SGAM is set to 1.

To free an extent, the GAM bit is set to 1 and the SGAM bit is set to 0.

**Table 2.5**   *GAM and SGAM Page Settings*

| Extent Status | GAM Bit Setting | SGAM Bit Setting |
|---|---|---|
| Free, not being used | 1 | 0 |
| Uniform or full mixed extent | 0 | 0 |
| Mixed extent with free pages | 0 | 1 |

**Note:** When allocating extents to a table, SQL Server 2000 "round-robins" the allocation from each file if there is more than one file in the filegroup to which the table belongs. This ensures that space is allocated proportionately from each file in the filegroup.

How does SQL Server 2000 keep track of which pages belong to a table or index? In previous versions of SQL Server (prior to SQL Server 7.0), data pages in a table were always chained together in a doubly linked list. This behavior changed in SQL Server 7.0 and so in SQL Server 2000 this is true only if the table has a clustered index (much more about clustered indexes in Chapter 3).

In SQL Server 2000 the extents used by a table or index are managed by IAM pages. A table or index has at least one IAM page, and, if the table or index is spread across more than one file, it will have an IAM page for each file. An IAM page can manage 512,000 pages, and, if the table size exceeds this within a file, another IAM is used. The IAM pages for a file or index are chained together. An IAM page must not only cater to uniform extents allocated to the table or index, but must also cater to single pages allocated from mixed extents.

To do this the first IAM page in the chain of IAM pages holds eight slots which can contain pointers to the eight pages that may be allocated from mixed extents. Other IAM pages in the IAM chain will not hold pointers in these slots. All IAM pages, though, will contain a bitmap with each bit presenting an extent in the range of extents held by the IAM. If the bit is set (1), the extent represented by that bit is allocated to the table or index; if it is not set (0), the extent represented by that bit is not allocated to the table or index.

To find the page ID of the first IAM page for a table or index, use the FirstIAM column in the sysindexes system table (the sysindexes system table will be discussed in Chapter 3). To do this use the following example:

```
SELECT object_name(id) AS Tablename , Name, FirstIAM FROM
sysindexes

Tablename    Name              FirstIAM
---------    -----             --------------
Authors              aunmind    0x7C0000000100
Publishers        UPKCL_pubind  0x650000000100
Titles        UPKCL_titleidind  0x690000000100
```

The Page ID is a hexadecimal number, which can be decoded as described previously in this chapter.

---

**Note:** The SQL Server documentation refers to a *heap*. A heap is a table that does not have a clustered index and, therefore, the pages are not linked by pointers. The IAM pages are the only structures that link the pages in a table together.

---

Finally, our last special page is a PFS page. A PFS page holds the information that shows whether an individual page has been allocated to table, index, or some other structure. It also documents how free an allocated page is. For each page, the PFS has a bitmap recording whether the page is empty, 1 percent to 50 percent full, 51 percent to 80 percent full, 81 percent to 95 percent full, or 96 percent to 100 percent full. Each PFS page covers an 8,000-page range. When a search is made to look for free space, the PFS page is consulted to see which page in an extent belonging to the table or index may have enough free space.

This results in a fundamental difference between SQL Server 2000 and versions prior to SQL Server 7.0. In these previous versions, if there were no clustered index on the table, new rows were always added at the end—that is, inserted into the last page. Now, rows can be inserted on any page in the table that has free space.

So, where in the database file do we find these special pages? The first page (0) contains a file header. The second page (1) is the first PFS page. The next PFS page will be found after another 8,000 pages. The third page (2) is the first GAM, and the fourth page (3) is the first SGAM. IAM pages are located in arbitrary positions throughout the file. This is shown in Figure 2.19.

This chapter has provided an overview of the SQL Server storage structures. In the next chapter we will look at tables and indexes in much more

**Figure 2.19**
*The PFS, GAM, and SGAM pages*

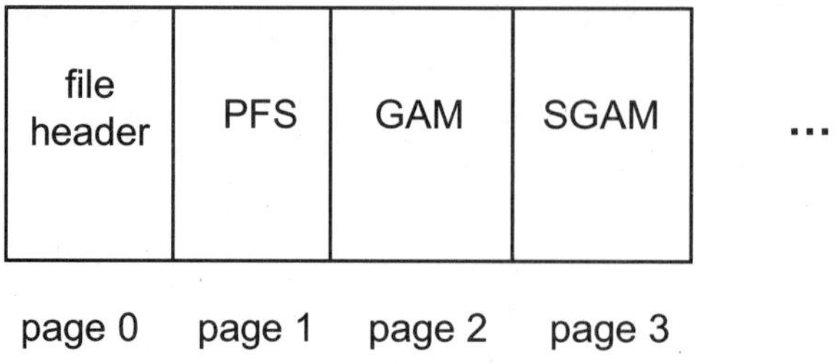

| file header | PFS | GAM | SGAM | ... |
|-------------|-----|-----|------|-----|

page 0     page 1     page 2     page 3

detail. But first of all, now that we have discussed databases, it is time to introduce the BankingDB database used in this book.

## 2.14   The BankingDB database

The BankingDB database is very simple. It consists of just three tables, which are created with the following Transact-SQL syntax:

```
CREATE TABLE customers
(
   customer_no        INT          NOT NULL,
   customer_fname     CHAR(20)     NOT NULL,
   customer_lname     CHAR(20)     NOT NULL,
   customer_notes     CHAR(400)    NOT NULL
   )


CREATE TABLE accounts
(
   account_no         INT          NOT NULL,
   customer_no        INT          NOT NULL,
   branch_no          INT          NOT NULL,
   balance            MONEY        NOT NULL,
   account_notes      CHAR(400)    NOT NULL
   )


CREATE TABLE branches
(
   branch_no          INT          NOT NULL,
   branch_name        CHAR(60)     NOT NULL,
   branch_address     CHAR(400)    NOT NULL,
   managers_name      CHAR(60)     NOT NULL
   )
```

The BankingDB database has customers who have one or many bank accounts. A bank account is managed by a branch of the bank at some geographical location. It is as simple as that.

There are 10,000 bank accounts for 5,000 customers. These are managed by 100 branches. Since we will be creating indexes frequently as we progress through the book, there are no indexes created in the basic database. For the same reason, the tables are also assumed to have no primary key constraints or foreign key constraints.

3

# *Indexing*

## 3.1    Introduction

There are many bells and whistles that can be tweaked to improve SQL Server performance. Some will provide a more positive benefit than others; however, to really improve performance, often with dramatic results, the database designer is well advised to concentrate his or her efforts in the area of indexing. The correct choice of index on a table with respect to the WHERE clause in a Transact-SQL statement, so that the query optimizer chooses the most efficient strategy, can have sensational results.

I was once asked to look at a query that performed a complex join and had not completed in over 12 hours. Who knows when the query would have completed had it not been cancelled by the user—it may still have been running at the end of the year! Examination of the query showed that a join condition was missing in the WHERE clause, as was an index on one of the large tables involved in the join. Making the appropriate changes meant that the query ran in less than eight minutes!

This magnitude of performance improvement is not likely to be achieved every day, but it makes an important point—namely, that focusing effort in the area of indexing and query optimization is likely to produce good results for the effort involved and should be high on the database tuner's hit list.

So, what are these indexes and why are they so important?

## 3.2    Data retrieval with no indexes

Imagine that this book had no index, and you were asked to find references to the topic page faults. You would have no choice but to open the book at page 1, scan the page looking for the topic, turn to page 2, and continue until you had scanned the last page of the book. You would have to continue your search to the last page in the book, since you would not know when you had found the last reference to the topic. You would have read and scanned every page in the book, which would probably have taken you a considerable length of time.

SQL Server has to behave in a similar fashion when asked to retrieve rows from a table that has no appropriate index. Suppose we were to execute the following Transact-SQL statement against the Accounts table, assuming there was no suitable index present:

```
SELECT * FROM accounts WHERE branch_no = 1100
```

How would SQL Server find the appropriate rows? It would have to search the Accounts table from the start of the table to the end of the table looking for rows that had a branch_no containing the value 1100. This might be fine for small tables containing just a few rows, but, if the table contained millions of rows, the above query would take a very long time to complete.

What is needed is a fast and efficient way of finding the data that conforms to the query requirements. In the case of a book, there is usually an index section from which the required topic can be found in an alphabetically ordered list, and the page numbers of the pages featuring that topic can then be obtained. The required pages can be directly accessed in the book.

The method used to directly retrieve the required data from a table in SQL Server is not unlike that used with books. Structures called indexes may be created on a table, which enable SQL Server to quickly look up the database pages that hold the supplied key value—in our example the value 1100 for the branch_no column.

Unlike a book, which normally has one index, a table may have many indexes. These indexes are based on one or more columns in the table. In SQL Server there are two types of index—clustered and nonclustered— which we shall now compare and contrast. The ultimate decision as to whether an index is used or whether a complete scan of the table is performed is made by a component of SQL Server known as the query optimizer, which we will discuss in detail in Chapter 4.

## 3.3   Clustered indexes

As a database designer you are allowed to create only one clustered index on a table—you have one chance to play this ace and so you must play it carefully. Why only one clustered index per table? Unlike its nonclustered cousin, described shortly, a clustered index imposes a physical ordering of the table data.

Creating a clustered index forces the data rows in the table to be reordered on disk so that they are in the same key sequence order as the clustered index key. For example, if we were to create a clustered index on the customer_lname column of the Customers table, the data rows would be sorted so that their physical order on the disk was in ascending order of the customers' last names—that is, Adamski would precede Tolstoy.

This order would be maintained as long as the clustered index was present. SQL Server would ensure that the insertion of a new data row would cause the row to be placed in the correct physical location in key sequence order.

The structure of a clustered index with its key defined on the customer_lname column of the Customers table is shown in Figure 3.1. The lowest level of the clustered index is composed of the data pages themselves, and in a clustered index the data pages are known as the leaf level of the index. The rest of the clustered index is composed of index pages. The

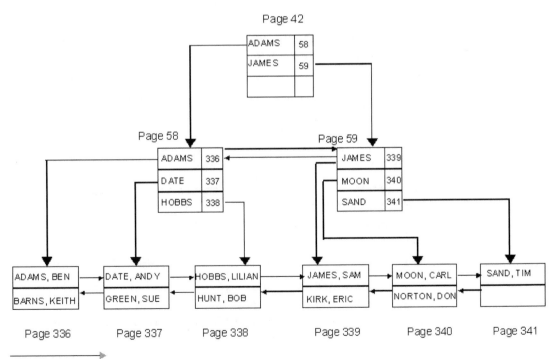

**Figure 3.1**    *Structure of the clustered index*

**Figure 3.2**
*Index pages are
linked together*

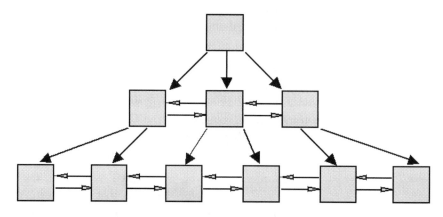

index page at the top of the index is known as the index root. Levels in the index between the root page and the leaf-level pages are known as intermediate-level pages. Another name for an index page is an index node. For simplicity we have shown the structure with the ability to hold two data rows per page and three index entries per page. In reality many more rows and index entries are likely to be found.

At any given level in the index the pages are linked together. This is shown in Figure 3.1, whereas Figure 3.2 emphasizes the linkage. Figure 3.2 shows how index pages are linked together, and this is true regardless of whether the index is a clustered index or nonclustered index.

The entries in the index pages contain a key value and a pointer to the next index page at the next lowest level starting with that key value, plus some control information. The pointer in a clustered index is a page number. In Figure 3.1, for example, the root page has an entry containing a key value, Adams, and a page number, 58, pointing to the intermediate index page 58, whose lowest key value is Adams.

**Note:** The pointer also contains the File ID as a prefix. This is needed because page numbers are only unique within a database file. A File ID plus a page number is referred to as a Page ID.

The reason why there can be only one clustered index on a table is that the clustered index governs the physical placement of the data and the data cannot be in two places at once. There can only be one sequence in which the data can be physically placed.

So how can a clustered index support our requirement to perform fast and efficient data retrieval? The clustered index will help us to avoid table scans, since the query optimizer will probably use the clustered index to retrieve data directly. Suppose we issued the following SELECT statement:

```
SELECT * FROM customers WHERE customer_lname =  'Green'
```

Let us assume that the query optimizer decides that the clustered index is the most efficient access path to the data. This is a realistic assumption, since the WHERE clause only specifies the customer_lname column on which the clustered index is based.

SQL Server will first obtain the page number of the root page from the sysindexes table—in our example, page 42. In this root page there will be a number of key values, and in our clustered index these are Adams and James. SQL Server will look for the highest key value not greater than Green, which will be Adams.

In a clustered index an index entry consists of the index key plus a pointer, which is a page number. The pointer held in the Adams key entry points to page 58, and so index page number 58 will be retrieved.

Since page 58 is still an index page, SQL Server will look for the highest key value not greater than Green. In index page number 58 this is Date. The pointer held in the Date key entry is to page 337, which is a data page, and so this page will be retrieved. The data page is now scanned for a row containing Green in the customer_lname column. The row is found and returned. Note that SQL Server did not know the row existed until the data page was obtained.

Clearly, the clustered index in our example has supported fast access to the data row. If we consider the number of I/Os required to traverse the index in this way we can see that one I/O is required to retrieve the root page, one I/O is required to retrieve the intermediate index page, and one I/O is required to retrieve the data page—a total of three I/Os. A table scan would probably result in many more I/Os.

Would the three I/Os required to traverse our index be physical reads to the disk? Probably not. The root page of an index is accessed by every query that needs to traverse the index and so is normally always found in cache if the index is accessed frequently. The intermediate nodes and data pages are less likely to be, but if the data cache is large enough it is possible that they will stay in the cache.

We have looked at a SELECT statement that retrieved a single row. What about a SELECT statement that retrieves a range of rows?

```
SELECT * FROM customers WHERE customer_lname BETWEEN
'Date' AND 'Kirk'
```

In the above example a range of values is specified based on the customer_lname column. It can be seen from Figure 3.1 that because our clustered index is based on the customer_lname column and the data is thus in key sequence order, the rows that meet the criteria are all stored together—that is, clustered. In our example, the six rows that meet the criteria of the SELECT statement are found in three data pages, and so only three I/Os would be required to retrieve these data pages.

If the clustered index had not been based on the customer_lname column, the rows would have not been clustered together (unless fate had intervened or the rows were loaded in that manner with no other clustered indexes on the table).

In the worst case, the six rows would have been stored across six data pages, resulting in six I/Os to retrieve them.

---

**Note:** In the BankingDB database there are about 15 customer rows per data page. As an example, eight I/Os would return 120 rows. As we will see, when a clustered index is not present to keep the rows in key sequence order, indexed access of these rows may require 120 I/Os. A not inconsiderable difference!

---

In a similar manner, clustered indexes support searches using the LIKE operator. Suppose we execute the following query:

```
SELECT * FROM customers WHERE customer_lname LIKE  'N%'
```

All the customers with last names beginning with N will be returned. Again, our clustered index on customer_lname will ensure that these rows are stored together, resulting in the least number of I/Os to retrieve them. Of course, duplicate last names would also be stored in the same cluster of pages.

Finally, what about returning the data in order? Suppose we execute the following query:

```
SELECT * FROM customers ORDER BY customer_lname
```

The query optimizer will know that the clustered index guarantees that the data is in key sequence order, and so there is no need to perform a sort of the rows to satisfy the ORDER BY clause, again saving disk I/O.

## 3.4 Nonclustered indexes

Similar to their clustered counterparts, nonclustered indexes are balanced trees with a hierarchy of index pages—starting with the index root page at the top, leaf-level pages at the bottom- and intermediate-level pages between the root page and the leaf-level pages. Again, at any given level in the index the pages are linked together, as shown in Figure 3.2.

**Note:** Data pages in a table without a clustered index will not be chained together, even if nonclustered indexes are present on the table. As was mentioned in Chapter 2, the data pages of the table will only be related through the IAM page(s) managing that table.

Unlike their clustered counterparts, nonclustered indexes have no influence on the physical order of the data, and the leaf level of a sorted index is not considered to be the data but is the lowest level of index pages. The structure of a nonclustered index with its key defined on the customer_fname column of the Customers table is shown in Figure 3.3.

The first observation we can make is that every data row in the table has a pointer to it from the index leaf level (the dashed lines). This was not the case with the clustered index in Figure 3.1, where the leaf level only contained pointers to the lowest keyed data row in each page. This means that nonclustered indexes are typically larger than their clustered counterparts, because their leaf level has to hold many more pointers. There are about 15 customer rows per data page, so the leaf level of the nonclustered index will need to hold 15 times more pointers than the lowest-level index page in the clustered index. The typical effect of this is that a nonclustered index on a key will usually have one more level of index pages than a clustered index on the same key.

What do the index entries in a nonclustered index look like? Similar to a clustered index, they contain a key value and a pointer to the relevant index page at the next lowest level. This pointer is a Page ID (File ID and database page number). The lowest index level, the leaf level, has index entries also containing a key value and a pointer. While in versions of SQL Server prior to 7.0 the pointer was always a Row ID, which pointed directly at the data row, this is no longer always true.

A Row ID is a Page ID plus a row number. In Figure 3.3 the leaf-level index page 96 has an entry for the key Ben, which points to Page ID 1:340, slot number 2.

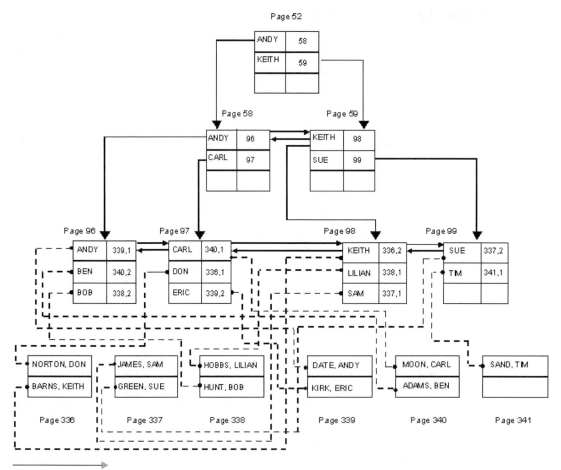

**Figure 3.3**   *Structure of a nonclustered index with no clustered index on the table*

So when is a pointer a Row ID and when is it not? If there is no clustered index present on the table, then the pointer is a Row ID. If there is a clustered index present on the table, then the pointer becomes something else. We shall see what this something is shortly and why this is so.

The most important observation to make about Figure 3.3 is that although the index levels are in key sequence order, the data is not. This means that any kind of range retrieval performed using the sorted index will have to use a logical read to follow each relevant leaf-level pointer to the data rows. This is an important point, which we will revisit later. Note also that once the leaf level has been accessed, SQL Server knows whether a row exists or not.

So far we have discussed the behavior of clustered indexes and nonclustered indexes with respect to data retrieval. Let us now look at the behavior of these indexes with respect to data insertion, update, and deletion.

## 3.5 The role of indexes in insertion and deletion

The existence of indexes on tables is usually considered with respect to query execution time. However, SQL Server indexes, in particular clustered indexes, also affect the behavior of SQL Server when rows are inserted. Consider the Customers table shown in Figure 3.4. The table has been allocated four pages from a mixed extent. Three pages are full, and the fourth page is partly filled.

We will assume, for clarity, that a database page only holds three rows and that only the customer_lname and customer_fname columns are shown.

Suppose we wish to add a new row. Where is it stored? Since the table has no indexes present and there is no free space anywhere else in the pages allocated to the table, the new row is inserted at the end of the table on the last page, as shown in Figure 3.5. We shall see shortly that this behavior is true even if there are nonclustered indexes present on the table. Only the creation of a clustered index can modify this behavior.

One can imagine that in a multiuser system many users will be attempting to insert customer rows. In previous versions of SQL Server prior to 7.0 this would have resulted in a hot spot at the end of the table, since a full implementation of row-level locking was not present. However, SQL Server 2000 has a full and robust implementation of row-level locking, and so the hot spot has been virtually eliminated. Locking is discussed in Chapter 6. What happens when rows are deleted from a table?

Suppose some rows are now deleted, as shown in Figure 3.6. Free space, shown in Figure 3.7, is left on the pages from which the rows are deleted.

**Figure 3.4**
*Customers table with no indexes present*

| Page 336 | Page 337 | Page 338 | Page 339 |
|----------|----------|----------|----------|
| HOBBS, LILIAN | ADAMS, BEN | STONE, JOHN | HUNT, BOB |
| GREEN, SUE | KIRK, ERIC | KENT, RON | |
| BARNS, KEITH | JAMES, SAM | MOON, CARL | |

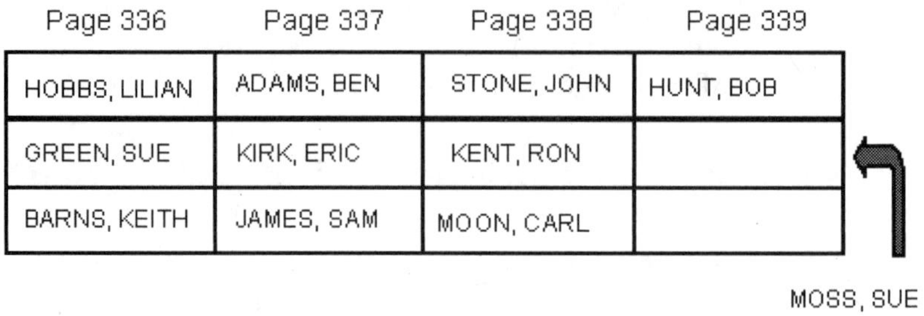

**Figure 3.5**
*Insertion at the end of a table*

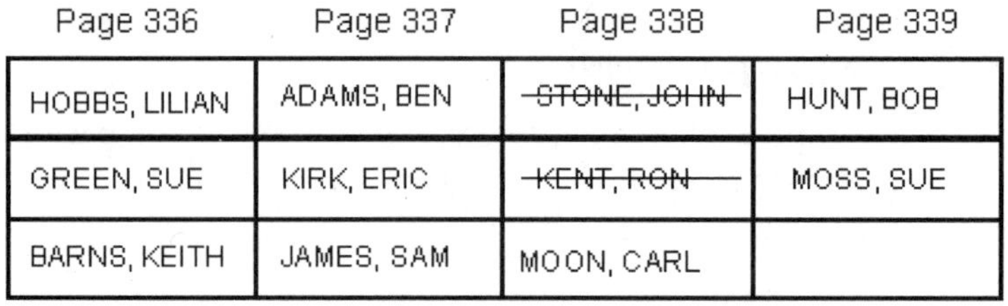

| Page 336 | Page 337 | Page 338 | Page 339 |
|---|---|---|---|
| HOBBS, LILIAN | ADAMS, BEN | STONE, JOHN | HUNT, BOB |
| GREEN, SUE | KIRK, ERIC | KENT, RON | |
| BARNS, KEITH | JAMES, SAM | MOON, CARL | |

MOSS, SUE

**Figure 3.6**
*Deleting rows from the table*

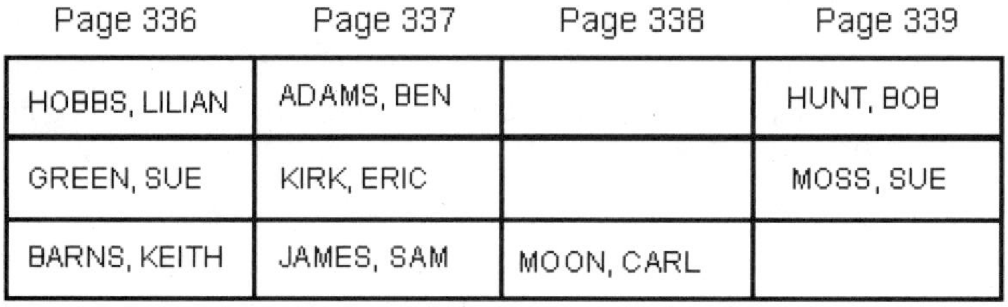

| Page 336 | Page 337 | Page 338 | Page 339 |
|---|---|---|---|
| HOBBS, LILIAN | ADAMS, BEN | ~~STONE, JOHN~~ | HUNT, BOB |
| GREEN, SUE | KIRK, ERIC | ~~KENT, RON~~ | MOSS, SUE |
| BARNS, KEITH | JAMES, SAM | MOON, CARL | |

**Figure 3.7**
*Space freed from row deletion*

| Page 336 | Page 337 | Page 338 | Page 339 |
|---|---|---|---|
| HOBBS, LILIAN | ADAMS, BEN | | HUNT, BOB |
| GREEN, SUE | KIRK, ERIC | | MOSS, SUE |
| BARNS, KEITH | JAMES, SAM | MOON, CARL | |

**Figure 3.8**
*Free space being reused*

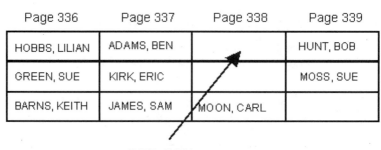

| Page 336 | Page 337 | Page 338 | Page 339 |
|---|---|---|---|
| HOBBS, LILIAN | ADAMS, BEN | | HUNT, BOB |
| GREEN, SUE | KIRK, ERIC | | MOSS, SUE |
| BARNS, KEITH | JAMES, SAM | MOON, CARL | |

DATE, ANDY

If a new row is now inserted, where will it go? In versions of SQL Server prior to 7.0, SQL Server would not have reused the space freed by the deletion of the rows. More sophisticated page management algorithms using more sophisticated page management structures (see Chapter 2) mean that space freed by deleting old rows can be reused by new rows. This is shown in Figure 3.8.

Once all the rows are removed from a page it becomes available for use by the table again. If all the rows are removed from an extent, it may be deallocated and so no longer belongs to the table.

---

**Note:** If a row size is used so that only one row can fit on a page, the deletion of a row will mean that there is no remaining row on the page. The page will immediately become available for reuse, and free space will not be wasted.

---

The previous discussion has shown that in a table with no indexes, rows will be inserted at the end of the existing data—that is, appended to the rows already present if there is no free space elsewhere in the table. However, if there is free space present in existing database pages in the table because some rows stored earlier have been deleted, then SQL Server can make use of this space to accommodate newly inserted data rows. In Figure 3.9, new rows can be inserted where free space has been left by deleted rows. The PFS management pages hold information about the free space in each page and so can be consulted when a page with sufficient free space is required.

This behavior stays the same if nonclustered indexes are present on the table, since they do not govern the physical placement of data. However, a

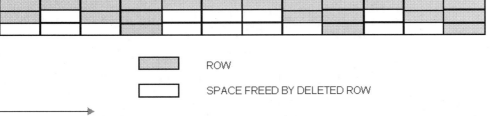

ROW

SPACE FREED BY DELETED ROW

**Figure 3.9**    *Pages with sufficient free space can be used for new rows*

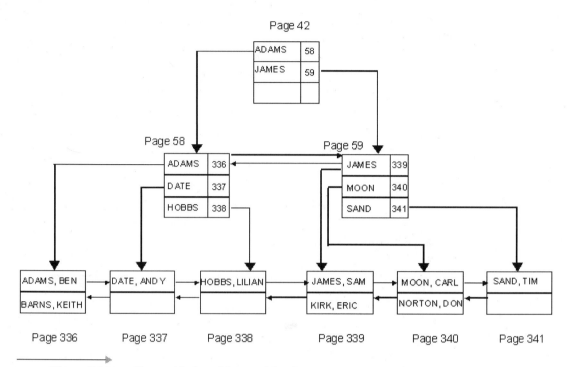

**Figure 3.10**   *Clustered index with some deleted rows*

clustered index will modify this behavior. This is because a clustered index will always ensure that new rows are inserted in key sequence order. In our Customers table example, this means in ascending order of the customer's last name. So let's delete some rows and see what happens.

We'll delete the customers who have the last names Green and Hunt. Pages 337 and 338 now have free space in them, as shown in Figure 3.10. Let's now insert two new customers, French and Hood. The clustered index forces these rows to be inserted in key sequence order, so French will need to be inserted after Date but before Hobbs, and Hood will need to be inserted after Hobbs but before James.

Well, we are lucky. It just so happens that there is free space on the pages where we want to insert the rows, and this space is therefore reused, as shown in Figure 3.11.

We can see that in our clustered index, space freed by deleting rows can be reused. Of course, if our clustered index key had been an increasing key value such as that generated in a column with the identity property, new rows would always be inserted at the end of the table and free space in a page may not be efficiently reused.

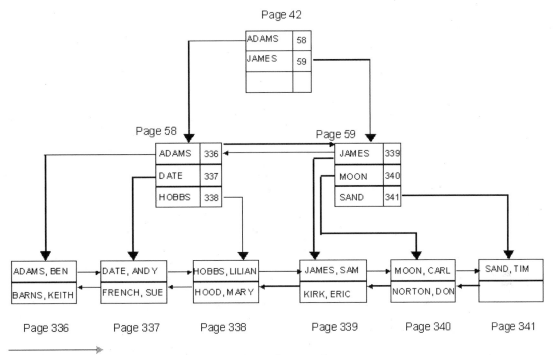

**Figure 3.11**   *Clustered index with some newly inserted rows*

Our example is, of course, a little contrived, since there will be many occasions where there is not going to be free space in the page where we want to insert the new row, and we will deal with this scenario now.

Suppose that our clustered index contains the entries shown in Figure 3.12. We want to insert a row with a key value of Jones, which SQL Server must store between the key values James and Kent, but there is obviously insufficient space in page 337 to hold the new row. In this case SQL Server must perform a page split. This involves acquiring a new empty page and chaining it into the existing chain of pages.

**Figure 3.12**
*Full clustered index leaf pages*

| Page 336 | Page 337 | Page 338 | Page 339 |
|---|---|---|---|
| ADAMS, BEN | HOBBS, LILIAN | KENT, RON | MOSS, SUE |
| BARNS, KEITH | HOOD, MARY | KIRK, ERIC | STONE, JOHN |
| GREEN, SUE | JAMES, SAM | MOON, CARL | |

**Figure 3.13**

*A 50:50 page split*

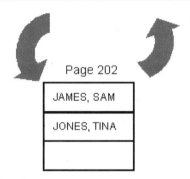

| Page 336 | Page 337 | Page 338 | Page 339 |
|---|---|---|---|
| ADAMS, BEN | HOBBS, LILIAN | KENT, RON | MOSS, SUE |
| BARNS, KEITH | HOOD, MARY | KIRK, ERIC | STONE, JOHN |
| GREEN, SUE | | MOON, CARL | |

Page 202

| |
|---|
| JAMES, SAM |
| JONES, TINA |
| |

This type of page splitting is known as a 50:50 split, since SQL Server ensures that approximately 50 percent of the rows on the existing page are moved onto the new page, as shown in Figure 3.13. This is only part of the work that SQL Server must do. The intermediate index pages in the clustered index must be updated so that the new page is referenced. This will involve adding a new entry into an index page at the next level up. Of course, if there is insufficient room for the new entry, the index page might split also! In our example, a new entry must be made for the key James pointing to page 202.

What about any nonclustered indexes that point to the table? Previously we mentioned that the index entries at the leaf level of a nonclustered index pointed directly at the data rows and these pointers, known as Row IDs, are of the form Page ID plus a row number on the data page. A Page ID is of the form File ID and database page number. We have just seen that when a page split occurs in a clustered index, rows can migrate from the old page to the newly chained-in page. So does this mean that the Row IDs for these rows are now incorrect? In versions of SQL Server prior to SQL Server 7.0 this is exactly what this would mean. The pointers in any nonclustered indexes present on the table pointing to the rows that had migrated would have to be changed to point to the row locations on the new page. This would result in a lot of nonclustered index update activity and a consequent increase in lock activity in these nonclustered indexes.

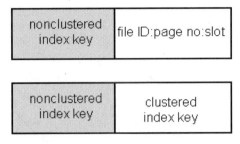

**Figure 3.14**
*Nonclustered index pointers with and without a clustered index present*

nonclustered index entry with
clustered index not present on table

nonclustered index entry with
clustered index present on table

For this reason, in SQL Server 2000, if a clustered index is present on a table, the nonclustered index pointers are no longer Row IDs. Instead, the nonclustered index pointers are the clustering index key. This is shown in Figure 3.14.

This needs a little more discussion! Instead of the index entries at the leaf level of a nonclustered index consisting of the nonclustered index key plus a Row ID pointer, each entry is composed of the nonclustered index key plus the clustered index key. A leaf-level index entry, therefore, no longer points directly at a data row; rather, it takes a route through the clustered index using the clustering key and then out to the data row. This is shown in Figure 3.15. The query specifies a column in the nonclustered index on the customer_fname column, and this index is chosen by the query optimizer. The index is traversed until the relevant index entry is found in the leaf-level index page. The pointer in this index entry is the clustered index key for this row. Since the clustered index is defined on the customer_lname column, this pointer is the customer's last name, in this case, Adams. The clustered index is now traversed using this key value, and the data row is fetched.

So, when is a pointer a Row ID and when is it not? If there is no clustered index present on the table, then the pointer is a Row ID. If there is a clustered index present on the table, the nonclustered index pointer (at the leaf level of the index) is the clustered index key. The primary reason for this approach is to avoid the work that must be performed by the server adjusting nonclustered index entries when a data page splits because of insertion into a clustered index, causing data rows to migrate to new pages.

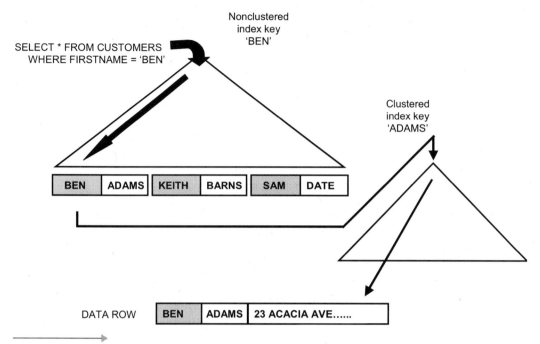

**Figure 3.15**    *Nonclustered index traversal with a clustered index present*

Since the nonclustered index leaf entries do not contain page numbers, if they contain the clustered index key, then the fact that data rows might move to a new page is irrelevant. The pointers will not need to be changed—in other words, they are stable. Because data page splits are a phenomenon only observed when a clustered index is present on a table, it follows that if there is no clustered index present on a table, data page splits cannot occur. The nonclustered index leaf entries are stable with respect to the insertion of new data rows, and the pointers can remain Row IDs, as in versions of SQL Server prior to 7.0.

This is all well and good, but suppose that we issue the following query:

```
SELECT * FROM customers WHERE customer_fname = 'John'
```

If we assume that there is a nonclustered index on the firstname column and a clustered index on the lastname column, then, from what we have just discussed, we can state that the pointer in the nonclustered index will be the clustered index key. Now suppose that for our customer John our pointer is Smith (John's last name). We traverse the nonclustered index searching for a key value of John and find the leaf- level index entry. We will assume for simplicity that there is only one customer with the first name John.

The pointer will contain the clustered index key Smith, and so the clustered index is now traversed from the top searching for this key. If there is only one customer with the last name Smith, we will traverse the clustered index and finally retrieve the data page containing our row. That's fine, but suppose in our Customer table we have more than one customer with the last name Smith. Perhaps we have a customer named Mary Smith. Now we have an interesting scenario. If the clustered index is now traversed from the top searching for a key of Smith, two rows will be found. Clearly this is nonsense, so how does SQL Server find the correct Smith?

The answer can be found in the way that duplicate clustered index key values are handled. If a clustered index is not created as a unique index, then duplicate key values will be allowed in the index. In our example this is not unreasonable—some customers will have the same last name. Internally, SQL Server will, however, add an extra column to the key, known as a uniqueifier. The first instance of a key value will not have a uniqueifier but subsequent instances will. The second instance will have a uniqueifier of 1, the third 2, and so on. In this way, SQL Server internally makes all the key values unique, and it is, in fact, the clustered index key and the uniqueifier that are held as the pointer in a nonclustered leaf-level index pointer. This pointer is then used to traverse the clustered index, and it will return a single, uniquely identified row. The uniqueifier will be completely transparent to the query and the application.

OK, let's now return to where we left off. We had just inserted a customer with the last name Jones, which caused a page spilt to occur. We might wish to insert another data row with a key value that is close to Jones. Are the split pages going to split again soon? We can see that if inserts continue, with key values greater than and less than James, there will be a delay before page splitting occurs again. This delay is caused by the fact that the page splitting left us with pages that had free space in them. We can store about 15 Customer rows into a data page, so in reality the page split will leave us with approximately seven rows per page and, therefore, room for another seven or eight rows more per page, which will delay the page splitting.

On average we can expect to find pages that range from 50 percent full having just split to 100 percent full just before they split, giving us an average page fullness of about 75 percent.

This is fine, but suppose the clustered index is based on an ever-increasing key value such as that provided by a column with the identity property or a column containing the date and time an order is taken. Insertion of new rows will always happen at the end of the clustered index. In this case

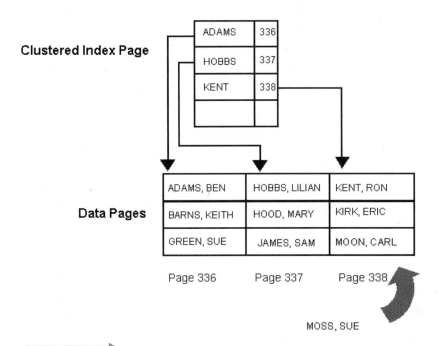

**Figure 3.16**    *Insertion at the end of the key range*

there is no point in SQL Server performing a 50:50 split when a new page is chained in, since space that is reserved physically before the last row inserted will never be used.

Figure 3.16 shows the insertion of a key value of Moss. There is no space in which to store this row on page 338, so a new page must be chained in. In this case SQL Server does not shuffle rows from page 338 onto the new page but instead inserts only the new row on the new page, as shown in Figure 3.17.

Note that an entry is added into the index page to point to the new key value on the new page.

The action of page splitting when a 50:50 split occurs is clearly going to give SQL Server some work to do. The new page must be obtained and chained in, rows must be shuffled, and entries in many cases will be inserted into a clustered index. Also, of course, new entries will have to be added to the nonclustered indexes to point to the new row.

It would clearly be beneficial to minimize page splitting, but how can we achieve this? One obvious way would be to not use clustered indexes, but the benefits they can bring to the performance of some queries can often outweigh the overhead of page splitting.

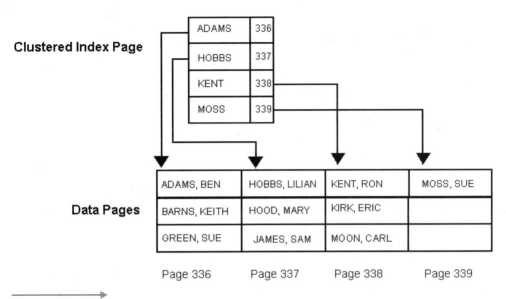

**Clustered Index Page**

| | |
|---|---|
| ADAMS | 336 |
| HOBBS | 337 |
| KENT | 338 |
| MOSS | 339 |

**Data Pages**

| ADAMS, BEN | HOBBS, LILIAN | KENT, RON | MOSS, SUE |
|---|---|---|---|
| BARNS, KEITH | HOOD, MARY | KIRK, ERIC | |
| GREEN, SUE | JAMES, SAM | MOON, CARL | |

Page 336        Page 337        Page 338        Page 339

**Figure 3.17**    *A page split that does not shuffle data*

Is there another way to minimize page splitting? Fortunately, there is. We can reserve space in a clustered index or a nonclustered index when we create the index using a fillfactor. During the creation of the index the index pages have free space reserved in them and, most importantly in a clustered index, free space is reserved in the data pages.

This free space is only reserved during the index creation process. Once the index has been created, the free space in the index and data pages can be used for newly inserted rows. The size of the index will be larger if space is reserved in it, and in the case of a clustered index the number of data pages in the table will also be greater, but this does mean that the point when SQL Server needs to page split will be delayed.

When SQL Server starts to split pages, fragmentation is said to occur. If many rows are inserted into a clustered index, such that page splits occur, many data pages will be chained into the table and the table will become fragmented. This affects both insertion and scan efficiency, and so we want to avoid it. We can tell if a table is becoming fragmented by using the DBCC SHOWCONTIG statement, which will be described shortly.

## 3.6    A note about updates

Obviously, if an indexed column is updated to a new value, the index must also be updated. In the case of a nonclustered index the index entry must change position since index keys are held in key sequence order. In the case of a clustered index, the data row may also have to change position, since the data rows are stored in key sequence order. But what happens to a data row when there is no clustered index present on the table?

Usually the update is performed in-place, which means that the row does not move to another page. Usually an update is logged as a single modification operation in the transaction log. In the case of the table having an update trigger or being replicated, the update is logged as a delete and insert operation. Even in this case the update will usually be an in-place update.

However, there comes a point where a variable-length column is updated to a size greater than its original size and there is no free space available on the page to accommodate it. In this case SQL Server 2000 will delete the row and insert it into a page that has free space. To avoid the overhead of having to adjust index pointers in nonclustered indexes to the new page, a forwarding pointer is left in the original location, which points to the new location. The index pointers will continue to point to the original location. This does mean that a retrieval of the row will incur an extra data page request for the forwarding pointer. If a subsequent update moves the row again, the pointer is adjusted to the new location. If a subsequent update means that the row can return to its original location, it will—and the forwarding pointer will disappear.

To detect the number of forwarding pointers in a table the DBCC SHOWCONTIG statement, which will be described shortly, may be used with the TABLERESULTS option.

Note that a table with a large number of forwarding pointers will experience performance degradation, especially if groups of rows are scanned, due to the extra accesses required. To tidy up the forwarding pointers the clustered index on the table can be rebuilt. If there is no clustered index, if possible create a dummy one and then drop it. Alternatively, unload the data into a file, truncate the table, and reload the data.

# 3.7   So how do you create indexes?

We have discussed the mechanics of indexes, and later we will discuss indexes with reference to performance, but it is time that we looked at how you create them. Indexes can be created via the following mechanisms:

- The Transact-SQL CREATE INDEX statement
- The SQL Enterprise Manager

- The Create Index Wizard

- Right mouse–clicking inside the Estimated Execution Plan tab in the Query Analyzer and choosing Manage Indexes

- Choosing the Tools menu item in the Query Analyzer and selecting Manage Indexes

- The Index Tuning Wizard (we will discuss this later in the book)

If you don't like any of the above options, you can always use the SQL-DMO (Distributed Management Objects) and the Index object to create an index!

**Note:** Indexes are also created when a primary or unique key constraint is added to a table.

First, let us look at the Transact-SQL options, and then we will look at the graphical approach provided by the SQL Enterprise Manager, Query Analyzer, and the Create Index Wizard. We will also have a quick peak at how this may be done in the SQL-DMO.

### 3.7.1   The Transact-SQL CREATE INDEX statement

The Transact-SQL syntax is as follows:

```
CREATE [ UNIQUE ] [ CLUSTERED | NONCLUSTERED ] INDEX
index_name
    ON { table | view } ( column [ ASC | DESC ] [ ,...n ]
)
[ WITH < index_option > [ ,...n] ]
[ ON filegroup ]

< index_option > :: =
    { PAD_INDEX |
        FILLFACTOR = fillfactor |
        IGNORE_DUP_KEY |
        DROP_EXISTING |
    STATISTICS_NORECOMPUTE |
    SORT_IN_TEMPDB
}
```

The different options will now be described.

To create a clustered index in Transact-SQL the CLUSTERED keyword is used:

```
CREATE CLUSTERED INDEX CI_AccountNo
    ON accounts (account_no)
```

The above example creates a clustered index on the account_no column of the Accounts table. The next example creates a unique clustered index, as follows:

```
CREATE UNIQUE CLUSTERED INDEX CI_AccountNo
    ON accounts (account_no)
```

The unique keyword ensures that only one row has a particular key value, in this case account_no. In other words, the uniqueness of the key is enforced. Note that the table may or may not already contain data. If it does, and if there are duplicate values, the above CREATE INDEX statement will fail:

```
CREATE UNIQUE CLUSTERED INDEX CI_AccountNo
    ON accounts (account_no)

Server: Msg 1505, Level 16, State 1, Line 1
CREATE UNIQUE INDEX terminated because a duplicate key
was found. Most significant primary key is '105000'.
The statement has been terminated.
```

Similarly, once the index has been successfully created, an attempt to insert or update a row that would result in a duplicate key value will fail:

```
INSERT INTO accounts (account_no, customer_no, branch_no,
balance, account_notes)
    VALUES (1916, 103424, 1012, 10765, 'A busy account')

Server: Msg 2601, Level 14, State 3, Line 1
Cannot insert duplicate key row in object 'accounts' with
unique index 'CI_AccountNo'.
The statement has been terminated.
```

This is fine, since we want the account_no column to contain no duplicate values, since this is the way we uniquely identify an account.

As mentioned previously, only one clustered index can be created on a table. This makes sense, since data can only be physically sorted in one order. Any attempt to create a second clustered index will fail:

```
CREATE CLUSTERED INDEX CI_AccountBalance
    ON accounts (balance)
```

```
Server: Msg 1902, Level 16, State 3, Line 1
Cannot create more than one clustered index on table
'accounts'. Drop the existing clustered index
'CI_AccountNo' before creating another.
```

To create a nonclustered index the CREATE INDEX statement is used, as it was for creating the clustered index, only in this case the NONCLUS-TERED keyword is specified:

```
CREATE NONCLUSTERED INDEX NCI_AccountBalance
    ON accounts (balance)
```

If neither CLUSTERED nor NONCLUSTERED is specified, a non-clustered index is created. The UNIQUE keyword has the same effect as it does for a clustered index. Hence, the following CREATE INDEX state-ment defaults to a nonunique, nonclustered index:

```
CREATE INDEX NCI_AccountBalance
    ON accounts (balance)
```

**Note:** The name of the index can be any name considered legal by SQL Server. I prefer to prefix the name with CI_ or NCI_ to signify a clustered or nonclustered index, respectively. I also find it useful to then use meaning-ful text that indicates the column name. This does, however, become unwieldy when you have an index that is comprised of many columns, so some compromises will have to be made. No naming scheme is ever perfect!

So far our examples have shown indexes that consist of only one col-umn. It is not uncommon to create an index that consists of more than one column. Such an index is known as a composite index. An index can be cre-ated consisting of no greater than 16 columns, which, in practical terms, is a limit few people are likely to hit. Also, the sum of the column sizes in the index cannot be greater than 900 bytes. It is not a good idea to choose a composite key of 900 bytes in length, because very few index entries will be able to fit into an index page and so many index pages will be used in the index. This will ultimately result in deep indexes consisting of many index levels. Traversing the index may then require many disk I/Os. In SQL Server 2000 it is, in fact, possible to create an index that contains columns defined with variable-length data types, such as VARCHAR, where the sum of the maximum sizes appears to exceed 900 bytes. However, if an attempt is made to insert a row so that the actual size of the index key would exceed the 900-byte limit, an error is returned.

For example, suppose a table consists of the following structure:

```
CREATE TABLE account_details
    (
    account_no      INT          NOT NULL,
    account_notes   VARCHAR(1000) NOT NULL
    )
```

If we attempt to create a nonclustered index on the account_notes column, SQL Server will successfully create the index but will warn us that the index key is potentially too large:

```
CREATE NONCLUSTERED INDEX NCI_AccountDetails
    ON account_details (account_notes)

Warning!. The maximum permissible key length is 900
bytes. The index 'NCI_AccountDetails' has maximum length
of 1000 bytes. For some combination of large values, the
insert/update operation will fail.
```

If we then attempt to insert a short string into the table, there is no problem:

```
INSERT INTO account_details VALUES (1000, 'This string is
less than 900')
```

However, if we attempt to insert a row with a string value large than 900 bytes, we are not allowed to do so:

```
INSERT INTO account_details
    VALUES (1001, 'This string is more than 900'+
REPLICATE('*',900))
Server: Msg 1946, Level 16, State 4, Line 1
Operation failed. The index entry of length 928 bytes for
the index 'NCI_AccountDetails' exceeds the maximum
permissible length of 900 bytes.
```

How do we specify an option to reserve space in index pages when an index is created? Remember that in the case of a clustered index the data pages are considered to be the lowest level of the index, whereas in the case of a nonclustered index the bottom level of the index is considered to be the lowest level of the index pages. In either case the lowest level of index is known as the leaf level.

The FILLFACTOR option is used to reserve space, and this option takes a value from 0 to 100. An index created with a FILLFACTOR of 100 will have its index pages completely filled. This is useful if no data is to be entered into the table in the future.

**Table 3.1**   *The Effect of Different FILLFACTOR Values*

| FILLFACTOR Value % | Nonleaf Page | Leaf Page |
| --- | --- | --- |
| 0 | one index entry | completely full |
| 1–99 | one index entry | ≤ FILLFACTOR % full |
| 100 | completely full | completely full |

An index created with a FILLFACTOR of 0 will have its leaf pages completely filled, but other levels in the index will have enough space for a minimum of another index entry. An index created with a FILLFACTOR of between 0 and 100 will have its leaf pages filled to the FILLFACTOR percentage specified, and, again, other levels in the index will have enough space for a minimum of another index entry.

The default FILLFACTOR value is 0, and this default value can be changed with the sp_configure system stored procedure or via the Database Settings tab in the Server Properties dialog box in the SQL Enterprise Manager. Table 3.1 shows the consequence of different FILLFACTOR values. A FILLFACTOR value of 0 specifies that the leaf-level page of the index should be completely filled, leaving no free space; however, the nonleaf pages should reserve space for one extra index entry. A FILLFACTOR value of 100 percent specifies that the leaf-level page of the index should be completely filled, leaving no free space. There should also be no free space reserved in the index pages. A FILLFACTOR value of 1 percent to 99 percent specifies that the leaf-level page of the index should be filled no more than the FILLFACTOR value. The nonleaf pages should reserve space for one extra index entry. Note that for nonunique clustered indexes, space is reserved for two index entries.

Care should be taken when choosing a FILLFACTOR, since its relevance will depend on the way the application uses the table data. There is little point in reserving space throughout an index if the row inserted always has a key greater than the current maximum key value. The following example creates an index with a FILLFACTOR of 50 percent, meaning that each data page (leaf page) will only be filled to 50 percent. Index pages at the other levels will have room for one or two more index entries.

```
CREATE CLUSTERED INDEX CI_AccountBalance ON accounts
(balance)
WITH FILLFACTOR =50
```

SQL Server will round up the number of rows placed on a page, so if the FILLFACTOR value would allow 3.3 rows, then 4 rows are stored.

Note that over time, as rows are inserted into the table, the effectiveness of the FILLFACTOR value will vanish, and a planned rebuilding of critical indexes at periodic intervals should be considered if heavy inserts are made to the table. Because SQL Server merges index pages with only one index entry to keep the index compact, the number of items on an index page is never less than two, even if a low value of FILLFACTOR is specified.

Another option, PAD_INDEX on the CREATE INDEX statement, is relevant to reserving space. The PAD_INDEX clause means that the FILL-FACTOR setting should be applied to the index pages as well as to the data pages in the index.

The IGNORE_DUP_KEY option is useful when a unique clustered or nonclustered index is to be created on a table that might have rows with duplicate key values inserted. If the IGNORE_DUP_KEY option is set, rows containing duplicate key values are discarded, but the statement will succeed. However, if the IGNORE_DUP_KEY option is not set, the statement as a whole will be aborted.

The DROP_EXISTING option can be a very useful performance optimization. Suppose we have a scenario where we have a table on which we have built a clustered index and perhaps two nonclustered indexes. As discussed earlier, if there is a clustered index present on a table, then the pointers at the leaf level of any nonclustered indexes on that table will be the clustered index key. Suppose we drop the clustered index from the table. The nonclustered index leaf pages can no longer contain index entries that use the clustered index key as the pointer value—there is no clustered index and therefore no clustered index key!

When the clustered index is dropped, SQL Server will rebuild all the nonclustered indexes on that table so that their index leaf pages will now contain index entries that use the Row ID as the pointer value. Remember, a Row ID is a Page ID (File ID plus page number) plus the position of the row on the page. The important point here is that SQL Server will rebuild all the nonclustered indexes on that table. This obviously can be a very time-consuming and resource-intensive process. But this is only the half of it.

Suppose the reason we wished to drop the clustered index was because we wanted to rebuild it. Perhaps we wanted to reorganize it so that page fragmentation was eliminated. Well, this means that after dropping the clustered index we are now going to create it again. Guess what's going to happen to all the nonclustered indexes on that table? You guessed! SQL Server will rebuild all the nonclustered indexes on that table so that their index leaf pages will now contain index entries that use the clustered index key as the pointer value.

This means that our clustered index reorganization has caused our nonclustered indexes to be rebuilt twice. What's annoying is that their leaf-level pointers have ended up as they started out anyway—clustered index key pointers. So what can we do to reduce the impact of rebuilding a clustered index?

Luckily for us the CREATE INDEX statement allows us to specify the DROP_EXISTING option. This allows us to issue a CREATE INDEX statement with the same name as an existing index. Using this option when you wish to rebuild a clustered index will give you a performance boost. The clustered index will be recreated on a new set of database pages, but, because the clustered index key values remain the same, the nonclustered indexes on the table do not have to be rebuilt. In fact, the recreation of the clustered index can make use of the fact that the data is already sorted in key sequence order so this data does not have to be sorted.

The DROP_EXISTING option can also be used if the clustered index key definition changes. Perhaps a new column is used. In this case the nonclustered index will have to be rebuilt—but only once.

The DROP_EXISTING option can also be used for a nonclustered index, and there will be a performance advantage over dropping and creating the nonclustered index. However, the real benefit is with rebuilding clustered indexes. Using this option will definitely use fewer resources than performing a DROP INDEX followed by a CREATE INDEX.

A CREATE INDEX using this option can also be used to rebuild the index that is created when a primary key constraint is defined on a table. This was previously accomplished with DBCC DBREINDEX. Comparing the resource use of both approaches, they seem identical—so there is probably no need to change existing scripts on this basis alone.

The STATISTICS_NORECOMPUTE option dictates that out-of-date index statistics are not automatically recomputed. This is an option I have never had to use. I have found that ensuring that index key distribution statistics are as up-to-date and accurate as possible is the best approach. Index key distribution statistics are discussed in Chapter 4.

The ON FILEGROUP option allows the database administrator to create the index on a filegroup different from the table itself. The use of filegroups was discussed in Chapter 2. The idea is that by using multiple filegroups, disk I/O to the index and table can be spread across separate disk drives for better performance. However, most database administrators typically use a form of disk striping to spread disk I/O. Disk striping is discussed in Chapter 5.

**Note:** Filegroups are also used to facilitate the backing up of large databases. However, if one filegroup contains a table and a separate filegroup contains an index for that table, then both filegroups must be backed up together.

Another index creation option that needs to be discussed is the column [ASC | DESC], which is part of the CREATE INDEX statement. Using these options determines whether an ascending or descending index is created. When an index is created, each column in the index key can be flagged with ASC or DESC. This specifies whether the index column has its data sorted in an ascending or descending manner. The default is ASC, which ensures that scripts written to create indexes in earlier versions of SQL Server behave correctly.

Suppose we create an index on the Accounts table, as in the following example:

```
CREATE NONCLUSTERED INDEX NCI_CustNoAccountNo
    ON accounts (customer_no ASC, account_no DESC)
```

The data in the customer_no key column will be held in ascending order, whereas the data in the account_no key column will be held in descending order. Why bother providing this capability? After all, the doubly linked lists that chain the index pages in an index level together allow SQL Server to rapidly move backward and forward along the sequence of keys. This is true, but if the query requests data to be sorted in the ascending order of one column and the descending order of another column, then just moving along the chain is not going to provide the optimum performance. If, however, the key columns are actually held in a sequence that matches the ORDER BY, then the chain can be followed in one direction and this will provide the optimum performance, so no additional sorting will be required.

The following query will be fully supported by the NCI_CustNo-AccountNo index without an additional sort step:

```
SELECT customer_no, account_no FROM accounts
    WHERE customer_no BETWEEN 1000 AND 1500
    ORDER BY customer_no ASC, account_no DESC
```

The following query will not be fully supported by the NCI_CustNoAccountNo index, and it will need an additional sort step:

```
SELECT customer_no, account_no FROM accounts
    WHERE customer_no BETWEEN 1000 AND 1500
    ORDER BY customer_no ASC, account_no ASC
```

A new metadata function named INDEXKEY_PROPERTY reports whether an index column is stored in ascending or descending order. The sp_helpindex system stored procedure has also been enhanced to report the direction of index key columns.

Finally, the SORT_IN_TEMPDB option can be used to place the data from intermediate sort runs used while creating the index into tempdb. This can result in a performance improvement if tempdb is placed on another disk drive or RAID array. The default behavior, if this option is not used, is to utilize space in the database in which the index is being created. This means that the disk heads are moving back and forth between the data pages and the temporary sort work area, which may degrade performance.

One aspect of index creation that can be seen from the CREATE INDEX syntax diagram is that SQL Server 2000 can create indexes on views. This is a significant enhancement to the product from a performance perspective and therefore is treated separately later in this chapter.

So, we have looked at the CREATE INDEX statement and the options that can be chosen. There are other ways in which we can create indexes and these are discussed in the following sections.

## 3.7.2   The SQL Enterprise Manager

To create a new index in the SQL Enterprise Manager the following sequence of events can be performed:

1.   Expand the server in the Console Pane.

2.   Expand the Databases folder.

3.   Expand the database holding the table of interest.

4.   Expand the Tables folder.

5.   Right-click the table on which you wish to create an index.

6.   Select All Tasks followed by Manage Indexes.

The Manage Indexes window is displayed, which lists the indexes that are currently resident on the table, whether or not they are clustered, and which columns constitute the index key. This is shown in Figure 3.18.

**Figure 3.18**
*Manage Indexes*
*window in the*
*SQL Server*
*Enterprise*
*Manager*

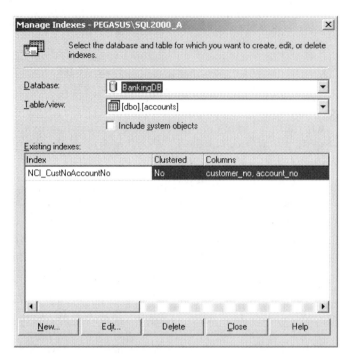

The New... button can be clicked in order to create an index, and this results in the Create New Index window being displayed, as shown in Figure 3.19.

The index can be named and the columns and index options chosen. From the Manage Indexes window, it is also possible to delete and edit an index.

Another means of creating an index through the SQL Server Enterprise Manager is through an alternate sequence of events, as follows:

1.    Expand the server in the Console Pane.

2.    Expand the Databases folder.

3.    Expand the database holding the table of interest.

4.    Expand the Tables folder.

5.    Right-click the table on which you wish to create an index.

6.    Select Design Table.

7.    In the Design Table window click the Table and Index Properties button.

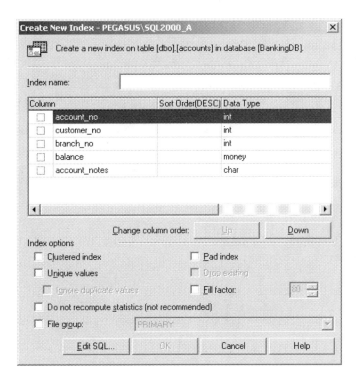

**Figure 3.19**
*Create New Index
window in the
SQL Server
Enterprise
Manager*

8.    In the Properties window select the Indexes/Keys tab and click
      New.

9.    Fill in the details as required to define the new index.

10.   Click Close and save the table design.

      The Indexes/Keys tab is shown in Figure 3.20.

      Personally, I find this route to creating an index confusing. I much prefer
      the All Tasks...Manage Indexes... approach.

### 3.7.3   The Query Analyzer

The Manage Indexes window, which can be accessed through the All
Tasks... Manage Indexes... route in the SQL Server Enterprise Manager, can
also be accessed via the Tools...Manage Indexes menu item in the Query
Analyzer. Right mouse–clicking any icon in the graphical query plan also
displays a menu, which allows Manage Indexes to be selected. Also, two
Query Analyzer templates can be used to create an index in Transact-SQL.
There is a basic-syntax and a full-syntax template. Use Edit and Insert Tem-
plate from the Query Analyzer menu.

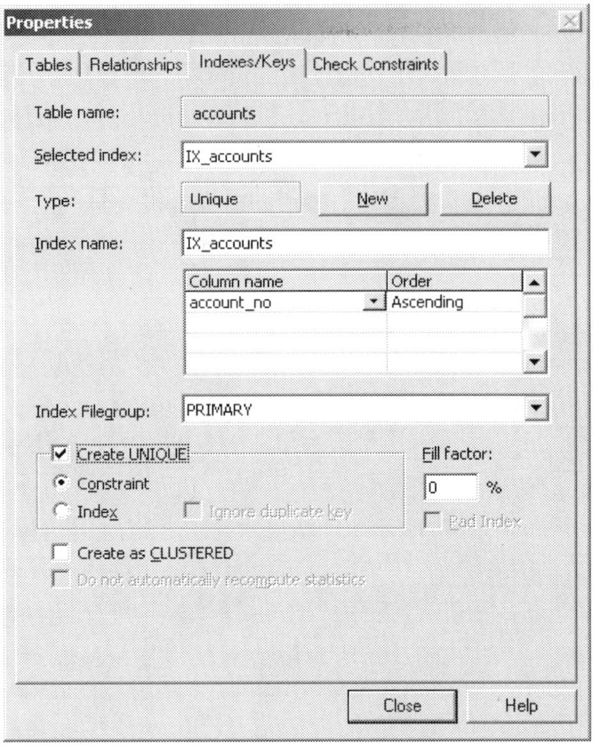

**Figure 3.20**
*Index/Keys*
*window in the*
*SQL Server*
*Enterprise*
*Manager*

### 3.7.4 The Create Index wizard

This wizard leads you through a logical sequence of steps in order to create an index. After the initial welcome screen you are invited to choose the database and table on which you wish to create the index. The next screen allows you to select the columns that are to participate in the index and whether their sort order is ascending or descending. Index options such as whether the index is to be clustered or unique and the FILLFACTOR are specified on the following screen. Finally, the last screen allows you to name the index and order the columns.

### 3.7.5 The SQL Distributed Management Framework (SQL-DMF)

The SQL Distributed Management Framework (SQL-DMF) is an integrated framework of objects, services, and components that may be used to manage SQL Server. Within the SQL-DMF resides SQL Distributed Management Objects (SQL-DMO). The SQL-DMO is a collection of objects that may be used for SQL Server database management. Index management can be performed through the SQL-DMO. Here is an example of Visual Basic code, which uses the SQL-DMO to create an index:

```
Private Sub cmdCommand1_Click()
On Error GoTo ErrorHandler

    Dim oSQLServer As SQLDMO.SQLServer
    Dim oTblCustomers As SQLDMO.Table
    Dim oIdxCustomerNo As SQLDMO.Index

    Dim bConnected As Boolean
    Set oSQLServer = New SQLDMO.SQLServer
    Set oIdxCustomerNo = New SQLDMO.Index
    Set oTblCustomers = New SQLDMO.Table

    bConnected = False
    oSQLServer.LoginTimeout = 30

    oSQLServer.Connect "KENENG01", "SA", ""
    bConnected = True

    Set oTblCustomers =
oSQLServer.Databases("BankingDB").Tables("Customers")

' Create a new Index object, then populate the object
' defining a unique, nonclustered index

    oIdxCustomerNo.Name = "NCI_CustomerNo"
    oIdxCustomerNo.Type = SQLDMOIndex_Unique
    oIdxCustomerNo.IndexedColumns = "[customer_no]"

' Create the index by adding the populated Index object
' to its containing collection.

    oTblCustomers.Indexes.Add oIdxCustomerNo

    oSQLServer.DisConnect

    Set oSQLServer = Nothing
    Set oTblCustomers = Nothing
    Set oIdxCustomerNo = Nothing

Exit Sub

ErrorHandler:

    MsgBox (Err.Description)
```

```
        If bConnected = True Then

            oSQLServer.DisConnect

            Set oSQLServer = Nothing
            Set oTblCustomers = Nothing

        End If

    End Sub
```

## 3.8    Dropping and renaming indexes

Both clustered and nonclustered indexes can be dropped with the DROP INDEX Transact-SQL statement:

```
DROP INDEX accounts.CI_AccountBalance
```

Note that the table name must also be specified. Indexes can also be dropped by using the graphical interfaces. As discussed previously, if there is a clustered index present on the table, then all the nonclustered indexes will use the clustered index key as a pointer in the leaf-level index pages. Therefore, dropping a clustered index may be a slow, resource-intensive operation, since all the nonclustered indexes will have to be rebuilt. On the other hand, dropping a nonclustered index will be a relatively fast operation, since no other indexes on the table will be affected.

It follows, therefore, that the order in which you drop indexes is important. Drop the nonclustered indexes first, before you drop the clustered index if there is one present on the table. Otherwise, you will waste time rebuilding the nonclustered indexes you are just about to drop.

Indexes can be renamed by using the sp_rename system stored procedure:

```
EXEC sp_rename 'accounts.CI_AccountBalance',
CI_AccountCurrentBalance
```

Note the use of the single quotes. Indexes may also be renamed by using the graphical interfaces.

## 3.9    Displaying information about indexes

Information can be graphically displayed by using the SQL Server Enterprise Manager or the Query Analyzer. There are also system stored procedures and functions that can be used to display information about indexes. These methods are discussed in the following sections.

### 3.9.1   The SQL Server Enterprise Manager

We have previously discussed how indexes can be created using the SQL Server Enterprise Manager All Tasks followed by Manage Indexes... route. The Manage Indexes window can be used to display information about an index. Just choose the index and click Edit. The Edit Existing window appears providing information about the chosen index. This is shown in Figure 3.21.

Similarly, if the table is right-clicked and Design Table chosen as discussed previously, the Table and Index Properties button can be clicked and the Indexes/Keys tab selected. A Properties window will then provide information about the selected index. This is shown in Figure 3.22.

In the Query Analyzer, the Manage Indexes window can be displayed from the Tools menu item.

**Figure 3.21**
*Edit Existing window in the SQL Server Enterprise Manager*

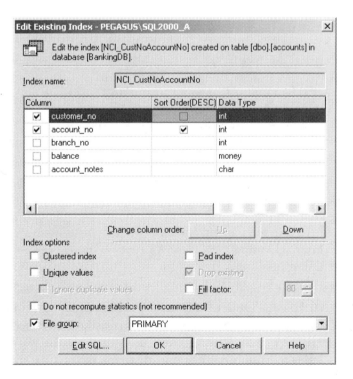

**Figure 3.22**

*Index/Keys window
in the SQL Server
Enterprise
Manager showing
an existing index*

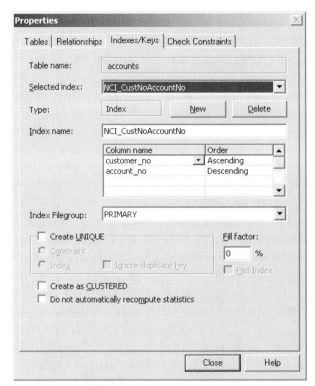

The Display Estimated Execution Plan window also provides access to the Manage Indexes window. When a query is present in the query pane, click the Display Estimated Execution Plan button or type CTRL+L. This displays the estimated query execution plan in the form of a number of icons. We will discuss these in the next chapter. For now we are only interested in obtaining information about our indexes. Just right-click anywhere in the display and choose Manage Indexes. The now-familiar Manage Indexes window will appear. I find the ability to display this window from here extremely useful, because when I am tuning an index strategy I am invariably using the Query Analyzer to display the estimated query execution plan.

In the Query Analyzer, the Object Browser window can be displayed by clicking the Object Browser button or pressing the F8 function key. A database hierarchy can be expanded so that the list of the indexes on the table can be viewed. Right-clicking an index provides the ability to script the index to various destinations. A section of the Object Browser is shown in Figure 3.23.

**Figure 3.23**
*A section of the
Object Browser
showing an index
object*

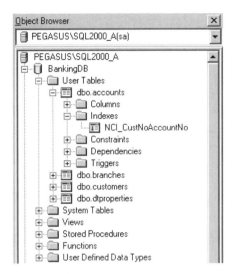

### 3.9.2    The system stored procedure sp_helpindex

The indexes that are present on a table can be listed by using the
sp_helpindex system stored procedure:

```
EXEC sp_helpindex accounts

index_name         index_description               index_keys
----------         -----------------               ----------
NCI_CustomerNo     nonclustered located on PRIMARY  customer_no
NCI_Balance        nonclustered located on PRIMARY  balance
```

### 3.9.3    The system table Sysindexes

The stored procedure sp_helpindex looks in the system table sysindexes,
which contains much useful information about indexes. Sysindexes is
present in every database. The definition of the table is shown in Table 3.2.

The following example shows a sysindexes entry for the clustered index
on the Accounts table. The column headings have been edited and moved
for clarity.

```
SELECT * FROM sysindexes WHERE name = 'CI_cusno'

id          status  first          indid  root
--          ------  -----          -----  ----
117575457   164000  x400A00000100  1      0xAF0C00000100
```

```
minlen   keycnt   groupid   dpages   reserved   used   rowcnt   rowmodctr   reserved3
------   ------   -------   ------   --------   ----   ------   ---------   ---------
424      2        1         2084     2159       2148   25000    0           0

reserved4  xmaxlen  maxirow  OrigFillFactor  StatVersion  reserved2
---------  -------  -------  --------------  -----------  ---------
0          441      34       60              0            0

FirstIAM      impid   lockflags   pgmodctr    keys
--------      -----   ---------   --------    ----
0xCF0900000100   0       0       0       0x380138000….

name       statblob        maxlen   rows
----       --------        ------   ----
CI_Cusno   0x040000005A…   8000     25000
```

The indid is 1, which shows that this is a clustered index. The number of data pages, dpages, is 2,084. There are 2,159 pages reserved for all the indexes and data, of which 2,148 are used. There are 25,000 rows.

The first page of the table is x400A00000100, the root page of the index is 0xAF0C00000100424, and the first IAM page is 0xCF0900000100. These can be decoded, as described in Chapter 2. The original FILLFACTOR was 60 percent.

**Table 3.2**    *Sysindexes Table Definition*

| Column | Datatype | Description |
| --- | --- | --- |
| id | int | ID of table (for indid = 0 or 255)—else, the ID of table on which the index is created. |
| status | smallint | Internal system-status information:<br>1 = Terminate command if attempt to insert duplicate key<br>2 = Unique index<br>4 = Terminate command if attempt to insert duplicate row<br>16 = Clustered index<br>64 = Index allows duplicate rows<br>2048 = Index created to support PRIMARY KEY constraint<br>4096 = Index created to support UNIQUE constraint |
| first | int | If indid = 0 or indid = 1, pointer to first data page.<br>If indid > 1 or ≤ 250, pointer to first leaf page.<br>If indid = 255, pointer to first text or image page. |
| indid | smallint | Index ID: 0 = Table, 1 = Clustered index, >1 = Nonclustered Index, 255 = text or image data |

**Table 3.2**    *Sysindexes Table Definition (continued)*

| Column | Datatype | Description |
|---|---|---|
| root | int | If indid > 0 or ≤ 250, pointer to root page. |
| | | If indid = 0 or indid = 255, pointer to last page. |
| minlen | smallint | Minimum length of a row |
| keycnt | smallint | Number of key columns in the index |
| groupid | smallint | ID of the filegroup in which the object is created |
| dpages | int | If indid = 0 or indid = 1, dpages is the count of used data pages. If indid > 1 or ≤ 250, dpages is the count of index leaf pages. |
| reserved | int | If indid = 0 or indid = 1, the total of pages allocated for all indexes and data pages. |
| | | If indid > 1 or ≤ 250, the total pages allocated to this index. |
| | | If indid = 255, the total pages allocated for text or image data. |
| used | int | If indid = 0 or indid = 1, the total of pages used for all indexes and data pages. |
| | | If indid > 1 or ≤ 250, the total pages used by this index. |
| | | If indid = 255, the total pages used for text or image data. |
| rowcnt | bigint | If indid ≥ 0 and indid ≤ 250, the number of rows in the table—else this is set to 0. |
| rowmodctr | int | Holds the total number of inserted, deleted, or updated rows since the last time statistics were updated for the table. |
| reserved3 | tinyint | Reserved |
| reserved4 | tinyint | Reserved |
| xmaxlen | smallint | Maximum size of a row |
| maxirow | smallint | Maximum size of a nonleaf index row |
| OrigFillFactor | tinyint | The original FILLFACTOR value used when the index was created |
| StatVersion | tinyint | Reserved |
| reserved2 | tinyint | Reserved |
| FirstIAM | binary(6) | Page ID of first IAM page for object |
| impid | smallint | Reserved |
| lockflags | smallint | Used to constrain locking in index |
| pgmodctr | int | Reserved |

**Table 3.2**    *Sysindexes Table Definition (continued)*

| Column | Datatype | Description |
| --- | --- | --- |
| keys | varbinary (1088) | List of the column IDs of the columns that make up the index key |
| name | sysname | Name of table (for indid = 0 or 255)—else index name. |
| statblob | image | Distribution statistics |
| maxlen | int | Reserved |
| rows | int | If indid ≥ 0 and indid ≤ 250, the number of rows in the table—else this is set to 0 (for backward compatibility). |

### 3.9.4   Using metadata functions to obtain information about indexes

There are a number of extremely useful functions that can be used to obtain information about the properties of an index. Probably the most useful one is the INDEXPROPERTY function.

This function takes the following form:

```
INDEXPROPERTY(table_ID, index, property)
```

The table_ID holds the object ID of the table (remember that the ID of an object can be obtained by using the object_id function passing the objects's name).

The index contains the name of the index whose properties you are investigating.

The property is the property to return and can be one of the values shown in Table 3.3.

An example of the INDEXPROPERTY function is as follows:

```
SELECT INDEXPROPERTY(OBJECT_ID('accounts'),
'NCI_Balance', 'IndexDepth')
```

There are other functions that can also be useful when displaying information about an index. The INDEXKEY_PROPERTY function returns information about an index key—for example, whether a column in the key is sorted in ascending or descending order. Another useful function is the OBJECTPROPERTY function. Some properties specified in this function are concerned with indexing, such as whether a table has a clustered index or not.

**Table 3.3**   *Property Values for the INDEXPROPERTY Function*

| Value | Description | Value Returned |
|---|---|---|
| IndexDepth | Depth of the index | Number of levels the index has |
| IndexFillFactor | Index specifies its own fill factor. | Fill factor used when the index was created or last rebuilt. |
| IndexID | Index ID of the index on the table or indexed view | Index ID<br>NULL = Invalid input |
| IsAutoStatistics | Index was generated by the auto create statistics option of sp_dboption. | 1 = True, 0 = False<br>NULL = Invalid input |
| IsClustered | Index is clustered. | 1 = True, 0 = False<br>NULL = Invalid input |
| IsFulltextKey | Index is the full-text key for a table. | 1 = True, 0 = False<br>NULL = Invalid input |
| IsHypothetical | Index is hypothetical and cannot be used directly as a data access path. Hypothetical indexes hold column-level statistics. | 1 = True, 0 = False<br>NULL = Invalid input |
| IsPadIndex | Index specifies space to leave open on each interior node. | 1 = True, 0 = False<br>NULL = Invalid input |
| IsPageLockDisallowed | Page locking is disallowed through sp_indexoption. | 1 = disallowed, 0 = allowed<br>NULL = Invalid input |
| IsRowLockDisallowed | Row locking is disallowed through sp_indexoption. | 1 = disallowed, 0 = allowed<br>NULL = Invalid input |
| IsStatistics | Index was created by the CREATE STATISTICS statement or by the auto create statistics option sp_dboption. Statistics indexes are used as a placeholder for column-level statistics. | 1 = True, 0 = False<br>NULL = Invalid input |
| IsUnique | Index is unique. | 1 = True, 0 = False<br>NULL = Invalid input |

## 3.9.5   **The DBCC statement DBCC SHOWCONTIG**

This DBCC statement is used to obtain information about an index or table that can be used to investigate performance degradation. It is a very useful tool for performance analysis. Some of the output is a little arcane and is not very useful, but that is more than made up for by the fact that DBCC SHOWCONTIG outputs useful information concerning the level of fragmentation that has occurred in a table—in other words, the level of page splitting. The following DBCC SHOWCONTIG output was from the Accounts table after it had been loaded with 12,500 rows with even values in the account_no column and a clustered index created on the account_no column.

```
DBCC SHOWCONTIG scanning 'accounts' table...
Table: 'accounts' (709577566); index ID: 1, database ID: 7
TABLE level scan performed.
- Pages Scanned                            : 695
- Extents Scanned                          : 88
- Extent Switches                          : 87
- Avg. Pages per Extent                    : 7.9
- Scan Density [Best Count:Actual Count]   : 98.86% [87:88]
- Logical Scan Fragmentation               : 12.52%
- Extent Scan Fragmentation                : 0.00%
- Avg. Bytes Free per Page                 : 380.2
- Avg. Page Density (full)                 : 95.30%
```

The first line of output, Pages Scanned, is the number of pages in the page chain; in our example, it is the number of pages in the table (dpages in sysindexes). Another way of looking at this item is that it has taken 695 pages to hold the 12,500 rows. Since a page will hold about 18 rows by the time you have taken away the 96-byte page header and other overhead from the 8-KB page size, this is in the right ballpark.

Extents Scanned is the number of extents read, which means that this is the number of extents used to hold the data rows. Since we have 695 pages, the best we can hope for is (number of pages/8 pages per extent) extents to hold the data. In our case 695/8 is 86.9, and, therefore, the best we can hope for is to hold the data in 87 extents. The data is actually held in 88 extents, slightly over our theoretical calculation but because of the initial allocation in mixed extents, this is reasonable.

Extent Switches is the number of times the DBCC statement moved off an extent while it was scanning the pages in the extent. We would expect an extent switch to happen after the whole extent had been scanned and a new extent needed to be scanned next. Our extent switches value is 87, which is expected, since the jump onto the first extent is not counted.

The Avg. Pages per Extent is merely the number of pages per extent, which is the (number of pages/number of extents). In our example this is (695/88), which gives us 7.9.

Perhaps the most useful line of output is the Scan Density [Best Count:Actual Count]. This is our measure of fragmentation. The Best Count is the ideal number of extents used to hold our data pages if everything is contiguously linked, whereas the Actual Count is the actual number of extents used to hold our data pages. The Scan Density is the ratio of these two values expressed as a percentage. In other words ([Best Count/ Actual Count] * 100). In our example Scan Density is (87/88 * 100), giving us 98.86 percent, which is close enough to perfect—we are pretty much utilizing our data pages and extents in the most effective way.

The Logical Scan Fragmentation and Extent Scan Fragmentation are not particularly useful, but they do represent the noncontiguity of pages and extents in the index leaf level The Avg. Bytes Free per Page and Avg. Page Density (full) are a measure of the average free bytes on the pages in the chain and the percentage of fullness, respectively. These are values that are affected by the FILLFACTOR used.

Next, 12,500 rows with odd values in the account_no column were loaded. This results in page splitting, since the even-numbered rows now have odd-numbered rows inserted between them.

Output after loading 12,500 rows with odd values in the account_no column:

```
DBCC SHOWCONTIG (accounts)

DBCC SHOWCONTIG scanning 'accounts' table...
Table: 'accounts' (709577566); index ID: 1, database ID: 7
TABLE level scan performed.
- Pages Scanned                         : 1389
- Extents Scanned                       : 176
- Extent Switches                       : 1388
- Avg. Pages per Extent                 : 7.9
- Scan Density [Best Count:Actual Count] : 12.53% [174:1389]
- Logical Scan Fragmentation            : 50.04%
- Extent Scan Fragmentation             : 1.14%
- Avg. Bytes Free per Page              : 374.6
- Avg. Page Density (full)              : 95.37%
```

After loading our second batch of 12,500 rows, we can see that the situation has deteriorated. We have doubled the number of rows in the table and the Pages Scanned value is now 1,389, which is double the number of pages scanned previously, 695. The number of extents used to hold the data is now 176, which, again, is not far off double the number we have just seen, which was 88. The most dramatic increase is in the number of extent switches performed, which is now 1,388—about 16 times greater than the previous value. This gives us a Scan Density of only 12.53 percent.

The bottom line is that there is much page fragmentation. Many pages have been inserted into the original page chain and SQL Server would have to jump around a lot to scan this table. Note also that the page fullness has not changed much. This is often not the case with real-world applications. After page splitting, pages are often found to be between two-thirds and three-quarters full. This is common when page splitting is occurring and is due to the fact that 50:50 splitting is taking place, as mentioned earlier in this chapter. An index rebuild, preferably with an appropriate FILLFAC-TOR value, would be advisable here.

The full syntax of the DBCC SHOWCONTIG statement is as follows:

```
DBCC SHOWCONTIG
[
( { table_name | table_id | view_name | view_id }
[ , index_name | index_id ] )
]
[ WITH
{ ALL_INDEXES
| FAST [, ALL_INDEXES]
| TABLERESULTS [, {ALL_INDEXES}] [, {FAST | ALL_LEVELS}]
}
]
```

IDs may be used instead of names, if preferred. The index name is optional and if omitted DBCC SHOWCONTIG reports information for the table—unless there is a clustered index on the table, in which case it reports information for that. So, if you want to report on a nonclustered index, it should be named. The option ALL_INDEXES outputs information on all the indexes on the table. The FAST option specifies whether to perform a fast scan of the index and output minimal information. A fast scan does not read the data on each page. The TABLERESULTS option displays results as a rowset and also outputs extra information. Some of this extra information can be very useful. For example, the number of rows referenced by forwarding pointers (as discussed in Chapter 4) is output. By default, information pertaining to a table's data pages (also by convention the clustered index leaf-level pages) or the nonclustered index leaf-level index pages is output. If the ALL_LEVELS option is specified, information pertaining to all index levels is output.

# 3.10   Creating indexes on views

Unlike previous versions of SQL Server, in SQL Server 2000 indexes can be created on a view, if its definition meets certain criteria. Unlike a nonindexed view, which does not physically hold data, an indexed view has its result physically stored in the database. Any modifications to the base data are reflected in the indexed view, so they are best created on tables that are changed infrequently.

The first index created on a view that is to be indexed must be a unique clustered index. Other indexes may then be created. For a view to be indexed it must satisfy a number of criteria.

One criterion is that it must be created with the SCHEMABINDING option. This option binds the view to the schema of the underlying base tables. This means that any views or tables participating in the view cannot be dropped, unless that view is dropped or changed so that it no longer has schema binding. Also, ALTER TABLE statements on tables that participate in views having schema binding will fail if these statements affect the view definition. Some, but not all, of the other criteria are as follows:

- The view must only use base tables in its definition—no views.

- Any user-defined functions in the view must use the SCHEMAB-INDING option.

- The ANSI_NULLS and QUOTED_IDENTIFIER options must have been set to ON for the connection that defined the view.

- The ANSI_NULLS option must have been set to ON for the connection that defined the tables referenced by the view.

- The base tables referenced in the view must be in the same database and have the same database owner.

- Base tables and user-defined functions referenced in the view must use a two-part name. No other combination of names is allowed.

- All functions referenced by expressions in the view must be deterministic. This means that for a given set of inputs, the same result is always returned.

- The select_list of the SELECT statement in the view must not include the * notation—the columns must be listed explicitly.

- Columns must not appear more than once, unless they appear the second time (or third time, etc.) in a complex expression. The select_list Col1, Col2 is valid and so is Col1, Col2, Col1+Col2 but not Col1, Col2, Col1.

- Also not allowed are derived tables, rowset functions, the UNION operator, subqueries, outer or self joins, the TOP clause, the ORDER BY clause, the DISTINCT keyword, and COUNT(*); however, COUNT_BIG(*) is allowed.

- The AVG, MAX, MIN, STDEV, STDEVP, VAR, or VARP aggregate functions. If AVG, MAX, MIN, STDEV, STDEVP, VAR, or VARP are specified in queries referencing the indexed view, the optimizer can often calculate the result if the view select_list contains SUM and COUNT_BIG. For example, AVG() can be calculated from SUM() / COUNT_BIG().

- A SUM function that references an expression that can be nullable is not allowed.

- The full-text search predicates CONTAINS or FREETEXT are not allowed.

- The view select_list cannot contain aggregate expressions unless a GROUP BY is present.

- If GROUP BY is present, the view select_list must contain a COUNT_BIG(*) expression, and the view definition cannot include HAVING, CUBE, or ROLLUP.

- A column that results from an expression that either evaluates to a float value or uses float expressions for its evaluation cannot be a key of an index in an indexed view.

We've not finished yet! Indexes created on the view have some restrictions also, as shown in the following list. Most importantly, the first index that is created on the view must be clustered and unique.

- The user executing the CREATE INDEX statement must be the owner of the view.

- The following options must be set to ON for the connection creating the index: CONCAT_NULL_YIELDS_NULL, ANSI_NULLS, ANSI_PADDING, ANSI_WARNINGS, and ARITHABORT. The QUOTED_IDENTIFIERS and NUMERIC_ROUNDABORT options must be set to OFF.

- Even if the CREATE INDEX statement does not reference them, the view cannot include text, ntext, or image columns.

- If the SELECT statement in the view definition specifies a GROUP BY clause, then the key of the unique clustered index can reference only columns specified in the GROUP BY clause.

An example view definition is as follows:

```
CREATE VIEW dbo.BranchTotalFunds
    WITH SCHEMABINDING
    AS
    SELECT branch_no,
    COUNT_BIG(*) AS AccountInstances,
    SUM(balance) AS TotalBalance
    FROM dbo.accounts
    GROUP BY branch_no
```

The following clustered index can now be created:

```
CREATE UNIQUE CLUSTERED INDEX CIV_BranchTotalFunds
    ON dbo.BranchTotalFunds (branch_no)
```

Although the clustered index key will only contain the branch_no column, being a clustered index, the complete set of data rows with all the columns will be stored at the clustered index leaf level in the database. Nonclustered indexes may also now be created on the indexed view if desired.

The query optimizer automatically makes use of indexed views—they do not have to be named explicitly—however, this is only true of the Enterprise Edition. We will discuss this behavior in Chapter 4.

## 3.11   Creating indexes with computed columns

In SQL Server 2000 it is possible to utilize computed columns in an index definition. The definition of the computed column must be deterministic. This means that for a given set of inputs, the same result is always returned.

A computed column definition is deterministic if the following occur:

- All functions referenced in the definition are deterministic and precise.

- All columns referenced in the definition are from the same table as the computed column.

- Multiple rows are not used to provide data for the computed column—for example, using SUM().

FLOAT data types are not precise. Also, various connection options, such as ANSI_NULL, must be set to ON when the table is created, and other options must be set to ON for the connection that creates the index.

As an example, the GETDATE() and @@IDENTITY functions are nondeterministic, whereas SQUARE() and DATEDIFF() are deterministic.

Suppose we create the following table:

```
CREATE TABLE accounts
    (
    account_no      INT         NOT NULL ,
    customer_no     INT         NOT NULL ,
    branch_no       INT         NOT NULL ,
    balance         MONEY       NOT NULL ,
    account_notes   CHAR (400)  NOT NULL ,
    taxed_balance   AS (balance * 0.9)
    )
```

The computed column is deterministic, since, for a given input, it produces the same output. Therefore, we can create an index using this column:

```
CREATE INDEX nci_taxed_balance ON accounts
(taxed_balance)
```

A SELECT statement that specifies the column in its WHERE clause will use this index if it makes sense to do so.

```
CREATE TABLE accounts
    (
    account_no      INT         NOT NULL ,
    customer_no     INT         NOT NULL ,
    branch_no       INT         NOT NULL ,
    balance         MONEY       NOT NULL ,
    account_notes   CHAR (400)  NOT NULL ,
    account_date    AS (GETDATE())
    )
```

We could not, however, create an index on the account_date column, since the computed column is nondeterministic.

# 3.12  Using indexes to retrieve data

Now that we have seen how indexes are put together and how they behave when data is retrieved and added, we can investigate how indexes are used to support good performance.

The choice of whether to use an index or not and if so which index is a decision that the query optimizer makes. We will discuss the query optimizer in detail in Chapter 4, but we need to look at the different mechanisms of using an index to understand what the query optimizer is considering when it is in the process of making its decision.

If there are no indexes present on a table, there is only one mechanism by which the data can be accessed and that is by means of a table scan. When a table scan is performed, each page in the table is read starting at the first page and ending at the last page. To read each page, a page request, SQL Server performs a logical read, also known as a logical I/O. If the page is not found in the data cache, this results in a physical read from disk. Each time a query is run the number of physical reads generated by the query is likely to change, because data will be cached from the previous execution of the query. For this reason, when comparing the work performed by different query optimizer strategies, it is better to compare the logical read values.

The table scan is a useful baseline, since we know that we can always access our data in the number of logical reads the table scan requires. Anything more is likely to be a poor strategy. However, be aware that the query optimizer in SQL Server 2000 considers other factors, such as CPU, when choosing a plan, and so the point at which the query optimizer chooses a table scan in preference to an indexed access is not just the point at which the logical reads used by an index plan exceed the pages in the table, as it was with SQL Server 6.5. With this in mind let us consider different types of index access.

We will use simplified diagrams for our two index types, as shown in Figures 3.24 and 3.25.

Figure 3.24 shows a simplified clustered index, and Figure 3.25 shows a simplified nonclustered index. Note that, as is commonly found, the clustered index contains one less level than the nonclustered index.

**Figure 3.24**
*A simplified
clustered index*

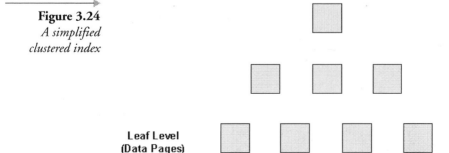

Leaf Level
(Data Pages)

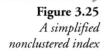

**Figure 3.25**
*A simplified
nonclustered index*

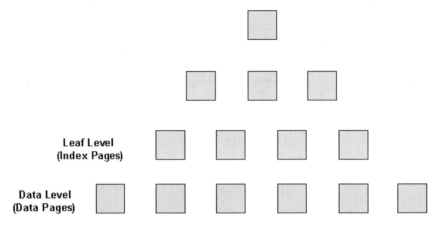

We will use a number of scenarios. First of all, we will use a scenario where we request a single row from the Accounts table using a clustered index on the account_no column and then a nonclustered index on the account_no column.

Our second scenario will perform a range retrieval from the Accounts table with the same indexing strategy.

Our third scenario will perform an access to the Accounts table that can be satisfied completely by the nonclustered index key columns.

Our fourth scenario will revisit the above scenarios; however, there will still be a nonclustered index on the account_no column of the Accounts table, but we will also add a clustered index on the customer_no column of the Accounts table.

Our fifth scenario will involve the use of multiple nonclustered indexes on our Accounts table.

## 3.12.1   Retrieving a single row

This is sometimes called a direct key lookup. We are attempting to retrieve a single row as opposed to a range of rows. Often this is a result of using the equality operator (=) on a primary key, for example:

```
SELECT balance WHERE account_no = 4000
```

In the case of the clustered index SQL Server will first obtain the page number of the root page from the sysindexes table. In this root page there will be a number of key values, and SQL Server will look for the highest key value that is not greater than the key we wish to retrieve.

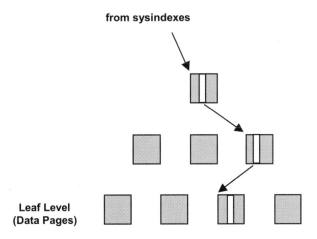

**Figure 3.26**
*A direct key lookup*
*in a clustered index*

from sysindexes

Leaf Level
(Data Pages)

---

**Note:** Remember that with both clustered indexes and nonclustered indexes, the index entries in the index pages are always held in key sequence at a given index level. Refer to Figures 3.1 and 3.3 to clarify this point.

---

As we have already seen, in a clustered index an index entry consists of the index key plus a pointer, which is a page number (ignoring the fileID), so the index key retrieved in the root page will point to an intermediate index page.

Again, SQL Server will look for the highest key value that is not greater than the key we wish to retrieve. In our diagram, the key found will now contain a page pointer to a data page, and this page will be retrieved. The data page is now scanned for a row containing the key we wish to retrieve. The rows in the data page in a clustered index are in key sequence, so the row is either found and returned or SQL Server will return a message stating "(0 row(s) affected)." This is shown in Figure 3.26.

In the case of a nonclustered index, the traversal of the index is performed in a similar manner. However, once the leaf level is reached the key value of the key we wish to retrieve is found, and this leaf-level index entry will contain the Row ID of the data row, so SQL Server will go directly to it in the appropriate data page. (See Figure 3.27.)

The nonclustered index has taken one more logical read. Is this important? Taken on its own probably not; however, if this is a query we are trying to optimize for an online transaction processing (OLTP) system with a large user population, it might just influence our design. On the whole

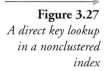

**Figure 3.27**
*A direct key lookup
in a nonclustered
index*

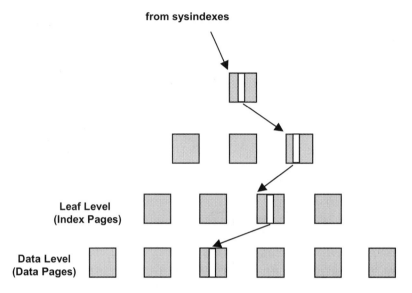

though, the difference between using a clustered index or a nonclustered
index for single row retrieval is slim.

## 3.12.2   Retrieving a range of rows

We shall now attempt to retrieve a range of rows, as opposed to a single row.
Often this is a result of using operators such as BETWEEN, <, >, and
LIKE—for example:

```
SELECT balance WHERE account_no BETWEEN 4001 AND 4500
```

In the case of the clustered index SQL Server will first obtain the page
number of the root page from the sysindexes table. In this root page there
will be a number of key values, and SQL Server will look for the highest key
value that is not greater than the lowest key we wish to retrieve.

The page pointer will be followed to the intermediate index page.

Again, SQL Server will look for the highest key value that is not greater
than the lowest key we wish to retrieve. In Figure 3.28, the key found will
now contain a page pointer to a data page, and this page will be retrieved.
The data page is now scanned for a row containing the lowest key we wish
to retrieve. The row is retrieved and so is the next row and so on until the
key value of a retrieved row is found to be higher than the range we require.

This is shown in Figure 3.28 with the query returning three rows. Note
that SQL Server is directed to the data page that contains the lowest key

**Figure 3.28**

*A range retrieval in
a clustered index*

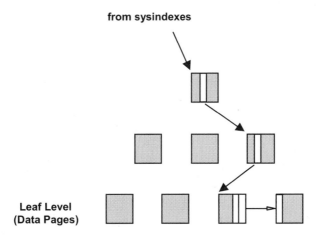

from sysindexes

Leaf Level
(Data Pages)

value in the range. Once there, SQL Server needs only to retrieve the rows sequentially until the range is exhausted. SQL Server can do this because the clustered index has ensured that the rows are in key sequence order.

In the case of a nonclustered index the traversal of the index is performed in a similar fashion. However, once the leaf level is reached the key value of the key we wish to retrieve is found, and this leaf-level index entry will contain the Row ID of the data row, so SQL Server will go directly to it in the appropriate data page. Now the leaf level of the nonclustered index is in key sequence order but the data is not. What this means is that the key values in the range are found next to one another in the index leaf pages, but it is highly unlikely that the data rows will be found next to one another in the data pages. In Figure 3.29 the query has returned three rows. The leaf level of the nonclustered index contains the three index entries next to one another, but the data rows are on different data pages.

This is a very important point and is a fundamental difference between the behavior of a clustered index and a nonclustered index with range retrievals. In our example the clustered index has required less logical reads to retrieve the data than the nonclustered index because in the clustered index the data rows are adjacent.

We have only retrieved three data rows in our example, but suppose we had retrieved 180 data rows. We can hold 18 rows from the Accounts table in one page, so the clustered index could theoretically retrieve the 180 data rows with ten logical reads to the data pages. The nonclustered index will take 180 logical reads to the data pages, which could equate to 180 physical reads if the data rows were all on their own separate data pages and none were found in the data cache (more on data caching in Chapter 5).

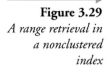

**Figure 3.29**
*A range retrieval in
a nonclustered
index*

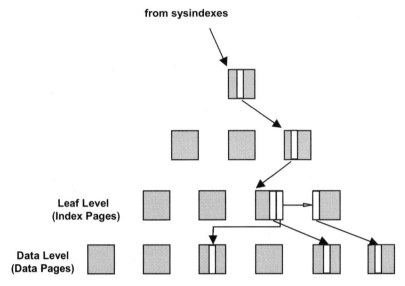

Suppose one data page happened to hold ten of the rows that satisfied the range. The nonclustered index would have ten pointers addressing that page and would still generate ten logical reads to it.

If the query optimizer decided that the number of logical reads needed to traverse the nonclustered index, scan the relevant leaf-level pages, and retrieve the data was greater than the number of pages in the table, a table scan would be performed—assuming that other factors such as CPU had been taken into consideration.

### 3.12.3   Covered queries

The leaf level of a clustered index contains the data rows, whereas the leaf level of a nonclustered index contains only the key and a pointer; as long as the key is only a small portion of the total row we can see that a database page will hold more key values than complete data rows. That is, an index page in the database can hold more index entries than a data page in the database can hold data rows.

We can use this fact to provide fast access for certain queries using a nonclustered index. Suppose we have created a composite index—that is, an index that consists of more than one column. An example of this might be the following:

```
CREATE INDEX NCI_AccountNoBalance
    ON accounts (account_no, balance)
```

**Figure 3.30**
*A covering index*

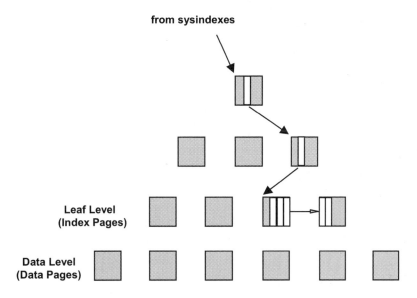

Now, suppose we execute the following query:

```
SELECT balance FROM accounts
     WHERE account_no BETWEEN 4001 AND 4500
```

The query optimizer will realize that this is a covered query and that the index named NCI_AccountNoBalance is a covering index. This means that SQL Server does not have to go to the data level to satisfy the query. It only needs to go down as far as the leaf level of the nonclustered index, as shown in Figure 3.30.

This is very efficient. In reality, there are 500 rows satisfying the query, but SQL Server only used four logical reads to satisfy the query. Although clustered indexes are often more efficient than their nonclustered cousins, when a nonclustered index is used as a covering index it is normally more efficient than an equivalent clustered index. As with a table scan, scanning the leaf level of an index activates the read ahead capability and a parallel data scan is initiated.

### 3.12.4   Retrieving a single row with a clustered index on the table

The important point to note here is that the nonclustered index on the Accounts table now has its leaf-level index entries containing the clustered index key as a pointer, not the Row ID. This was discussed earlier in the chapter. This means that access to data rows via the nonclustered index will take a route from the nonclustered index leaf-level pointer to the data rows via the clustered index. Let us look at our query again:

```
SELECT balance WHERE account_no = 4000
```

SQL Server will first obtain the page number of the root page of the nonclustered index on account_no from the sysindexes table. In this root page there will be a number of key values, and SQL Server will look for the highest key value that is not greater than the key we wish to retrieve. As before, the index key retrieved in the root page will point to an intermediate index page.

Again, SQL Server will look for the highest key value that is not greater than the key we wish to retrieve. Having located that, the next-level index page will be retrieved, which will be the leaf-level index page. The leaf-level index entry for account number 4,000 will contain the clustered index key, which will be a customer number.

The root index page of the clustered index will now be retrieved. Using the customer number value to traverse the clustered index, the data row will

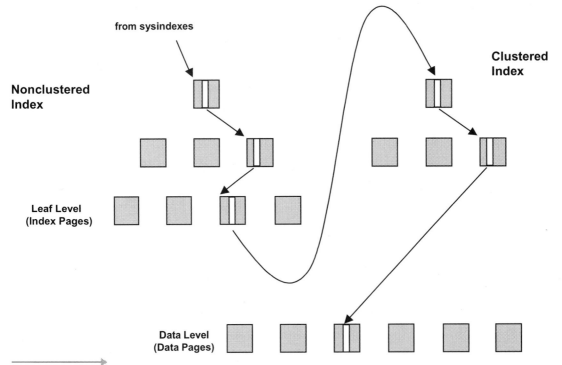

**Figure 3.31**   *A nonclustered index with a clustered index*

be retrieved in exactly the same way as any single row retrieval from a clustered index. This is shown in Figure 3.31.

How does this retrieval strategy compare with our single row retrieval described earlier using a Row ID? Clearly it is less efficient. Instead of following the index pointer directly to the data, we now have to take a trip through the clustered index as well. In reality this is unlikely to be too much of an overhead. A clustered index is a compact index with typically few levels, so we are adding an overhead of a small number of page requests. For a single row retrieval this is not likely to be significant.

### 3.12.5    Retrieving a range of rows with a clustered index on the table

Again, the basic index retrieval strategy is similar to the range retrieval with a nonclustered index, described earlier. In this case, however, instead of requesting a data page containing the row for each leaf-level index entry found in range, the clustered index will be accessed to fetch each of the rows in the range. In other words, instead of requesting 180 data pages to fetch our 180 rows, as before, we are now accessing the clustered index 180 times. This is not efficient at all. Again, range retrieval via a nonclustered index is not efficient. Once more than a few rows are returned by the range retrieval, a table scan is likely to be performed by the query optimizer.

### 3.12.6    Covered queries with a clustered index on the table

This is an interesting scenario. Suppose we wish to execute the following query:

```
SELECT customer_no FROM accounts
    WHERE account_no BETWEEN 4001 AND 4500
```

We will assume that we have a nonclustered index on the account_no column of the Accounts table and a clustered index on the customer_no column of the Accounts table as well.

At first glance, this query does not appear to be covered by the nonclustered index. It is a single column index on account_no. However, we know that the leaf-level pointer is the clustered index key, so the leaf-level index entry contains both the account_no column and the customer_no column. Therefore, the query can indeed be satisfied by the nonclustered index without the data rows being fetched, and the query is, in fact, covered.

The fact that the clustered index key is part of the index entry in a non-clustered index can result in the query optimizer choosing a very efficient strategy.

### 3.12.7   Retrieving a range of rows with multiple nonclustered indexes on the table

Suppose we wished to execute the following query:

```
SELECT * FROM accounts
WHERE
balance BETWEEN 100 AND 200
AND
customer_no BETWEEN 1000 AND 1200
```

If there are no appropriate indexes on the table, SQL Server would perform a table scan. If there is a nonclustered index present on the balance column, then the query optimizer might choose to use that index if the number of rows returned was not too large. If there is a nonclustered index present on the customer_no column, then the query optimizer might choose to use that index if the number of rows returned is not too large.

If one of the indexes is present and is chosen, then SQL Server would process the range retrieval by processing the appropriate range in index key values in the leaf level of the nonclustered index and issuing a data page request for each pointer (we'll assume there is no clustered index on the table, so we are dealing with Row IDs). When each data row is fetched, the remaining criteria would be applied to the data row. We say that it is filtered.

One problem with this technique is that it can be wasteful. Suppose we have a nonclustered index present on the balance column alone and that the query optimizer chooses that index to perform the previous query. The index may have 100 leaf-level index key values satisfying the balance range, and 100 data page requests (logical reads) will be performed. SQL Server will then apply the customer number range filter and could eliminate most of the data rows from the result set. We have used the nonclustered index to fetch a set of rows, most of which are ultimately discarded. Fetching data pages is a relatively expensive operation.

Now suppose we create a second nonclustered index on the customer_no column. The query optimizer can often make use of both of these indexes in the plan. The result of the query is the set intersection of the set of accounts that have a balance between 100 and 200 and the set of accounts that have a customer number between 1,000 and 1,200. This is shown in Figure 3.32.

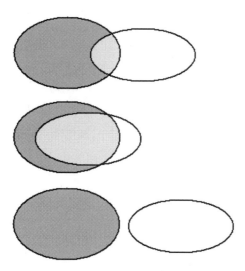

**Figure 3.32**
*Index intersection*

From an indexing perspective we can think of this as the set intersection of the valid set of Row IDs from the nonclustered index on balance and the valid set of Row IDs from the nonclustered index on customer_no. As Figure 3.32 shows, the sets of Row IDs may overlap a little, overlap greatly, or not overlap at all. In the latter case, this means that no rows satisfy both criteria. The query optimizer can perform this set intersection in memory (typically) and so find the set of Row IDs that point to data rows satisfying both query conditions before the data pages have been accessed. This will often avoid having many data page requests performed needlessly. How does SQL Server perform the set intersection operation on the Row IDs? It uses a hashing algorithm, which we will discuss in Chapter 4. In Chapter 4 we will also discuss a query optimizer plan, which utilizes index intersection.

So, typically how much benefit can this use of multiple indexes provide? This depends on a number of considerations, but the main one concerns the size of the reduction in the data page requests. Remember: If there are too many, the query optimizer will probably decide a table scan is a more efficient means of querying the data.

If we look at Figure 3.32, we can see that the intersection of the two sets of Row IDs in the second case results in a set that contains most of the Row IDs. In this case the number of data page requests will not be reduced greatly by the use of both indexes.

The intersection of the two sets of Row IDs in the first case results in a set that contains few of the Row IDs. In this case the number of data page requests will be reduced by the use of both indexes and this is a win.

In the third case the two sets of Row IDs do not intersect. This results in a set that contains no Row IDs. In this case the number of data page requests will be reduced to zero by the use of both indexes in the query plan, since clearly no rows satisfy the query. This is a big win.

We have just looked at a variety of scenarios using clustered and non-clustered indexes. In Chapter 4 we will look more closely at the query optimizer itself and how these fundamental scenarios are used.

# 3.13   Choosing indexes

The choice of indexes can dramatically affect performance and can mean the difference between data being retrieved in seconds, with few disk I/Os or minutes, even hours, with many disk I/Os. Choosing the optimum number of indexes to support the critical queries is therefore an extremely important task.

## 3.13.1   Why not create many indexes?

If queries can be assisted by indexes, why not create lots of indexes on every table? Unfortunately, as in so many areas of database technology, there are swings and roundabouts concerning the use of indexes. On one hand, indexes can speed up access to data, but, on the other hand, they can slow down table insertions, updates, and deletions. This is because SQL Server has more work to do maintaining all the indexes to ensure that they always truly reflect the current data in the table. Indexes also take up disk space.

Clearly, if disk space is plentiful and the database is read only, there are good reasons to create many indexes. In reality most databases experience a mixture of read and write activity, so the correct choice of indexes is critical to good performance. The choice of appropriate indexes should be a product of good upfront design and transaction analysis.

We have already seen the effect that inserts can have on a clustered index. If the index key is not an increasing key value—that is, the newly inserted key is not always higher than existing key values—data rows will be inserted throughout the page chain. This will cause page splitting to occur.

Either way, row insertion means that SQL Server must perform work to maintain the clustered index. If there are also nonclustered indexes on the table, which is usually the case, each nonclustered index must also be maintained when row insertions occur. Every nonclustered index must accommodate a new index entry, which may cause page splitting to occur in the index pages.

What about row deletion? In a clustered index a row may be deleted from a data page, and, if there is no index entry pointing to it because it is not the lowest key value in the page, little maintenance activity need be performed. In the case of nonclustered indexes there will always be maintenance activity if a row is deleted. Every nonclustered index must remove the index entry. If this leaves a single row in an index page, SQL Server will merge the index page with another in order to keep the index compact. Again, this means work for SQL Server.

The behavior of updates was discussed earlier. It is possible that an update to a row can result in the row being deleted and then reinserted, which has the overhead of deletion and insertion.

The bottom line is that too many indexes on a table can be disastrous for the performance of transactions that write to the table. How many indexes should there be on a table? There is no correct answer, but for a volatile table I start to worry if someone wants to put more than three on it. That's not to say that it will be a problem. I'm just saying I worry, which means I don't leave things to chance—I test them!

## 3.13.2 Online transaction processing versus decision support

Online transaction processing (OLTP) systems have characteristics that are different from decision support systems (DSSs), and you should have a good appreciation of where your application fits into this spectrum.

OLTP systems tend to involve a high frequency of short, predefined transactions that affect small amounts of data. More often than not, OLTP systems change data by insertion, update, and deletion. OLTP systems frequently support large user populations and provide guaranteed response times in the subsecond range.

DSS systems tend to be read only. They tend to involve a low frequency of long, complex, ad hoc queries that affect large amounts of data. Usually DSS systems do not support large user populations, and the response time of queries may be measured in minutes or even hours. Unlike OLTP systems, DSS systems are often not mission critical. This is shown in Figure 3.33.

**Figure 3.33**   *The OLTP DSS spectrum*

Examples of OLTP systems are sales order entry systems and travel booking systems; examples of DSS systems might be anything from MIS reporting systems to large data warehousing systems.

Given the differences in the two application types it is clear that the indexing strategies are going to be different. In the case of OLTP there are likely to be high transaction rates involving transactions that change data. Having too many indexes will adversely affect the performance of OLTP systems, so the designer should limit the number of indexes to those that are really necessary. In the case of DSS the system is likely to be predominantly read only, and therefore the designer can use as many indexes as are needed to support the query mix.

Unlike OLTP transactions, DSS queries are ad-hoc by nature, and the designer will often be unable to perform much upfront transaction analysis in order to arrive at a fixed indexing strategy; therefore, using a good mix of indexes is frequently necessary.

### 3.13.3  Choosing sensible index columns

When the query optimizer is investigating different access strategies, it will cost each strategy to determine the number of logical reads the strategy will use. This will be an estimate, but, depending on the choice of columns in an index, the query optimizer might decide very quickly that an index is not worth bothering with.

When we are choosing index columns, we should be looking for a combination of columns that support our queries, as well as the number of duplicate values in the index column or columns. Suppose we were to index a column that could contain only the code M (male) and F (female). Would this be a good column to index? It would not be a good column to index, because probably half the rows would contain M and half would contain F. We can say that the following query is not very selective:

```
SELECT * FROM clients WHERE gender = 'F'
```

If there is a nonclustered index on gender, it is highly unlikely that the query optimizer would use it.

Another example would be the state column in a table holding client information. If we executed the following query on a 100,000-row table, how many rows would be returned?

```
SELECT * FROM clients WHERE state = 'CA'
```

If our company is based in San Francisco, we might expect that most of our clients were in California, and therefore 90 percent of the rows in the table might be returned. However, if our company is based in Ulan Bator, we might expect that few of our clients were in California, and therefore 5 percent of the rows in the table might be returned.

We can define selectivity as the percentage of the rows returned. For example:

```
selectivity = (the number of rows returned / the count of
rows in the table) * 100
```

If 5,000 of the rows in our 100,000-row table were returned, the selectivity of our query would be:

```
selectivity = (5000 / 100000) * 100 = 5%
```

If 90,000 of the rows in our 100,000-row table were returned, the selectivity of our query would be:

```
selectivity = (90000 / 100000) * 100 = 90%
```

The more selective a query the fewer rows returned and the more likely that an index will be chosen by the query optimizer. In the example where 90 percent of the rows in the table are returned, the query optimizer would probably choose a table scan in preference to a nonclustered index on the state column. In the example where 5 percent of the rows in the table are returned, the query optimizer would probably choose to use a nonclustered index on the state column.

**Note:** The terminology here can be quite confusing. If a query is highly selective, few rows are returned, but the selectivity will be a low percentage value. If a query is not highly selective, many rows are returned, but the selectivity will be a high percentage value.

How does the query optimizer know that 5 percent or 90 percent of the rows in a table will be returned by a query? We shall see later that each index usually has key distribution statistics to help the query optimizer estimate the number of rows returned.

Another value associated with selectivity is density. The density is the average fraction of duplicate index key values in the index. We can easily work out the density by finding the reciprocal of the count of unique values in the index key. Suppose in our example we had clients in 40 states; then the index density would be $1/40 = 0.025$.

Once the index density is known, by multiplying the total count of rows in the table by it, we can obtain the likely number of rows hit by specifying a given value, in our example:

```
row hits = 100000 * 0.025 = 2500
```

This is obviously an approximation, since it does not take into account the fact that we might have many or few column values of CA, so index density is only used when key distribution statistics cannot be.

---

**Note:** Again, these terms can be confusing. A high selectivity refers to few duplicates, but a high density refers to many duplicates.

---

SQL Server holds multiple index densities for a composite index, and we can picture the fact that adding more columns to an index is likely to increase the number of unique values in the index key.

Suppose, in our example, that the index is not based on the state column alone but is based on the state and city columns. Whereas previously 10,000 clients may have been located in California, only ten may be located in Oakland. The selectivity of a query specifying both the state and city columns will be higher than the selectivity of a query specifying only the state column.

SQL Server will hold the index densities for the state column and the state and city columns combined—that is, two density values. The query optimizer can access these values when working out its strategy.

How can we easily find information about the density of an index key? DBCC comes to the rescue with the DBCC SHOW_STATISTICS statement:

```
DBCC SHOW_STATISTICS (accounts, 'NCI_BranchNoCustNo')

Statistics for INDEX 'NCI_BranchNoCustNo'.

Updated                  Rows    Rows Sampled    Steps    Density    Average key length
-------                  ----    ------------    -----    -------    ------------------
Feb 29 2000 11:58AM      10000   10000           295      0.0        11.999647


All density       Columns
-----------       -------
9.9999998E-3      branch_no
1.9999999E-4      branch_no, customer_no

Statistics for INDEX 'NCI_BranchNoCustNo'.
Updated                  Rows    Rows Sampled    Steps    Density    Average key length
-------                  ----    ------------    -----    -------    ------------------
Oct 19 2000  9:31PM      25000   25000           100      0.0        8.0


All density       Average Length    Columns
-----------       --------------    -------
9.9999998E-3      4.0               branch_no
7.9999998E-5      8.0               branch_no, customer_no


RANGE_HI_KEY    RANGE_ROWS    EQ_ROWS    DISTINCT_RANGE_ROWS    AVG_RANGE_ROWS
------------    ----------    -------    -------------------    --------------
1000            0.0           250.0      0                      0.0
1001            0.0           250.0      0                      0.0
1002            0.0           250.0      0                      0.0
1003            0.0           250.0      0                      0.0
1004            0.0           250.0      0                      0.0
1005            0.0           250.0      0                      0.0
1006            0.0           250.0      0                      0.0
```

This DBCC statement displays information about the key distribution statistics. Most of this information will be discussed with respect to the query optimizer later in the book. However, there is some information, referred to as All Density, which is the index density we have been discussing. Our index is a composite index of two columns, branch_no and customer_no. The branch_no column has a density value of 9.9999998E-3—that is, approximately 0.01. This is representative of the fact that we have 100 unique branch_no values (density = 1/100).

The density of both columns combined is very low (1.9999999E-4 or 0.0002). Suppose there are 10,000 rows in the Accounts table. A query containing the following:

```
WHERE branch_no =  1000
```

would return (10,000 * .01 = 100) rows, whereas a query containing:

```
WHERE branch_no =  1000 AND customer_no = 34667
```

would return (10,000 * 0.0002 = 2) rows.

Let us have a look at another example to emphasize a point. Let us assume that we have a nonclustered index on the balance column in the Accounts table. Here is a fragment of the DBCC SHOW_STATISTICS output:

```
DBCC SHOW_STATISTICS (accounts, NCI_Balance)

Statistics for INDEX 'NCI_Balance'.

Updated                 Rows    Rows Sampled  Steps   Density       Average key length
-------                 ----    ------------  -----   -----------   ------------------
Oct 19 2000  9:46PM     25000   25000          106    4.0426468E-5  12.0


All density      Average Length     Columns
-----------      --------------     -------
4.0471085E-5      8.0               balance
3.9999999E-5      12.0              balance, customer_no
```

If we look at the All Density information, we can see that statistics are displayed not only for the balance column but also for the balance, customer_no combination. Why is this? This is a single column index containing only the balance column. This is because the database administrator has just created a clustered index on the Accounts table on the customer_no column.

Therefore, all nonclustered indexes use this clustered index key as the pointer at the index leaf level. Since the leaf-level index entry for our NCI_Balance index is then effectively balance, customer_no, SQL Server can keep meaningful index density information using both columns. Note that in our previous example the index NCI_BranchNoCustNo would be holding the customer_no column redundantly if there was a clustered index present on the Accounts table on the customer_no column.

This raises an interesting point. If a clustered index is dropped from a table, we know that the nonclustered indexes will be rebuilt so that their leaf-level pointers become Row IDs. This means that they no longer contain the clustered index key, which previously made the nonclustered indexes effectively composite indexes. Therefore, be prepared for some query optimizer strategy changes if you change a clustered index into a nonclustered index at some point.

### 3.13.4   **Choosing a clustered index or a nonclustered index**

As we have seen, a table can only have one clustered index, so it is important that we use it carefully—it's our ace and we want to play it at the right time. So when is a clustered index useful?

Consider using a clustered index when the following occur:

- The physical ordering supports the range retrievals of important queries, or equality returns many duplicates.

- The clustered index key is used in the ORDER BY clause or GROUP BY clause of critical queries.

- The clustered index key is used in important joins to relate the tables—that is, it supports the foreign key.

- The clustered index columns are not changed regularly.

However, remember that there is a downside to using a clustered index. Every nonclustered index leaf-level pointer will become the clustered index key. If the clustered index is large, this may significantly impact the size and efficiency of the nonclustered indexes on the table. Also, creating a clustered index on a large table will require a large amount of free space in the database to accommodate the mechanics of the clustered index creation algorithm. A 1-GB table will require free space equal to 1-GB plus at least 0.2 GB during the creation phase.

Consider using a nonclustered index when the following occur:

- Once or more rows will be retrieved—that is, the query is highly selective.

- The nonclustered index key is used in the ORDER BY clause or GROUP BY clause of critical queries.

- The nonclustered index key is used in important joins to relate the tables.

- A covered query is required.

- Multiple indexes can be used for index intersection.

Also consider that many applications will require the selection of a row by its primary key. This is a single row selection and therefore would normally benefit from the creation of an index containing the same columns as the primary key. Since it is less common to request ranges of primary keys, a nonclustered index is probably the best option.

There are occasions when neither a clustered index nor a nonclustered index should be used. If the table is small the query optimizer will probably choose a table scan anyway, and if the index has a low selectivity, the query optimizer might ignore it.

Creating an index in these instances just increases disk space use and maintenance overhead.

The choice of index and index columns is often a compromise, in my experience, regardless of the database product. This choice is perhaps the most critical one the database designer must face, since incorrect indexes will result in potentially greater disk I/O, CPU, locking contention, and a lower caching efficiency. A piece of good news, though. As we shall see later in this book, SQL Server possesses an Index Tuning Wizard, which can assist us when designing our indexing strategy.

**4**

# *The Query Optimizer*

## 4.1    Introduction

When we execute a query, either by typing in a Transact-SQL statement or by using a tool such as Microsoft Access, it is highly likely we will require that rows be read from one or more database tables. Suppose we require that SQL Server performs a join of two tables: table A containing a dozen rows and table B containing a million rows. How should SQL Server access the required data in the most efficient manner? Should it access table A looking for rows that meet the selection criteria and then read matching rows from table B, or should it access table B first? Should it use indexes, if any are present, or perform a table scan? If indexes are present and there is a choice of index, which one should SQL Server choose?

The good news is that SQL Server contains a component known as the query optimizer, which will automatically take a query passed to it and attempt to execute the query in the most efficient way. The bad news is that it is not magic, and it does not always come up with the best solution. A database administrator should be aware of the factors that govern query optimization, what pitfalls there are, and how the query optimizer can be assisted in its job. Database administrators who know their data well can often influence the optimizer with the judicious use of indexes to choose the most efficient solution.

What do we mean by efficient in the context of the query optimizer? Basically, the query optimizer is looking to minimize the number of logical reads required to fetch the required data. The query optimizer is the SQL Server AutoRoute Express, choosing the best route to the data. Unfortunately, the query optimizer doesn't show you the golf courses on the way!

The query optimizer's main task, therefore, is to minimize the work required to execute a query, whether it is a query that retrieves data from a single table or a query that retrieves data from multiple tables participating in a join.

Note that, although we have referred only to queries, the query optimization process is necessary for SELECT, INSERT, UPDATE, and DELETE Transact-SQL statements, since the UPDATE and DELETE Transact-SQL statements will often contain a WHERE clause and the INSERT statement may contain a SELECT clause.

## 4.2    When is the query optimized?

When a query is submitted to SQL Server, various phases of processing occur. First of all, the query is parsed—that is, it is syntax checked and converted into a parsed query tree that the standardization phase can understand. The standardization phase takes the parsed query tree and processes it to remove redundant syntax and to flatten subqueries. This phase essentially prepares the parsed query tree for query optimization. The output of this phase is a standardized query tree. This phase is sometimes known as normalization.

The query optimizer takes the standardized query tree and investigates a number of possible access strategies, finally eliminating all but the most efficient query execution plan. In order to formulate the most efficient query execution plan, the query optimizer must carry out a number of functions. These are query analysis, index selection, and join order selection.

Once the most efficient query execution plan is produced, the query optimizer must translate this into executable code that can execute under Windows operating systems. This code can then access the appropriate indexes and tables to produce the result set.

Figure 4.1 shows a simplified diagram of how query optimization takes place. In reality the process is much more complex but this gives us a basic idea.

How does the query optimizer work out the most efficient query execution plan? We will look at the way it does this now. We will see that it takes in the information available to it in the form of the query itself, indexes and key distribution statistics, size of the table and rows per page, and then calculates the logical read cost given a possible access path.

**Figure 4.1**
*Phases in query processing*

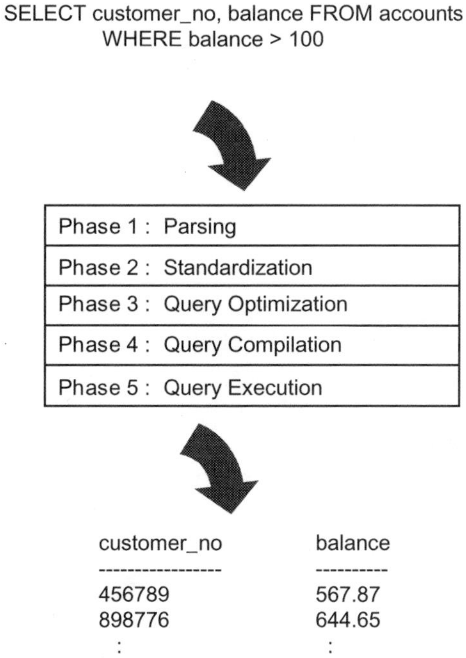

SELECT customer_no, balance FROM accounts
WHERE balance > 100

| Phase 1 : Parsing |
| Phase 2 : Standardization |
| Phase 3 : Query Optimization |
| Phase 4 : Query Compilation |
| Phase 5 : Query Execution |

```
customer_no          balance
-----------------    ----------
456789               567.87
898776               644.65
    :                    :
```

# 4.3   Query optimization

The query optimization phase is the phase we will concern ourselves with in this chapter. This phase can be broken down into a number of logical steps, as follows:

- Query analysis
- Index selection
- Join order selection

Let us discuss each step in sequence.

## 4.3.1   Query analysis

The first step the query optimizer performs during the query optimization phase is query analysis. In this step the query optimizer examines the query for search arguments (SARGs), the use of the OR operator, and join conditions.

## Search arguments

A search argument is the part of a query that restricts the result set. Hopefully, if indexes have been chosen carefully, an index can be used to support the search argument. Examples of search arguments are as follows:

```
account_no = 7665332

balance > 30

lname = 'Burrows'
```

The AND operator can be used to connect conditions, so another example of a valid search argument would be as follows:

```
balance > 30 AND lname = 'Burrows'
```

Examples of common operators that are valid in a search argument are =, >, <, ≤, and ≥. Other operators such as BETWEEN and LIKE are also valid, because the query optimizer can represent them with the common operators listed above. For example, a BETWEEN can always be represented as ≥ AND ≤. For example:

```
balance BETWEEN 1000 AND 10000
```

becomes:

```
balance >= 1000 AND balance <= 10000
```

A LIKE can always be represented as ≥ AND <. For example:

```
lname LIKE 'Burr%'
```

becomes:

```
lname >= 'Burr' AND lname < 'Burs'
```

---

**Note:** The expression balance BETWEEN 1000 AND 10000 is not equivalent to balance BETWEEN 10000 AND 1000. The query optimizer will not detect the mistake and switch the values.

---

There are a number of expressions that are not considered to be search arguments. The NOT operator is an example:

```
NOT IN ('CA', 'NH', 'TX')

customer_no <> 9099755

balance <> 78000
```

Another example of this is the use of NOT EXISTS.

NOT is not considered to be a search argument, because it does not limit the search. Whereas account_no = 100,000 specifies a single value in a table that may potentially be efficiently retrieved using an index, account_no <> 100,000 will cause SQL Server to look at every row in the table to ensure that the account_no column does not contain this value.

There are other expressions that are not considered to be search arguments. If a column is used instead of an operator, the expression is not considered to be a search argument. For example:

```
loan < loan_agreed
```

How can SQL Server use such an expression to restrict the result set? It cannot, since the loan_agreed value is not known until the row is read; until it is known, it cannot be used to compare against the loan column. This will normally result in a table scan or index scan if the query is covered.

Another example of an expression that cannot be considered for query optimization is one that involves mathematics or functions. For example:

```
balance * 1.175 > 10000

UPPER(lname) = 'SHARMAN'
```

Against my database, using mathematics as in the first example, the query optimizer chose to use a nonclustered index on balance as long as the number of rows returned was low. The query optimizer had done the math and estimated correctly the number of rows returned whose balance would be greater than 10,000/1.175. However, using a function such as CEILING() caused a table scan to be performed, as in:

```
SELECT * FROM accounts WHERE CEILING(balance) = 100
```

String functions, as in the second example, caused the query optimizer to resort to a table scan. A number of common string functions cause a table scan to be performed—for example, LEFT().

The bottom line is that using a function or expression on the left side of the operator will probably cause the query optimizer to use a table scan. This is one reason why it is very important to check the query execution plan that the query optimizer has produced—it may not be what you expect! We'll see how to check the query execution plan shortly.

As long as we have just a column on the left side of an appropriate operator, we have a search argument. We can often compare the column with an expression, so that the query optimizer will be able to use the distribution steps in the index key distribution statistics for the index rather than just the density values. Distribution statistics will be covered shortly. This is true as long as the expression can be evaluated before the query execution phase—in other words, before the query actually runs. An example of such a search argument would be as follows:

```
monthly_yield = items_processed/12

yearly_amount = daily_rate * 365
```

However, consider the following query:

```
sell_by_date > DATEADD (DAY, -10, GETDATE())
```

The query optimizer will choose a table scan. Again, this is common when a function is used. So check the query execution plan carefully!

**Note:** How can we make sure that the index is used? There are various techniques, which we will discuss shortly. We could put the query in a stored procedure and pass the result of the function as a parameter. We may be able to create a computed column on the table and index it. Depending on what we want to achieve, this may or not make sense. However, we can only index a computed column if the computation is deterministic. This was discussed in the previous chapter. The function GETDATE() is not deterministic. We can also force the query optimizer to use an index. This technique is discussed later but should be used with care.

If the query optimizer cannot evaluate the expression until the query runs—that is, until after the query optimization phase has completed, then SQL Server has no chance of making use of distribution steps. A classic example of this is where variables are used:

```
DECLARE @bal MONEY

SELECT @bal = 9990.23

SELECT * FROM accounts WHERE balance > @bal
```

In the BankingDB database, the previous example used a table scan instead of the nonclustered index on balance. If we do not use a variable, the nonclustered index is used, as follows:

```
SELECT * FROM accounts WHERE balance >  9990.23
```

Note that this is different from stored procedure parameters, which will be discussed later in this chapter.

### OR clauses

The query optimizer also checks the query for ORs. The OR clause links multiple search arguments together. For example, we might have a query that looks like the following:

```
SELECT * FROM customers WHERE
   age > 40          OR
   height < 2        OR
   weight < 200      OR
   state = 'NH'      OR
   city = 'Manchester'
```

Any row matching any of the above conditions will appear in the result set. A customer will be displayed who lives in the city of Manchester in the United Kingdom or who lives in Nashua in New Hampshire. In other words, it is likely that many rows in the table will meet one or more of these criteria.

Compare the previous query with the following query:

```
SELECT * FROM customers WHERE
   age > 40          AND
   height < 2        AND
   weight < 200      AND
   state = 'NH'      AND
   city = 'Manchester'
```

The number of rows in the table that meet all the criteria is likely to be far less. The ANDs restrict the result set, whereas the ORs widen it. For this reason a query containing ORs is handled in a particular way, which will be discussed later in the chapter. Because of this, the query optimizer looks for OR clauses in the query analysis step.

There may be OR clauses in the query that are hiding. Take the following query, for example:

```
SELECT lname, fname FROM employees
   WHERE
   state IN ('CA', 'IL', 'KS', 'MD', 'NY', 'TN', 'TX')
```

At first glance there are no ORs in this query. The query optimizer sees this, however, as a number of OR clauses, as follows:

```
SELECT lname, fname FROM employees
   WHERE
        state = 'CA'     OR
        state = 'IL'     OR
        state = 'KS'     OR
        state = 'MD'     OR
        state = 'NY'     OR
        state = 'TN'     OR
        state = 'TX'
```

### Join clauses

After looking for search arguments and OR clauses the query optimizer looks for any join conditions. When more than one table is processed in a query, a join clause is usually found. The join clause can be in the WHERE clause or in the ON clause of the SELECT statement if ANSI-standard join clauses are used.

SQL Server join example:

```
SELECT fname, lname FROM customers, accounts
   WHERE customers.customer_no = accounts.customer_no AND
   balance > 10000
```

ANSI join example:

```
SELECT fname, lname FROM customers INNER JOIN accounts
   ON customers.customer_no = accounts.customer_no
   WHERE balance > 10000
```

Note that in SQL Server 2000 the following ANSI-standard join clauses are supported:

- Join

- Cross join

- Inner join

- Left outer join

- Right outer join

- Full outer join

Sometimes a table can be joined with itself. This is known as a self-join, or reflexive join. Although only one table is being accessed, the table is mentioned in the query more than once and so a join clause is used. The classic self-join is the Employees table containing a column, supervisor_id, that holds a value found in the employee_id column elsewhere in the table. In other words, a supervisor is an employee. The Employees table might be defined as follows:

```
CREATE TABLE employees
   (
   employee_id   CHAR(8),
   lname         CHAR(10),
   fname         CHAR(10),
   supervisor_id CHAR(8)
   )
```

A query to retrieve the last name of the employee and the last name of the supervisor would be as follows:

```
SELECT e1.lname AS employee, e2.lname AS supervisor
   FROM employees e1 INNER JOIN employees e2
   ON e1.supervisor_id = e2.employee_id
```

## 4.3.2 Index selection

Having identified the search arguments in the query, the next step the query optimizer performs during the query optimization phase is index selection. In this step the query optimizer takes each search argument and checks to see if it is supported by one or more indexes on the table. The selectivity of the indexes is taken into consideration, and, based on this, the query optimizer can calculate the cost of a strategy that uses that index in terms of logical reads and CPU. This cost is used to compare strategies that use different indexes and a strategy that uses a table scan.

### Does a useful index exist?

To obtain information on the indexes present on a table and their characteristics, SQL Server can check the sysindexes system table. From the sysindexes table the query optimizer can quickly establish the indexes present on the table by checking the rows that have a value in the id column equal to the object ID of the table (as defined in the sysobjects system table) and an indid column value > 0 and < 255. Other columns in the sysindexes table help the query optimizer determine on which columns the index is based.

The query optimizer will look for an index based on the same column as the search argument. If the index is a composite index, the query optimizer determines if the first column in the index is specified in the search argument.

If a search argument has no matching index, then no index can be used to support the search argument and so the query optimizer will look for indexes supporting other search arguments. If it is the only search argument, then a table scan will be performed.

### How selective is the search argument?

Suppose the following query is presented to the query optimizer:

```
SELECT account_no FROM accounts WHERE
    branch_no = 1005 AND
    balance > 5000 AND
    customer_no BETWEEN 10000 AND 110000
```

If there are indexes present on the branch_no, balance and customer_no columns, how can the query optimizer decide which indexes are the most efficient to use—that is, which indexes will use the least number of logical reads and CPU to return the data? The query optimizer may choose to use no indexes, since a table scan is estimated to be a more efficient access mechanism, or it may choose to use one or more indexes.

The query optimizer has a number of mechanisms by which it can determine this information. The most accurate method is to use statistical information available in the key distribution statistics associated with the index. We will look at these distribution statistics shortly. If the key distribution statistics do not exist, the query optimizer applies a weighting to each operator. For example, the = operator has a weighting of 10 percent, which means that the query optimizer will assume that 10 percent of the rows in the table will be returned.

The approximate weightings of some common operators are shown in Table 4.1.

As you might imagine, these weightings are very general estimates and can be wildly inaccurate, so it is always best if the query optimizer is able to use the distribution statistics associated with an index.

**Table 4.1**    *Weightings of Common Operators*

| Operator | Weighting |
|----------|-----------|
| =        | 10%       |
| <        | 33%       |
| >        | 33%       |
| BETWEEN  | 12%       |

If we have a unique index matching the search argument, then the query optimizer knows immediately the number of rows returned by the = operator. Because of the unique index, the query optimizer knows that at most one row can be returned (of course, zero rows could be returned), so this figure is used rather than the 10 percent weighting.

### Key distribution statistics

Key distribution statistics are usually created when an index is created. The one exception to this is when an index is created on an empty table; otherwise, the index has key distribution statistics held for it. Note that the indexes on a table that has been truncated will have no key distribution statistics held for them. From now on we'll just refer to key distribution statistics as index statistics. We cannot just refer to them as statistics, since this is ambiguous. Why? Because a little later on we'll meet another type of distribution statistics known as column statistics.

Where are these index statistics held? They are held as a column in the sysindexes system table for the relevant row representing the index whose index statistics we wish to keep. This column is named statblob and is an IMAGE datatype. Since it is an IMAGE datatype, there is plenty of room to hold lots of statistics, if required, although SQL Server keeps the number of statistics held to a fairly small but significant value. In my experience, for most indexes, the number of samples held in this column is in the low hundreds, typically about 300.

If this column is empty (holds NULL), then there are no index statistics associated with the index.

The statblob column holds index statistics information for the index to allow the query optimizer to quickly estimate the proportion of rows that will be returned by a search argument. Suppose we execute the following query on the Accounts table, which holds information for 25,000 accounts:

```
SELECT account_no FROM accounts WHERE balance > 9999
```

Will 25,000 rows be returned, or 1,000 rows, or 25 rows, or 0 rows? The query optimizer needs to know this information so it can decide whether a nonclustered index on the balance column should be considered interesting or whether a table scan is likely to be more efficient. Remember that returning a range of rows using a nonclustered index is going to result in a request for a data page (logical read) for every row returned. If the query optimizer can accurately estimate how many rows are likely to be returned, it knows with reasonable accuracy how many data page requests will be needed, and, therefore, it can calculate the cost of the query and compare this with the cost of a table scan.

In the BankingDB database there are, on average, less than five accounts that have a balance greater than 9,999, and so an indexed access should be more efficient than a table scan. But how can the query optimizer know this? It could count the number of rows that satisfied the search argument before it actually executed the query, but that would defeat the object of the exercise!

This is where the statblob column comes to the rescue. It holds a series of samples across the index key range that the query optimizer can check. Based on these samples the query optimizer can quickly estimate the percentage of the rows in the table that will be returned by the search argument using that index.

The statblob column actually holds a number of key values. This number is a function of the key size and the number of rows in the table. Although, in theory, the statblob column could hold up to 2 GB of key distribution statistics for an index, only a very large table would need that, and the effort in reading the index statistics would be far greater than the data. Of course, in practice, only a small amount of data space is needed in the statblob column, since few key values are actually held. For example, a nonclustered index on the account_no column in the Accounts table, which is a four byte (integer) key, has index statistics information consisting of 200 steps. By comparison, a nonclustered index on the account_notes column, which is a CHAR(400), has index statistics information consisting of 74 steps. The more steps, the more accurate the statistics, so, in this respect at least, it is better to have a smaller key value.

Suppose we have an index key that is an integer, such as the account_no column in our Accounts table. The initial key value found in the index is the first one to be sampled and stored in the statblob column, so we will have the statblob column contents shown in Figure 4.2.

We can see that the number of distribution steps is typically going to be less than the number of key values stored in the statblob column. Apart from the choice of key size we cannot influence the number of key values held. However, as we shall see shortly, we can choose how much of our data is actually sampled in order to generate our index statistics.

What about composite indexes? SQL Server only stores key values for the first column. This means that it is better to choose the most selective column as the first column of an index—that is, the column with the least

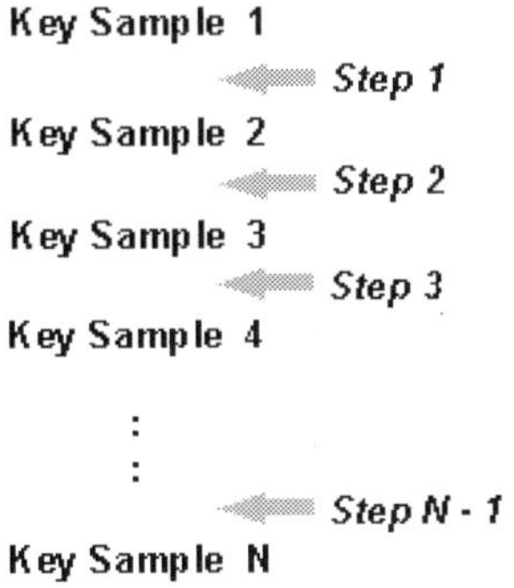

**Figure 4.2**
*Distribution steps
and keys in the
statblob column*

Key Sample 1
                        Step 1
Key Sample 2
                        Step 2
Key Sample 3
                        Step 3
Key Sample 4

            :
            :
                        Step N - 1
Key Sample N

number of duplicate values. Of course, the first column of the index needs to be specified in the query, and choosing the most selective column will need to be done with this in mind.

I find that many database designers choose the key order in a composite index starting with the first column being the least selective, the next column being the next least selective, and so on, even if the query is going to specify all of the columns in its WHERE clause. Why is this? Usually it is because it is the most natural approach to take.

Consider a three-column composite index on the columns region, state, city. There is a natural hierarchy here—cities belong to states, which in turn belong to regions. There are few regions, more states, and many more cities. It's natural to create the index in the region, state, city column order just as you would in a report. But we can see that if we do this, we are going to populate the statblob column with few distinct values. This could result in the query optimizer choosing a table scan to execute the following statement when the nonclustered index would have been a better choice.

```
SELECT qty FROM sales
   WHERE
   region = 'North' AND
   state = 'CO' AND
   city = 'Denver'
```

As we saw in the previous chapter, we can use the utility DBCC SHOW_STATISTICS to investigate index statistics. The format of this DBCC statement is as follows:

```
DBCC SHOW_STATISTICS (table_name, target)
```

The target is an index name or a statistics collection name. We will talk about statistics that are not index statistics later.

For example, to show the index statistics on the nonclustered index nci-Balance, the following code segment would be used:

```
DBCC SHOW_STATISTICS (accounts, nciBalance)

Statistics for INDEX ' nciBalance'.
Updated                 Rows   Rows Sampled   Steps   Density        Average key length
-------                 ----   ------------   -----   -------        ------------------
Oct 20 2000  5:50PM     25000  25000          106     4.0426468E-5   8.0


All density   Average Length      Columns
-----------   --------------      -------
4.0471085E-5   8.0                balance
```

| RANGE_HI_KEy | RANGE_ROWS | EQ_ROWS | DISTINCT_RANGE_ROWS | AVG_RANGE_ROWS |
|---|---|---|---|---|
| .9500 | 0.0 | 1.0 | 0 | 0.0 |
| 88.1000 | 237.0 | 2.0 | 235 | 1.0085106 |
| 237.0600 | 357.0 | 1.0 | 353 | 1.0084746 |
| 282.3600 | 127.0 | 1.0 | 127 | 1.0 |
| 316.1400 | 107.0 | 2.0 | 107 | 1.0 |
| 413.7800 | 225.0 | 2.0 | 224 | 1.0044643 |
| 699.9500 | 735.0 | 2.0 | 729 | 1.0082304 |
| 723.5500 | 64.0 | 2.0 | 64 | 1.0 |
| : | | | | |
| : | | | | |
| 9696.2000 | 383.0 | 1.0 | 379 | 1.0078948 |
| 9739.9200 | 126.0 | 2.0 | 124 | 1.008 |
| 9998.5700 | 603.0 | 1.0 | 596 | 1.0100503 |
| 9998.8500 | 0.0 | 1.0 | 0 | 0.0 |

The index statistics shown above are associated with the nonclustered index based on the balance MONEY data type column in the Accounts table. The index statistics indicate that there are 111 steps and that 25,000 rows from the Accounts table were sampled to create these statistics. There are 25,000 rows in the Accounts table in total, so, in fact, all the rows were sampled. This is expected behavior when a CREATE INDEX statement generates the index statistics. Later we will see that other mechanisms to update the key distribution statistics will not necessarily sample all the rows.

If we look at the All Density value, we can see that it is 4.0471085E-5. As discussed in Chapter 3, the density is the average fraction of duplicate index key values in the index. Since the density is the reciprocal of the count of unique values in the index key, the count of unique values in our non-clustered index must be 1 / 4.0471085E-5, which yields 24,709 unique values, which is correct as checked with a SELECT DISTINCT (balance) query.

Multiplying the total count of rows in the table by the index density, 4.0465478E-5, we can obtain the likely number of rows hit by specifying a given value, in our example:

```
row hits = 25000 * 4.0471085E-5 = 1.011777125
```

This means that a query specifying balance = value would usually return one row.

---

**Note:** Just to remind us of the terminology, this is an example of high selectivity and low density.

---

The output from DBCC SHOW_STATISTICS needs a few more words of explanation. The Density value, 4.0426468E-5, is close to the All Density value of 4.0471085E-5. The difference is due to the fact that the Density value considers nonfrequent values. These are values that appear only once in a step. If a value appears more than once, it is considered to be a frequent value. The All Density value includes frequent values. The Average Length is the average length of the index key. If the index were a composite index, there would be an entry for the first column, first plus second column, and so on. The Average Key Length is the average length of the total composite index key (including a clustered index key pointer if there is a clustered index on the table). The average in this context is necessary because columns in the key can be variable-length datatypes.

The next section of data contains the sample steps themselves. Remember that they only apply to the first column in the key. The column RANGE_HI_KEY is the upper bound value of a histogram step—that is, the highest value in the step. The first step is the lowest value for the column in the table. The column RANGE_ROWS is the number of rows from the sample that fall within a histogram step, excluding the upper bound. By definition, this must be zero in the first sample. We can see that the seventh step contains the value 735 and that the values are quite varied across other steps. The column EQ_ROWS is the number of rows from the sample that are equal in value to the upper bound of the histogram step. In our data this varies between 1.0 and 2.0. For our seventh step this is 2.0.

The column DISTINCT_RANGE_ROWS is the number of distinct values within a histogram step, excluding the upper bound. For our seventh step there are 729 distinct values within the step, excluding the value 699.9500 (the upper bound). Finally, the column AVG_RANGE_ROWS is the average number of duplicate values within a histogram step, excluding the upper bound. This is defined as:

```
(RANGE_ROWS / DISTINCT_RANGE_ROWS for DISTINCT_RANGE_ROWS
> 0)
```

For our seventh step this value is 1.0082304.

To check out some of these column values let us focus on the seventh step. Suppose we execute the SQL statement:

```
SELECT COUNT (balance) FROM accounts
    WHERE balance BETWEEN 413.7800 AND 699.9500
```

This SELECT specifies the two RANGE_HI_KEY values for our seventh step and the one before. We find that 739 rows are returned. However, the BETWEEN operator is inclusive, but the definition of the RANGE_ROWS column excludes the upper bound; the upper bound of the previous sample will not be included in the RANGE_ROWS column. So we need to rewrite the query, as follows:

```
SELECT COUNT (balance) FROM accounts
    WHERE balance > 413.7800 AND balance < 699.9500
```

We now find that 735 rows are returned, which is the correct value.

Suppose we execute the following query:

```
SELECT COUNT (balance) FROM accounts WHERE balance=
699.9500
```

We find that the value 2 is returned, which agrees with the value in the EQ_ROWS column for this step. Finally, let us execute this statement:

```
SELECT COUNT (DISTINCT (balance)) FROM accounts
    WHERE balance > 413.7800 AND balance < 699.9500
```

This returns 729, which agrees with the value in the DISTINCT_RANGE_ROWS column for this step. We can then calculate RANGE_ROWS / DISTINCT_RANGE_ROWS, which is 735/729, giving 1.0082304. This agrees with the value in the AVG_RANGE_ROWS column for this step.

### Column statistics

As well as maintaining statistics on indexed columns—to be precise, the first column of an index key—SQL Server will optionally maintain statistics on nonindexed columns. This includes columns in a composite index key other than the first. As long as the database option auto create statistics is set to on, if a column on which index statistics are not being maintained is referenced in a WHERE clause, statistics will be gathered if it would help the query optimizer.

This behavior can be suppressed by setting the database option auto create statistics to off. If this option is set to off, the fact that the query optimizer would like statistics information for the column is usually made obvious by a warning in the estimated query execution plan output in the Query Analyzer. A Missing Column Statistics event will also be evident in the SQL Server Profiler if it is being traced. If auto create statistics is set to on, an Auto Stats event will occur.

There are many occasions when SQL Server will automatically create column statistics. Basically, it will do so if they are missing and the query optimizer would really like to have them. Here is an example of such an occasion. Suppose we have created a nonclustered index with a composite key consisting of the customer_no and balance columns. We now execute the following query:

```
SELECT account_no  FROM accounts WHERE customer_no = 100
AND balance = 100
```

The query optimizer knows the statistical distribution of key values in the customer_no column but not in the balance column. It will create statistics for this column because they are helpful in finding the most efficient query plan.

To find the column statistics that have been created automatically by the query optimizer, look for statistics with names similar to _WA_Sys_balance_0519C6AF. To display statistics use the system stored procedure sp_helpstats or Tools →Manage Statistics in the Query Analyzer.

Of course, you can manually create column statistics. Use Tools → Manage Statistics in the Query Analyzer or the CREATE STATISTICS Transact-SQL statement. Alternatively, the system stored procedure sp_createstats can be used to create single-column statistics for all eligible columns for all user tables in the current database.

### Updating index and column statistics

When do index and column statistics get updated? Statistics are not automatically updated when transactions that change the index commit. This would cause the statblob column to become a bottleneck. The statblob column is accurate when it is first constructed as part of the index creation (assuming there is data in the table at that time). After that, on a volatile index, the key distribution statistics will diverge from reality. It is the

responsibility of the database administrator to ensure that the key distribution statistics are updated to reflect reality, and there are various ways to
achieve this. The most common method is to use the Transact-SQL statement UPDATE STATISTICS. The format of this statement is as follows:

```
UPDATE STATISTICS table
    [
        index
        | (statistics_name[,...n])
    ]
    [   WITH
        [
            [FULLSCAN]
            | SAMPLE number {PERCENT | ROWS}]
            | RESAMPLE

        ]
        [[,] [ALL | COLUMNS | INDEX]
        [[,] NORECOMPUTE]
    ]
```

If both the table name and index name are specified, the statistics for that
index are updated. If only the table name is specified, the statistics for all
indexes present on the table are updated. The same is true for column statistics, which are referred to by statistics_name. The FULLSCAN and SAM-
PLE number {PERCENT | ROWS} clause allows the database administrator
to choose how much data is actually sampled from the table. The
FULLSCAN option is used to specify that all the rows in a table should be
retrieved to generate the key distribution statistics.

The SAMPLE number {PERCENT | ROWS} option is used to specify
the percentage of the table or the number of rows to sample when generating statistics. This is typically used when a large table is being processed.
SQL Server will make sure that a minimum number of rows are sampled to
guarantee useful statistics. If the PERCENT, ROWS, or number option
results in too small a number of rows being sampled, SQL Server automatically corrects the sampling based on the number of existing rows in the
table.

Note that updating index statistics for a nonclustered index can be performed by scanning the leaf-level index pages of the nonclustered index,
which may well be a lot faster than scanning the table rows. When updating
column statistics, it is likely that the table will need to be scanned.

If neither of these options is specified, SQL Server automatically computes the required sample size for the scan.

The RESAMPLE option specifies that an inherited sampling ratio will be applied to the indexes and columns. In other words, the sampling ratio from the old statistics will be used. When a table has undergone major changes (e.g., numerous deletes), SQL Server 2000 may override the inherited sampling factor and implement a full scan instead.

The ALL | COLUMNS | INDEX option specifies whether the UPDATE STATISTICS statement updates column statistics, index statistics, or both. If no option is specified, the UPDATE STATISTICS statement updates all statistics.

The NORECOMPUTE option specifies that statistics that become out of date will not be automatically recomputed. When statistics become out of date is a function of the number of changes (INSERT, UPDATE, and DELETE operations) that hit indexed columns. If this option is used, SQL Server will not automatically rebuild statistics. To switch automatic statistics recomputation back on, the UPDATE STATISTICS statement can be executed omitting the NORECOMPUTE option, or the system stored procedure sp_autostats can be used.

One might imagine that omitting the table name would cause the key distribution statistics on all of the indexes on all of the tables in the database to be updated. Not so, this will result in a syntax error. Microsoft provides a convenient way to accomplish this with the system stored procedure sp_updatestats. This will run UPDATE STATISTICS against all user tables in the current database. For example:

```
USE BankingDB

EXEC sp_updatestats
```

will update both index- and column-level statistics.

Another way of achieving this might be to use a Transact-SQL cursor, as follows:

```
DECLARE tables_cursor CURSOR FOR
    SELECT table_name FROM information_schema.tables
        WHERE table_type = 'BASE TABLE'

OPEN tables_cursor

DECLARE @tablename NVARCHAR(128)

FETCH NEXT FROM tables_cursor INTO @tablename

WHILE (@@fetch_status <> -1)
```

```
BEGIN

    EXEC ('UPDATE STATISTICS ' +  @tablename)
    FETCH NEXT FROM tables_cursor INTO @tablename

END

PRINT 'The statistics have been updated.'

CLOSE tables_cursor

DEALLOCATE tables_cursor
```

The above cursor creates a result set of all the user tables and then proceeds to update the key statistics of all the indexes on each one. Obviously, using sp_updatestats is more straightforward, but the cursor can be modified easily to only update the statistics of certain tables—for example, only those beginning with cust. This may be useful on a database consisting of large tables.

Another method of updating statistics is to use the Database Maintenance Plan wizard. This is a wizard that allows a database administrator to easily and quickly set up a routine to back up and integrity check a database, as well as to reorganize indexes and update statistics. The section of the wizard that is concerned with data optimization is shown in Figure 4.3.

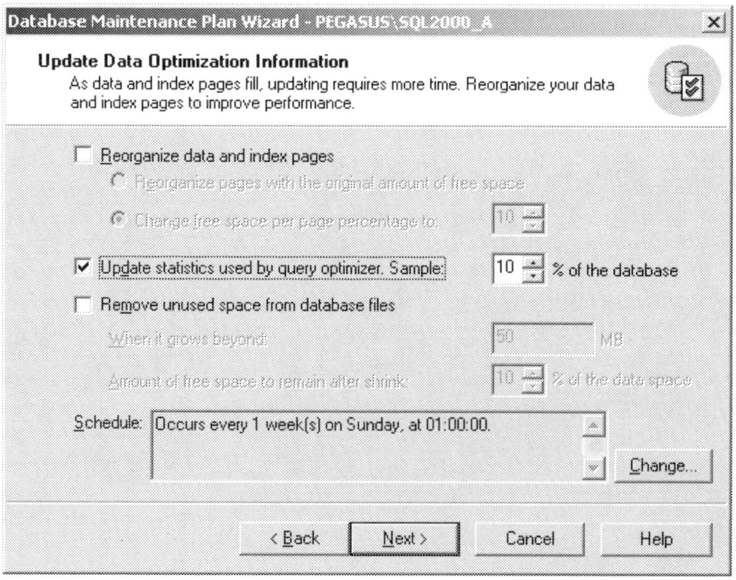

**Figure 4.3**
*The Database Maintenance Plan wizard*

A possible reason for not using this wizard is that it will run UPDATE STATISTICS on all the tables in the database, and this may become a problem with a database consisting of large tables.

Updating distribution statistics can also be achieved using the Distributed Management Objects (DMO) interface. The Table object has methods named UpdateStatistics and UpdateStatisticsWith, which can be used to update the distribution statistics of all the indexes and columns on a table. The Index object and Column object also support these methods.

How can we easily tell when distribution statistics were last updated? This information is displayed by DBCC SHOW_STATISTICS. However, there is also a function called STATS_DATE that can be used. The format of this function is as follows:

```
STATS_DATE    (table_id, index_id)
```

To check the date the distribution statistics were last updated on all the indexes and column statistics on a given table, the following Transact-SQL can be used:

```
SELECT
    ind.name AS 'Index/Column Statistics',
    STATS_DATE(ind.id, ind.indid) AS 'Date Last Updated'
    FROM sysobjects tab INNER JOIN sysindexes ind
    ON tab.id = ind.id
    WHERE tab.name = 'accounts'
```

This might give the following output:

```
Index/Column Statistics    Date Last Updated
------------------------------------------------
nciBalance                 2000-10-10 20:38:27.927
stat_branch_no             2000-10-10 20:38:28.627
```

Note that if there is no distribution statistics created for an index, because the index was created on an empty table, the Date Last Updated column will contain null. This should be a red warning light to a database administrator, who should run UPDATE STATISTICS without delay!

Another method that can be used to check when distribution statistics were last updated is to use the system stored procedure sp_autostats, described shortly.

Whichever method is chosen, the distribution statistics for an index or column on a table should be updated regularly or the query optimizer will start to use inaccurate information. An extreme example of this would be an index that was created on a table containing a single row that then had a million rows added. Most cases are not so extreme, but it is easy to forget to update statistics if no automated mechanism such as a scheduled task is set up. When the query optimizer chooses a strategy that you would not expect, the date the statistics were last updated is often the first information to check.

However, there is a safety net for the database administrator who forgets to update statistics. SQL Server 2000 contains functionality to automatically update statistics. This functionality is enabled globally for all the distribution statistics in a database by the database option auto update statistics.

Individual distribution statistics can have the automatic updating of statistics turned on or off by the use of the UPDATE STATISTICS statement with the NORECOMPUTE option. If UPDATE STATISTICS is executed with the NORECOMPUTE option, the automatic updating of statistics is turned off for the index or column distribution statistics referenced in the statement. If UPDATE STATISTICS is executed without the NORE-COMPUTE option, the automatic updating of statistics is turned on for the index or column distribution statistics referenced in the statement.

The automatic updating of statistics may also be turned on or off by the sp_autostats system stored procedure. If this is executed with just the table name parameter, information is displayed regarding all the index- and column-level distribution statistics relevant to that table, as follows:

```
EXEC sp_autostats accounts

IndexName               AUTOSTATS    Last Updated
-------------------------------------------------

[nciBalance]            ON           2000-10-1020:38:27.927
[stat_branch_no]        ON           2000-10-1020:38:28.627
```

An index or column statistics name can be specified to limit the output:

```
EXEC sp_autostats @tblname=accounts, @indname= nciBalance

IndexName               AUTOSTATS    Last Updated
-------------------------------------

[nciBalance]            ON           2000-10-1020:38:27.927
```

Note that this system stored procedure also displays when the statistics were last updated.

### *When can we not use statistics?*

Statistics cannot be used by the query optimizer if they are not there! As we have said, this occurs if the index was created on an empty table. In this case the STATBLOB column in the sysindexes table will contain NULL. If a table is truncated, the STATBLOB column will also be set to NULL. It follows, therefore, that if an index is created on an empty table, which is then populated with data, an UPDATE STATISTICS operation should be executed, or the query optimizer may create an inefficient query execution plan based on false assumptions. An UPDATE STATISTICS operation should also be run after a table has been truncated and repopulated. Of course, SQL Server 2000 may jump in and automatically update the distribution statistics if the appropriate database options are set, but why leave it to chance!

Not having distribution statistics present means that the query optimizer has little idea how many rows are likely to satisfy the query and, therefore, whether an index should be used. This is of particular importance when dealing with nonclustered indexes, since the query optimizer may decide not to use it and use a table scan instead. As an example, our Accounts table was created with a nonclustered index on the balance column. The table contained 25,000 rows. It was then truncated and repopulated with the 25,000 rows. The following query was then executed:

```
SELECT * FROM accounts WHERE balance = 100
```

The estimated query execution plan showed that the query optimizer had decided to use a table scan, and it had estimated that 1,988 rows would be returned. In fact, zero rows were returned, since no accounts had a balance of exactly zero. A bad decision, since the nonclustered index would have been the most efficient access method.

Even if statistics are present, they may not be used. When we discussed search arguments earlier in this chapter, we introduced cases where the query optimizer cannot evaluate the expression in the WHERE clause until the query runs—that is, until after the query optimization phase has completed. An example of this is using a variable, as follows:

```
DECLARE @bal MONEY

SELECT @bal = 4954.99

SELECT * FROM accounts WHERE balance = @bal
```

In this case distribution steps cannot be used when the query optimizer creates a query execution plan for the Transact-SQL batch, and the query optimizer will use the index density information present in the statblob column. Index density was discussed in Chapter 3 and is the average fraction of duplicate index key values in the index. It is the reciprocal of the count of unique values in the index key.

Suppose we have a Supplier table with a country_code column and we deal with suppliers from 20 countries. The index density would then be $1/20 = 0.05$.

By multiplying the total count of rows in the table by the index density, we can obtain the likely number of rows hit by specifying a given value. Suppose our table contains 5,000 suppliers:

```
row hits = 5000 * 0.05 = 250
```

However, this does not take into account the fact that we might have many or few column values of UK; therefore, index density is a poor substitute for statistics.

An even worse substitute are the weightings we saw earlier in this chapter (shown in Table 4.1). These are used if there are no statistics.

### Translating rows to logical reads

When the query optimizer has found a particular index interesting and has used the selectivity of the search argument to assess the number of rows returned, it translates this value into logical reads.

The way it does this translation depends on the index type—clustered or nonclustered—and whether there is actually an index present.

### No index present

If we have no suitable index on the table, a table scan must be performed, as shown in Figure 4.4.

The number of logical reads a table scan will use is easy to calculate. All we have to do is find the number of database pages used by the table. We

**Figure 4.4**
*Logical reads required for a table scan*

Data Pages

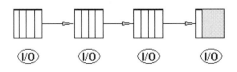

can find this information from the sysindexes system table by looking at the dpages column. In the BankingDB database the Accounts table uses 1,389 pages.

This is an extremely important number. We immediately know that we can retrieve all the rows from the Accounts table in 1,389 logical reads. This establishes a baseline value against which the query optimizer measures the cost of index access in terms of logical read.

### A clustered index present

What if we can use a clustered index? SQL Server will have to traverse the index until the appropriate data page is reached. Because the data is in key sequence, this data page and any other relevant pages will then be retrieved. The cost of using a clustered index is the cost of the index traversal plus the data pages scanned, as shown Figure 4.5.

We can estimate the number of data pages scanned by knowing the approximate number of rows per page. I tend to use the DBCC SHOW-CONTIG statement with the TABLERESULTS option to find the average record size and then divide this into 8,000 to get the approximate number of rows per page. In the BankingDB database the Accounts table holds about 18 rows per page. Knowing this, you can estimate the number of data pages scanned if you know roughly how many rows will be returned by the query. But what about the index pages?

To find the number of logical reads used to traverse the clustered index we need to know the number of levels in the index. This is known as the depth of the index. Again, I tend to use the DBCC SHOWCONTIG statement with the TABLERESULTS option and the ALL_LEVELS option to

**Figure 4.5**
*Logical reads
required for a
clustered index*

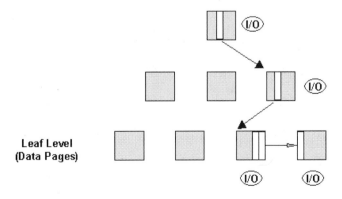

Leaf Level
(Data Pages)

find the number of levels in an index. The number of levels in an index will be the number of logical reads used to traverse the index. Most indexes will consist of a small number of levels, so the number of logical reads used to traverse an index can often be ignored.

### A nonclustered index present

If there is a nonclustered index present, SQL Server will have to traverse the index until the appropriate leaf pages are reached. The pointers from the leaf pages will then have to be followed to each row pointed at by a an index entry in the leaf page. Each data row may reside on its own data page, or a data page may host a number of the rows we wish to retrieve. This is irrelevant. Each row retrieved will result in a data page request—that is, a logical read. The cost of using a nonclustered index is then the cost of the index traversal plus the leaf pages scanned plus the cost of retrieving each row, as shown in Figure 4.6.

This could result in many logical reads. If the query returns a range of rows, say 2,000, the query optimizer will assume that this will cost the number of logical reads to traverse the nonclustered index plus the number of logical reads to scan the relevant leaf pages plus 2,000 logical reads to retrieve the data rows. We can immediately see that in the case of our Accounts table, this is greater than our baseline value for a table scan. In other words, all other things being equal, the table scan would be the most efficient retrieval method.

**Figure 4.6**
*Logical reads required for a nonclustered index*

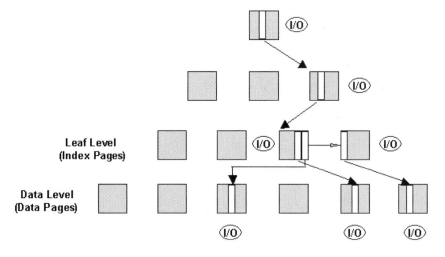

Leaf Level
(Index Pages)

Data Level
(Data Pages)

**Figure 4.7**
*Logical reads
required for a
nonclustered index
and a single row
retrieval*

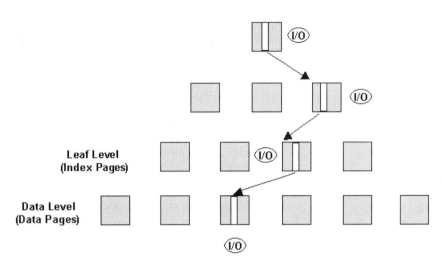

Leaf Level
(Index Pages)

Data Level
(Data Pages)

**Note:** In fact, the query optimizer does not consider only logical reads. It also considers CPU. For this reason, a comparison alone between logical reads and the number of pages in the table is an oversimplification.

Clearly, if the query is only going to return one row—for example, when we use the = operator with a unique index, the cost is the index traversal plus the cost of retrieving the single data page, as shown in Figure 4.7. Compared with performing the same operation using a clustered index, the nonclustered index will usually take only one extra logical read.

We have previously mentioned the covered query, where all the information necessary is satisfied from the index leaf level without visiting the data. SQL Server will have to traverse the index until the leaf level is reached and then the relevant leaf-level pages are scanned, as shown in Figure 4.8.

### A nonclustered index present and a clustered index present

We have already mentioned in Chapter 3 that the presence of a clustered index on a table results in the leaf-level index page pointers in any nonclustered indexes on the table to become the clustered index key instead of the Row ID.

So now, as well as SQL Server 2000 traversing the nonclustered index, it must also traverse the clustered index. Of course, a query that returns a

**Figure 4.8**
*Logical reads
required for a
covering
nonclustered index*

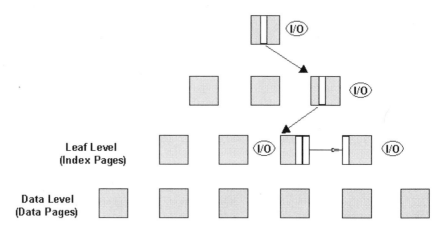

**Figure 4.8**
*Logical reads
required for a
covering
nonclustered index*

range of rows will return a range of pointers from the nonclustered index, all of which will have to access the clustered index. The number of logical reads performed to access the nonclustered index will therefore be increased by the logical reads needed to access the clustered index.

However, there is a positive side to this. As we have stated, the presence of a clustered index on a table results in the leaf-level index page pointers in any nonclustered indexes on the table to become the clustered index key instead of the Row ID. In other words, the leaf-level index entries in the clustered index will now hold the nonclustered index key plus the clustered index key, and so there is more chance of the nonclustered index covering the query.

### Multiple nonclustered indexes present

We have discussed the fact that range retrieval in a nonclustered index may result in a large number of data page requests such that a table scan is chosen in preference. But what if the WHERE clause of the query contains more than one filter. For example:

```
SELECT * FROM accounts
    WHERE
    balance BETWEEN 100 AND 200
    AND
    customer_no BETWEEN 1000 AND 2000
```

If we have a nonclustered index on the balance column and the range is reasonably selective, we should expect the query optimizer to choose a query execution plan that selects the data rows based on the index and then discards the ones where the customer_no column holds a value that is not in range. If the range is not selective, we will expect a table scan. But what if there is also a nonclustered index present on the customer_no column? As we discussed in Chapter 3, the query optimizer may be able to perform an index intersection. If the query optimizer believes that using both indexes will reduce the number of data page requests, then it will do just that.

### 4.3.3 Join order selection

If the query contains more than one table or the query performs a self-join, the query optimizer will derive the most efficient strategy for joining the tables. The order in which tables are joined can have a large impact on performance. For example, suppose we wanted to run the following query, which joins the Accounts table with the Customers table.

```
SELECT * FROM accounts INNER JOIN customers
ON
accounts.customer_no = customers.customer_no
WHERE
balance > 9990
```

Both tables have a nonclustered index on customer_no. Suppose the Customers table was accessed first. There is no restriction on the customer_no column and so all 12,500 customer rows would be retrieved, and for each of these rows the Accounts table would be accessed. It would, therefore, be accessed 12,500 times, and since each customer has two accounts, 25,000 account rows would be retrieved. Each one would then be tested for the restriction > 9,990.

Suppose, instead, the Accounts table was accessed first. The restriction would be applied, removing the majority of rows in the Accounts table and leaving only 21 rows with the balance column containing a value > 9,990. This means that the Customers table will only be accessed 21 times, considerably reducing the logical reads needed to execute the query. In fact in our BankingDB database this join order needed 96 logical reads against the 51,695 logical reads needed by the first join order!

The query optimizer can use information in the statblob column to help it choose an efficient strategy. We have already seen that the statblob column contains index density information, and it is this information the query optimizer uses to estimate how many rows from one table will join with rows from another table—that is, the join selectivity. The statblob column not only holds index density for a single column in a composite index but also the index densities of some of the column combinations. If the composite index contained three columns—COL1, COL2, and COL3, then the index densities held would be for the following combinations:

```
COL1                   index density value (a)

COL1, COL2             index density value (b)

COL1, COL2, COL3  index density value (c)
```

Suppose the statblob column is not populated. In this case the query optimizer uses a formula to work out the join selectivity. It is simply the reciprocal of the number of rows in the smaller table. If we had a query that joined the Accounts table (25,000 rows) with the Customers table (12,500 rows), the join selectivity would be (1/12500) = 0.00008. For each row in the Customers table we would expect a match to (0.00008 * 250000) = 2 rows in the Accounts table.

## 4.3.4    How joins are processed

Prior to SQL Server 7.0, there was only one basic join mechanism available to the query optimizer to join two tables together. This was the nested loops join. In SQL Server 2000 there are three, as follows:

1.    Nested loops joins

2.    Merge joins

3.    Hash joins

The nested loops join is still the best general-purpose join available, but the merge and hash joins can be utilized by the query optimizer to produce a more efficient join plan in certain circumstances.

### Nested loops joins

In the nested loops join, tables are processed as a series of nested loops, which are known as nested iterations. In a two-table join every row selected from the outer table (the table in the outer loop) causes the inner table (the table in the inner loop) to be accessed. This is known as a scan (not to be confused with table scan). The number of times the inner table is accessed is known as its scan count. The outer table will have a scan count of 1; the inner table will have a scan count equal to the number of rows selected in the outer table. Figure 4.9 illustrates a three-table join.

The outer table will use indexes to restrict the rows if it can, whereas the inner table will use indexes on the join columns and potentially any other indexes that might be efficient in limiting the rows returned. However, the

**Figure 4.9**
*A join of three tables implemented as a nested loop*

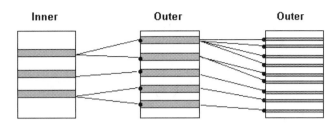

| Inner | Outer | Outer |

index on the join column is the most important index, since, without it, the inner table will be table scanned for each relevant row in the outer table.

For example, consider an inner join between the Customers table and the Accounts table. There are 12,500 rows in the Customers table and 25,000 rows in the Accounts table. Suppose the Accounts table has a nonclustered index on the customer_no column. The query optimizer will choose the Customers table as the outer table (there is no index that is useful, and, besides, this is the smaller table). The Customers table will be passed through once. Its scan count will be one—that is, it is processed once, or, if you prefer, it is visited once.

There are 12,500 qualifying rows in the Customers table and so the Accounts table will be visited 12,500 times. It will have a scan count of 12,500. Luckily, there is a useful index on the customer_no column of the Accounts table so the table will not be table scanned 12,500 times! Later on we will look at how we can return statistical information about the scan count and the logical read (pages requested) count. But for now just let me say that this join indeed results in the following statistics:

| Table | Logical Read | Scan Count |
|-------|--------------|------------|
| Customers | 736 | 1 |
| Accounts | 50,859 | 12,500 |

Note that the logical read count of the Customers table is 736, because there are 736 data pages in this table. The logical read count for the Accounts table is approximately four per scan count, indicating that for each access of the Accounts table, via the index, four logical reads were used (three for index pages and one for the data page).

The nested loops join does not depend on an equality operation relating the two tables together. The operator, for example, can be < or >.

If the outer table supplies only a few rows to the query—that is, it is a small table or is filtered by a WHERE clause and the inner table has an index on the join column—a nested loops join can be very efficient, usually more so than a merge or hash join. However, when large tables are being joined, a merge or hash join may be more efficient.

How many ways are there of joining two tables: A and B? There are in fact two ways: AB and BA. What about three tables? There are six ways: ABC, ACB, BAC, BCA, CAB, and CBA. What about four tables? The answer is four, or 1 * 2 * 3 * 4 = 24.

The number of ways, then, to join X tables is X!, or factorial X. If a query were to join 16 tables, we are talking about 20,922,789,888,000 possible ways of performing this join. A join of ten tables would have 3,628,800 possible combinations, and SQL Server 2000 can join a maximum of 256 tables in a SELECT statement!

Luckily, the query optimizer uses techniques internally to minimize the number of possible combinations, but the fact still remains that the more tables in a join the longer the query optimizer will take to work out the most efficient access strategy. Also, any inefficiency will be magnified enormously, since we are basically placing loops within loops within loops within a nested loops join.

The bottom line is: If you are going to execute a query that joins many tables, test it! Check what the final query execution plan is. Check the number of logical reads. Check the elapsed time. If you are not happy, then break the join down into parts, perhaps joining a subset of the tables into a temporary table and then joining that with the remaining tables.

One useful rule of thumb is to make sure that if the number of tables in the query is N, then the number of join conditions is at least N − 1. For example, suppose we join three tables—TAB1, TAB2, and TAB3—and the join is over a column we will call C1. Suppose the query is as follows:

```
SELECT * FROM TAB1, TAB2, TAB3 WHERE
   TAB1.C1 = TAB2.C1
```

Applying our rule of thumb we can see that there are three tables in the join, so there should be at least two join conditions. There is only one join condition in the query, which is below the minimum number. This will result in SQL Server performing a lot of extra work joining all the rows in TAB3 with all the rows in the result set from the join of TAB1 and TAB2 or some combination of this. Depending on the form of the SELECT statement, the answer returned may be correct—for example, if a DISTINCT was used. The time taken to process the query, though, would be much greater than necessary.

Applying our rule of thumb we can see that the query should be written as follows:

```
SELECT * FROM TAB1, TAB2, TAB3 WHERE
   TAB1.C1 = TAB2.C1 AND
   TAB2.C1 = TAB3.C1
```

However, if it makes sense to add a third join condition, then do not be afraid to do so, since it will give the query optimizer more options to work with:

```
SELECT * FROM TAB1, TAB2, TAB3 WHERE
   TAB1.C1 = TAB2.C1 AND
   TAB2.C1 = TAB3.C1 AND
   TAB1.C1 = TAB3.C1
```

Of course, if you use the ANSI join syntax (recommended) with the ON clause you cannot miss the join condition.

### Merge joins

Merge joins can be efficient when two large tables of similar size need to be joined and both inputs are already sorted by virtue of their indexes, or a sort operation is not expensive for sorting one or more of the inputs. The result from a merge join is sorted on the join column, and if this ordering is needed by the query, the merge join can supply it. The equality operator must be used in the query to join the tables; otherwise, a merge join cannot be used.

There are two types of merge join: a one-to-many (regular) and a many-to-many. In the case of a one-to-many, one input will contain unique join column values, whereas the other will contain zero, one, or many matching values. In the case of a many-to-many merge join, both inputs may contain duplicate join column values.

A many-to-many merge join requires that a temporary worktable is used, and this is apparent when looking at the logical read information that can be returned from a query (discussed later). In my experience, the added work required to process this worktable often means that the query optimizer uses one of the other join techniques—for example, a hash join in preference to the many-to-many merge join. If the join column from one input does contain unique values, the query optimizer will not know this unless a unique index is present on that column.

If the two join columns from the two input tables both have a clustered index created on them, the query optimizer knows that the rows are physi-

**Figure 4.10**
*Basic merge join
algorithm*

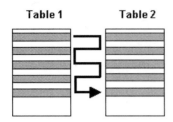

Table 1              Table 2

cally sorted on the join column. In this case the query optimizer does not need to perform a sort on any of the inputs. Joining these two tables will probably be performed with a merge join, especially, if the merge join is a one-to-many. The presence of an ORDER BY clause on the query will increase the likelihood that a merge join is used.

If the two join columns from the two input tables both have a nonclustered index created on them, then the query optimizer knows that the rows are not physically sorted on the join column. In this case the query optimizer will need to perform a sort on the inputs. Joining these two tables with a merge join is less likely, unless an ORDER BY clause on the query is used. In this case the query optimizer will decide if a merge join is more efficient than nested loops or hash.

So how does a merge join work? Basically, the two tables being joined are visited once each. The scan count for each table is one. This is shown in Figure 4.10.

The algorithm for a one-to-many merge join is as follows:

- Read a row from Table 1.

- Read a row from Table 2.

- If the join column values are equal, return all the matching rows.

- If the value from Table 1 is < the value from Table 2, read the next row from Table 1.

- If the value from Table 2 is < the value from Table 1, read the next row from Table 2.

The query optimizer carries on, stepping along each table until the processing is complete.

### Hash joins

In my experience, hash joins are used by the query optimizer frequently in SQL Server 2000—somewhat more, in fact, than merge joins. Of course, this may not be the case with your application. With a hash join, there are two inputs: the build input and the probe input. The build input is typically the smaller table, although this may not be the table that uses fewer data pages on disk. Rather, it is the table with the least rows after selection criteria in the WHERE clause have been considered by the query optimizer. An interesting consideration with hash joins is that there need be no useful indexes on the tables to be joined. This means that the hash join mechanism can be used to join any two nonindexed inputs. This is very useful, because this is exactly the form that intermediate results in the query execution plan take. We will see examples of this later. The equality operator must be used in the query to join the tables; otherwise, a hash join cannot be used.

Assuming that the query optimizer has chosen the smaller table to be the build input, it now reads each row in turn from the table. For each row read, the value in the join column is processed by a hashing algorithm. Hashing algorithms apply some function to the input value to arrive at an output value. The important consideration is that when the same value is input to the hashing algorithm later, the value output is the same as was previously output.

In a hash join, the value returned by the hashing algorithm is used to identify a cell in memory known as a hash bucket. The row from the build input is then written into this hash bucket (at least the columns of interest to the query are). The number of hash buckets is a function of the size of the build input. It is best if the query optimizer can hold all of the hash buckets (the build input) in memory. It is not always possible to do this, and therefore several variations of the basic hash algorithm exist to facilitate the storing of hash buckets to disk. Two of these mechanisms are known as a Grace Hash Join and a Recursive Hash Join.

Once the build input has completed, the probe input phase starts. Each row in the probe input (the bigger table) is read, and the value of the join column is input to the same hash algorithm. The resulting value again identifies a hash bucket. The query optimizer then checks the hash bucket to see if there are any rows in it from the build input with the same join column value. If there are, the row is retrieved from the hash bucket and, with the row from the probe phase, returned to the query. If there is no match, the row may be discarded depending on the type of join being performed.

With a hash join, both tables are visited just once—that is, each has a scan count of one. Memory is needed for the hash buckets, so hash joins tend to be memory and CPU intensive. They typically perform better than merge joins if one table is large and one is small, and they are better than

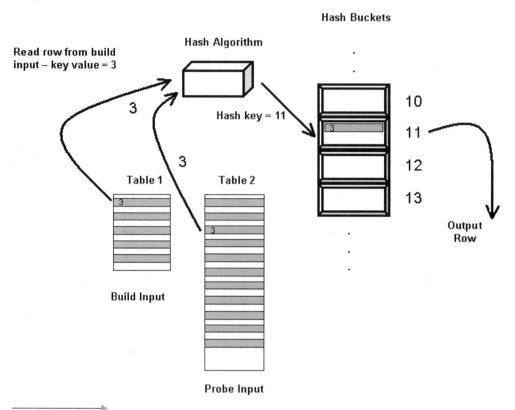

**Figure 4.11**    *Basic hash join algorithm*

nested loops joins if both tables are large. However, because the build input is performed before any rows are returned, hash joins are not efficient when the first row of the join must be retrieved quickly.

Figure 4.11 shows a build input being processed. A row has been read with a value of 3 in the join column. This is hashed to a value of 11, and the row (relevant columns) is written into the hash bucket. Later, the probe input is processed. A row is read with a value of 3 in the join column. This is hashed to a value of 11, and the query optimizer checks to see if there is a matching row in the hash bucket from the build input. There is, so the rows are concatenated and returned to the query.

The hash join mechanism, as previously mentioned, can be used to join nonindexed inputs. One example of this is when the query optimizer has created a plan that involves two sets of index pointers, and pointers need to be found that exist in both sets—that is, the set intersection. Hashing is also useful when the query contains an aggregate operator—for example, SUM or MAX with a GROUP BY. Using SUM as an example, suppose we want to find the sum of the bank balances for the accounts managed by each branch on a per branch basis, as follows:

```
SELECT branch_no, SUM(balance)
    FROM accounts
    GROUP BY branch_no
```

The query optimizer may choose to create a query execution plan using a hashing mechanism. The build input creates a set of hash buckets and then reads each row in turn. The branch number of the first account (the GROUP BY column) will be hashed, and the branch number and account balance values will be written into the appropriate hash bucket. This process will continue for each row. However, if a branch number is found to be present already in a hash bucket, the balance will be added to the value present. Finally, when all the rows have been retrieved, the hash buckets are scanned and the branch number values returned with their sums.

**Note:** This mechanism will produce a nonordered output, so, as always, use an ORDER BY clause if you wish the output to be ordered.

### 4.3.5   **Tools for investigating query strategy**

We have now discussed the steps that the query optimizer performs during query optimization, namely:

- Query analysis

- Index selection

- Join order selection

To facilitate performance, tuning, and optimization it is essential that we are able to see the decisions that the query optimizer has made so that we can compare the decisions with what we expect. We also need to be able to measure the work done in executing the query so we can compare the effectiveness of different indexes.

**Note:** You should always calculate a rough estimate of the logical reads a query should use. If the logical reads used differ by a large amount, it could be that your estimate is very inaccurate or, more likely, the query execution plan is not what you expected!

There are a number of tools at our disposal for checking what the query optimizer is doing. There are various options we can set in the Query Analyzer, the graphical query execution plan, and the SQL Server Profiler. The SQL Server Profiler is discussed in Chapter 7. We will focus our discussion here on the graphical query execution plan, but, first, let us investigate the SET statements and options available to us.

### SET SHOWPLAN_TEXT { ON | OFF }

When SET SHOWPLAN_TEXT is set on, information is displayed pertaining to the query execution plan used. The query is not executed. This statement must be the only statement in the query batch.

Suppose we execute the following query when SET SHOWPLAN_TEXT ON has been executed:

```
SELECT * FROM accounts WHERE balance = 0
```

The following output will result:

```
StmtText
----------------------------------------
select * from accounts where balance = 0

(1 row(s) affected)

StmtText
----------------------------------------------------------
    |--Table Scan(OBJECT:([BankingDB].[dbo].[accounts]),
WHERE:([accounts].[balance]=Convert([@1])))
```

Note that the output has been wrapped to fit on the page. The text of the query is repeated and then information pertaining to the query execution plan is displayed. This contains information such as the logical and physical operators used (described shortly) and other information pertinent to the plan. Since this statement is designed to be used primarily with Microsoft MS-DOS applications, such as the osql command-line utility, we will not spend any more time on it.

### SET SHOWPLAN_ALL { ON | OFF }

When SET SHOWPLAN_ALL is set on, detailed information is displayed pertaining to the query execution plan used. The query is not executed. This statement must be the only statement in the query batch.

Suppose we execute the following query when SET SHOWPLAN_ALL ON has been executed:

```
SELECT * FROM customers C INNER JOIN accounts A
   ON C.customer_no = A.customer_no
   WHERE balance = 100
```

The output will be returned in the form of a rowset that can be accessed by programs. There is too much information returned to display it across the page, so we will break it down into its constituent parts. Rather than use the previous SQL statement, we will use a slightly more complex one involving an inner join of the Customers and Accounts tables. We are not too concerned with the reason a particular plan was chosen here—the goal of this example is merely to show the output from this SET statement. Ultimately, I find the graphical query execution plan much easier to use and I will focus on that shortly.

```
StmtText

SELECT * FROM customers C INNER JOIN accounts A ON C.customer_no = A.customer_no WHERE balance = 100
 |--Bookmark Lookup(BOOKMARK:([Bmk1000]), OBJECT:([BankingDB].[dbo].[customers] AS  [C]))
     |--Nested Loops(Inner Join, OUTER REFERENCES:([A].[customer_no]) WITH PREFETCH)
         |--Table Scan(OBJECT:([BankingDB].[dbo].[accounts] AS [A]), WHERE:([A].[balance]=100.00))
         |--Index Seek(OBJECT:([BankingDB].[dbo].[customers].[nciCustomerNo] AS [C]), SEEK:([C].[customer_no]=
     [A].[customer_no]) ORDERED FORWARD)
```

I have wrapped the output so this StmtText column can be read completely. This is how it looks with no wrap, so it can easily be matched with the other columns I will discuss. I have had to truncate the text to fit it on the page.

```
SELECT * FROM customers C INNER JOIN accounts A ON C.customer_no = A.customer_no WHERE balance = 100
 |--Bookmark Lookup(BOOKMARK:([Bmk1000]), OBJECT:([BankingDB].[dbo].[customers] AS  [C]))
     |--Nested Loops(Inner Join, OUTER REFERENCES:([A].[customer_no]) WITH PREFETCH)
         |--Table Scan(OBJECT:([BankingDB].[dbo].[accounts] AS [A]), WHERE:([A].[balance]=100.00))
         |--Index Seek(OBJECT:([BankingDB].[dbo].[customers].[nciCustomerNo] AS [C]), SEEK:([C].[customer_no]=
```

This StmtText column repeats the SQL statement in the first row of the column. Subsequent rows in the display, known as PLAN_ROWS, contain a description of the operation taking place. This column contains the physical operator and may or may not also contain the logical operator. So what are physical and logical operators? The physical operator describes the physical mechanism by which the operation was performed. In our example we can see physical operators such as Nested Loops, Table Scan, and Index Seek. Logical operators describe the relational operation being performed—in our example, an Inner Join. Often, there is no separate logical operator, since the logical operation results in a number of steps—each representing physical operations. In our example, there is no logical operator mentioned in the line that represents the Table Scan physical operation.

Other information is also often present in the StmtText column. In our example, we can see that the row containing the Index Seek physical operator also names the index in question—nciCustomerNo—and the column used in the predicate—customer_no—as well as the table name. The row containing the Nested Loops physical operator also specifies WITH PREFETCH, which means that asynchronous read ahead is being utilized (see Chapter 5). The information in the StmtText column is also repeated in other columns, as we shall now see.

Note that the output is in the form of a hierarchical tree with the SQL statement itself at the top of the tree. I find that decoding the hierarchy can sometimes be confusing, but, again, as we shall see, the graphical query execution plan will help us here. It is often best, however, to start looking at the deepest level in the hierarchy. This represents the basic operations against tables and indexes, which together form the basic building blocks of the query execution plan. Other steps will utilize these basic steps until the result of the query is returned. To assist in understanding the hierarchy, the  next set of columns lend a helping hand.

| StmtId | NodeId | Parent | PhysicalOp | LogicalOp |
|--------|--------|--------|-----------------|-----------------|
| 17 | 1 | 0 | NULL | NULL |
| 17 | 3 | 1 | Bookmark Lookup | Bookmark Lookup |
| 17 | 5 | 3 | Nested Loops | Inner Join |
| 17 | 7 | 5 | Table Scan | Table Scan |
| 17 | 8 | 5 | Index Seek | Index Seek |

The StmtId is a number that identifies the statement in the batch of SQL statements if there is more than one SQL statement in the batch. This groups all the steps together for the one statement. The NodeId is a number that identifies the step in the query execution plan, and the Parent is the node ID of the parent step. Using these numbers, the position of a step in the hierarchical tree can be ascertained. The PhysicalOp and LogicalOp columns contain the physical and logical operators as described above.

```
Argument
--------
1
BOOKMARK:([Bmk1000]), OBJECT:([BankingDB].[dbo].[customers] AS [C])
OUTER REFERENCES:([A].[customer_no]) WITH PREFETCH
OBJECT:([BankingDB].[dbo].[accounts] AS [A]), WHERE:([A].[balance]=100.00)
OBJECT:([BankingDB].[dbo].[customers].[nciCustomerNo] AS [C]),
OBJECT:([BankingDB].[dbo].[customers].[nciCustomerNo] AS [C]), SEEK:([C].[customer_no]=[A].[customer_no])
ORDERED FORWARD
```

This column displays extra information concerning the operation, as described previously.

The next set of columns includes the values used by the operator; they are typically columns from a SELECT list or WHERE clause. Internal values may also be represented here. In our example, the * has been expanded to the actual list of columns.

```
DefinedValues
-------------
NULL
[C].[customer_no], [C].[customer_fname], [C].[customer_lname], [C].[customer_notes]
NULL
[A].[account_no], [A].[customer_no], [A].[branch_no], [A].[balance], [A].[account_notes]
[Bmk1000]
```

Next we see columns that are concerned with the estimated cost of the query.

| EstimateRows | EstimateIO   | EstimateCPU  | AvgRowSize | TotalSubtreeCost |
|--------------|--------------|--------------|------------|------------------|
| 1988.1769    | NULL         | NULL         | NULL       | 1.4232613        |
| 1988.1769    | 6.2500001E-3 | 2.1869945E-3 | 886        | 1.4230624        |
| 1988.1769    | 0.0          | 8.3105788E-3 | 445        | 1.4146254        |
| 1988.1769    | 0.60027075   | 0.01378925   | 435        | 1.22812          |
| 1.0          | 6.3284999E-3 | 7.9603E-5    | 19         | 0.1661949        |

The EstimateRows column contains the number of rows the query optimizer expects the operator to return. In our example, we are looking at 1,988 rows estimated for all the operators except the Index Seek. The 1,988 estimate comes from the fact that the query optimizer estimates that this number of Account table rows will have a balance of 100. The value of 1 from the index seek indicates that the query optimizer knows that for each row from the Accounts table a maximum of one row can be returned from the Customers table (it has a unique index on the customer_no column).

How many rows are actually returned? How many customer accounts have a balance of exactly 100? The answer in our database is, in fact, zero! The query optimizer estimate is very inaccurate. Why? We shall see shortly!

The EstimateIO column contains the estimated I/O cost for the operator. In our example, the cost estimates are small numbers, so what do the values represent? The numbers are weighted by some undocumented weighting factor. Microsoft does not publish the weighting factor, since they want the ability to adjust it to their heart's desire. This means that it is practically impossible to translate the EstimateIO value into logical reads. However, it is possible to compare these numbers with one another, and we know the lower the number the lower the cost.

The EstimateCPU column contains the estimated CPU cost for the operator. In our example, the cost estimates are again small numbers, and, again, the numbers are weighted by some undocumented weighting factor. This means that it is not possible to translate the EstimateCPU value into CPU milliseconds. Again, it is possible to compare these numbers with one another, and, again, the lower the number the lower the cost. Using these two estimates we can easily see the most expensive operation in terms of I/O and CPU in a query.

The AvgRowSize is the estimated average row size (in bytes) passing through the operator. In our example, rows from the Accounts table are estimated to be 435 bytes in length. The output of the Index Seek operator is an index entry (key plus pointer) of 19 bytes. Once the Customers table row has been retrieved from the data page (the Index Lookup) and joined with the Accounts table row, the combined size is estimated at 886 bytes.

The TotalSubtreeCost column contains the estimated total cost of the operator and the cost of all its children. This is derived from the EstimateIO and EstimateCPU columns, and, again, some mystery weighting factor is used. This number, though, represents a cost value that combines the I/O and CPU cost and is very useful when looking for the operation in a query that is using the lion's share of the query resource. The OutputList column represents a list of the columns that will be displayed by the query.

```
OutputList
----------
NULL
[C].[customer_no], [C].[customer_fname], [C].[customer_lname], [C].[customer_notes], [A].[account_no],
[A].[customer_no], [A].[branch_no], [A].[balance], [A].[account_notes]
[Bmk1000], [A].[account_no], [A].[customer_no], [A].[branch_no], [A].[balance], [A].[account_notes]
[A].[account_no], [A].[customer_no], [A].[branch_no], [A].[balance], [A].[account_notes]
[Bmk1000]
```

| Warnings | Type | Parallel | EstimateExecutions |
|---|---|---|---|
| NULL | SELECT | 0 | NULL |
| NULL | PLAN_ROW | 0 | 1.0 |
| NULL | PLAN_ROW | 0 | 1.0 |
| NO STATS:([accounts] [customer_no],<br>[accounts].[balance]) | PLAN_ROW | 0 | 1.0 |
| NULL | PLAN_ROW | 0 | 1988.1769 |

The Warnings column contains any warning messages issued by the query optimizer for the operation. In our example, the only operation to be associated with a warning is the Table Scan operation, where the Accounts table is being scanned looking for rows with a balance of 100. We shall look at this warning in the graphical query execution plan shortly, but for now let us just say that the query optimizer is telling us why the estimate of the number of rows returned is so inaccurate—can you guess what the warning means?

The Type column merely flags a row as being the parent row for the query—a SELECT, INSERT, UPDATE, or DELETE, for example, or a row representing an element of the query execution plan—PLAN_ROW.

The Parallel column contains a value of 0 or 1 specifying whether the operator can execute in parallel (1) or not (0).

The EstimateExecutions column is the estimated number of times the operator will execute during the query. In our example, the Table Scan operator will execute once. However, for each row in the Accounts table being scanned, the Customer table will be accessed (it is the inner table in a nested loops join). For this reason, the EstimateExecutions column for the Index Seek operator contains the value 1988.1769.

So, as we have seen, the SET SHOWPLAN_ALL statement produces a large amount of information concerning the query execution plan. As I've hinted at a number of times now, I feel this information is best displayed through the graphical query execution plan. Before we take a look at this there are more SET statements that are useful—so let's have a look at them.

### SET STATISTICS PROFILE { ON | OFF }

The SET SHOWPLAN_TEXT and SET SHOWPLAN_ALL statements we have just looked at both display information concerning the query execution plan adopted by the query optimizer. Neither statement actually allows the query to execute. This has a number of ramifications. Consider the following stored procedure:

```
CREATE PROCEDURE usp_testplan
AS
CREATE TABLE #t1 (c1 int)
SELECT c1 from #t1
RETURN
```

Suppose we now issue a SET SHOWPLAN_ALL ON and execute the stored procedure, as follows:

```
EXEC usp_testplan

Server: Msg 208, Level 16, State 1, Procedure
usp_testplan, Line 4
Invalid object name '#t1'.
```

Because the SET statement suppresses the execution of the stored procedure, the temporary table #t1 is not created, and it is not therefore possible to display plan information for the SELECT statement.

Another problem caused by the SET statement suppressing query execution is that we cannot produce information about the logical reads actually used by the query, nor can we see how many rows pass through an operator as opposed to an estimated number.

Enter SET STATISTICS PROFILE. This statement does not suppress the execution of the query. As well as returning the same information as SET SHOWPLAN_ALL, it also displays two extra columns—Rows and Executes—which contain the actual number of rows returned and the actual number of times the operator executed during the query. In other words, the equivalent of the EstimateRows column and the EstimateExecutions column, respectively.

### SET STATISTICS IO { ON | OFF }

Another SET statement that is useful when investigating different query optimizer strategies is SET STATISTICS IO. This displays the count of table accesses (scans), logical and physical reads, and read ahead reads for each Transact-SQL statement, as follows:

```
SET STATISTICS IO ON

SELECT C.customer_lname, A.account_no, A.balance
   FROM customers C INNER JOIN accounts A
   ON C.customer_no = A.customer_no
   WHERE
   balance BETWEEN 100 AND 120


customer_lname     account_no     balance
--------------     ----------     -------
Burrows            107540         118.0400
   :
   :
(56 row(s) affected)

Table 'customers'. Scan count 56, logical reads 181,
physical reads 0, read-ahead reads 0.
Table 'accounts'. Scan count 1, logical reads 1569,
physical reads 0, read-ahead reads 0.
```

In the above example, the Accounts table experienced a scan count of 1 and the Customers table experienced a scan count of 56. The phrase scan count has nothing to do with the use of table scans; it merely states how many times the table was accessed in the query. In our example, the Accounts table is processed as the outer table of the (nested loops) join and is therefore accessed only once. For each qualifying row in the Accounts table, the Customers table is accessed. In this example there are 56 qualifying rows in the Accounts table, so the scan count of the Customers table is 56.

There are 1,569 pages in the Accounts table. As this is table scanned, SQL Server 2000 must retrieve every page—hence, the logical read value of 1,569. The Customers table experiences 181 logical reads, approximately three per scan. This is because the index is two levels deep, so two index pages and one data page will be fetched on each scan.

Since the data and index pages are already cached in memory, the physical reads counter is zero. A physical read represents a database page request that is not found in cache, so SQL Server 2000 has to fetch it from disk. Read-ahead reads will be discussed in Chapter 5.

**Note:** The scan count may sometimes be larger than you expect. For example, you may expect the scan count for a table to be one. However, the query optimizer has created a parallel execution plan and two parallel threads access the table—hence, it has a scan count of two.

### SET STATISTICS TIME { ON | OFF }

The SET STATISTICS TIME ON statement displays the time (in milliseconds) that SQL Server took to parse the statement, compile the query optimizer strategy, and execute the statement, as follows:

```
SELECT C.customer_lname, A.account_no, A.balance
   FROM customers C INNER JOIN accounts A
   ON C.customer_no = A.customer_no
   WHERE
   balance BETWEEN 100 AND 120

SQL Server parse and compile time:
   CPU time = 10 ms, elapsed time = 10 ms.

customer_lname    account_no    balance
--------------    ----------    -------
Burrows           107540        118.0400
   :
   :
(56 row(s) affected)


SQL Server Execution Times:
   CPU time = 29 ms,  elapsed time = 29 ms.
```

I personally do not use this statement. Whereas logical reads is a constant and will be the same for a given access strategy at any time irrespective of other work on the server, this is not true for the statistics time. For that reason I do not find it very useful. If I really want to compare the elapsed times of queries, I often use my own statements, as follows:

```
DECLARE
  @time_msg CHAR(255),
  @start_time DATETIME

SELECT @start_time = GETDATE()

-- Execute the query we wish to test

SELECT C.customer_lname, A.account_no, A.balance
  FROM customers C INNER JOIN accounts A
  ON C.customer_no = A.customer_no
  WHERE
  balance BETWEEN 100 AND 120

-- Calculate the query duration

SELECT @time_msg = 'Query time (minutes:seconds) ' +
         CONVERT(CHAR(2),
DATEDIFF(ss,@start_time,GETDATE())/60) +
         ':'  +
         CONVERT(CHAR(2),
DATEDIFF(ss,@start_time,GETDATE())%60)

print @time_msg
```

```
customer_lname      account_no     balance
--------------      ----------     -------
Burrows             107540         118.0400
  :
  :
(56 row(s) affected)

Query time (minutes:seconds) 0 :16
```

Of course, the Query Analyzer makes life easy for us now, since we can merely look in the bottom right area of the query window where the elapsed time of a query is displayed. Still, the above code is useful in scripts.

**Note:** The SQL Server 2000 Profiler will also display the CPU, duration, and I/O usage of a query. It can also display the query execution plan. This will be described in Chapter 7.

### The graphical query execution plan

We have been discussing SET statements so far in this chapter that allow us to check the query execution plan that the query optimizer has created. As mentioned on a number of occasions, I find this easier to do with the graphical query execution plan, and this will now be our focus. As with SET SHOWPLAN_TEXT and SET SHOWPLAN_ALL, displaying the estimated execution plan does not cause the query to execute. However, as with SET STATISTICS PROFILE, it is possible to execute the query and view the query execution plan afterwards.

To display the estimated execution plan the keyboard shortcut CTRL+L can be used, or choose Display Estimated Execution Plan from the Query menu. Alternatively, just click the Display Estimated Execution Plan button on the toolbar. Let us take a trip around the graphical display, and then we will look at the graphical query execution plans we might encounter when analyzing our queries. We'll use the inner join we previously used for the SET SHOWPLAN_ALL statement, as follows:

```
SELECT * FROM customers C INNER JOIN accounts A
   ON C.customer_no = A.customer_no
   WHERE balance = 100
```

The estimated execution plan for this statement is shown in Figure 4.12.

The query execution plan is read from right to left. We can see the operators that were rows in the SET SHOWPLAN_ALL output. The hierarchical tree is displayed on its side with the top of the tree on the left—the SELECT statement. On the far right of the display the children at the lowest branches of the tree are displayed. The children at the same level are displayed vertically above one another. The flow of rows, index pointers, and so on is illustrated by the arrows joining the operators. Note that these

**Figure 4.12**
*A graphical estimated execution plan*

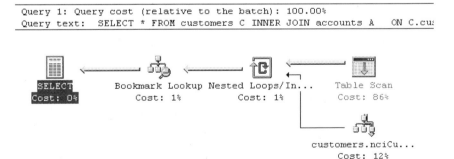

Query 1: Query cost (relative to the batch): 100.00%
Query text:   SELECT * FROM customers C   INNER JOIN accounts A     ON C.cu:

SELECT
Cost: 0%

Bookmark Lookup   Nested Loops/In...
Cost: 1%              Cost: 1%

Table Scan
Cost: 86%

customers.nciCu...
Cost: 12%

arrows vary in width. This variation is proportional to the number of rows passed to the next operator up the tree.

At the top of the display is a heading specifying that this is query 1. We only have one query in our query batch, but if there were more than one query these would be labeled accordingly. The query text is also displayed. More interestingly, the query optimizer has also estimated the cost of the query relative to the cost of the batch. This is useful when you want to see which query in the batch is the one that is the most expensive. In our example, having only one query, the cost is 100 percent of the batch.

Different operations within a query are also costed relative to one another. In our example the cost of the Table Scan is 86 percent of the cost of the query. Clearly, this operator is worthy of some investigation if the query is performing badly.

The operators are named and represented by an icon. In the case of the nested loops join, the icon represents a nested loop, and the name of the physical and logical operator are displayed in the format physical/logical. In the case of the table scan, the physical operator Table Scan is displayed. There is no logical operator as such; therefore it takes the same name as the physical operator and just physical is displayed. In the case of the indexed access of the Customers table, the icon representing an Index Seek is displayed and the index name in the format table.index is displayed underneath. How do we know what these icons represent? In the background of the display, if an icon or arrow is right-clicked, a menu appears. If Help is chosen, a list of operators appears. Click on an operator and an explanation is displayed. You will also notice that the displayed menu contains options for zooming, fonts, and managing indexes and statistics.

What about the detailed information that was produced by SET SHOWPLAN_ALL? Can the graphical execution plan produce this information also? It can and all we have to do is move the mouse pointer over the operator we are interested in—no click is needed. This is shown in Figure 4.13.

As can be seen, lots of information pertaining to the operator is displayed. Pretty much all the cost information and any other text that was displayed in the SET SHOWPLAN_ALL are displayed in this window. Note what happens when we move the mouse pointer over the Table Scan operator. This is shown in Figure 4.14.

A warning message is displayed (in red—but you can't see that!) telling us that statistics are missing from the table. If we recall, the SET

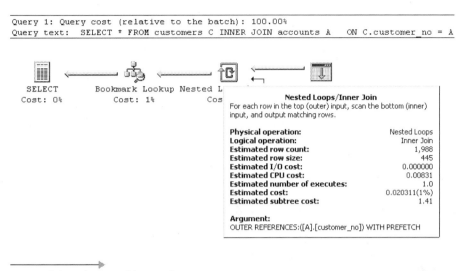

```
Query 1: Query cost (relative to the batch): 100.00%
Query text:  SELECT * FROM customers C INNER JOIN accounts A   ON C.customer_no = A
```

**Nested Loops/Inner Join**
For each row in the top (outer) input, scan the bottom (inner) input, and output matching rows.

| | |
|---|---|
| **Physical operation:** | Nested Loops |
| **Logical operation:** | Inner Join |
| **Estimated row count:** | 1,988 |
| **Estimated row size:** | 445 |
| **Estimated I/O cost:** | 0.000000 |
| **Estimated CPU cost:** | 0.00831 |
| **Estimated number of executes:** | 1.0 |
| **Estimated cost:** | 0.020311(1%) |
| **Estimated subtree cost:** | 1.41 |

**Argument:**
OUTER REFERENCES:([A].[customer_no]) WITH PREFETCH

**Figure 4.13** *Placing the pointer over an operator*

SHOWPLAN_ALL output also had a warning in the Warnings column of its output for this operator. We'll look at what the warning means shortly, but for now let us just register that the graphical query execution plan displays warnings and, in this case, suggests a course of action. Again, we can't see this, but on the graphical display shown in Figure 4.12, the Table Scan

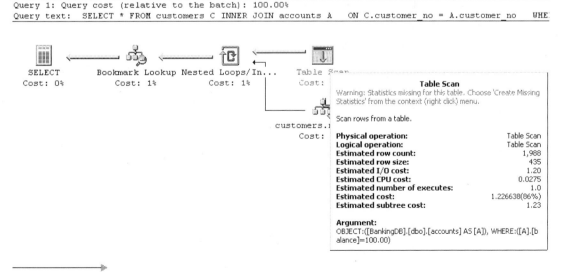

```
Query 1: Query cost (relative to the batch): 100.00%
Query text:  SELECT * FROM customers C INNER JOIN accounts A   ON C.customer_no = A.customer_no   WHE
```

**Table Scan**
Warning: Statistics missing for this table. Choose 'Create Missing Statistics' from the context (right click) menu.

Scan rows from a table.

| | |
|---|---|
| **Physical operation:** | Table Scan |
| **Logical operation:** | Table Scan |
| **Estimated row count:** | 1,988 |
| **Estimated row size:** | 435 |
| **Estimated I/O cost:** | 1.20 |
| **Estimated CPU cost:** | 0.0275 |
| **Estimated number of executes:** | 1.0 |
| **Estimated cost:** | 1.226638(86%) |
| **Estimated subtree cost:** | 1.23 |

**Argument:**
OBJECT:([BankingDB].[dbo].[accounts] AS [A]), WHERE:([A].[balance]=100.00)

**Figure 4.14** *Placing the pointer over the Table Scan operator*

**Figure 4.15**
*Placing the pointer
over an arrow*

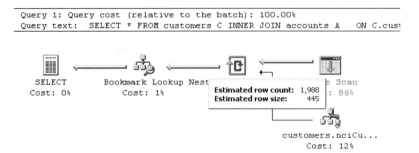

```
Query 1: Query cost (relative to the batch): 100.00%
Query text:   SELECT * FROM customers C INNER JOIN accounts A    ON C.cust
```

and Cost: 86 percent text are also displayed in red to draw our attention to the fact that this operator has warnings associated with it.

If the mouse pointer is placed over an arrow, a window pops up—as shown in Figure 4.15.

This window displays information about the estimated number of rows being passed to the next operator and the estimated row size.

Now that we know the format of the Display Estimated Execution Plan window, we can investigate some query optimizer strategies. These strategies will be examples of the query optimizer and index behavior we have discussed in this and the previous chapter. We will start with simple examples and then move to more complex examples.

To refresh our memories, the BankingDB database definition is as follows:

```
CREATE TABLE customers
    (
    customer_no      INT          NOT NULL,
    customer_fname   CHAR(20)     NOT NULL,
    customer_lname   CHAR(20)     NOT NULL,
    customer_notes   CHAR(400)    NOT NULL
    )

CREATE TABLE accounts
    (
    account_no       INT          NOT NULL,
    customer_no      INT          NOT NULL,
    branch_no        INT          NOT NULL,
    balance          MONEY        NOT NULL,
    account_notes    CHAR(400)    NOT NULL
    )
```

```
CREATE TABLE branches
   (
   branch_no        INT          NOT NULL,
   branch_name      CHAR(60)     NOT NULL,
   branch_address   CHAR(400)    NOT NULL,
   managers_name    CHAR(60)     NOT NULL
   )
```

The Customers table contains 12,500 rows. Each customer has two accounts, so the Accounts table contains 25,000 rows. The Branches table contains 100 rows. We will define indexes on the tables as we go along. There are no indexes to start with. Also, the automatic updating and creation of index statistics has been disabled.

To summarize, the tables after creation with no indexes are shown in Table 4.2.

Note that the number of pages used by a table will vary depending on what we have just done to the table. For example, creating a clustered index on the Accounts table will increase the Average Page Density and reduce the Average Bytes Free per Page (as reported by DBCC SHOWCONTIG). This results in 1,390 pages being allocated to the Accounts table.

Let us now check the estimated query execution plan for various queries. Before we execute the first query, we will make sure that the database option Auto create statistics is set to off.

### Query 1: Find the accounts whose balances are $100

```
SELECT * FROM accounts WHERE balance = $100
```

Figure 4.16 displays the graphical query execution plan for query 1.

We can see immediately that the Table Scan operator is used. This is not unreasonable, since we have no indexes present. The query optimizer has no choice but to perform a table scan. Every page in the Accounts table will be retrieved to search for the accounts with a balance of $100. If we check the

**Table 4.2**   *Attributes of the Tables in the BankingDB Database*

| Table Name | Rows | Data Pages |
|------------|--------|------------|
| Accounts | 25,000 | 1,570 |
| Customers | 12,500 | 834 |
| Branches | 100 | 8 |

**Figure 4.16**
*Graphical query
execution plan for
query 1*

```
Query 1: Query cost (relative to the batch): 100.00%
Query text:  select * from accounts where balance=$100.00
```

```
SELECT                Table Scan
Cost: 0%              Cost: 100%
```

Set statistics IO output, set within the Current Connection Properties button in the Query Analyzer, we can verify this as follows:

```
Table 'accounts'. Scan count 1, logical reads 1570,
physical reads 0, read-ahead reads 0.
```

Indeed, the logical reads number is the same value as the data pages in
the table.

There are, in fact, zero rows returned by this query, but if we place the
mouse pointer over the (fairly wide) arrow, the pop-up window shows that
the estimated number of rows passed to the SELECT statement operator at
the top of the tree is somewhat more than this, as Figure 4.17 shows.

The estimated rows value is 1,988, but the actual number of rows
returned is zero. The query optimizer's estimate is very inaccurate Why is
this?

The clue lies with the Table Scan operator. The Table Scan and Cost:
100 percent are actually displayed in red indicating that a warning is associated with this operation. If we pass the mouse pointer over the operator, we
can see a warning message—as shown in Figure 4.18.

The query optimizer is telling us that there are no statistics that it can
use. Since there are no indexes, this is no surprise. The query optimizer is
also telling us, though, that there are no column statistics either. Because of
this lack of statistics, the query optimizer has used its internal magic num-

```
Query 1: Query cost (relative to the batch): 100.00%
Query text:  select * from accounts where balance=$100.00
```

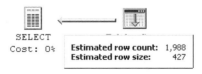

```
SELECT
Cost: 0%    Estimated row count:  1,988
            Estimated row size:     427
```

**Figure 4.18**
*Graphical query execution plan for query 1 showing a warning*

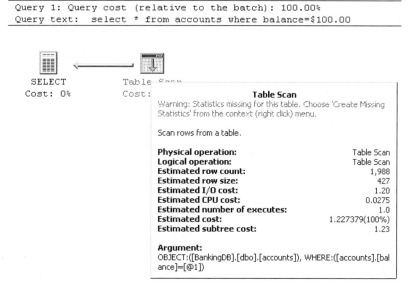

```
Query 1: Query cost (relative to the batch): 100.00%
Query text:  select * from accounts where balance=$100.00
```

SELECT
Cost: 0%

Table Scan
Cost:

**Table Scan**
Warning: Statistics missing for this table. Choose 'Create Missing Statistics' from the context (right click) menu.

Scan rows from a table.

| | |
|---|---|
| **Physical operation:** | Table Scan |
| **Logical operation:** | Table Scan |
| **Estimated row count:** | 1,988 |
| **Estimated row size:** | 427 |
| **Estimated I/O cost:** | 1.20 |
| **Estimated CPU cost:** | 0.0275 |
| **Estimated number of executes:** | 1.0 |
| **Estimated cost:** | 1.227379(100%) |
| **Estimated subtree cost:** | 1.23 |

**Argument:**
OBJECT:([BankingDB].[dbo].[accounts]), WHERE:([accounts].[balance]=[@1])

bers to estimate that the equality operation (balance = $100) will return about 8 percent of the table. I have seen this figure closer to 10 percent, but the fact is, it was completely wrong.

The query optimizer warning also tells us how to solve the problem. It suggests that we might choose Create Missing Statistics from the context (right-click) menu. This will create column-level statistics for the balance column and is equivalent to executing the Transact-SQL statement CREATE STATISTICS.

If we take this option, the Create Missing Statistics dialog box is displayed—as shown in Figure 4.19.

We'll sample all of the data, but we'll leave the name of the statistics group to be the default of statistic_balance.

Now, if we look at the estimated execution plan again, we'll see that the arrow is narrower, as shown in Figure 4.20.

Passing the mouse pointer over the arrow shows the estimated number of rows to be one, which is somewhat more accurate. This example showed us a scenario where the query optimizer flagged the fact that it would really like some statistics. In reality this is not likely to be the case. The query optimizer would normally have created the statistics itself without asking us to create them for it. The only reason it didn't this time was because we sup-

**Figure 4.19**
*Create missing
statistics dialog box*

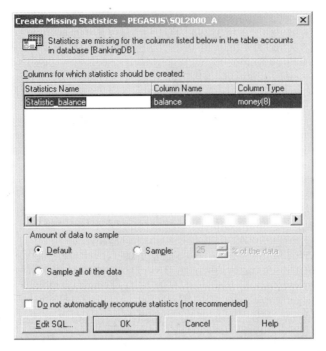

pressed this capability by setting the database option Auto create statistics to off. Note that, as discussed previously, these automatically created column statistics will have a name that is prefixed with _WA.

OK, so did this improve the efficiency of the plan? Will the rows be retrieved any faster? No, of course not. Since there are no indexes, a table scan still has to be performed and column-level statistics in this scenario are not useful. However, in many scenarios this is not the case—column-level statistics are very useful and later we will see the query optimizer create column-level statistics dynamically.

Let us give the query optimizer more options to play with. We'll create a nonclustered index on the balance column. There are no reasons why two

**Figure 4.20**
*Estimated
execution plan after
missing statistics
have been created*

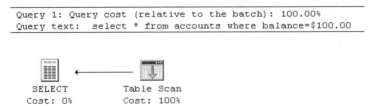

```
Query 1: Query cost (relative to the batch): 100.00%
Query text:  select * from accounts where balance=$100.00
```

SELECT          Table Scan
Cost: 0%        Cost: 100%

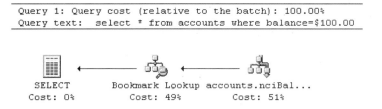

**Figure 4.21**
*Graphical query execution plan for query 1 with a nonclustered index present on the balance column*

bank accounts should not have the same balance value, so this index cannot be a unique index.

If we execute our query now, the estimated execution plan will be as shown in Figure 4.21.

We can immediately see that the Table Scan operator has disappeared. If we read from right to left, the first operator we come to is an Index Seek. Passing the mouse pointer over this operator gives us the window that contains cost information. There is a one-line explanation of the operator: Scanning a particular range of rows from a nonclustered index.

If we look at the Argument: at the bottom of the window, we see that it names the index and it also contains a SEEK:() predicate. The predicate is [accounts].[balance]=100; in other words, the filter in the WHERE clause of the query. What this means is that the index is traversed using the filter value.

In Chapter 3, the algorithm used by SQL Server was to look for the highest key value not greater than the lowest key we wish to retrieve. Using this algorithm SQL Server traverses the nonclustered index to the leaf-level index pages. Any index entries satisfying the search predicate will now be retrieved. In other words, a set of pointers will be retrieved. This is the role of the Index Seek operator—to collect the pointers for qualifying rows ready to read the data pages containing those rows. This was shown in Figure 3.29. The index seek actually traverses the three levels of index pages ready to access the data pages.

If we continue to read from right to left, the next operator we come to is a Bookmark Lookup. Passing the mouse pointer over this operator the window appears that contains cost information. There is a one-line explanation of the operator: Use a Bookmark (RID or Clustering Key) to look up the corresponding row in the Table or Clustered Index.

If we look at the Argument: we see at the bottom of the window that it names the table whose data pages we are reading. So, this Bookmark

**Figure 4.22**
*Graphical query*
*execution plan for*
*query 1 showing*
*estimated rows*
*when a*
*nonclustered index*
*is used*

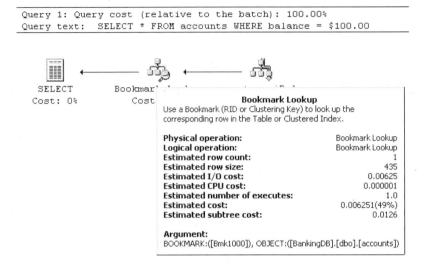

```
Query 1: Query cost (relative to the batch): 100.00%
Query text:   SELECT * FROM accounts WHERE balance = $100.00
```

Lookup operator is using a bookmark (which is a fancy name for a pointer) to look up the data rows from the table. Of course, as we have discussed previously, if there was a clustered index present on the table, the pointer in the nonclustered index leaf entries would be the clustered index key. There is no clustered index present on our table, so the pointer addresses the row on the data page directly with a Row ID.

Again, referring back to Figure 3.29, each index entry that matches the search predicate will point to a data row, and a logical read will be required to fetch the data page in which the row resides.

If we position the mouse pointer on the Bookmark Lookup icon, we see that the Estimated row count is one. This is shown in Figure 4.22.

The query optimizer has estimated that one pointer is going to be passed to the Bookmark Lookup operator. In other words, the query optimizer estimates that one row will be returned. Of course, one pointer will return exactly one row, and so the arrow connecting the Bookmark Lookup operator to the SELECT statement will also have an Estimated row count of one. This is a pretty accurate estimate, since we know zero rows will actually be returned.

It is interesting to note the relative costs of the two operators. They're pretty much the same. Fetching one data page in the Bookmark Lookup and fetching some index entries in the Index Seek are fairly trivial operations with approximately equal costs.

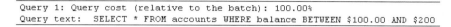

**Figure 4.23**
*Graphical query execution plan for query 2 showing estimated rows when a nonclustered index is used for a range retrieval*

```
Query 1: Query cost (relative to the batch): 100.00%
Query text:   SELECT * FROM accounts WHERE balance BETWEEN $100.00 AND $200
```

```
   SELECT          Bookmark Lookup accounts.nciBal...
  Cost: 0%            Cost: 99%          Cost: 1%
```

We can quickly change things so that fetching data pages in the Bookmark Lookup is not trivial, and we'll do this with query 2. Before we do, let us just look at the Set statistics IO output for query 1 with our nonclustered index:

    Table 'accounts'. Scan count 1, logical reads 2, physical
    reads 0, read-ahead reads 0.

This is somewhat less than the table scan. We have used just two logical reads.

### Query 2: Find the accounts whose balances are between $100 and $200

The following range retrieval actually returns 253 rows from the Accounts table.

    SELECT * FROM accounts
        WHERE balance BETWEEN $100 AND $200

The estimated execution plan is shown in Figure 4.23.

The plan is similar to the plan for query 1. The operators are the same but the arrows are wider. This is because the query optimizer has estimated that a larger number of rows will be returned by this query. The estimate is 263 rows, which is fairly accurate. Note, however, the distribution of costs across the operators. The Index Seek costs 1 percent of the query, whereas the Bookmark Lookup now costs 99 percent. This illustrates an important point—once a query starts to retrieve more than a few rows, the nonclustered index starts to become expensive, since a data page will need to be retrieved for each qualifying row. This is because each retrieval is a logical read. If we look at the Set statistics IO output for query 2 with our nonclustered index, we see the following code:

    Table 'accounts'. Scan count 1, logical reads 256,
    physical reads 0, read-ahead reads 0.

**Figure 4.24**
*Graphical query execution plan for query 2 showing the estimated execution plan when a nonclustered index is used for a larger range retrieval*

```
Query 1: Query cost (relative to the batch): 100.00%
Query text:   SELECT * FROM accounts WHERE balance BETWEEN $100.00 AND $220
```

```
 SELECT               Table Scan
 Cost: 0%             Cost: 100%
```

We can see that the logical read value has increased. As the number of rows satisfying a range retrieval becomes large, so does this logical read value. Eventually, the query optimizer will decide that a table scan is more efficient than using the index. Let us test this theory. We will increase the range slightly, as follows:

```
SELECT * FROM accounts
    WHERE balance BETWEEN $100 AND $220
```

The estimated execution plan is shown in Figure 4.24.

The following code is the new Set statistics IO output for query 2:

```
Table 'accounts'. Scan count 1, logical reads 1570,
physical reads 0, read-ahead reads 0.
```

For a small increase in the range, the query optimizer has decided that a table scan is now a more efficient option.

### Query 3: Find the accounts whose balances are between $100 and $200 and whose customer numbers are between 7000 and 8000

```
SELECT * FROM accounts
    WHERE balance BETWEEN $100 AND $200
    AND
    customer_no BETWEEN 7000 AND 8000
```

In this query, not only is there a filter on the balance column, but there is also a filter on the customer_no column. The query plan is shown in Figure 4.25.

The query optimizer has again chosen the nonclustered index on the balance column to find the rows that satisfy the range of balances. As in the previous query, the Bookmark Lookup operation will retrieve the data pages to fetch the Account table rows. However, now a Filter operator is applied

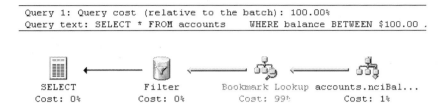

**Figure 4.25**
*Graphical query execution plan for query 3 showing the addition of a filter operator*

to find the rows that also satisfy the range of customer numbers. The query optimizer text for the Bookmark Lookup is in red, indicating a warning. This is shown in Figure 4.26. The reason for the warning is that the query optimizer would like to know how many Account table rows have a customer number in the range, but it has no column statistics for this column. It therefore has to estimate how many rows the Filter operation will return. The only reason it didn't automatically create the missing column statistics is because we suppressed this capability by setting the database option Auto create statistics to off.

This indexing strategy may be very wasteful. Consider the case where the customer number filter discards most of the rows that satisfied the balance range. In this case the Bookmark Lookup will retrieve many data pages, only to find that they did not contain rows that had a qualifying customer number. So what can we do? One possibility is to change the index

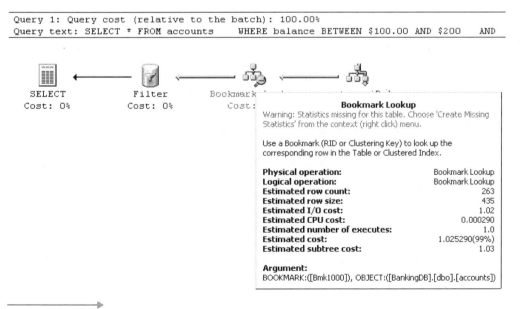

**Figure 4.26** *Graphical query execution plan for query 3 showing the bookmark warning*

**Figure 4.27**
*Graphical query execution plan for query 3 with a composite index*

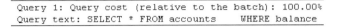

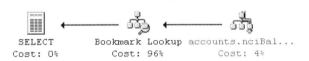

on the balance column to a composite index containing the balance and customer_no columns. If we do this, the query plan becomes the one shown in Figure 4.27. We can see that the Filter operator has now disappeared. The query optimizer can select the qualifying rows before the data pages are requested. It is interesting to note that the query plan contains a Missing Statistics warning on the Index Seek operator.

Why is this? As we have previously discussed, index statistics are only held for the first column of a composite index. The query optimizer would like us to let it have statistics for the second column, the customer_no column. The query optimizer could have calculated the statistics for itself, but, again, it didn't automatically create the missing column statistics because we suppressed this capability by setting the database option Auto create statistics to off.

So, the composite index is a useful index for our query. In fact, the addition of the customer_no column to the index results in 22 logical reads being performed instead of 256 when just the balance column was present. However, there is one problem with this composite index. Consider the following query:

```
SELECT * FROM accounts
    WHERE customer_no BETWEEN 7000 AND 8000
```

Because we are not supplying a value for the balance column, the query optimizer cannot use the index. In fact, a table scan is performed.

So what other options do we have? Let us create a new nonclustered index on the customer_no column and return our original index consisting of just the balance column. We now have two indexes. This will support the above query if the range is not too large. But what about our original query?

```
SELECT * FROM accounts
    WHERE balance BETWEEN $100 AND $200
    AND
    customer_no BETWEEN 7000 AND 8000
```

Let us look at the query plan, which is shown in Figure 4.28.

**Figure 4.28**
*Graphical query execution plan for query 3 with two nonclustered indexes*

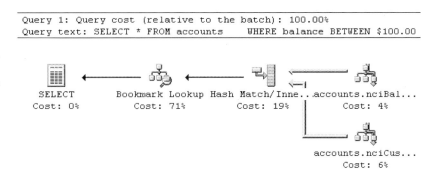

We can see that something interesting has happened. First of all, we can see that on the right side of the query plan there are two operators at the same level in the tree, with both having the Hash Match physical operator (Inner Join logical operator) as a parent. These two operators are both Index Seek operators. The query optimizer has been able to utilize both indexes to perform an index intersection, as described in Chapter 3. What has happened is that the query optimizer has obtained two sets of pointers from each index for key values satisfying each key range. It knows that for a row to satisfy the WHERE clause, a pointer must be present in both sets.

To determine this, a Hash Match operation is performed on the two sets of pointers using the hash algorithm described earlier in the chapter. Once the qualifying pointers have been obtained, a Bookmark Lookup operation is performed to retrieve the relevant data pages to fetch the rows. The important point to note here is that no data rows are fetched and then discarded. The Hash Match operation ensures that all nonqualifying rows are eliminated before data pages are fetched. This query plan used 28 logical reads and the indexing strategy supports queries specifying only the balance column, only the customer_no column, or both. Since there are two indexes, row inserts and deletes will be more costly than in the case of the single composite index. Note that the query optimizer could perform index intersections using more than two indexes, but I have seldom seen this happen.

### Query 4: Find the accounts whose customer numbers are between 7000 and 8000, displaying the customer number and branch Number

```
SELECT customer_no, branch_no FROM accounts
    WHERE customer_no BETWEEN 7000 AND 8000
```

In this example, we have moved away from the * in the SELECT list and explicitly specified two columns. Generally, I would not advise the use of *

**Figure 4.29**
*Graphical query
execution plan for
query 4 with a
composite
nonclustered index*

```
Query 1: Query cost (relative to the batch): 100.00%
Query text:  SELECT customer_no, branch_no FROM accounts
```

```
 SELECT              accounts.nciCus...
Cost: 0%              Cost: 100%
```

in code. Using * could cause problems if one day someone adds an extra column (that someone might be the wizard that sets up merge replication as it adds a rowguid column). It also does not provide good documentation. We are interested in indexing strategies, and there may be a detrimental effect here. A query that might otherwise be covered will certainly not be if the developer is lazy and uses the * when a small number of columns are actually needed.

If we execute the above query, a table scan is performed even though there is a nonclustered index on the customer_no column. This is because 2,002 customers are returned by the query and so the query optimizer has decided to perform a table scan using 1,570 logical reads. Now let us change the index on the customer_no column to a composite index containing the branch_no column as the second key column. The resulting query plan is shown in Figure 4.29.

The index is now covering the query so no data pages need to be retrieved, since the leaf-level index pages will satisfy the query. The logical reads used has dropped to seven—a not inconsiderable drop! Suppose we execute the following query:

```
SELECT customer_no, branch_no FROM accounts
    WHERE branch_no BETWEEN 1000 AND 1010
```

The index can still cover the query, but all the leaf-level index pages will have to be scanned. This still only requires 60 logical reads. Let us drop all the indexes on the Accounts table and create a clustered index on the branch_no column and a nonclustered index on the customer_no column. Let us repeat the following query:

```
SELECT customer_no, branch_no FROM accounts
    WHERE customer_no BETWEEN 7000 AND 8000
```

The query plan is shown in Figure 4.30. This looks a little surprising at first. The query optimizer has chosen the nonclustered index that contains

**Figure 4.30**
*Graphical query execution plan for query 4 with a nonclustered index and a clustered index*

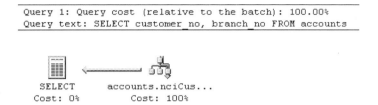

```
Query 1: Query cost (relative to the batch): 100.00%
Query text: SELECT customer_no, branch_no FROM accounts
```

```
SELECT              accounts.nciCus...
Cost: 0%            Cost: 100%
```

the customer_no column. Previously it performed a table scan. Furthermore, only eight logical reads were used. What has happened?

Let us think back to our discussion on clustered indexes, nonclustered indexes, and pointers. If a clustered index is present on the table, then the nonclustered index leaf-level pointers will be the clustered index key. In other words, our nonclustered index on the customer_no column will contain the branch_no column as a pointer. Therefore, the nonclustered index is actually covering our query.

### Query 5: Find the accounts that are managed by branch 1000

Since we have a clustered index on the branch_no column, let us investigate it.

```
SELECT * FROM accounts
   WHERE branch_no = 1000
```

The query plan is shown in  4.31. The operator is a Clustered Index Seek, which means that the query processor will traverse the index using the key value until the appropriate data page is found. If necessary, the next pointers on the data pages will then be followed to retrieve all the qualifying rows. This query returned 250 rows for a cost of only 16 logical reads.

Suppose the following query is executed:

```
SELECT * FROM accounts
   WHERE customer_no = 1000
```

**Figure 4.31**
*Graphical query execution plan for query 5 with a clustered index*

```
Query 1: Query cost (relative to the batch): 100.00%
Query text: SELECT * FROM accounts     WHERE branch_no = 1000
```

```
SELECT              accounts.ciBran...
Cost: 0%            Cost: 100%
```

**Figure 4.32**
*Graphical query
execution plan for a
clustered index seek*

```
Query 1: Query cost (relative to the batch): 100.00%
Query text: SELECT * FROM accounts    WHERE customer_no = 1000
```

```
SELECT          accounts.ciBran...
Cost: 0%         Cost: 100%
```

The query plan is shown in Figure 4.32.

Since there is no index on the customer_no column, we might expect to see a table scan operation. However, we do not. Instead, we see a Clustered Index Scan operator. When there is a clustered index present on a table, the table scan operation becomes a clustered index scan operation. Traditionally the leaf level of a clustered index is considered to be the data pages of the table, so a clustered index scan is effectively a table scan.

### Query 6: Find the accounts whose balance falls between $100 and $150 or between $5,000 and $5,050

In this query we are using the OR operator. Whereas the AND operator tends to introduce extra filter expressions that limit the rows in the query result, the OR operator tends to do the opposite.

```
SELECT * FROM accounts
WHERE
balance BETWEEN $100 AND $150
OR
balance BETWEEN $5000 AND $5050
```

This query returns 262 rows. There are no indexes except the nonclustered index on the balance column. The estimated query execution plan is shown in Figure 4.33.

This is exactly the same estimated query execution plan as for query 2. The nonclustered index has been used because it is more efficient than a

**Figure 4.33**
*Graphical query
execution plan for
ORed filters on the
same column*

```
Query 1: Query cost (relative to the batch): 100.00%
Query text: SELECT * FROM accounts    WHERE    balance
```

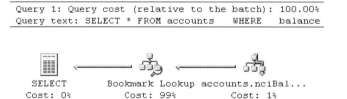

```
SELECT          Bookmark Lookup accounts.nciBal...
Cost: 0%          Cost: 99%        Cost: 1%
```

table scan. Choosing two ranges on the same column is the same as having a larger, single range as far as the query optimizer is concerned. If we increase the number of ORed expressions, we will increase the number of rows returned until a table scan is performed. A table scan is performed if the following query, which returns 381 rows, is executed.

```
SELECT * FROM accounts
WHERE
balance BETWEEN $100 AND $150
OR
balance BETWEEN $5000 AND $5050
OR
balance BETWEEN $6000 AND $6050
```

### Query 7: Find the accounts whose balance falls between $100 and $150 or that belong to customer numbers in the range 500 to 550

In this query, we are using the OR operator again; however, this time two different columns are being used. This means that an account may satisfy either condition or it may indeed satisfy both conditions. The query is as follows:

```
SELECT * FROM accounts
    WHERE
    balance BETWEEN 100 AND 150 OR
    customer_no BETWEEN 500 AND 550
```

There is a nonclustered index present on the balance column and a nonclustered index present on the customer_no column.

The query returns 233 rows, and its estimated query execution plan is shown in Figure 4.34.

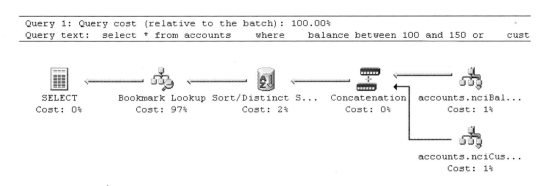

```
Query 1: Query cost (relative to the batch): 100.00%
Query text:  select * from accounts     where     balance between 100 and 150 or     cust
```

SELECT        Bookmark Lookup  Sort/Distinct S...   Concatenation   accounts.nciBal...
Cost: 0%         Cost: 97%         Cost: 2%           Cost: 0%         Cost: 1%

                                                                      accounts.nciCus...
                                                                         Cost: 1%

**Figure 4.34**      *Graphical query execution plan for ORed filters on different columns*

There are similarities between this query execution plan and the query execution plan shown in Figure 4.28, where two similar filter expressions were ANDed.

On the right hand of the query plan there are two operators at the same level in the tree, both having the Concatenation operator as a parent. These two operators are both Index Seek operators. The query optimizer has been able to utilize both indexes. What has happened is that the query optimizer has obtained two sets of pointers from each index for key values satisfying each key range. It knows that pointers from either set will point to account rows that will satisfy the query, and the Concatenation operator will append the multiple inputs to form a single output. In fact, if the mouse cursor is placed over the arrows entering the Concatenation operator, the Estimated row count values are 125 and 99. If the mouse cursor is placed over the arrow leaving the Concatenation operator, the Estimated row count value is 225.

The estimated query execution plan must take care of one other eventuality—the two inputs may both return the same row if it satisfies both filter conditions. The Sort/Distinct Sort operator takes care of this by removing any duplicate rows.

Again, if changes to the ORed expressions increase the number of rows returned, a table scan will be performed. A table scan will also occur if any of the ORed expressions are not supported by an index.

### Query 8: Find the accounts for customer number 1000

Here we will start to use joins. To keep things simple we will use the * in the SELECT list. Note that this will ensure that columns will be required from both tables. We will perform the following join:

```
SELECT * FROM customers C INNER JOIN accounts A
   ON C.customer_no = A.customer_no
   WHERE C.customer_no = 1000
```

The query plan is shown in Figure 4.35.

The indexes present on the Customers and Accounts tables are both nonclustered indexes on the customer_no column. In the case of the Customers table the nonclustered index is unique. We can see that, reading from right to left, there are two inputs to the plan with the parent being the Nested Loops physical operator. If the mouse pointer is placed over this operator, the resulting display explains how it processes the join. This is shown in Figure 4.36.

**Figure 4.35**
*Graphical query execution plan for a nested loops inner join*

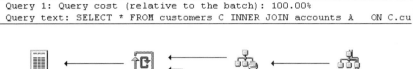

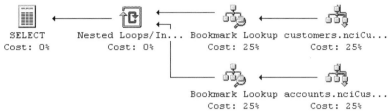

It states: For each row in the top (outer input), scan the bottom (inner) input and output matching rows. So this is our classic nested loops join described earlier in the chapter. The query optimizer has determined that the (unique) index on the customer_no column in the Customers table is highly selective, since it can, at most, return one row. The Customers table has therefore been chosen to be the outer input. So, for each qualifying row in the outer input—that is, for each Customer row—the customer number will be used to access the inner input—that is, the Accounts table. The non-clustered index on the customer_no column in the Accounts table will be used to fetch the matching rows from the Accounts table. Note the Set statistics IO display, which is as follows:

```
Table 'accounts'. Scan count 1, logical reads 4, physical
reads 0, read-ahead reads 0.
Table 'customers'. Scan count 1, logical reads 3,
physical reads 0, read-ahead reads 0.
```

**Figure 4.36**
*Graphical query execution plan showing the nested loops description*

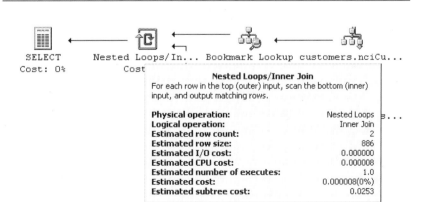

Often the inner table will have a scan count greater than one, but, because the outer input can only produce a maximum of one row, the scan count is, in fact, one. This means that the query optimizer estimates that the inner table will be only be accessed once. Suppose we changed the query, as follows:

```
SELECT * FROM customers C INNER JOIN accounts A
    ON C.customer_no = A.customer_no
    WHERE C.customer_no BETWEEN 1000 AND 1003
```

In this case, four customers are returned from the Customers table, and the scan count of the Accounts table is, therefore, four, as shown in the following code:

```
Table 'accounts'. Scan count 4, logical reads 16,
physical reads 0, read-ahead reads 0.
Table 'customers'. Scan count 1, logical reads 6,
physical reads 0, read-ahead reads 0.
```

Why did the query optimizer choose a nested loops join? Ultimately because it decided that it was the most efficient plan in terms of cost. There was a highly selective index on both tables.

However, suppose we increase the range of customer numbers, as follows:

```
SELECT * FROM customers C INNER JOIN accounts A
    ON C.customer_no = A.customer_no
    WHERE C.customer_no BETWEEN 1000 AND 1999
```

Now, if we check the query plan, we can see that the query optimizer has decided that the nested loops join method is not the most efficient. There are 1,000 customers that satisfy the query and a nested loop would result in the inner table being accessed 1,000 times. The query optimizer has

**Figure 4.37**
*Graphical query execution plan showing a hash join*

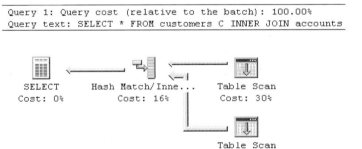

```
Query 1: Query cost (relative to the batch): 100.00%
Query text: SELECT * FROM customers C INNER JOIN accounts
```

```
SELECT          Hash Match/Inne...     Table Scan
Cost: 0%            Cost: 16%          Cost: 30%

                                       Table Scan
                                       Cost: 54%
```

decided that a hash join is a better bet. The query plan is shown in Figure 4.37.

Again, we observe two inputs, but we can see that these are table scans. The parent operator for the table scans is the Hash Match physical operator. If the mouse pointer is placed over this operator, the resulting display explains how it processes the join. This is shown in Figure 4.38.

It states: Use each row from the top input to build a hash table, and each row from the bottom input to probe into the hash table, outputting all matching rows. This is the hash join we described earlier in this chapter. The Set statistics IO output is shown in the following code. Notice that each table has a scan count of just one.

```
Table 'accounts'. Scan count 1, logical reads 1570,
physical reads 0, read-ahead reads 0.
Table 'customers'. Scan count 1, logical reads 840,
physical reads 0, read-ahead reads 0.
```

Now both tables are accessed via a table scan. Does this mean that the indexes are redundant? At first sight you might think the answer would be yes—but you would be wrong! The reason is this: The query optimizer needs to know how many customers satisfy the query. It uses this information to work out the table to use for the build input and the table to use for the probe input and then, ultimately, the cost. Without these indexes it would need column statistics. We have none, and we have not allowed the

**Figure 4.38**
*Graphical query execution plan showing the hash join*

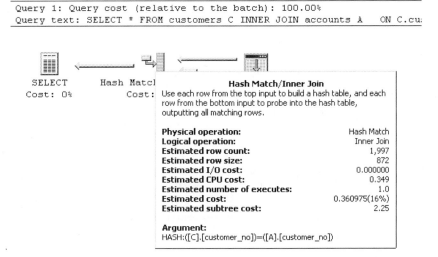

Query 1: Query cost (relative to the batch): 100.00%
Query text: SELECT * FROM customers C INNER JOIN accounts A   ON C.cu:

SELECT        Hash Matcl          **Hash Match/Inner Join**
Cost: 0%      Cost:      Use each row from the top input to build a hash table, and each
                         row from the bottom input to probe into the hash table,
                         outputting all matching rows.

                         **Physical operation:**                        Hash Match
                         **Logical operation:**                          Inner Join
                         **Estimated row count:**                           1,997
                         **Estimated row size:**                              872
                         **Estimated I/O cost:**                         0.000000
                         **Estimated CPU cost:**                            0.349
                         **Estimated number of executes:**                    1.0
                         **Estimated cost:**                      0.360975(16%)
                         **Estimated subtree cost:**                         2.25

                         **Argument:**
                         HASH:([C].[customer_no])=([A].[customer_no])

**Figure 4.39**
*Graphical query
execution plan
showing the hash
join*

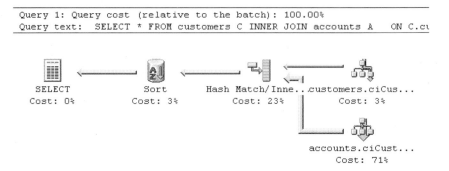

```
Query 1: Query cost (relative to the batch): 100.00%
Query text:   SELECT * FROM customers C INNER JOIN accounts A    ON C.cu
```

query optimizer to create them automatically. Therefore, with no indexes, there are no statistics and the query optimizer might choose an inefficient plan.

When is the query optimizer likely to choose a merge join? Let us change the query so there is a requirement for the output to be sorted on the customer_no column, as follows:

```
SELECT * FROM customers C INNER JOIN accounts A
    ON C.customer_no = A.customer_no
    WHERE C.customer_no BETWEEN 1000 AND 1999
    ORDER BY c.customer_no
```

Let us also ensure that a clustered index on customer_no is created on each table. We have now created two inputs that are effectively sorted on customer_no. If we execute the query, the resulting query plan would be as shown in Figure 4.39. The query optimizer has still decided that a hash join is the most efficient method.

If we force a merge join strategy (we will see how later) we can compare the costs, as shown in the following chart.

| Join Type | Estimated Cost | Logical IO | CPU (ms) |
| --- | --- | --- | --- |
| Hash | 1.54 | 2,408 | 120 |
| Merge (M:M) | 1.61 | 7,409 | 631 |

The hash join is a clear winner, so the query optimizer created the most efficient plan. But why was the merge join more expensive? After all, the sorts are effectively already done. The clue is in the Set statistics IO output, which is as follows:

```
Table 'Worktable'. Scan count 1999, logical reads 5000,
physical reads 0, read-ahead reads 0.
Table 'accounts'. Scan count 1, logical reads 225,
physical reads 0, read-ahead reads 0.
Table 'customers'. Scan count 1, logical reads 62,
physical reads 0, read-ahead reads 0.
```

A worktable has been used that increased the cost. Why? Because the clustered index we created on the Customers table was not unique. The query optimizer used a many-to-many merge join and hence a worktable was used. Note that when the mouse pointer is passed over the Merge Join operator, the pop-up window will contain argument text, which will specify that the merge join was many-to-many. What happens if we recreate the clustered index as a unique clustered index? The query plan is shown in Figure 4.40.

A merge join has been used. The costs Merge (1:M) are shown in the following chart, compared with the previous costs.

| Join Type | Estimated Cost | Logical IO | CPU (ms) |
|---|---|---|---|
| Hash | 1.54 | 2,408 | 120 |
| Merge (M:M) | 1.61 | 7,409 | 631 |
| Merge (1:M) | 1.20 | 287 | 60 |

We can see that by being careful with our index creation we have enjoyed a not inconsiderable cost reduction. Hopefully, most of you will use primary key constraints and so, in the case above, the index would have been created as a unique index automatically.

**Figure 4.40**
*Graphical query execution plan showing merge join*

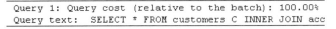

```
Query 1: Query cost (relative to the batch): 100.00%
Query text:   SELECT * FROM customers C INNER JOIN acc
```

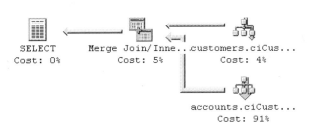

```
SELECT          Merge Join/Inne...customers.ciCus...
Cost: 0%         Cost: 5%            Cost: 4%

                                    accounts.ciCust...
                                    Cost: 91%
```

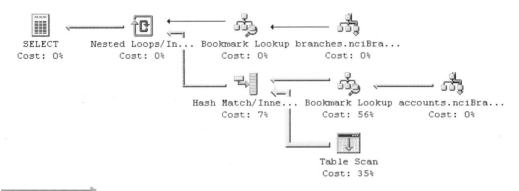

```
Query 1: Query cost (relative to the batch): 100.00%
Query text:   SELECT * FROM customers C    INNER JOIN accounts A ON C.customer_no = A.cus
```

**Figure 4.41**    *Graphical query execution plan showing a three-table join*

### Query 9: Find the accounts and customers for branch number 1000

This is just an example of a three-table join as opposed to the two-table joins we have seen so far.

```
SELECT * FROM customers C
    INNER JOIN accounts A ON C.customer_no = A.customer_no
    INNER JOIN branches B ON A.branch_no = B.branch_no
    WHERE B.branch_no = 1001
```

The estimated query execution plan is shown in Figure 4.41. There is nothing special about this query plan except that it demonstrates that the more tables in the query, the more inputs to the plan.

### Query 10: Find the sum of the account balances managed by each branch

This is an example of aggregation. The query optimizer has to create a plan so that, for each branch number, a total is calculated for the values in the balance column in the Accounts table.

```
SELECT branch_no, SUM(balance) FROM accounts
    GROUP BY branch_no
```

We will remove all the indexes from the Accounts table. The query plan is shown in Figure 4.42.

The Accounts table is table scanned. Even if there were an index on the branch_no column, it would not be used, since all the branches are

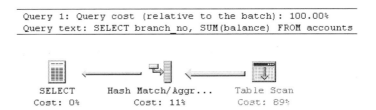

**Figure 4.42**
*Graphical query execution plan showing a group by using hash aggregation*

```
Query 1: Query cost (relative to the batch): 100.00%
Query text: SELECT branch_no, SUM(balance) FROM accounts
```

```
   SELECT          Hash Match/Aggr...       Table Scan
   Cost: 0%          Cost: 11%              Cost: 89%
```

included in the query. The Table Scan operator consequently passes 25,000 rows to the next operator. This interesting operator is the Hash Match Aggregate operator. This operator performs aggregation, as described earlier in this chapter.

The build input creates a set of hash buckets and then reads each row in turn. The branch number of the first account (the GROUP BY column) will be hashed, and the branch number and account balance values will be written into the appropriate hash bucket. This process will continue for each row. However, if a branch number is found to be already present in a hash bucket, the balance will be added to the value present. Finally, when all the rows have been retrieved, the hash buckets are scanned and the branch number values returned with their sums

The Set statistics IO output for this operation is as follows:

```
Table 'accounts'. Scan count 1, logical reads 1570,
physical reads 0, read-ahead reads 0.
```

In other words, the only logical reads performed are those needed to execute the table scan. Suppose we now create a clustered index on the branch_no column of the Accounts table.

If we execute the query again, we see that the query plan changes. This is shown in Figure 4.43.

The query optimizer has decided to make use of the fact that the clustered index on the branch_no column will ensure that the Accounts table rows are stored in branch number order. It can scan the clustered index and

**Figure 4.43**
*Graphical query execution plan showing a group by using a clustered index*

```
Query 1: Query cost (relative to the batch): 100.00%
Query text: SELECT branch_no, SUM(balance) FROM accounts
```

```
   SELECT         Stream Aggregat...    accounts.ciBran...
   Cost: 0%         Cost: 3%              Cost: 97%
```

**Figure 4.44**
*Graphical query
execution plan
showing a group by
using a
nonclustered index*

```
Query 1: Query cost (relative to the batch): 100.00%
Query text: SELECT branch_no, SUM(balance) FROM accounts
```

```
   SELECT           Stream Aggregat...  accounts.nciBra...
   Cost: 0%           Cost: 37%            Cost: 63%
```

pass the sorted rows to the Stream Aggregate operator. This operator computes the sum of the balances using the sorted input stream.

The logical read count is similar to that used for the table scan and hash aggregate. The costs are also similar. The estimated cost for the table scan/hash aggregate is 1.36, whereas the estimated cost for the clustered index scan/stream aggregate is 1.16. The clustered index scan/stream aggregate is therefore estimated to be a cheaper alternative to hashing.

Suppose we drop the clustered index and replace it with a nonclustered index with a composite key of the branch_no and balance columns. This will cover the query. The estimated query execution plan is shown in Figure 4.44.

This is very efficient. The Set statistics IO output is as follows:

```
Table 'accounts'. Scan count 1, logical reads 73,
physical reads 0, read-ahead reads 0.
```

This is a significant reduction in logical reads from the other two query plans. The estimated cost is only 0.188. Using a covering index for aggregate operations is clearly a strategy worth pursuing.

### Query 11: Find the count of the accounts with various restrictions

It is worth a quick look at the COUNT operator, since it may or may not be able to use nonclustered indexes present on a table in various circumstances. Consider the following query:

```
SELECT COUNT(customer_no) FROM accounts
```

The COUNT function used in conjunction with a column counts the number of non-NULL values in the column—in other words, the number of rows that do not have a NULL value in that column. If there are no indexes present on the table, the query optimizer must perform a table scan to execute the count. However, suppose that there is a nonclustered index on the customer_no column. The query optimizer chooses the estimated query execution plan shown in Figure 4.45.

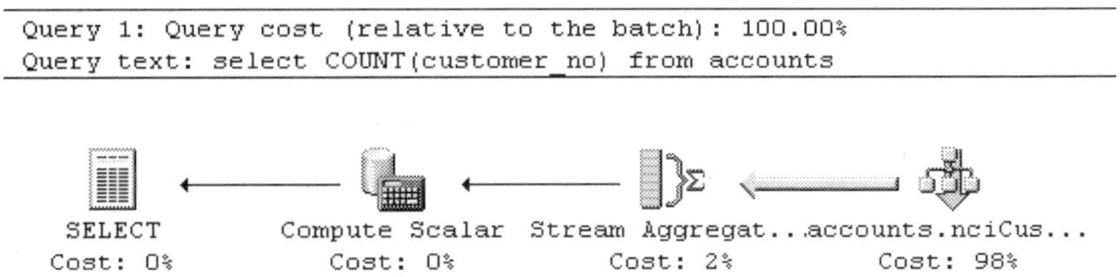

**Figure 4.45**
*Graphical query execution plan showing a COUNT(customer _no) using a nonclustered index on the customer_no column*

```
Query 1: Query cost (relative to the batch): 100.00%
Query text: select COUNT(customer_no) from accounts
```

```
     SELECT          Compute Scalar   Stream Aggregat...  accounts.nciCus...
     Cost: 0%          Cost: 0%          Cost: 2%            Cost: 98%
```

The output from Set statistics IO is as follows:

```
Table 'accounts'. Scan count 1, logical reads 48,
physical reads 0, read-ahead reads 0.
```

This is much more efficient than the 1,570 logical reads used by a table scan of the Accounts table. What has happened is that the query optimizer has chosen to scan the leaf-level index pages, counting the index entries that are not NULL. This makes sense, since we already know that the leaf-level index pages contain exactly one entry per data row. Since an index page will typically hold many more index entries (just key plus pointer) than a data page will hold data rows, the index leaf level will consist of far fewer pages. A scan of the index is likely to be much faster than a scan of the table.

The estimated query execution plan shows the Index Scan operator followed by the Aggregate and Compute Scalar operators, which will count the index entries.

Now, suppose that the index on the customer_no column is dropped and replaced by a nonclustered index on the balance column. The estimated query execution plan that the query optimizer now uses is shown in Figure 4.46.

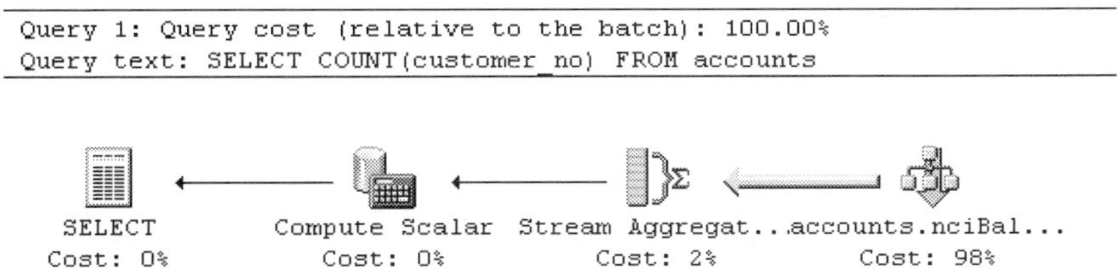

**Figure 4.46**
*Graphical query execution plan showing a COUNT(customer _no) using a nonclustered index on the balance column*

```
Query 1: Query cost (relative to the batch): 100.00%
Query text: SELECT COUNT(customer_no) FROM accounts
```

```
     SELECT          Compute Scalar   Stream Aggregat...  accounts.nciBal...
     Cost: 0%          Cost: 0%          Cost: 2%            Cost: 98%
```

Again, the estimated query execution plan shows a scan of a nonclustered index—in this case, the index on the balance column. How can this index be used when the query is counting the accounts with a non-NULL value in the customer_no column? After all, the customer_no column does not even appear in the nonclustered index. The answer lies in the fact that the column in the Accounts table does not actually allow NULL values. Therefore, it is not necessary to test for NULL values, and any nonclustered index can be scanned to obtain the count. If the customer_no column had allowed NULL values, the query optimizer would have had to perform a table scan to check this column, since the nonclustered index on the balance column would not have contained the necessary information. Suppose the following query is executed:

```
SELECT COUNT(DISTINCT customer_no) FROM accounts
```

The COUNT and DISTINCT used in conjunction with a column counts the number of non-NULL values in the column with duplicates eliminated. The estimated query execution plan is shown in Figure 4.47.

We can see that a Table Scan operator is performed, and this is followed with a Hash Match / Aggregate operator to eliminate the duplicates. The important point to note here is that the DISTINCT keyword requires that duplicate customer numbers are removed and that the nonclustered index on the balance column does not contain the necessary information. Again, a table scan must be performed.

Now consider the following query:

```
SELECT COUNT(*) FROM accounts
```

This form of the COUNT function is not interested in any column, so the question of NULL or duplicate values is irrelevant. Consequently, the query optimizer will produce an estimated query execution plan, which uti-

---

Query 1: Query cost (relative to the batch): 100.00%
Query text: SELECT COUNT(DISTINCT customer_no) FROM accounts

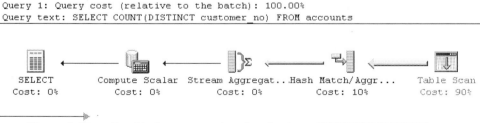

| SELECT | Compute Scalar | Stream Aggregat... | Hash Match/Aggr... | Table Scan |
|--------|----------------|--------------------|--------------------|------------|
| Cost: 0% | Cost: 0% | Cost: 0% | Cost: 10% | Cost: 90% |

**Figure 4.47**   *Graphical query execution plan showing a COUNT(DISTINCT customer_no) using a table scan*

**Figure 4.48**
*Graphical query execution plan showing a COUNT(*) using a nonclustered index*

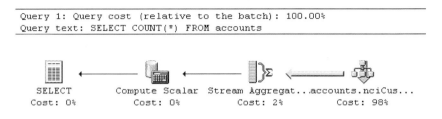

```
Query 1: Query cost (relative to the batch): 100.00%
Query text: SELECT COUNT(*) FROM accounts
```

SELECT          Compute Scalar   Stream Aggregat...  .accounts.nciCus...
Cost: 0%          Cost: 0%          Cost: 2%          Cost: 98%

lizes the nonclustered index with the smallest leaf level. Suppose we execute this query with both the nonclustered indexes on the balance column and the customer_no column present on the Accounts table. The estimated query execution plan is shown in Figure 4.48. The nonclustered index on the customer_no column is used, since the key is a four-byte INTEGER rather than an eight-byte MONEY data type and therefore the index leaf level is smaller.

To summarize, when using the COUNT function, remember that choosing between the different formats may dramatically impact performance, since this may restrict the query optimizer's use of available indexes. Also remember that a covering nonclustered index may help out other aggregate functions such as AVG, MIN, MAX, and SUM.

### Query 12: Display account details in sorted order

If the result of a query is to be ordered by a column or group of columns, the query optimizer can use various techniques to sort it.

Suppose we execute the following query:

```
SELECT customer_no, balance FROM accounts
    ORDER BY customer_no
```

There are no indexes presently on the Accounts table, and so the estimated query execution plan must involve table scan. This is shown in Figure 4.49.

**Figure 4.49**
*Graphical query execution plan showing an ORDER BY using a table scan*

```
Query 1: Query cost (relative to the batch): 100.00%
Query text: SELECT customer_no, balance FROM accounts ORDER
```

SELECT          Sort          Table Scan
Cost: 0%          Cost: 58%          Cost: 42%

**Figure 4.50**
*Graphical query
execution plan
showing an
ORDER BY using
a clustered index*

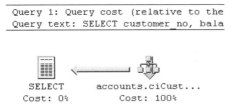

```
Query 1: Query cost (relative to the
Query text: SELECT customer_no, bala
```

SELECT          accounts.ciCust...
Cost: 0%          Cost: 100%

The stream of rows resulting from the table scan is passed to a Sort operator. This sorts the output according to the ORDER BY clause of the query. SQL Server will attempt to perform the sort in memory, but, if the query has insufficient memory, disk space will be used. This situation can be detected by the Sort Warnings event in the SQL Profiler. Suppose we create a clustered index on the customer_no column and repeat the query. The estimated query execution plan is shown in Figure 4.50.

The Sort operator has disappeared, and the Table Scan operator has been replaced by the Clustered Index Scan operator. The query optimizer, knowing that the clustered index will return the data in key sequence order (customer_no column order), can scan the clustered index and therefore avoid any sort.

Suppose the clustered index on the customer_no column is replaced by a nonclustered index. The estimated query execution plan is shown in Figure 4.51.

Note that this is the same estimated query execution plan as that shown in Figure 4.49. In other words, the addition of the nonclustered index makes no difference—a table scan is still performed. This should come as no surprise, because of what we already know. The query optimizer has decided that a table scan and sort are less costly than the many data page requests that would result by scanning the nonclustered index leaf level and

**Figure 4.51**
*Graphical query
execution plan
showing an
ORDER BY using
a table scan rather
than a nonclustered
index*

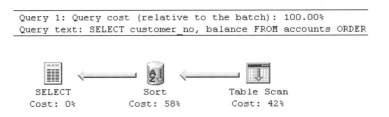

```
Query 1: Query cost (relative to the batch): 100.00%
Query text: SELECT customer_no, balance FROM accounts ORDER
```

SELECT          Sort          Table Scan
Cost: 0%        Cost: 58%     Cost: 42%

**Figure 4.52**
*Graphical query execution plan showing an ORDER BY using a nonclustered index*

```
Query 1: Query cost (relative to the batch): 100.00%
Query text: SELECT customer_no, balance FROM accounts
```

SELECT          Bookmark Lookup  accounts.nciCus...
Cost: 0%        Cost: 99%        Cost: 1%

fetching the data pages. However, if the range of rows is reduced, the non-clustered index will be used. Suppose the following query is executed:

```
SELECT customer_no, balance FROM accounts
    WHERE customer_no BETWEEN 1000 AND 1100
    ORDER BY customer_no
```

The estimated query execution plan is shown in Figure 4.52.

There is no Sort operator, because the query optimizer knows that the leaf level of the nonclustered index is in account_no column order, so scanning it will return the data rows in the correct sequence.

Suppose we execute the following query:

```
SELECT customer_no, balance FROM accounts
    WHERE customer_no BETWEEN 1000 AND 1100
    ORDER BY customer_no, balance
```

The estimated query execution plan is shown in Figure 4.53.

Since we only have a nonclustered index present on the customer_no column in the Accounts table, the query optimizer will need to place a Sort operator in the query plan to ensure that the data is sorted by the balance column also. A composite index will fix this. Let us create a nonclustered index on a composite key of the customer_no and balance columns. If we execute the query again, the Sort operator disappears, as shown in Figure 4.54.

**Figure 4.53**
*Graphical query execution plan showing an ORDER BY using a nonclustered index plus a sort*

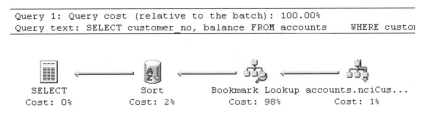

```
Query 1: Query cost (relative to the batch): 100.00%
Query text: SELECT customer_no, balance FROM accounts      WHERE custo
```

SELECT       Sort        Bookmark Lookup  accounts.nciCus...
Cost: 0%     Cost: 2%    Cost: 98%        Cost: 1%

**Figure 4.54**
*Graphical query execution plan showing an ORDER BY using a composite nonclustered index*

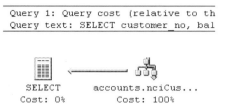

```
Query 1: Query cost (relative to th
Query text: SELECT customer_no, bal
```

```
SELECT              accounts.nciCus...
Cost: 0%            Cost: 100%
```

Suppose we now ask for the result to be sorted in descending order of balance, as follows:

```
SELECT customer_no, balance FROM accounts
    WHERE customer_no BETWEEN 1000 AND 1100
    ORDER BY customer_no, balance DESC
```

We can see from the estimated query execution plan shown in Figure 4.55 that the Sort operator has returned.

Figure 4.55 illustrates an important fact. SQL Server can index scan equally well in both directions on a single-column index. This is because, as we know, the index pages at a given level are linked by next and prior pointers pointing to the next and previous index pages at that level.

However, if an ORDER BY clause specifies different directions for the key columns, a Sort operator is needed. If such a sort is a frequent requirement, the index can be defined with a mix of ascending and descending keys. In our example, we can create the index as follows:

```
CREATE INDEX nciCustomerNoBalance
    ON accounts (customer_no, balance DESC)
```

The index keys will now be stored in ascending order of customer number but descending order of balance. The resulting estimated query execution plan is shown in Figure 4.56.

**Figure 4.55**
*Graphical query execution plan showing an ORDER BY using a composite nonclustered index and a descending order*

```
Query 1: Query cost (relative to the batch): 100.00%
Query text: SELECT customer_no, balance FROM accounts
```

```
SELECT            Sort              accounts.nciCus...
Cost: 0%          Cost: 67%         Cost: 33%
```

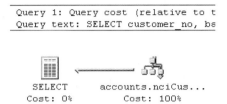

**Figure 4.56**
*Graphical query execution plan showing an ORDER BY using a composite nonclustered index and a descending index key*

We can see that the Sort operator has again disappeared.

Finally, let us return to our earlier query:

```
SELECT customer_no, balance FROM accounts
    ORDER BY customer_no
```

Again, we will ensure that only a nonclustered index on the customer_no column of the Accounts table is present. We know that the estimated query execution plan for this query involves a Table Scan operator, as was shown in Figure 4.50. The query optimizer decided that this plan was cheaper than using the nonclustered index. In fact, the query uses 1,570 logical reads.

In the case of a table scan and sort no rows will be returned until the result set has been sorted. If the nonclustered index was chosen by the query optimizer, the first row could be returned immediately. This behavior can be forced with the FASTFIRSTROW query optimizer hint, as follows:

```
SELECT customer_no, balance FROM accounts
    WITH (FASTFIRSTROW)
    ORDER BY customer_no
```

The query plan is shown in Figure 4.57.

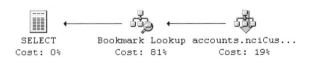

**Figure 4.57**
*Graphical query execution plan showing an ORDER BY using a nonclustered index and a FASTFIRSTROW query optimizer hint*

The query returns the first row instantly, but overall the query now uses 25,048 logical reads.

The penalty, therefore, for this rapid return of the first row is usually a slower query response time overall caused by more logical reads.

### Query 13: Display the total balances managed by each branch but making use of indexed views

We discussed indexed views in Chapter 3. Let us look at how the query optimizer can make use of an indexed view. First of all, let us remind ourselves of how normal views are used. Basically, their definition is expanded and merged with the query definition of the query that is using the view. Traditional (nonindexed) views contain no data. For example, take the following traditional view definition:

```
CREATE VIEW dbo.BranchTotalFunds
AS
SELECT branch_no, COUNT_BIG(*) AS AccountInstances,
SUM(balance) AS TotalBalance
FROM dbo.accounts
GROUP BY branch_no
```

We will use this view in a query, as follows:

```
SELECT * FROM BranchTotalFunds
   WHERE TotalBalance > $1350000.00
```

The query plan is shown in Figure 4.58.

Note that the estimated query execution plan specifies a table scan against the base table—the view has been expanded into its constituent parts. Now let us create an indexed view, as follows:

```
CREATE VIEW dbo.BranchTotalFunds
WITH SCHEMABINDING
AS
SELECT branch_no, COUNT_BIG(*) AS AccountInstances,
SUM(balance) AS TotalBalance
FROM dbo.accounts
GROUP BY branch_no

CREATE UNIQUE CLUSTERED INDEX ciBranchNo ON
dbo.BranchTotalFunds (branch_no)
```

**Figure 4.58**
*Graphical query
execution plan for a
query using a
traditional view*

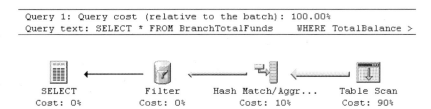

```
Query 1: Query cost (relative to the batch): 100.00%
Query text: SELECT * FROM BranchTotalFunds     WHERE TotalBalance >
```

SELECT          Filter     Hash Match/Aggr...     Table Scan
Cost: 0%        Cost: 0%       Cost: 10%          Cost: 90%

We had to create a unique clustered index on the view to make it an indexed view. We will also create a nonclustered index on the indexed view, as follows:

```
CREATE INDEX nciTotalBal ON dbo.BranchTotalFunds
(TotalBalance)
```

First of all, let us execute the following query:

```
SELECT * FROM BranchTotalFunds
```

The query plan is shown in Figure 4.59.

We immediately notice that the estimated query execution plan shows the BranchTotalFunds view being used. There is no aggregation needed, because the view holds the result of its defining query physically in the database. The access to the data is via a clustered index scan on the ciBranchNo index.

Suppose we execute the following query again:

```
SELECT * FROM BranchTotalFunds
   WHERE TotalBalance > $1350000.00
```

The query plan is shown in Figure 4.60.

We can see that the BranchTotalFunds view is being used and so is the nonclustered index on it. We have basically indexed the aggregate result.

**Figure 4.59**
*Graphical query
execution plan for a
simple query using
an indexed view*

```
Query 1: Query cost (relative to the batch)
Query text: SELECT * FROM BranchTotalFunds
```

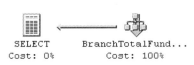

SELECT        BranchTotalFund...
Cost: 0%         Cost: 100%

**Figure 4.60**
*Graphical query
execution plan for a
query using an
indexed view*

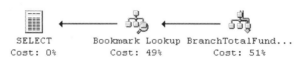

```
Query 1: Query cost (relative to the batch): 100.00%
Query text: SELECT * FROM BranchTotalFunds     WHERE
```

SELECT          Bookmark Lookup  BranchTotalFund...
Cost: 0%          Cost: 49%         Cost: 51%

Using an indexed view can really speed up queries that need to perform this type of access. Now consider the following query:

```
SELECT branch_no, SUM(balance) AS TotalBalance
FROM accounts
GROUP BY branch_no
```

The indexed view is not mentioned anywhere in this query. The query plan is shown in Figure 4.61. Notice that the query optimizer has recognized that even though it is not explicitly mentioned, the indexed view can be used instead of directly accessing the base table. Later in this chapter we will see mechanisms that allow us to override this behavior.

### Query 14: Querying accounts through a partitioned union view

In this example we have decided that our Accounts table is growing too large and so we will split it into three physical tables. Perhaps these will be stored on three separate physical RAID arrays. To avoid application logic having to concern itself with which table to access when it needs to access customer accounts, we will also make use of a union view. Here is the Transact-SQL that defines the new tables:

```
CREATE TABLE accounts1
    (
    account_no    INT         NOT NULL
       PRIMARY KEY (account_no)
       CHECK (account_no BETWEEN 0 and 10000),
    customer_no   INT         NOT NULL,
    branch_no     INT         NOT NULL,
```

**Figure 4.61**
*Graphical query
execution plan for a
query on a table
with an indexed
view*

```
Query 1: Query cost (relative to the
Query text: SELECT branch_no, SUM(ba
```

SELECT          BranchTotalFund...
Cost: 0%         Cost: 100%

```
balance         MONEY NOT  NULL,
account_notes CHAR (400) NOT NULL
)

CREATE TABLE accounts2
  (
account_no      INT        NOT NULL
    PRIMARY KEY (account_no)
    CHECK (account_no BETWEEN 10001 and 20000),
customer_no     INT        NOT NULL,
branch_no       INT        NOT NULL,
balance         MONEY      NOT NULL,
account_notes CHAR (400) NOT NULL
  )

CREATE TABLE accounts3
  (
account_no      INT        NOT NULL
    PRIMARY KEY (account_no)
    CHECK (account_no > 20001),
customer_no     INT        NOT NULL,
branch_no       INT        NOT NULL,
balance         MONEY      NOT NULL,
account_notes CHAR (400) NOT NULL
  )
```

Here is the Transact-SQL that defines the view:

```
CREATE VIEW AllAccounts AS
   SELECT account_no, branch_no, balance FROM accounts1
   UNION ALL
   SELECT account_no, branch_no, balance FROM accounts2
   UNION ALL
   SELECT account_no, branch_no, balance FROM accounts3
```

Notice the CHECK constraint in each table definition. They specify valid ranges of rows and, taken together, they completely describe all the possible valid account numbers in our bank without overlap. Since the ranges do not overlap, an account number may only be found in one table. Also note that negative account numbers are not allowed. We have also created a primary key constraint on each table using the account_no column as the primary key column. The primary key index is clustered.

Let us now investigate the estimated query execution plan of a query that has no WHERE clause. This is shown in Figure 4.62.

```
SELECT * FROM AllAccounts
```

**Figure 4.62**
*Graphical query execution plan for a query with no WHERE clause against a union view*

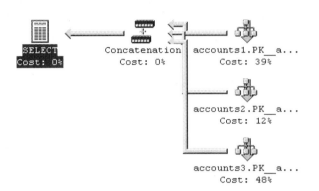

Query 1: Query cost (relative to the batch): 100.00%
Query text: SELECT * FROM AllAccounts

We can see that each table participates in the query and feeds the results of its clustered index scan into the Concatenation operator, which appends the input tables into a single output table. The slight variation in width of the arrows feeding into the Concatenation operator is due to the fact that each table contributes a different number of rows because of the CHECK constraint.

Let us now execute the following query:

```
SELECT * FROM AllAccounts
    WHERE
    account_no = 15000
    OR
    account_no = 25000
```

The estimated query execution plan is shown in Figure 4.63.

**Figure 4.63**
*Graphical query execution plan for a query with a WHERE clause against a union view*

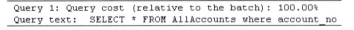

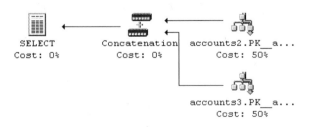

Query 1: Query cost (relative to the batch): 100.00%
Query text:  SELECT * FROM AllAccounts where account_no

We can see that the estimated query execution plan only refers to two tables. Because of the CHECK constraint, the query optimizer knows that the table Accounts1 cannot hold rows that participate in the query.

For the query optimizer to know this information it must trust the CHECK constraint. This means that when the CHECK constraint is created, the existing data must be checked for validity. If the option is selected to not choose the existing data, then the query optimizer will not trust the constraint and all tables will be checked. To find out if a constraint was created so that existing data were checked, use the OBJECTPROPERTY function with the CnstIsNotTrusted property name. For example, as follows:

```
SELECT
    OBJECT_PROPERTY (OBJECT_ID('CK_accounts1'),
                     'CnstIsNotTrusted')
```

If this returns zero, then the constraint did check the existing data on creation. The constraint name can be found from EXEC sp_helpconstraint tablename.

---

**Note:** I would normally name the constraint myself to ensure consistent naming.

---

As far as partitioning goes, this is just the tip of the iceberg. In SQL Server 2000 the partitions can be distributed across servers and a union view created on each server. Each union view will consist of its local partition and the remote partitions on the other servers. These will have been set up as linked servers. As long as the criteria are met to set up this sort of configuration, the distributed union views can also be updated.

This distributed union view capability gives SQL Server 2000 the ability to partition tables across many federated servers. Microsoft refers to this capability as scale-out. With scale-out as the workload increases, more servers are added. This allows massive scalability increases. In comparison, scale-up, which refers to adding CPUs and other hardware resources to an existing server, does not provide for such a large scalability increase—the hardware limitations of a single server are quickly hit. We will not discuss how to partition tables across multiple servers here. This is well documented, and only organizations with very heavy workloads will need to implement such a configuration.

## 4.3.6   Influencing the query optimizer

As we have already seen, the query optimizer is a sophisticated piece of software that can consider multiple factors and create the most efficient query plan. However, there will be situations when you may wish to force the query optimizer to create a plan that it would not otherwise have chosen. Perhaps what it considers the most efficient plan is not really the case in some specific situations that you understand well. As we shall now see, it is possible to override the query optimizer, but this should be considered only as a last resort. Perhaps rewriting the query or changing the index design strategy might be a better long-term option.

The query optimizer can be overridden by using a query optimizer hint. These hints can be grouped into four categories:

1.   Join hints

2.   Table hints

3.   View hints

4.   Query hints

### Join hints

Join hints are used to force the query optimizer to create a query plan that adopts a particular join technique when joining two tables. We already know that there are three join techniques available; these are nested loops, merge, and hash. We can specify a join hint, which will force two tables to be joined using one of these techniques. A fourth join hint, REMOTE, can also be specified to dictate on which server a join is to be performed in a distributed join query.

The join hint syntax is simple to use; the join type is specified as part of the join, as follows:

```
SELECT * FROM accounts INNER HASH JOIN customers
ON
accounts.customer_no = customers.customer_no
WHERE
balance > 9990
```

In the above example, a hash join technique is forced.

The REMOTE join hint dictates that the join operation is performed on the server hosting the right table. This is useful when the left table is a local table with few rows and the right table is a remote table that has many rows, since this may avoid a lot of data being shipped to the local server.

### Table hints

Table hints are very useful, since they dictate the access method to use when retrieving data from a table. This can be a table scan, a single index, or multiple indexes. An example of the syntax used is as follows:

```
SELECT * FROM accounts WITH (INDEX (nciBalance))
    WHERE
    balance BETWEEN 100 AND 200
    AND
    customer_no BETWEEN 1000 AND 2000
```

The above example forces the query optimizer to adopt a plan that uses the nonclustered index nciBalance to access the Accounts table. The following example forces the query optimizer to adopt a plan that uses the nonclustered indexes nciBalance and nciCustomerNo to access the Accounts table—in other words, to perform an index intersection.

```
SELECT * FROM accounts WITH (INDEX (nciBalance,
nciCustomerNo))
    WHERE
    balance BETWEEN 100 AND 200
    AND
    customer_no BETWEEN 1000 AND 2000
```

Suppose a table scan must be forced. The following syntax forces the query optimizer to adopt a plan that uses a table scan if there is no clustered index present on the table or that uses a clustered index scan if there is.

```
SELECT * FROM accounts WITH (INDEX (0))
    WHERE
    balance BETWEEN 100 AND 200
    AND
    customer_no BETWEEN 1000 AND 2000
```

If there is a clustered index present on the table, a clustered index scan or seek can be forced, as shown in the following example:

```
SELECT * FROM accounts WITH (INDEX (1))
    WHERE
    balance BETWEEN 100 AND 200
    AND
    customer_no BETWEEN 1000 AND 2000
```

Another table hint that we have briefly discussed is FASTFIRSTROW. As mentioned in our previous discussion concerning ORDER BY, in the case of a table scan and sort no rows will be returned until the result set has been sorted. If the nonclustered index is chosen by the query optimizer, the first row can be returned immediately. This behavior can be forced with the FASTFIRSTROW query optimizer hint, as follows:

```
SELECT customer_no, balance FROM accounts
    WITH (FASTFIRSTROW)
    ORDER BY customer_no
```

### View hints

View hints are similar to table hints but are used with indexed views. The only view hint is NOEXPAND, which forces the query optimizer to process the view like a table with a clustered index. The index on the view, which should be used, may be specified. An example of the syntax used is as follows:

```
SELECT * FROM BranchTotalFunds
    WITH (NOEXPAND,INDEX (nciTotalBal))
    WHERE TotalBalance > $1350000.00
```

A query hint, described in the following section, can be used to expand the indexed view.

### Query hints

A query hint is used throughout the whole query. Query hints can be used to specify many plan behaviors. For example, the following query hint forces the query optimizer to use hashing when calculating an aggregate.

```
SELECT branch_no, SUM(balance)
FROM accounts
GROUP BY branch_no
OPTION (HASH GROUP)
```

If an ordering (sorting) rather than a hashing technique should be used, then this can be forced as follows:

```
SELECT branch_no, SUM(balance)
FROM accounts
GROUP BY branch_no
OPTION (ORDER GROUP)
```

A query hint can be used to force the query optimizer to adopt different techniques when performing UNION operations. The following example will force the use of a Concatenation operator to perform the union, and thus a Sort/Distinct operator will subsequently eliminate the duplicate rows if any.

```
SELECT * FROM AccountsEurope WHERE balance > 9990
UNION ALL
```

```
SELECT * FROM AccountsUSA WHERE balance > 9990
OPTION (CONCAT UNION)
```

The following example will force the use of a Hash/Union operator to perform the union, and thus a Sort/Distinct operator will not be needed to eliminate the duplicate rows.

```
SELECT * FROM AccountsEurope WHERE balance > 9990
UNION ALL
SELECT * FROM AccountsUSA WHERE balance > 9990
OPTION (HASH UNION)
```

Finally, the following example will force the use of a Merge/Union operator to perform the union, and thus a Sort/Distinct operator will not be needed to eliminate the duplicate rows. Normally, the Merge/Union operator would exploit the sorted order of the inputs in a manner similar to a merge join, as follows:

```
SELECT * FROM AccountsEurope WHERE balance > 9990
UNION ALL
SELECT * FROM AccountsUSA WHERE balance > 9990
OPTION (MERGE UNION)
```

We have already seen that a JOIN clause can include a join hint. The join hint is relevant to the two tables being joined by that particular join operator. The type of join may also be specified as a query hint, in which case the join type will be applied to all the joins in the query, as follows:

```
SELECT * FROM accounts
    INNER JOIN customers
    ON accounts.customer_no = customers.customer_no
    INNER JOIN branches
    ON accounts.branch_no = branches.branch_no
    WHERE balance > 9990
    OPTION (HASH JOIN)
```

Note that a join hint will override the query hint.

To force a query plan to deliver the first rows quickly, perhaps at the expense of the whole query, the FAST query hint can be used, as in the following example:

```
SELECT customers.customer_no, customer_lname, balance
    FROM customers INNER JOIN accounts
    ON customers.customer_no = accounts.account_no
    WHERE customers.customer_no > 12400
    ORDER BY customers.customer_no
    OPTION (FAST 10)
```

This query hint will force the query optimizer to create a plan that will be optimized to return the first ten rows.

Perhaps a more practical hint is one that can force the query optimizer to change the join order to that specified by the query syntax, as follows:

```
SELECT customers.customer_no, customer_lname, balance
    FROM customers INNER JOIN accounts
    ON customers.customer_no = accounts.account_no
    WHERE accounts.balance BETWEEN 100 AND 200
    OPTION (FORCE ORDER)
```

In the above example, the outer table will become the Customers table even though it is the Accounts table that is filtered.

The next query hint is used to specify the number of CPUs used to parallelize the query on a multiprocessor computer. If there is only one processor, this hint is ignored. The following hint limits the number of CPUs that can be used for parallelism to two.

```
SELECT branch_no, SUM(balance)
FROM accounts
GROUP BY branch_no
OPTION (MAXDOP 2)
```

If MAXDOP is set to 1, parallel query plan is suppressed.

The KEEP PLAN and KEEPFIXED PLAN options are similar in that they control when query plans are recompiled. This is discussed later in the chapter. The KEEPFIXED PLAN option ensures that the query optimizer does not recompile a query due to changes in statistics or to the indexed column. A query will only be recompiled if the table schema changes or sp_recompile is executed specifying the table. The KEEPPLAN option is used to reduce the recompilation thresholds, which determine how many inserts, deletes, and index column updates cause a query to be recompiled. The recompilation thresholds used for querying temporary tables in a stored procedure are less than those for a permanent table, and therefore this option is useful when it is necessary to reduce stored procedure recompilations for stored procedures that use temporary tables. This is discussed later in the chapter.

The EXPAND VIEWS option is used with indexed views. This option effectively ensures that the indexes on an indexed view are not used. The view is expanded into its definition, which is the traditional behavior with nonindexed views, as follows:

```
SELECT * FROM BranchTotalFunds
   WHERE TotalBalance > $1350000.00
   OPTION (EXPAND VIEWS)
```

The ROBUST PLAN option ensures that the query plan will not fail due to size limitations when the maximum row sizes are used in the query. For example, plan A may be more efficient than plan B. However, due to the fact that plan A uses intermediate tables to store intermediate results, if any of the variable-length rows used in the query are at their maximum size, the use of the intermediate tables will fail due to size limitations. The ROBUST PLAN option will ignore plan A and choose plan B, which, although less efficient, will not have the same potential problems due to the way the plan executes—perhaps it does not use intermediate storage of results.

### 4.3.7   Stored procedures and the query optimizer

Stored procedures are found everywhere in SQL Server. There are many system stored procedures, and a typical SQL Server development department will also create and use many stored procedures. There are a number of benefits to using stored procedures, such as the following:

- Function encapsulation

- Security

- Performance

By function encapsulation I mean that complex logic can be placed into a stored procedure and hidden from the client software, which then only has to call the stored procedure, passing appropriate parameters. The stored procedure logic can be changed, perhaps to encompass a database modification, without having to change client application software or at least minimizing any change. We can say that stored procedures insulate the client application software from the database structure.

Many sites take a stance that updates to database data can only be made through stored procedures and cannot be made directly to the tables by the client issuing Transact-SQL statements. This model of processing is shown in Figure 4.64.

This brings us to the second benefit of stored procedures: security. Taking the model shown in Figure 4.64, we can see that in order to implement it, we need a security mechanism that allows us to prohibit client software from directly accessing tables and other objects but allows indirect access in

**Figure 4.64**
*Insulating clients*
*from the database*
*structure via stored*
*procedures*

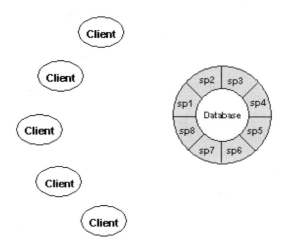

a way that we can define and control. Stored procedures provide this benefit by means of ownership chains.

As long as the owner of the stored procedure is the owner of all the objects referenced by the stored procedure, then execute access on that stored procedure can be granted to database users. They can perform all of the actions defined in the stored procedure even though they have no direct access to the underlying objects. For example, a database user may be granted execute access to a stored procedure that deletes from one table and inserts into another. As long as the ownership of the stored procedure and tables is the same, the database user needs no permissions on the tables.

The most important benefit of stored procedures from the perspective of this book is performance, and it is this aspect of stored procedures on which we will now concentrate. Generally speaking, stored procedures save us the time and effort spent syntax checking Transact-SQL and optimizing it. They reduce network load because they minimize the amount of traffic sent to and from the server.

The stages in stored procedure processing are shown in Figure 4.65. This figure can be compared with Figure 4.1, which shows the stages in query processing. The principal difference is that when a Transact-SQL query is submitted, all the above phases are performed. If the query is submitted 100 times, these phases are performed for each submission unless the query plan for the statement can be reused. We will discuss plan reuse for statements later.

With a stored procedure, the query plan is generally always reused—with a few exceptions. When the stored procedure is initially created, the syntax is

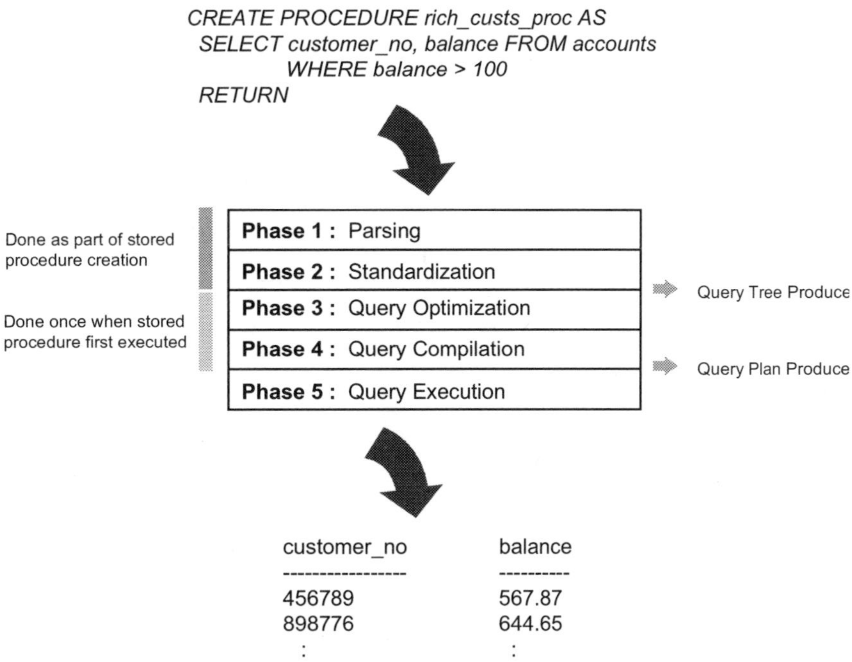

**Figure 4.65**
*Stages in stored procedure processing*

checked, and, if correct, the stored procedure code is stored in the syscomments system table, which is resident in every database. Also, the stored procedure name is stored in the sysobjects system table, which is also resident in every database.

When a stored procedure is first executed after SQL Server starts (in other words it is not cached in any way), the stored procedure is retrieved from syscomments. We can see that we immediately have a performance gain, since we do not have to perform the syntax checking, which, for a large stored procedure, may be nontrivial. Existence checking must be performed at this point, since SQL Server allows us to create the stored procedure even if tables and views, which are referenced in it, do not exist at creation time. This is known as delayed name resolution.

Assuming all the objects referenced exist, the query optimizer creates a query plan for the Transact-SQL in the stored procedure and compiles it into executable code. Once the query plan has been created and compiled, it is cached in an area of memory known as the procedure cache. It is then available for the next user.

If another user wishes to execute the stored procedure, SQL Server can now skip the above phases, since the query plan is ready and waiting in the cache. This can increase the performance benefit of the stored procedure quite substantially. How useful the performance advantage of skipping these phases is depends on how long it takes to perform these phases relative to the execution time of the stored procedure and how often the stored procedure is executed. For a complex stored procedure, which is frequently executed, the performance advantage is significant.

**Note:** Microsoft recommends that the owner name be specified when a stored procedure is executed. This enables SQL Server to access the execution plan for the specific procedure more efficiently. Therefore, it is better to issue:

```
EXEC dbo.usp_GetAuthors
```

than

```
EXEC usp_GetAuthors
```

The query plan of a stored procedure can be utilized by many users at the same time. The stored procedure is effectively split into a read only section, which many users can share, and multiple sections, which are private to a user. They are reusable but cannot be shared simultaneously between users. These sections can be used, for example, to hold a user's read/write variables. This is known as an execution context. This approach means that the bulk of the stored procedure plan, the executable code, is held in cache as a single copy. Actually, even this is not quite true. Two copies of the plan may be held on a multiprocessor computer: a nonparallel plan and a parallel plan.

### A stored procedure challenge

There is one disadvantage to the stored procedure mechanism compared with executing Transact-SQL queries outside of a stored procedure.

Suppose we execute the following query outside of a stored procedure, assuming that there is a nonclustered index on the balance column.

```
SELECT account_no, balance FROM accounts
    WHERE balance BETWEEN 8000 AND 8100
```

What strategy will the query optimizer choose? The nonclustered index on the balance column is, in fact, chosen. This is a reasonable plan given what we already know. If we execute the query, the following Show Stats IO output is displayed after 239 rows have been returned.

```
Table 'accounts'. Scan count 1, logical reads 241,
physical reads 0, read-ahead reads 0.
```

The query optimizer has chosen to use a nonclustered index to access the data and has taken 241 logical reads to do so. Now suppose we execute the following query:

```
SELECT account_no, balance FROM accounts
    WHERE balance BETWEEN 8000 AND 9000
```

What strategy will the query optimizer now choose? As we might expect, the query optimizer has decided to use a table scan. Again, this is a reasonable plan given what we already know. As the number of rows returned increases, it becomes more efficient to execute a table scan rather than use the nonclustered index. If we execute the query, the following Show Stats IO output is displayed after 2,426 rows have been returned.

```
Table 'accounts'. Scan count 1, logical reads 1570,
physical reads 0, read-ahead reads 0.
```

So, the query optimizer has now chosen to use a table scan, taking 1,570 logical reads to do so.

Now let us place the query in a stored procedure, as follows:

```
CREATE PROCEDURE dbo.usp_accounts_per_range (@minbal
MONEY, @maxbal MONEY)
AS
SET STATISTICS IO ON
SELECT account_no, balance FROM accounts
       WHERE balance BETWEEN @minbal AND @maxbal
RETURN
```

Let us execute it with the following EXEC statement:

```
EXEC dbo.usp_accounts_per_range @minbal=8000, @maxbal =
8100
```

```
account_no    balance
----------    -------
7880          8000.43
12053         8000.43
    :
    :
Table: accounts  scan count 1,  logical reads: 241,
physical reads: 0,  read ahead reads: 0
```

This is exactly the same number of logical reads as before. The query optimizer has chosen a query plan that uses the nonclustered index as it did for the standalone query.

Now let us execute the stored procedure with the following EXEC statement:

```
EXEC dbo.usp_accounts_per_range @minbal=8000, @maxbal =
9000

account_no    balance
----------    -------
7880          8000.43
12053         8000.43
  :
  :

Table: accounts  scan count 1,  logical reads: 2433,
physical reads: 0,  read ahead reads: 0
```

The number of logical reads has increased from 1,570 executing the query as a standalone statement to 2,433 executing the query in a stored procedure. Why is this?

The problem is caused by the fact that the query plan was created and loaded into cache by the first execution. The query optimizer created the query plan based on the parameters passed to it, so in this case it created a query plan for the SELECT statement, as follows:

```
SELECT account_no, balance FROM accounts
   WHERE balance BETWEEN 8000 AND 8100
```

The next time the stored procedure was executed no query optimization was done and the query plan utilizing the nonclustered index was used. This is not the most efficient query plan for the range, as can be seen from the logical reads.

In its worst manifestation we can imagine that the first stored procedure execution happens to use a query plan that is not efficient for all subsequent stored procedure executions. So how can we deal with this situation?

One mechanism available to us is to make sure that the stored procedure always creates and uses a new query plan. We can force a stored procedure to create and use a new query plan, but there are also times when a stored procedure is automatically recompiled.

We will look shortly at how we can force a stored procedure to create and use a new query plan, but first let us look at some of the situations that result in SQL Server automatically recompiling a plan. To check if a stored procedure plan is recompiled the SP:Recompile SQL Server Profiler event can be monitored. The SQL Server Profiler is discussed further in Chapter 7.

### Changes to the table structure

If the structure of a table referenced by the stored procedure is changed, typically by the use of an ALTER TABLE statement, the schema_ver and base_schema_ver columns in the sysobjects system table are incremented. This informs SQL Server that it needs to recompile the stored procedure plan the next time the stored procedure executes. Examples of structure changes are the addition and deletion of columns and constraints.

### Changes to indexes

If indexes are created and dropped, the schema_ver and base_schema_ver columns are incremented. This will cause a stored procedure recompilation even if the indexes are not relevant to the queries in the stored procedure.

### Executing update statistics

If UPDATE STATISTICS is run against a table referenced by the stored procedure, stored procedure recompilation will take place the next time the stored procedure is executed. Running UPDATE STATISTICS increments the base_schema_ver and stats_schema_ver columns.

### Aging the stored procedure out of cache

We will discuss how stored procedures are aged out of cache later. If this happens, then the next time the stored procedure executes it must be compiled and cached again.

### Table data modifications

SQL Server will detect that a certain fraction of the data in a table has changed since the original plan was compiled. Once this threshold has been crossed a recompilation will occur. To keep track of the changes to the table data, the rowmodctr column in the sysindexes system table is incremented whenever one of the following conditions occurs to the table in question.

- A row is inserted.

- A row is deleted.

- An indexed column is updated.

When a predefined threshold has been crossed, the statistics for the table will be automatically updated when it is accessed next, assuming the database option Auto update statistics is set to on. This automatic updating of statistics will reset the rowmodctr column.

This threshold tends to depend on the size of the table. For SQL Server 7.0 Microsoft documented the algorithm as follows:

- If the number of rows in the table is less than six and the table is in the tempdb database, an automatic update of statistics is performed with every six modifications to the table.

- If the number of rows in the table is greater than six, but less than or equal to 500, an automatic update of statistics is performed with every 500 modifications.

- If the number of rows in the table is greater than 500, an automatic update of statistics is performed when (500 + 20 percent of the table) changes have occurred.

So the stored procedure is recompiled when the threshold is crossed. As was mentioned earlier, the SP:Recompile SQL Server Profiler event can be monitored to check for recompilations; however, trace flag 205 can also be used to output information about when a statistics-dependent stored procedure is being recompiled. I tend to set this in the Startup Parameters section of the General Tab in Server Properties in the SQL Server Enterprise Manager together with trace flag 3605 to ensure logging of trace messages to the error log. A typical pair of messages logged follows:

```
Recompile issued : ProcName: usp_GetAccts    LineNo:2
StmtNo: 3

Schema Change: Tbl Dbid: 7 Objid: 1993058136 RowModCnt:
25000.000000 RowModCntMax: 0 RowModLimit: 22000
```

The first message specifies the stored procedure. The second message holds the table name in the form of its object ID. The item RowModCnt is the total number of modifications to the table, and RowModLimit is the threshold, which, when exceeded, results in the statistics being updated for the table and the stored procedure being recompiled. It is possible to ensure that the query optimizer does not recompile a query due to changes in statistics or to the indexed column by using the KEEPFIXED PLAN query option. In this case a query will only be recompiled if the table schema changes or sp_recompile is executed specifying the table.

### Mixing data definition language and data manipulation language statements

If Data Definition Language (DDL) statements and Data Manipulation Language (DML) statements are mixed together in a stored procedure, the stored procedure will be recompiled when the DML statements are executed. The following example displays a stored procedure.

```
CREATE PROC dbo.usp_DDL_DML
AS
CREATE TABLE #table1 (c1 INT)
SELECT COUNT(*) FROM #table1
CREATE INDEX i1 ON #table1(c1)
SELECT COUNT(*) FROM #table1

CREATE TABLE #table2 (c1 INT)
SELECT COUNT(*) FROM #table2
CREATE INDEX i2 ON #table2(c1)
SELECT COUNT(*) FROM #table2
RETURN
```

This will result in four stored procedure recompilations. When the stored procedure compilation takes place the first time around, the temporary tables #table1 and #table2 have not yet been created. The stored procedure must execute for this to happen. The SELECT statements that access #table1 and #table2 are not yet able to have a plan created. When the stored procedure executes, #table1 is created and then accessed by the first SELECT statement. Since a plan does not exist for this query, the stored procedure is recompiled in order to create a plan for this query.

The index is then created for #table1. A SELECT statement is then executed against #table1, but, as we have previously mentioned, this is treated as a schema change and therefore the stored procedure is recompiled again. The same recompilations occur because of #table2, and thus four recompilations are performed. It would have been better to place all the DDL statements at the beginning of the stored procedure and then execute the DML statements. Doing this results in one stored procedure recompilation.

### Temporary tables

Another reason that stored procedures may be recompiled concerns the use of temporary tables. SQL Server will recompile a stored procedure if a few changes have been made to a temporary table created in the stored procedure. At the time of writing, only six changes to the temporary table have to be made inside the stored procedure before it is recompiled. This means that changes to a temporary table will result in recompilation far more frequently than in the case of a permanent table, as previously discussed. If you wish to apply the same recompilation thresholds to temporary tables as were applied to permanent tables, use the KEEP PLAN query option on any query that uses the temporary table.

### Forcing recompilation

How can we manually cause a stored procedure to be recompiled? There are a number of mechanisms.

- The sp_recompile stored procedure
- CREATE PROCEDURE WITH RECOMPILE
- EXECUTE WITH RECOMPILE

The sp_recompile system stored procedure ensures that each stored procedure and trigger that uses the specified table are recompiled the next time the stored procedure and triggers are run.

```
EXEC sp_recompile accounts

Object 'accounts' was successfully marked for
recompilation.
```

It is also possible to specify a stored procedure name instead of a table name, in which case only that stored procedure will be recompiled the next time it is run.

The sp_recompile system stored procedure actually increments the schema_ver and base_schema_ver column in the sysobjects system table. Note that triggers are also affected. Triggers are just a special kind of stored procedure that are automatically executed when inserts, updates, and deletes happen to a table. As such, they have their query plans stored in cache like any other stored procedure.

When we create a procedure, we can use the WITH RECOMPILE option. This means that every execution of a stored procedure causes a new query plan to be created. Using this option means that we do not have the problem of a query plan resident in cache that is inefficient for various parameter combinations. However, because we generate a new query plan for each execution of the stored procedure, the performance benefit of stored procedures is negated.

A less-severe option is to execute a stored procedure with the WITH RECOMPILE option. This causes a new query plan to be created for just that execution.

These options will help us avoid the problem described previously with an inefficient query plan loaded into procedure cache, but they do mean that new query plans get created. Another option is to break up the stored procedure into smaller pieces.

```
CREATE PROC dbo.usp_few_accounts_per_range (@minbal
MONEY, @maxbal MONEY)
AS
SET STATISTICS IO ON
SELECT account_no, balance FROM accounts
    WHERE balance BETWEEN @minbal AND @maxbal
RETURN

GO

CREATE PROC dbo.usp_many_accounts_per_range (@minbal
MONEY, @maxbal MONEY)
AS
SET STATISTICS IO ON
SELECT account_no, balance FROM accounts
    WHERE balance BETWEEN @minbal AND @maxbal
RETURN

GO

CREATE PROC dbo.usp_accounts_per_range (@minbal MONEY,
@maxbal MONEY)
AS
IF (@maxbal - @minbal) <= 100
    EXEC dbo.usp_few_accounts_per_range @minbal, @maxbal
ELSE
    EXEC dbo.usp_many_accounts_per_range @minbal, @maxbal
RETURN

GO
```

The stored procedure usp_accounts_per_range is executed passing the minimum and maximum balance. It tests to see if the difference between the minimum and maximum balance is less than or equal to 100, and, if it is, it executes the stored procedure usp_few_accounts_per_range. If the difference is greater than 100, it executes the stored procedure usp_many_accounts_per_range. In this way the two stored procedures that access the data are compiled with their own execution plan. In this example the stored procedure usp_few_accounts_per_range gets a query plan that uses a nonclustered index, whereas the query plan for usp_many_accounts_per_range uses a table scan.

This method can work well, but it did require the developer writing the stored procedures to know that a balance range greater than 100 was best dealt with by a table scan, and, of course, this distribution can change over time.

Another approach is to recompile not the whole stored procedure but only the troublesome statement. This can be brought about by using the EXECUTE statement with a character string.

```
CREATE PROC dbo.usp_example_proc (@bal MONEY)
AS
DECLARE @balstr VARCHAR(10)
SELECT @balstr = CONVERT(VARCHAR(10), @bal)
  :
EXECUTE ('SELECT account_no, balance FROM accounts WHERE
balance > ' + @balstr)
  :
RETURN
```

The Transact-SQL statement inside the EXECUTE statement goes through the same phases that any standalone Transact-SQL statement goes through—that is, parsing through to query compilation. This does not happen until the EXECUTE statement is performed. Other Transact-SQL statements in the stored procedure are compiled just once. To see the plan used for the Transact-SQL statement in the EXECUTE you need to look at the query plan after the stored procedure has been executed. In other words, choose Show Execution Plan from the Query menu in the Query Analyzer.

Another possibility is to use query optimizer hints. We have already seen optimizer hints and how they can be used to force the query optimizer to use a particular index. Optimizer hints can also be used with queries in stored procedures to ensure that a particular query plan is always used.

### Aging stored procedures from cache

Versions of SQL Server prior to SQL Server 7.0 used two areas of cache—one for stored procedure plans and one for database pages, in particular data and index pages. SQL Server 7.0 and SQL Server 2000 use a single unified cache for database pages, stored procedure plans, and the query plans of SQL statements that are not stored procedures. The cache can grow and shrink dynamically as the memory allocated to SQL Server grows and shrinks.

Different stored procedures will require different amounts of effort to compile. Some will be simple and cheap to compile and some will be complex and expensive to compile. To ensure that a stored procedure plan that is expensive to compile is not as easily aged out of cache as a simple stored procedure, the cost of the stored procedure compilation is stored with the plan.

If memory is tight, a component of SQL Server known as the lazywriter frees up cache pages. It does this by looking at the buffers in cache and checking the cost value associated with them. The lazywriter will decrement the cost of a buffer page by one. If the lazywriter finds that the cost of a page is zero, it will be freed. Conversely, if a stored procedure plan is used, the cost is set to the initial creation cost. This means that a frequently used stored procedure will not have its cost decremented over time to zero by the lazywriter. Also, a stored procedure that was expensive to compile and therefore has an associated large cost will take a long time to have its cost decremented to zero. Therefore, a stored procedure that is expensive to compile but not used frequently may stay in cache, as would a stored procedure that is cheap to compile but is used frequently.

How do you monitor the cache? This will be discussed in Chapter 5.

## 4.3.8   Non-stored procedure plans

If you wish to ensure that a query plan is created and stored in cache, then placing the query inside a stored procedure will guarantee this. However, SQL Server does not only place stored procedure plans in cache. It will store the plans of SQL statements that are not part of a stored procedure in cache and attempt to reuse them.

SQL Server distinguishes between RPC events and SQL language events. RPC events are parameterized in some way. If the developer has used sp_executesql to submit the query or has used the prepare/execute model from the database API, it is an RPC event. Parameterization is typically used by a developer who wishes to submit a SQL statement for multiple execution, and in this case it makes sense to try to keep the query plan of the SQL statement.

A SQL language event is typically a SQL statement that is sent direct to the server. It has not been prepared and has not been submitted using sp_executesql. In this case the developer probably does not intend that the SQL statement be resubmitted multiple times.

**Note:** The SQL Server Profiler distinguishes between these events—for example, RPC:Starting, Prepare SQL, and SQL: StmtStarting.

When an RPC statement is received by SQL Server, the query plan is created and placed into cache. So that the query plan can be retrieved for a subsequent statement, some mechanism must be used to allow the plan to be identified. In the case of a stored procedure this was not necessary, since the stored procedure has a unique name. In the case of a SQL statement, which has no such name, the statement text is hashed to produce a hash key, which identifies it in cache. The hash key seems to be particularly sensitive to the statement text. The following two statements will have different keys even though the only difference is the case of the WHERE keyword (the server is case insensitive).

```
SELECT account_no FROM accounts where balance=100

SELECT account_no FROM accounts WHERE balance=100
```

Even the number of spaces in the statement is significant when hashing the statement text. Different plans will also be stored for identical statements that have different connection settings. Suppose two connections both execute the following SQL statement.

```
SELECT account_no FROM accounts WHERE balance=100
```

Suppose one connection has its ANSI_NULL setting set to TRUE and one connection has it set to FALSE. There will be two plans cached.

For nonparameterized (ad hoc) SQL language statements, the query optimizer may actually attempt to change a hard-coded value into a parameter marker in order to facilitate reuse of the query plan. This is known as autoparameterization. However, the query optimizer is very conservative and few statements will undergo this process. The reason for this is the same as our previous discussion of stored procedure plans. A plan that is efficient for one parameter value may be extremely inefficient for another value. At least with stored procedures, the developer is in control and can use one of the techniques suggested earlier to avoid this problem. This is not the case with non-stored procedure statements, so the responsibility falls with SQL Server to avoid using inefficient plans.

To achieve this, it only autoparameterizes when it knows it is safe to do so. A typical case would be the following statement.

```
SELECT balance FROM accounts WHERE account_no = 1000
```

There is a unique nonclustered index on the account_no column. An obvious efficient plan is to use this nonclustered index. Since this index is unique, a maximum of one row only can be returned.

Now consider the following statement.

```
SELECT account_no FROM accounts WHERE balance between 100
and 120
```

It would be very risky to replace the values 100 and 120 by parameter markers. Two different values from a subsequent query such as 50 and 5,000 would probably benefit from an entirely different plan.

It's worth it at this point to mention the system stored procedure sp_executesql. This allows the developer to build a Transact-SQL statement that can be executed dynamically. Unlike the EXECUTE statement though, sp_executesql allows the setting of parameter values separately from the Transact-SQL string. This means that sp_executesql can be used instead of stored procedures to execute a Transact-SQL statement a number of times when only the parameters change. Because the Transact-SQL statement itself does not change—rather, the parameter values change—it is highly probable that query optimizer will reuse the query plan it creates and saves for the first execution. Again, it is up to the developer, being familiar with the data, to decide whether reusing plans is a good strategy for a particular statement.

Here is an example of using sp_executesql.

```
DECLARE @MoneyVariable MONEY
DECLARE @SQLString NVARCHAR(500)
DECLARE @ParameterDefinition NVARCHAR(500)

-- Create the SQL String - only need to do this once

SET @SQLString =
    N'SELECT account_no FROM accounts WHERE balance =
@bal'
SET @ParameterDefinition = N'@bal MONEY'

-- Execute the string with the first parameter value

SET @MoneyVariable = 100
EXECUTE sp_executesql @SQLString, @ParameterDefinition,
                      @bal = @MoneyVariable

-- Execute the string with the next parameter value

SET @MoneyVariable = 200
EXECUTE sp_executesql @SQLString, @ParameterDefinition,
                      @bal = @MoneyVariable
```

Note that the query plans of the nonstored procedure SQL statements are placed in the cache and aged in a manner similar to stored procedures, described previously. Ad hoc statements that are not autoparameterized, however, will be placed in the cache with a cost of zero, so their plans will be removed from cache as soon as memory becomes short.

### 4.3.9    The Syscacheobjects system table

To check for plans in cache the system table syscacheobjects can be queried. Here is a fragment of the output of syscacheobjects.

```
SELECT cacheobjtype, objtype, sql FROM syscacheobjects
```

| cacheobjtype | objtype | sql |
| --- | --- | --- |
| Compiled Plan | Adhoc | SELECT account_no FROM accounts where balance=100 |
| Compiled Plan | Adoc | SELECT account_no FROM accounts WHERE balance=100 |
| Compiled Plan | Adhoc | SELECT account_no FROM accounts WHERE balance between 100 and 120 |
| Executable Plan | Prepared | (@1 smallint)SELECT [balance]=[balance] FROM [accounts] WHERE [account_no]=@1 |
| Compiled Plan | Prepared | (@1 smallint)SELECT [balance]=[balance] FROM [accounts] WHERE [account_no]=@1 |
| Executable Plan | Prepared | (@bal MONEY)SELECT account_no FROM accounts WHERE balance = @bal |
| Compiled Plan | Prepared | (@bal MONEY)SELECT account_no FROM accounts WHERE balance = @bal |
| Executable Plan | Proc | usp_accounts_per_range |
| Compiled Plan | Proc | usp_accounts_per_range |

The column sql holds the statement text. The column cacheobjtype represents the type of object in the cache. We can see that the two statements previously mentioned that have their WHERE keyword in different case are represented by separate plans. The statement that was too dangerous to autoparameterize with the balance between 100 and 120 values is held as a separate plan. All three statements are held as ad hoc objects in the objtype column. This column holds the type of object.

One of our statements was autoparameterized.

```
SELECT balance FROM accounts WHERE account_no = 1000
```

This is held as a prepared object, as is the statement that was submitted through sp_executesql. Finally, we can see that a stored procedure is also held in cache. Because different users will usually have different parameter values when executing stored procedures and prepared statements, they must also be given an execution context as well as a completely shared plan.

In this chapter we have looked extensively at the query optimizer. Knowledge of the material in this chapter combined with that in Chapter 3 will be invaluable to you when designing an indexing strategy or tracking down a performance problem with a query.

# 5

# *SQL Server 2000 and Windows 2000*

This chapter discusses SQL Server 2000 performance with respect to the CPU, memory, and disk resources found on a Windows 2000 server.

## 5.1 SQL Server 2000 and CPU

### 5.1.1 Introduction

The first resource on a Windows 2000 server that is usually monitored is the CPU. CPUs have been gaining in power dramatically over the last few years, and Windows 2000 supports multiprocessor systems with up to 32 processors (with Microsoft Windows 2000 Datacenter).

Although a multiprocessor system may not reduce CPU bottlenecks when a single threaded process is consuming the CPU, multithreaded processes such as SQL Server 2000 will benefit greatly.

CPU is a system resource. The more CPU power available the better the system is likely to perform. Windows 2000 schedules CPU time to the threads of a process, and, if more threads require CPU time than there is CPU time available, a queue of waiting threads will develop. Sometimes a processor bottleneck is actually masking another bottleneck, such as memory, so it is important to look at CPU use in conjunction with other resource use on the system. This first part of the chapter provides an overview of CPU usage and looks at how SQL Server 2000 makes use of the CPU. It then looks at how CPU bottlenecks can be observed.

### 5.1.2 An overview of Windows 2000 and CPU utilization

To understand the way that Windows 2000 uses the CPU we first of all need to consider the difference between a process and a thread. A process can be considered to be an object containing executable code and data; an address space, which is a set of virtual addresses; and any other resources allocated to the code as it runs. It also must contain a minimum of one thread of execution.

A thread is the item inside a process that is scheduled to run, not the process itself as in some older operating systems. A Windows 2000 process can contain any number of threads, and a process that contains more than one thread is known as a multithreaded process. Windows 2000 is able to simultaneously schedule a number of threads across multiple CPUs. These can be threads belonging to many processes or threads belonging to just one process.

Each running instance SQL Server 2000 is a multithreaded process, and so it is able to schedule a number of threads simultaneously across multiple processors to perform a multitude of functions. SQL Server 2000 may have threads concurrently executing across multiple processors with one servicing a user connection, one performing a backup, and one writing pages from cache to disk. Also, SQL Server 2000 is able to perform queries in parallel as well as various database operations in parallel, such as index creation. Although SQL Server 2000 can be parallelizing operations across multiple processors, it can be restricted to only using a subset of the available processors on the server.

The order in which threads are scheduled is governed by a priority associated with those threads. Windows 2000 always schedules the highest-priority thread waiting for processor time to run first in order to make sure that the highest-priority work gets done first. Each process is allocated to one of four base priority classes.

1.  Idle

2.  Normal

3.  High

4.  Real time

The base priority of a process can change within its base priority class. The base priority of a process thread varies within the base priority of its parent process. As a general rule, the base priority of a thread varies only within a range of two greater than or two less than the base priority of its process. The dynamic priority of a thread governs when it will be scheduled. The dynamic priority of a thread is constantly being adjusted by Windows 2000. For example, the dynamic priority of a thread is typically increased when an I/O operation it has been waiting for completes and the thread now needs processor time. The dynamic priority of a thread can equal or grow beyond its base priority, but it can never drop below it.

By default, SQL Server 2000 runs at normal priority.

SQL Server 2000 also has the concept of fibers. Normally, SQL Server 2000 executes work using Windows 2000 threads. Work is allocated to threads. The Windows 2000 operating system code that manages threads runs in kernel mode. Switching threads requires switches between the user mode of the application code and the kernel mode of the thread manager. This context switching can be expensive on systems with multiple CPUs that are very busy. For that reason, SQL Server 2000 can be configured to use fibers by means of the lightweight pooling server configuration option. Setting this option can be accomplished using sp_configure or setting the option on the Processor tab of the SQL Server Properties (Configure) window in the SQL Server Enterprise Manager.

Lightweight pooling allows SQL Server 2000 to manage scheduling within the normal Windows 2000 thread structures. Fibers are managed by code running in user mode, and switching fibers does not require the user-mode to kernel-mode context switch needed to switch threads. Each Windows 2000 thread can support multiple fibers, and SQL Server performs the scheduling of these fibers. For most SQL Server systems, using lightweight pooling is unlikely to produce any noticeable benefit.

## 5.1.3    How SQL Server 2000 uses CPU

There are various ways that SQL Server 2000 can be configured with respect to how it makes use of the CPU. These can be grouped into the following categories.

- Priority

- Use of symmetric multiprocessing systems

- Thread use

- Query parallelism

Let us consider each of these in turn.

### Priority

On the Windows 2000 Server running SQL Server 2000 it is likely that little interactive use will take place. The server will communicate with client workstations. Usually, when there is interactive use made of a workstation, it is preferable to increase the priority of the foreground application—that

**Figure 5.1**

*The performance options window*

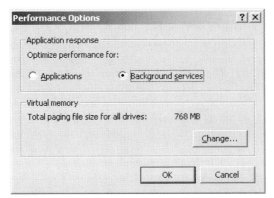

is, the application running in the window that is currently displayed at the top of the other windows.

By default, Windows 2000 Server has longer, fixed quanta with no priority boost for foreground applications, allowing background services to run more efficiently. Windows 2000 Professional, however, defines short, variable quanta for applications and gives a foreground application a priority boost (a quantum is the maximum amount of time a thread can run before the system checks for another thread of the same priority to run).

Whether a priority boost for foreground applications occurs or not can be overridden. This can be done using the System icon in the Control Panel, choosing the Advanced tab, and mouse-clicking the Performance Options button. This is shown in Figure 5.1.

SQL Server 2000 is never a foreground application, and so, on the server, the performance should be optimized for Background services. On the client workstation, however, boosting the foreground priority by optimizing for Applications makes sense. Again, the choice of the Windows 2000 platform will likely accomplish this by default. Of course, using the Query Analyzer, for example, on the server directly will not benefit from any priority boost, so you might find that you do not get great performance. This does not mean that SQL Server 2000 is running slowly; it means that the Query Analyzer is not priority boosted and so will be contending equally with it for the CPU.

Another method of changing the priority of SQL Server 2000 is to change the advanced server configuration option priority boost. This governs whether or not SQL Server 2000 should run at a higher priority than other processes on the same server. Setting this option can be accomplished using sp_configure or setting the option on the Processor tab of the

SQL Server Properties (Configure) window in the SQL Server Enterprise Manager.

Setting priority boost to 1 causes SQL Server 2000 to execute at a higher priority and to be scheduled more often. In fact, its priority will be changed from Windows 2000 base priority 7 to base priority 13. This will probably have a negative impact on other applications running on the server (including other instances of SQL Server), and therefore this parameter should be used with care unless the server has been designated as being dedicated to SQL Server 2000 (in which case why bother setting it anyway!). To use our previous example, executing the Query Analyzer locally on a server that has priority boost set to 1 would result in degraded Query Analyzer performance.

### Use of symmetric multiprocessing systems

With respect to multiprocessor systems, the edition of SQL Server 2000 and the operating system platform on which it is running governs the maximum number of processors that can be supported. For example, using SQL Server 2000 Enterprise Edition on Microsoft Windows 2000 Datacenter, up to 32 processors can be supported. On the other hand, using SQL Server 2000 Standard Edition on Microsoft Windows 2000 Server, up to four processors can be supported. Multiprocessor support is not available on SQL Server 2000 Windows CE Edition, nor is it available if SQL Server 2000 is running on Windows 2000 Professional, Windows NT 4.0 Workstation, or Windows 98.

For query parallelism, described shortly, the maximum number of processors that can be used to execute a query can be specified as a server configuration option, max degree of parallelism. Setting this option can be accomplished using sp_configure or setting the option on the Processor tab of the SQL Server Properties (Configure) window in the SQL Server Enterprise Manager. This also limits the degree of parallelism for utility execution such as DBCC CHECKDB.

Which processors on a multiprocessor system can SQL Server 2000 use? Generally, Windows 2000 does not guarantee that any thread in a process will run on a given processor. However, it uses a soft affinity algorithm, which tries to run a thread on the last processor that serviced it. A thread may still migrate from processor to processor if the favored processor is busy, which causes reloading of the processor's cache. Under heavy system loads, this is likely to degrade performance. Specifying the processors that should and should not run SQL Server 2000 threads can boost performance by reducing the reloading of processor cache. This is only likely to make a difference with four or more processors under load. By specifying the processors manually a hard affinity algorithm is used.

The association between a processor and a thread is called processor affinity. SQL Server 2000 enables a processor affinity mask to be specified as a server configuration option. By setting bits in the mask, the system administrator can decide on which processors SQL Server 2000 will run. The number of the bit set represents the processor. For example, setting the mask to the value 126 (hexadecimal 0x7E) sets the bits 01111110, or 1, 2, 3, 4, 5, and 6. This means that SQL Server 2000 threads should run on processors 1, 2, 3, 4, 5, and 6. On an eight-processor system this means that SQL Server 2000 threads should not run on processors 0 and 7.

In the SQL Server Enterprise Manager, the CPU affinity can be set in the Processor control section on the Processor tab of the SQL Server Properties (Configure) window.

---

**Note:** It is also possible to use the Set Affinity option in the Task Manager to allocate a process to specific CPUs.

---

For most database administrators, using a hard affinity option is unlikely to be an option that gains much in the way of performance.

### Thread use

When a SQL Server client executes a request, the network handler places the command in a queue and the next usable thread from the worker pool of threads acquires the request and handles it. If no free worker thread is available when a request arrives, SQL Server 2000 creates a new thread dynamically, until it reaches the server configuration option maximum worker threads.

The default value for maximum worker threads is 255, which will often be greater than the number of users connected to the server. However, when there are a large number of connections (typically hundreds), using a thread for every user connection may deplete operating system resource. To avoid this SQL Server 2000 can use a technique called thread pooling. With thread pooling a pool of worker threads will handle a larger number of user connections.

If the maximum worker threads value has not been exceeded, a new thread is created for each user connection. Once the maximum worker threads value has been exceeded, user connections will share the pool of worker threads. A new client request will be handled by the first thread in the pool that becomes free.

### Query parallelism

In SQL Server 2000, a single query can execute in parallel over multiple CPUs. For workloads that have a small number of complex queries running on SMP computers, this should bring a performance boost. For OLTP workloads, which consist of many small transactions, parallelism is unlikely to enhance performance.

Parallel query processing is aimed at improving the performance of single, complex queries. The query optimizer decides if a query plan can be executed in parallel based on various criteria. If it can, the query plan will contain extra operators, known as exchange operators, which will enable the query plan to be executed in parallel. At run time, SQL Server will decide, again based on various criteria, how many processors the query will use—that is, how many threads will be used. This is known as the Degree of Parallelism (DOP).

Parallel query processing is pretty much out of the box. There are, however, two server configuration options that affect parallel query processing.

1.    Max degree of parallelism

2.    Cost threshold for parallelism

The max degree of parallelism option controls the number of CPUs SQL Server can use for parallel queries—that is, the maximum number of threads a query can use. The cost threshold for parallelism controls the threshold over which the query optimizer will generate a parallel query plan. If a query is short, such as an OLTP query, the overhead of setting up a parallel query is not worth the gain.

The query optimizer will not generate a parallel query plan if the computer is only a single processor. Before the query starts to execute, SQL Server uses its knowledge of CPU use and the available memory to decide the degree of parallelism for the query. It may be that SQL Server decides not to run the query in parallel at all.

If the estimated cost of executing the query is less than the cost threshold for parallelism, the query optimizer will not generate a parallel plan. This is also true if the query optimizer determines that only a few rows will be returned. To summarize, the query optimizer will only generate a parallel query plan if it considers that it is worth doing so, and at run time the query will only be executed in parallel if SQL Server decides that there are sufficient free resources to do so.

There are SQL statements that will not be executed with a parallel query plan. INSERT, UPDATE, and DELETE statements will use a serial plan, but their WHERE clause may use a parallel plan. Static and keyset cursors can use a parallel plan but not dynamic cursors.

To control parallel query execution, as previously mentioned, the maximum number of processors that can be used to execute a query can be specified as a server configuration option, max degree of parallelism. Setting this option can be accomplished using sp_configure or setting the option on the Processor tab of the SQL Server Properties (Configure) window in the SQL Server Enterprise Manager. The default is to use all the processors.

To specify the cost threshold for parallelism the cost threshold for parallelism server configuration can be specified using sp_configure or setting the *Minimum query plan threshold . . .* value on the Processor tab of the SQL Server Properties (Configure) window in the SQL Server Enterprise Manager. The default is five seconds.

There is also a query optimizer hint, which can be used to influence parallel query execution. The MAXDOP query hint allows the max degree of parallelism to be set on a statement-by-statement basis. However, this is not supported for CREATE INDEX statements.

The CREATE INDEX in SQL Server 2000 can be executed in parallel. Assuming that the max degree of parallelism option is sufficiently high, and the workload on the server is not great, the CREATE INDEX statement can be executed across all the CPUs. To give each CPU an equal portion of work to do, a fast, random initial scan is performed to check on the data value distribution of the table column that will be used for the index column. This initial thread then dispatches the number of threads determined by the max degree of parallelism option. Each thread builds its own index structure based on the range of data it is working with. The initial thread then combines these smaller index structures into a single index structure.

Let us now look at how we can detect processor bottlenecks.

## 5.1.4  Investigating CPU bottlenecks

The tools used to observe CPU bottlenecks are typically the System Monitor and the Task Manager. There are also a number of tools in the Windows 2000 Resource Kit. We will focus on using the System Monitor in this section, although the Processes and Performance tabs in the Task Manager are

**Table 5.1** *Selected Counters for the System, Processor, and Process Objects*

| CPU-Related Counters | Explanation |
| --- | --- |
| System: Processor Queue Length | The number of threads that need CPU time but have to wait. This counts only ready threads, not those being handled. This counter belongs to the system object, because there is only one queue even when there are multiple processors on the server. |
| Processor: % Processor Time | This is the percentage that a processor is busy. There is an instance of this counter for every processor on the server. The _Total instance can be used to display the value of total processor utilization system-wide. |
| Processor: % User Time | This is the percentage that a processor is busy in user mode. User mode means application code and subsystem code. |
| Processor: % Privileged Time | This is the percentage that a processor is busy in privileged mode. Privileged mode means operating system services. |
| Process: % Processor Time | This is the percentage of CPU time that a process is busy. |

also quite useful. These are shown later in Figures 5.14 and 5.15 when we investigate memory. Note that Chapter 7 discusses the general use of the System Monitor. The System, Processor, and Process objects are a useful place to start and it's worth a look at some of their counters, as shown in Table 5.1.

In Figure 5.2 the System Monitor is being used to monitor the following counters:

- Processor: % Processor Time

- System: Processor Queue Length

The counter Processor: % Processor Time is highlighted (in white). We can see that the processor appears to be 100 percent utilized. This in itself is not necessarily going to cause a bottleneck; however, we can see that the Processor Queue Length is quite high. It averages around six (note the scale factor of ten so it can be seen on the display) and peaks at around ten. To check the average and maximum, this counter was selected instead of the counter Processor: % Processor Time counter. This means that on average, six threads are waiting for the CPU; this is a clear indication that we have a processor bottleneck.

The lows and highs in the Processor Queue Length counter display are caused by the randomness that ready tasks are being generated. This is not uncommon. Queues usually appear when the processor is very busy, but they can appear when CPU utilization not high. This can happen if

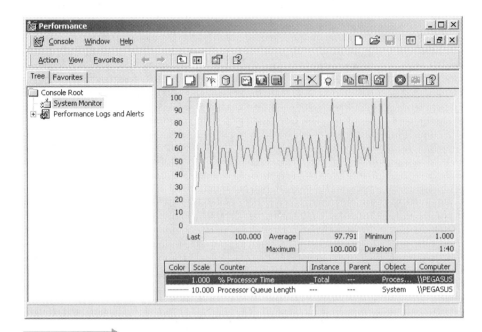

**Figure 5.2**   *A busy processor*

requests for the processor's time arrive randomly and if threads demand irregular amounts of time from the processor.

So what is causing the bottleneck? Is it one process or many processes? We can monitor the processor use of each process to get a feel for the answer. In Figure 5.3 the System Monitor is being used to monitor the Process: % Processor Time counter.

We have selected the Histogram display to make it easier to look at the processes using the processor. It is pretty clear that one process is monopolizing the processor. This is the highlighted process and we can see that it is SQL Server. The only problem is that we do not know which SQL Server! We may have many instances of SQL Server running, and in each case the instance will be named sqlservr in the System Monitor. There are various approaches to finding out which instance is which. One approach I find useful is to create a System Monitor report showing the Process: % Processor Time counter and the Process: ID Process counter. This is shown in Figure 5.4.

Note that we can confirm that the instance sqlservr with process ID 1000 is using up the CPU. Another way (often easier) is to check the Processes tab in the Task Manager. This is shown in Figure 5.5.

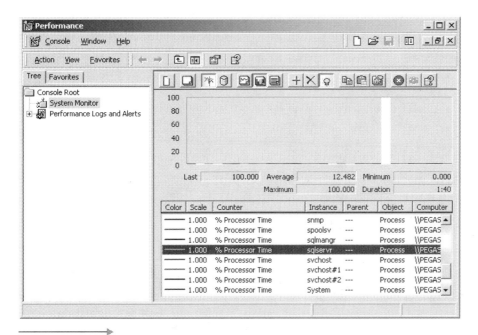

**Figure 5.3**   *Monitoring processor time for individual processes*

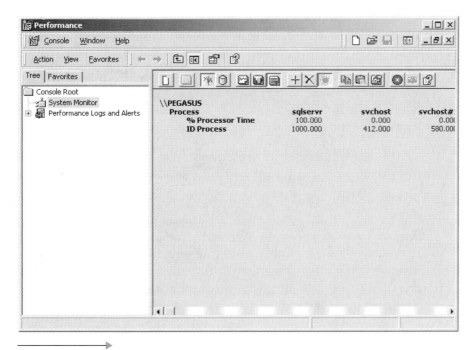

**Figure 5.4**   *Checking process ID for the SQL Server instance*

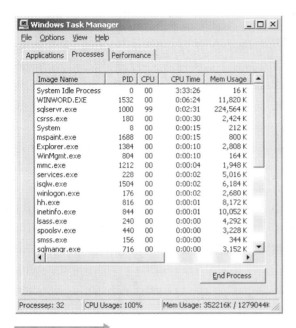

**Figure 5.5**    *The Task Manager processes tab*

If we click on the CPU column heading, the display will be sorted with the process using most of the CPU displayed first. We can easily read off the process ID from the PID column.

Whichever method we use to find the process ID, once we have obtained it we now need to translate it into a SQL Server instance. An easy way to do this is to connect to the SQL Server instance you suspect in the Query Analyzer and execute the following statement.

```
SELECT SERVERPROPERTY('ProcessID')
```

This will return the process ID. If it is not correct, connect to the next instance and check that. Most servers will not be running more than a few instances.

Once we have established the SQL Server instance that is monopolizing the processor, we need to further investigate why this is so, and, if it is not a database or application design problem, perhaps consider moving the instance of SQL Server 2000 onto its own server. If no process stands out in this display, this might be an indication that the processor is just too slow.

Can we drill down further into SQL Server 2000? We can look at the individual threads. In Figure 5.6 the System Monitor is being used to monitor the Thread: % Processor Time counter for all the SQLSERVR process's

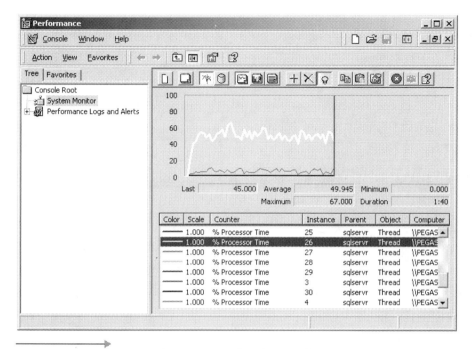

**Figure 5.6**   *A single SQL Server thread monopolizing the CPU*

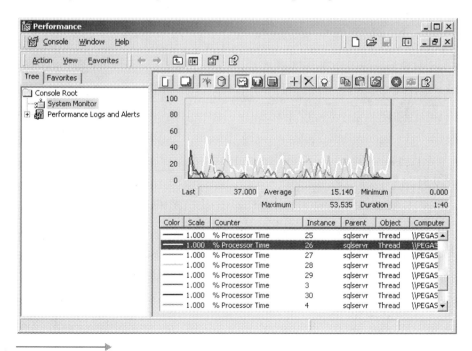

**Figure 5.7**   *Many SQL Server threads using the CPU*

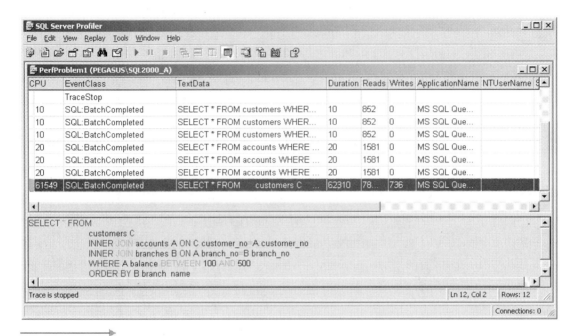

**Figure 5.8**    *The SQL Profiler showing a single thread monopolizing the CPU*

threads. We can clearly see that one thread with thread instance number 26 is using most of the CPU.

Compare this with Figure 5.7. Here we see that many SQL Server threads are running the CPU. So looking at the Thread: % Processor Time counter can be useful to help distinguish between the case of one busy connection versus many busy connections, but I find that at this point I really want to start using the SQL Profiler.

Chapter 7 discusses the SQL Profiler in detail. We wish to check for connections that are using a large proportion of the CPU and which SQL statements on those connections are using the most CPU.

For our requirement we can create a trace with the SQLServerProfiler-Standard template. The default events are sufficient, since they include the events that we need. We can choose to filter out low CPU use events, but we must be careful not to filter out information that might prove useful in our investigation. In Figure 5.8, a graphic SQL Profiler display is shown.

The data columns have been grouped by the data column CPU, and we can immediately see that although many queries are using between 10 and 20 milliseconds of CPU, one query is using nearly 62 seconds of CPU. We can see that the duration of this query is about 62 seconds also. In fact,

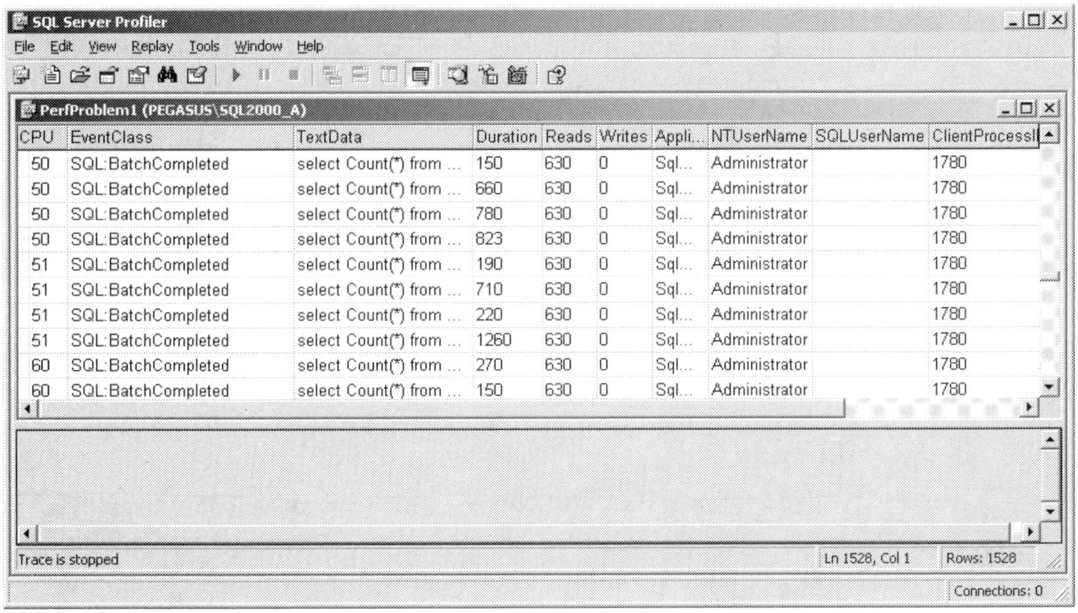

**Figure 5.9** *The SQL Profiler showing many threads using the CPU*

virtually this entire query is CPU. The SQL Profiler identifies the query syntax, application name, and so on so we can easily identify the problem query in our application. We can then, of course, investigate the query plan using the Query Analyzer and hopefully improve it.

We could have saved the trace into a table and then searched the table for events taking, for example, greater than one second of CPU. In practice, I find myself taking this approach most of the time.

In Figure 5.9, many queries are using between 50 and 60 seconds of CPU. No one query stands out. If the queries have a duration, reads, writes, and a CPU use that is expected, then it may be that the queries are efficient. If the processor is constantly busy and there is a significant queue, it may be the case that the CPU is just not powerful enough.

## 5.1.5 Solving problems with CPU

Having determined that there is indeed a CPU bottleneck and that there is a queue of threads waiting for processor time, the next step is to find out what is using up the CPU. Other bottlenecks should be investigated, such as memory, to ensure that they are not manifesting themselves as a CPU bottleneck. If there is no particular candidate process to home in on, then the CPU is probably too slow and either a faster CPU can be purchased or an additional CPU. If it is obvious which application is monopolizing the CPU and it is not SQL Server 2000, then it might be an idea to move that application to another server. Moving SQL Server off a Domain Controller may help if that is where it is installed.

If SQL Server 2000 is monopolizing the CPU, then it should be possible to track down a query that is inefficient and using too much CPU. If there is no particular candidate query to home in on, then the CPU is probably too slow and an additional CPU might be the most cost-effective solution.

Another consumer of CPU is the network interface card. Replacing 8- or 16-bit cards with 32-bit cards will save some CPU. Network interface cards that use bus-mastering direct memory access (DMA) are less of a burden on the CPU.

If SQL Server does not seem to be the main consumer of the CPU, it is always worth checking the counters System: Context Switches/sec and Processor: Interrupts/sec. The System: Context Switches/sec counter measures the average rate per second at which context switches among threads on the computer occur. On a multiprocessor system experiencing processor bottlenecks, high context switches may be reduced by using fibers, which can be enabled by setting the lightweight pooling server configuration option.

The Processor: Interrupts/sec counter measures the average rate per second at which the processor handles interrupts from applications or hardware devices. High activity rates can indicate hardware problems. According to the Windows 2000 Resource Kit, expect to see interrupts in the range upward from 1,000 per second for computers running Windows 2000 Server and upward from 100 per second for computers running Windows 2000 Professional.

One very important factor to consider is the processor cache. Use the largest processor cache that is practical. Typically, choose from 512 KB to 2 MB for the L2 cache. Benchmarks have shown that upgrading to a faster processor but with a smaller cache usually results in poorer performance.

Multiprocessors need some further consideration. Adding extra processors to the server may well increase performance if SQL Server is bottlenecking on CPU. It is recommended that the addition of CPUs be accompanied by the addition of other resources such as memory and disk. It is recommended to scale memory with processors. For example, if a single-processor system requires 128 MB of memory and a second processor is added to increase the throughput, double the memory to 256 MB.

Because of the extra processors, the acceptable queue length will be longer. If the CPUs are mostly utilized, a queue value equal to about three per processor is not unreasonable. A four-processor server, for example, might have a queue length of 12.

If SQL Server is running in lightweight pooling mode—that is, using fibers, the queue length should not exceed one, because there is a single thread on each processor in which fibers are scheduled.

## 5.2   SQL Server 2000 and memory

### 5.2.1   Introduction

Another important resource on a Windows 2000 server is memory. Over the last few years the amount of memory found on servers and workstations has rapidly increased. Windows 2000 Datacenter Server, for example, supports up to 64 GB of physical memory.

Having large amounts of physical memory is not enough in itself. The software running on the server must be able to benefit from it, and it is therefore vital that the server operating system manages memory in an efficient and intelligent fashion. Windows 2000 employs a virtual memory manager to do just that, and it can provide excellent memory management on a wide range of memory configurations with multiple users.

SQL Server 2000 uses the virtual memory management features of Windows 2000 to enable it and other processes to share the physical memory on the server and to hold memory pages on disk in a page file.

Physical memory is a system resource. The more physical memory the better the system is likely to perform. If there is not enough physical memory on the server, then performance will be degraded as processes fight for memory. This section provides an overview of the Windows 2000 virtual memory model and looks at how SQL Server 2000 uses memory. It then looks at how memory bottlenecks can be observed.

### 5.2.2   An overview of Windows 2000 virtual memory management

Similar to a number of modern server operating systems, Windows 2000 uses a flat, linear 32-bit memory model. Each process is able to address 4 GB of virtual memory. The upper 2 GB of virtual memory are reserved for system code and data, which are accessible to the process only when it is running in privileged mode. The lower 2 GB are available to the process when it is running in user mode. However, SQL Server 2000 Enterprise Edition provides support for using Windows 2000 Address Windowing Extensions (AWEs).

This enables SQL Server 2000 running on Windows 2000 Advanced Server to address 8 GB of memory and SQL Server 2000 running on Windows 2000 Datacenter Server to address 64 GB of memory.

Information held in physical memory can usually be categorized as either code or data. The pages given to a Windows 2000 process by the virtual memory manager are known as the working set of the process, and this working set holds pages containing any code and data recently used by the process. The working set of a process can grow or shrink as the virtual memory manager transfers pages of code and data between hard disk and physical memory. This is known as paging. All virtual memory operating systems page, and the secret is to make sure that the amount of physical memory and the memory requirements of processes are such that paging does not become a burden on the system. In this situation, paging can cause disk bottlenecks and start to consume the processor.

If a page of code or data is required by a process, and it is not present in the working set of the process, a page fault results. The page is then brought into its working set. Whether the working set of the process then grows is determined by the availability of free memory on the server. If there is an abundance of free memory, the working set of the process will grow as the new page is added. If there is a lack of free memory, pages in the working set that have not been used for a while will be removed. This is known as working set trimming. If pages are continually being taken out of the working set of a process to make room for new pages, it is likely that the removed pages will be needed again soon. The process will again page fault and the cycle will be repeated.

We can see that if memory is running low, code and data pages will be continually removed from, and added to, the working set of the process, resulting in many page faults. This can lead to a disk bottleneck and wasted CPU, since the system spends more time paging than doing useful work on behalf of the user.

There are two types of page fault. A hard page fault happens when the code or data page needs to be retrieved from disk. A soft page fault happens when it is discovered elsewhere in physical memory. Soft faults use CPU, but hard faults cause disk reads and writes to occur.

When a page is removed from the working set, it may need to be written to disk if it has been changed. If it has not been changed, this need not happen. The area on disk that pages are read from and written to is known as the page file. The file name of the page file is pagefile.sys, and its default size is equal to 1.5 times the amount of physical memory. If memory is committed to a process (known as committed memory), space will be reserved for it in the page file.

### 5.2.3   How SQL Server 2000 uses memory

An instance of SQL Server 2000 is a single Windows 2000 process as is an instance of the SQL agent process that manages components such as the replication and alert subsystems. The amount of memory you can give to SQL Server 2000 really depends upon the amount of memory available on your Windows 2000 server, and this is a function of the amount of physical memory on the server and the memory requirements of other processes running on the server. Ideally, if it is possible, dedicate a single Windows 2000 Server to run a single instance of SQL Server 2000, and then SQL Server 2000 will not compete for memory resources with anything else. Of course, it can compete with Windows 2000 itself for memory, but this will degrade performance and so the dynamic memory configuration in SQL Server 2000 leaves free memory for the operating system. If you decide to configure the memory requirements of SQL Server 2000 manually, you are advised to leave ample memory for the operating system.

Remember that multiple instances of SQL Server can run on one Windows 2000 server—a default instance with up to 16 named instances. Each of these instances will compete for memory.

So what is memory used for in an instance of SQL Server 2000? The short answer is lots of things. There is a pool of 8 KB buffers that are used for database pages—for example, data and index pages and also query plans. Memory is required for user connections and locks. Most importantly, memory is required for the queries themselves.

Different queries can have very diverse memory requirements. A simple query such as a single row lookup will require little memory to execute. Such queries are typically found in online transaction processing systems (OLTPs). Other queries, such as the ad hoc queries found in data warehouse type systems, may need to perform large sorts. Some queries will need to perform hash joins on large amounts of data. The queries that need to sort and hash will benefit from lots of memory. If the sort can fit into memory, or the hash buckets can fit into memory, query performance will be improved.

When the query optimizer creates a plan for a query, it calculates the minimum memory a query will need and the maximum amount of memory it would benefit from. When a query needs to be executed, it is passed to a special scheduler. This scheduler checks to see if the query indeed does perform a sort or hash operation. If it does not, it is scheduled to run immediately. Queries that have a sort or hash operation will then be scheduled based on their memory requirements. Queries with small sorts or joins will be scheduled almost immediately. Queries with large sorts or joins will be scheduled in such a way that only a few can run concurrently.

### Configuring memory for SQL Server 2000

SQL Server 2000 will dynamically configure its memory requirements. It will expand to use up the free memory on the Windows 2000 server as long as it needs memory and that amount of memory is available on the server. It will not use all the free memory, since some will be needed by the operating system—typically about 4 MB to 10 MB. As other processes start up and need memory, the available free memory will drop and SQL Server will then release memory.

Two server configuration options, min server memory (MB) and max server memory (MB), can be used to specify upper and lower bounds for the memory a SQL Server 2000 instance will use. When the instance is started, it takes as much memory as it needs to initialize. This may well be below the min server memory (MB) value. However, once it has crossed this value, it should not drop below it. This ensures that even if the instance is not busy, some memory will be kept ready for starting queries. This ensures that their performance is not degraded by the instance trying to suddenly acquire memory it has given up. The max server memory (MB) value places an upper limit on the memory the instance will use.

These two server options can be set so that their values are equal. In this situation, once the instance has grown its memory to that value, it should not increase or decrease it.

These server configuration options can be set with the system stored procedure sp_configure or with the SQL Server Enterprise Manager. In the SQL Server Enterprise Manager the SQL Server 2000 instance name is right mouse-clicked and Properties chosen. The Memory tab is then selected. This is shown in Figure 5.10.

**Figure 5.10**
*The SQL Server
properties memory
tab*

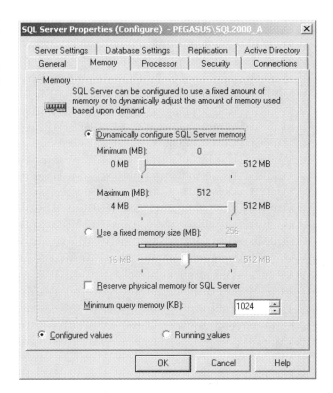

The slider controls that set the min server memory (MB) and max server memory (MB) server configuration option values can be seen. These can be adjusted and are meaningful when the Dynamically configure SQL Server memory option is selected. If preferred, the Use a fixed memory size (MB) option can be selected, which effectively sets min server memory (MB) and max server memory (MB) values equal and stops dynamic configuration.

**Note:** Address Windowing Extensions (AWEs) can be enabled in SQL Server 2000 Enterprise Edition to allow SQL Server to address large amounts of physical memory (8 GB on Windows 2000 Advanced Server and 64 GB on Windows 2000 Datacenter Server). In this case, dynamic memory management does not occur.

Once the server has been allocated memory, it uses it for a variety of objects—for example, user connections, locks, and the buffer pool (cache).

There are various methods to investigate the apportionment of memory. The System Monitor (described in Chapter 7) has a number of objects and

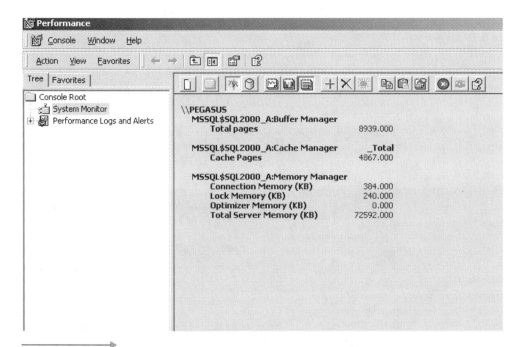

**Figure 5.11**    *System Monitor counters useful for checking memory use of objects*

counters to help us. Figure 5.11 shows the System Monitor in report format displaying some useful object counters.

In Figure 5.11 we can see three objects—Buffer Manager, Cache Manager, and Memory Manager. They belong to the instance of SQL Server 2000 named SQL2000_A. Some useful counters belonging to these objects are displayed.

The Buffer Manager: Total Pages counter represents the total number of 8-KB pages (buffers) in the buffer pool. This holds, for example, database pages and stored procedure query plans. There are currently 8,939 buffers in the pool.

The Cache Manager: Cache Pages counter, for the _Total instance, represents the total number of 8-KB pages (buffers) in the buffer pool used by cached objects, such as stored procedure plans, trigger plans, prepared SQL plans, and ad hoc SQL plans. If required, the number of pages used by each of these cached object types can be monitored individually. There are currently 4,867 pages used for cached objects.

The Memory Manager: Connection Memory (KB) counter represents the amount of memory in kilobytes used by connections. There are currently 384 KB used by connections. Generally, a new connection will take about 24 KB depending on the network packet size. The formula for connection memory is: ((3 * the network packet size) + 12 KB), with the default network packet size being 4 KB.

The Memory Manager: Lock Memory (KB) counter represents the amount of memory in kilobytes used by locks. There are currently 240 KB used by locks. Generally, a lock will take about 96 KB.

The Memory Manager: Optimizer Memory (KB) counter represents the amount of memory in kilobytes used for query optimization. There is no query optimization being performed at the time of the monitoring.

The Memory Manager: Total Server Memory (KB) counter represents the amount of dynamic memory that the instance is currently using. We can see that if we add up the Buffer Manager: Total Pages counter (remember, each page is 8 KB) and the Memory Manager counters, the value is not far from 72,592 KB. The figure arrived at is less, because we have not monitored all consumers of dynamic memory.

Another useful tool is DBCC MEMUSAGE. This has not been documented since SQL Server 6.5, and its output has changed dramatically since then. However, if we use it with that thought in mind, we get the following output.

```
dbcc memusage (names)

Buffer Cache Top 20

Database Name   Object Name   Index Name   Buffers   Dirty
-------------   -----------   ----------   -------   -----
BIG             accounts                   5556      0
Master          syscharsets                33        0
Master          syscomments                24        0
Master          sysmessages                14        0
BIG             accounts      UNKNOWN      11        0
   :
   :
```

This gives us an insight into the number of data and index pages used by the largest objects in cache.

To look at the sizes of cached objects, such as stored procedure plans, the syscacheobjects system table can be queried, as discussed in Chapter 4. Here is a fragment of output showing the pages used by different objects in cache.

```
SELECT cacheobjtype, objtype, pagesused, sql
  FROM master..syscacheobjects
  ORDER BY pagesused DESC
```

| Cacheobjtype    | objtype | pagesused | sql             |
| --------------- | ------- | --------- | --------------- |
| Executable Plan | Proc    | 2164      | usp_test        |
| Compiled Plan   | Proc    | 206       | usp_test        |
| Compiled Plan   | Proc    | 52        | sp_helpdb       |
| Executable Plan | Proc    | 42        | sp_helpdb       |
| Compiled Plan   | Proc    | 31        | sp_helpconstraint |

## 5.2.4   Investigating memory bottlenecks

If memory starts to get tight on the server, performance will start to suffer. This is most likely to happen on a server that is running applications other than just SQL Server 2000, since they will contend for memory.

Before we investigate memory bottlenecks, we need to look at the tools we can use to do so. The first piece of information we will want to know is likely to be how much physical memory the server has. We can easily check this by choosing About Windows from the Help menu in Windows Explorer, as shown in Figure 5.12.

Another handy tool is the Task Manager, which is present in Windows 2000. There are a number of tabs that can be chosen, and these are Applica-

**Figure 5.12**
*Memory available
as shown by
Windows Explorer*

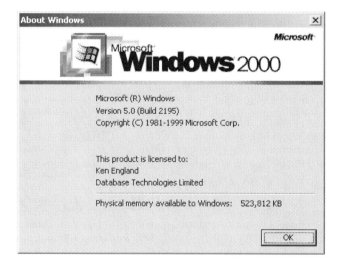

**Figure 5.13**
*The Windows
2000 Task
Manager
applications tab*

tions, Processes, and Performance. The Applications tab is shown in Figure 5.13. This tab shows the status of programs that are running on the system. SQL Server 2000 is not shown, since it is running as a service. The Processes tab displays information about processes that are running on the system, as shown in Figure 5.14. Information such as the memory usage and the page faults is shown for each process. Columns can be added or removed from this tab. The Performance tab, shown in Figure 5.15, displays a graph of CPU and memory use history as well as a textual display.

The most useful tool is the System Monitor, which we have already met. There are a number of useful System Monitor objects concerning memory, such as Memory and Process. There are also a number of tools in the Windows 2000 Resource Kit.

Let us now focus on using the System Monitor to investigate memory bottlenecks. The memory object is a useful place to start, and it is worthwhile to look at some of the memory object's counters, as shown in Table 5.2.

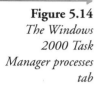

**Figure 5.14**
*The Windows
2000 Task
Manager processes
tab*

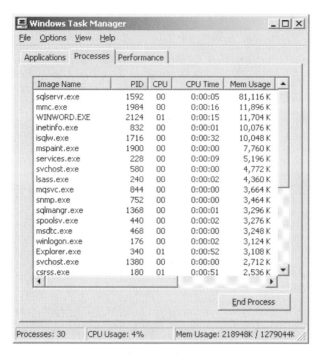

**Figure 5.15**
*The Windows
2000 Task
Manager
performance tab*

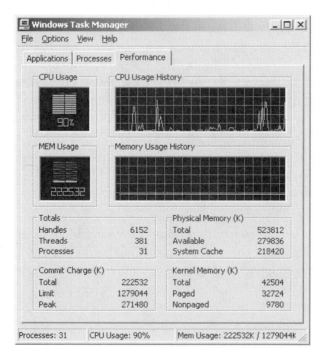

**Table 5.2**    *Selected Counters for the Memory Object*

| Memory Object Counter | Explanation |
| --- | --- |
| Page Faults/sec | This counter includes both hard page faults and soft page faults. Hard page faults result in disk I/O. Soft page faults mean pages are found elsewhere in memory. |
| Pages Input/sec | This is a measure of the number of pages brought in from disk every second. The difference between this value and Page Faults/sec represents soft page faults. |
| Pages Output/sec | This is a measure of the number of pages written to disk every second to make room in the working set of the process for newly faulted pages. If the process modifies pages, they must be written out. They cannot be discarded. |
| Pages/sec | This is total of Pages Input/sec plus Pages Output/sec. |
| Page Reads/sec | This indicates the reads from disk per second to satisfy page faults. This is an important counter. As a rule of thumb, if this counter exceeds five pages per second there is a memory shortage. A single read operation can actually bring in more than one page. |
| Page Writes/sec | This indicates the writes to disk per second to satisfy page faults. This is another important counter, since it measures real disk I/O work being done by the system because of page faulting. A single write operation can actually write out more than one page. |
| Available Bytes<br>Available KBytes<br>Available MBytes | This shows how much memory remains that can be given to processes. The three counters only differ in the units used. |

In Figure 5.16 the System Monitor is being used to monitor the following counters:

- Memory: Page Reads/sec

- Memory: Page Writes/sec

- Memory: Pages Input/sec

- Memory: Page Faults/sec

The line that peaks the highest is Page Faults. This is to be expected, since it represents both hard and soft faults.

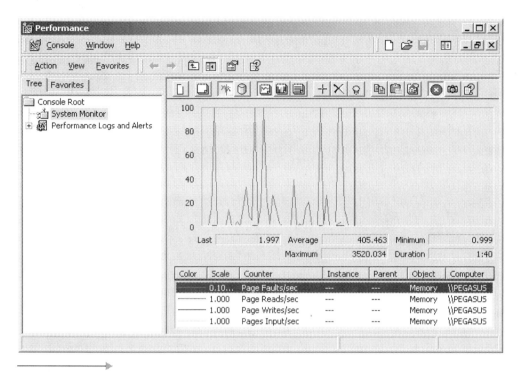

**Figure 5.16**   *Memory pages being read in from disk*

The averages for these counters are shown in the following chart (the averages cannot be deduced from the screenshot alone).

| Counter | Average |
|---------|---------|
| Page Reads/sec | 0.2 |
| Pages Input/sec | 0.8 |
| Page Faults/sec | 405 |

The Page Faults/sec counter represents the sum of hard and soft page faults. The Pages Input/sec counter represents hard faults, so about 0.2 percent of the faults are hard faults. The 0.8 pages that are input per second are brought in by 0.2 page reads per second, so approximately four pages are being brought in by every disk read. Although the majority of page faults are soft, 0.2 I/Os per second are hitting the disk to retrieve pages, which is trivial.

It is useful to also examine the disk activity to see how hard paging is hitting the disks. Some useful counters are as follows:

- % Disk Time

- Avg. Disk Queue Length

- Disk Reads/sec

The % Disk Time is the percentage of elapsed time that the selected disk drives are busy servicing requests. Avg. Disk Queue Length is the average number of read and write requests queued on the selected disks. Disk Reads/sec is the rate of read operations on the disk. These are shown in Figure 5.17. The averages for these counters are shown in the following chart.

| Counter | Average |
| --- | --- |
| Page Reads/sec | 0.4 |
| Pages Input/Sec | 1.6 |
| Page Faults/sec | 282 |
| % Disk Read Time | 23.8 |
| Avg. Disk Queue Length | 0.2 |
| Disk Reads/sec | 9 |

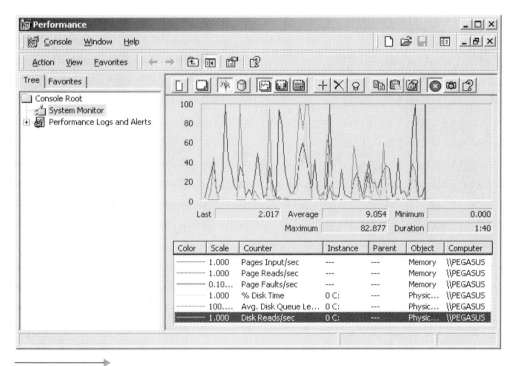

**Figure 5.17**   *Memory counters with disk counters*

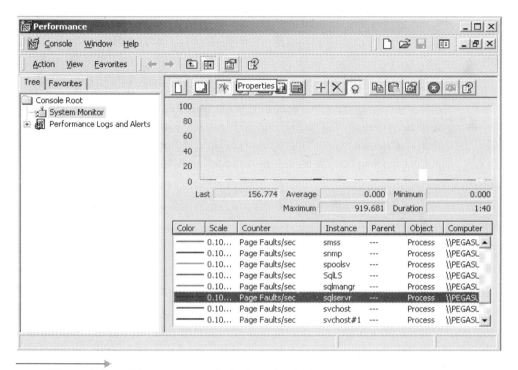

**Figure 5.18**    *Monitoring page faults for individual processes*

We can immediately compare Page Reads/sec with Disk Reads/sec. This shows us that only a small part of our disk activity is caused by paging. The disk is busy about 24 percent of the time. The Avg. Disk Queue Length is small: about 0.2.

A similar investigation can be performed for page writes. It is also worth looking at which individual processes are faulting heavily. This can be done by monitoring the Page Faults/sec counter on the process object for all the process instances. If this is viewed in histogram format, processes that are page faulting heavily stand out immediately, as shown in Figure 5.18.

Another area worth monitoring is the page file, to see if it is filling. Ensure that there is enough free space to let it expand if it needs to.

## 5.2.5  Solving problems with memory

The two main approaches to solving memory problems are: making best use of available memory and adding more physical memory to the server.

To make more use of available memory, remove anything that is not needed but is consuming memory resource. For example, Windows services, drivers, and network protocols that are not used. As was mentioned earlier: If possible, dedicate the server to a single instance of SQL Server 2000.

Increasing the size of the paging file and adding another paging file may help. The addition of extra memory should also be accompanied by an increase in paging file size and, if possible, an increase in secondary cache size. In my experience, the addition of more memory is often the simplest and quickest fix to memory problems and is often the most cost effective.

# 5.3    SQL Server 2000 and disk I/O

## 5.3.1    Introduction

A bottleneck that is often experienced with database management systems concerns the disk subsystem. By definition a database is a shared repository of information, and, consequently, many users are likely to be reading and writing to the database. Depending on whether the database supports an online transaction processing (OLTP) system or a decision support system (DSS), users may update small amounts of data or may perform read only queries on large amounts of data.

The disks themselves are different from most other components in the server in that they typically have moving parts. The disk surface rotates and the disk heads move in and out across the disk surface. Relative to memory access this takes a long time, and therefore SQL Server 2000 uses many techniques to help it minimize disk access. In fact, as we have seen, the query optimizer attempts to choose an access strategy that limits the number of disk I/Os performed.

Care should be taken when investigating disk I/O bottlenecks, since there can be many causes. One cause is a memory bottleneck, which results in high levels of paging to disk, as was described in the previous section.

## 5.3.2    An overview of Windows 2000 and disk I/O

To perform its disk I/O SQL Server 2000 issues reads and writes to Windows 2000 and lets Windows 2000 deal with the business of reading and writing to the underlying disk subsystem. Various techniques are employed to keep the physical disk I/Os efficient. For example, Windows 2000 (and Windows NT) utilize a technique known as scatter-gather I/O. This technique enables Windows 2000 to transfer data into or out of areas of memory, which are not contiguous, in a highly efficient fashion. Unlike

Windows 98, Windows 2000 (and Windows NT) can also make use of asynchronous I/O, which gives SQL Server the ability to issue I/Os to disk and, instead of waiting for the I/O to complete, carry on with other work. The I/O completion can then be checked later.

To provide high levels of disk I/O throughput, Windows 2000 provides various levels of RAID (Redundant Arrays of Inexpensive Disks), and SQL Server 2000 can make use of this capability. Various vendors also provide hardware-based RAID solutions. These increase the cost of the system but tend to provide better performance and are becoming increasingly popular. For that reason, we will assume we are using hardware-based RAID arrays.

Commonly supported RAID levels are as follows:

- RAID 0—disk striping
- RAID 1—disk mirroring
- RAID 5—disk striping with parity

In a RAID 0 stripe set, data is spread across all the drives in the set. If you were to create a database file on a RAID 0 stripe set, the disk controller would actually break the file into pieces (known as chunks) as you created it. Each piece would be placed on the next disk in the set circling round when it moved off the last one. We can imagine a three-disk stripe set now providing three sets of disk heads to access the file. This is the bonus of RAID 0: performance. RAID 0 provides very good performance for both reading and writing. The downside of RAID 0 is that the loss of a single disk will affect the whole stripe set. The RAID 0 array will appear to be a single disk to Windows NT/2000 and SQL Server.

RAID 5 is very similar to RAID 0. However, as well as writing data onto a disk drive in the stripe set, parity information is written to another stripe set member. Not only do we stripe data, but we stripe parity information. This gives us a level of redundancy. We can lose one disk and the data information on that disk can be recreated from the parity on other disks when a request for data on the failed disk is made. The downside of RAID 5 is that although read performance is good, write performance is worse than RAID 0, since two disks must be written to. Hardware-based implementations of RAID 5 can help to absorb this write performance degradation. Again, the RAID 5 array will appear to be a single disk to Windows NT/2000 and SQL Server.

In RAID 1 data is duplicated on a mirror disk drive (some RAID implementations allow more than one mirror). Writes are performed to both

**Table 5.3** *RAID Levels 0, 1, and 5*

| RAID Type | Characteristics | Number of Disks | Reliability | Performance |
|---|---|---|---|---|
| RAID 0: disk striping | Data is spread over all the disks in the stripe set with no redundancy. | N | Less than a single disk | High for read and write |
| RAID 1: disk mirroring | Data duplicated on each member | 2N | Higher than RAID 0 or 5 or single disk | Good for read but less than a single disk for write |
| RAID 5: disk striping with parity | Similar to RAID 0, but parity information is stored with data for redundancy | N + 1 | Higher than RAID 0 or single disk | Similar to RAID 0 for read but less than a single disk for write |

members of the set. This configuration gains us redundancy. We can lose one of the members and still continue working with the other one. There is no performance advantage in using RAID 1 for writing; in fact, it can be slightly slower, but it may well give some performance boost to reading. A downside of RAID 1 is that twice as much disk space is necessary and, therefore, twice the cost.

It is also possible to use two disk controllers—one for each mirror set member. This means that a disk controller failure can be tolerated. This is known as duplexing. As with the other RAID configurations, the RAID 1 array will appear to be a single disk to Windows NT/2000 and SQL Server.

Table 5.3 summarizes the different RAID levels.

What happened to RAID levels 2, 3, and 4? Generally, these are considered to be evolutionary steps toward RAID 5 and thus are not often used with database systems.

**Figure 5.19**
*A RAID configuration utilizing RAID 0 and 1 for the data and RAID 1 for the log*

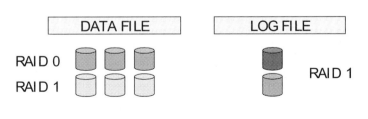

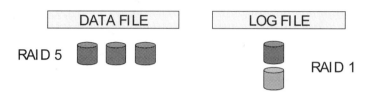

**Figure 5.20**
*A RAID
configuration
utilizing RAID 5
for the data and
RAID 1 for the log*

Choosing the appropriate RAID implementation is a compromise between performance, fault tolerance, and cost. Figures 5.19 and 5.20 show two common configurations.

Both of the configurations store the log on a separate RAID array from the data using a separate disk controller. This means that the data file can be lost while the transaction log remains unaffected.

The configuration in Figure 5.19 places the data file on a RAID 0 array for optimum read and write performance. The RAID 0 array is mirrored to provide fault tolerance. This is often known as RAID 1+0, or RAID 10. This provides the best performance and fault tolerance but at the greatest cost. The transaction log is placed on a RAID 1 array. The transaction log is usually written to sequentially so, as long as nothing competes for disk bandwidth on this array, this configuration provides good write performance (and read). The transaction log is mirrored, since losing it may result in the loss of work.

The configuration in Figure 5.20 places the data file on a RAID 5 array. This will provide optimum read performance, but write performance will be degraded. This will be a lower-cost solution than the previous configuration. The transaction log is placed on a RAID 1 array as before.

Suppose the size of our data was greater than the size of the RAID arrays available to us. In this case we could use multiple data files, placing each file on each RAID array. Space for our tables would be allocated from each file on each RAID array. SQL Server would be able to issue read requests simultaneously to each RAID array when the table was scanned.

### 5.3.3   How SQL Server 2000 uses disk I/O

We have already mentioned the fact that SQL Server maintains a pool of 8-KB buffers. This buffer pool is sometimes referred to as a unified cache, since it holds both cached objects, such as stored procedure plans, and database pages, such as data and index pages. The buffers used for cached objects are often referred to as the procedure cache, and the buffers used for database pages are referred to as the data cache.

The goal of the data cache is to minimize physical accesses to the disk subsystem. There is a single data cache for each instance of SQL Server 2000 that all the instance's databases share. In this section we will look at the data cache and the various techniques used to make reading from it and writing to it more efficient.

### An overview of the data cache

As we discussed earlier, a portion of SQL Server 2000 memory is used for the data cache. As long as there is enough memory available on the server to allow SQL Server 2000 to dynamically grow its memory allocation, the data cache can grow.

The idea behind the data cache is quite simple. If a user connection requests a row, SQL Server 2000 will translate this into a page request and it will then look for the page in the data cache to see if this page has previously been retrieved from disk. This request for a page represents a logical read.

If the page cannot be found, it must be retrieved from the database on disk, and this disk access represents a physical read. The page is read into a free buffer and the data requested by the connection obtained. The page is now in cache, and, assuming that it does not leave the cache for any reason, it will be available for any connection requesting it. The next connection requesting that page will issue a logical read, which will be satisfied from the data cache. This is a memory access, as opposed to a disk access, and is consequently much faster than the original request that brought in the page from disk.

We can envision a situation where a whole database gets brought into the cache, and this is quite feasible—the only limiting factor being the size of the data cache. In reality, 20 percent of most databases get accessed 80 percent of the time, so we find that the most accessed pages in the database find themselves in the data cache. Note that increasing the size of the data cache does not bring us a linear performance increase. Once we can hold the most accessed pages in a database or group of databases in the data cache, the allocation of more memory to the data cache brings us little gain.

An empty data cache is created when SQL Server 2000 is started. At this point most database page requests end up as physical reads. After awhile a steady state is reached, with the data cache holding the most frequently used pages, as shown in Figure 5.21. The percentage of time a requested database

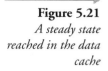

**Figure 5.21**
*A steady state
reached in the data
cache*

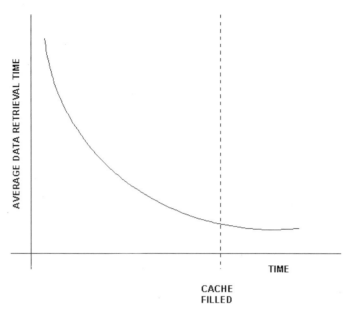

page is found in the data cache is known as the cache hit ratio. The cache
hit ratio is defined as follows:

```
cache hit ratio (%) = ((logical read - physical read)/
logical read) * 100
```

What happens if we fill the data cache and then we need to read in a
new page? We will discuss the mechanisms employed shortly, but SQL
Server 2000 will have to make room in the data cache for the new page. If
the new page has been changed by a user connection, then it is known as a
dirty page and it cannot be discarded, because it reflects the latest state or
version of that page. It must be written back to the database on disk. However, if the page has not been changed, it can be discarded. SQL Server
2000 keeps track of which pages have not been used for the longest length
of time. This is important, because this is taken into account when SQL
Server 2000 jettisons pages from the cache.

How does SQL Server 2000 find out if a page is resident in the data
cache? It could look at every used buffer in the data cache, but this would
be very expensive for large data caches consisting of tens of thousands of
buffers. Instead, it uses an internal hashing scheme to quickly locate buffers.

What happens if we change pages in the data cache? How do they get to
disk? There are a number of mechanisms involved. First of all, we need
to consider the fact that usually the data cache is finite in size and even-

tually all the buffers in it could be used. In other words, there are no free buffers. If there are no free buffers, then SQL Server has no room to place new pages that are read in from disk. To avoid and preempt this situation, SQL Server periodically frees up buffers in the data cache. When a buffer is freed, it is first checked to see if it is dirty. A dirty page is one where changes have not yet been written to disk and therefore the buffer cannot just be discarded. The dirty page must be written to the data file. If the page is not dirty, then its contents can be discarded and the buffer is placed into a chain of free buffers.

It would not make sense to free a buffer containing a page that was frequently accessed instead of a buffer containing a page that had not been accessed for a long time. To avoid this situation, each buffer contains a reference count, which is incremented each time the page in the buffer is accessed. The more the page is accessed, the greater the reference count. When the data cache is searched in order to find buffers that can be freed, the reference count is decremented. When a buffer is found with a reference count of zero, it is freed. This mechanism ensures that frequently accessed pages stay in the cache. Of course, if we have a large data cache and lots of memory on the server so that the data cache can expand, there is no reason to free up buffers constantly.

Note that SQL Server 2000 uses a write-ahead log algorithm. This means that the transaction log is always written to before the data file, and this ensures that a change can always be rolled back in a recovery situation.

So what writes the dirty pages to disk? There is no one process that does this. Often it is the worker threads that perform the function of scanning the buffer pool looking for pages to discard. They do this while waiting for their own disk accesses to complete. If they need to write a page, this is performed as an asynchronous I/O.

A system process known as the lazywriter also performs the same function. The lazywriter thread is activated at periodic intervals. It then scans the data cache in order to find buffers that can be freed. It basically performs the same activities at the worker threads. Because the worker threads have been freeing up buffers, the lazywriter system process is not kept busy. However, on the Windows 98 platform, where asynchronous I/O is not supported, the worker threads cannot perform this function and therefore the lazywriter system process can become very busy.

Another system process that contributes is the checkpoint process. The checkpoint thread's goal in life is not to free up buffers but rather to ensure that the contents of dirty pages eventually get written to the data files on

**Table 5.4**   *Some Useful Counters for Observing Page Transfers to and from Disk*

| | |
|---|---|
| Lazywrites/sec | Number of buffers written per second by the lazywriter |
| Checkpoint pages/sec | Number of pages flushed to disk per second by a checkpoint |
| Page Reads/sec | Number of physical database page reads per second |
| Page Writes/sec | Number of physical database page writes per second |
| Database Pages | Number of database pages in the buffer pool |
| Free Pages | Number of free pages |

disk. It does this to keep recovery time short; otherwise, an automatic SQL Server recovery, performed perhaps because of a power failure, would potentially take a long time rolling forward changes from the transaction log to the data files. The checkpoint thread writes the pages asynchronously to disk with what are sometimes referred to as batch writes. This is a very efficient mechanism, especially if it is used in conjunction with hardware-based RAID arrays.

To monitor the lazywriter and checkpoint processes, SQL Server 2000 provides us with a number of useful counters associated with the Buffer Manager object, as shown in Table 5.4.

Another Buffer Manager counter that is very useful is Buffer Cache Hit Ratio. This is the cache hit ratio described previously.

Figure 5.22 shows checkpoint activity occurring on the server. The highlighted counter is the Checkpoint pages/sec counter. Notice that during the checkpoint, another counter is also active. This is the Page Writes/sec counter. In this example both counters had a maximum value of 1,807.

### Keeping tables and indexes in cache

As described previously, tables and indexes that are accessed frequently stay in the data cache, while other, least used pages are flushed out first. In this way the pages that are often required are the pages that connections get fast access to. However, it is possible that fast access is required to tables and indexes that are not accessed frequently enough to keep them in the data cache.

To keep a table and its indexes in data cache the sp_tableoption system stored procedure can be used, as follows:

```
EXEC sp_tableoption 'branches', 'pintable', true
```

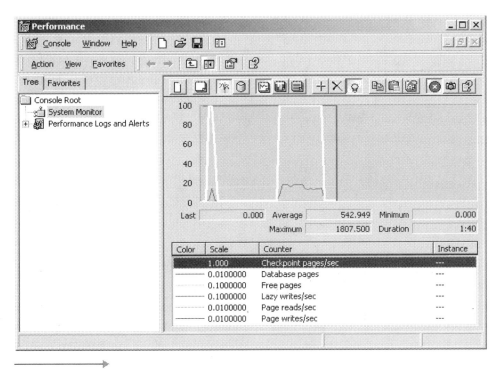

**Figure 5.22**   *Checkpoint activity observed in the System Monitor*

Note that the table name can use wildcard characters. This statement does not load pages from the table into the data cache, but once they are read into data cache by normal activity, they stay there and are not removed. This can result in little data cache being left for other tables and indexes, so table pinning should be used with care.

To turn the option off, just use the false keyword, as follows:

```
EXEC sp_tableoption 'branches', 'pintable', false
```

### Read-ahead scans

Read-ahead processing is a mechanism used by SQL Server 2000 to reduce the number of stalls a thread experiences waiting for a physical read to complete. It is a concept similar to instruction prefetch in a CPU. If SQL Server 2000 realizes that a table scan or an index scan is taking place—in other words, sequential scanning of pages—it can start to prefetch pages into the data cache before the thread requests those pages. This means that when the thread requests a page, it is found in the data cache and the thread does not stall waiting for a physical read from disk to complete.

**Figure 5.23**
*Performing a table
scan with no read
ahead*

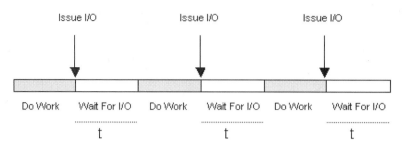

If a read-ahead mechanism was not employed, a thread issuing many disk I/Os while executing a table scan or index scan would spend a large amount time waiting for the disk read to complete, as shown in Figure 5.23.

We know that disk I/O takes a long time relative to memory access, and this is represented by "t" in Figure 5.23.

If we employ a read-ahead mechanism, which can read the pages into cache using other threads before the user's thread requests them, we have eliminated the stall caused by the physical read and only the data cache access is required, as shown in Figure 5.24.

The read-ahead mechanism also reads in units of extents, so it reads in eight pages in one disk I/O, which clearly is more efficient than reading eight pages with eight single-page reads.

So what can we benefit from the read-ahead capability? Basically, anything that performs a sequential scan of data pages, including the following.

- Table scans

- Nonclustered index leaf scans

- DBCC statements, such as DBCC CHECKDB

- Transact-SQL statements, such as UPDATE STATISTICS

How does SQL Server 2000 know, for example, that a table scan is taking place? It knows because that was the decision the query optimizer made.

**Figure 5.24**
*Performing a table
scan with read
ahead*

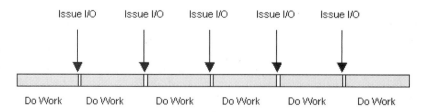

How does SQL Server 2000 know which pages to read next? Because the extents in a table or index are managed by IAM pages (described in Chapter 2), SQL Server can easily retrieve the relevant IAM page or pages and find the extents that need to be read. A sorted list is then built of the extents to be read and this drives the read ahead. Contiguous extents can then be read very efficiently

To observe read-ahead processing in action, the Set statistics IO option can be set in the Query Analyzer. For example, suppose we execute the following query against the Accounts table—this time increased to 400,000 rows.

```
SELECT COUNT(*) FROM accounts
```

The output from Set statistics IO is as follows:

```
Table 'accounts'. Scan count 1, logical reads 24306,
physical reads 136, read-ahead reads 24087.
```

This shows that 24,306 logical reads were required to perform the table scan but only 136 physical reads. The number of read-ahead reads performed was 24,087. This means that 24,087 pages were read into the data cache by the read-ahead mechanism. The low value of physical reads performed by this query is due to read ahead.

Note what happens if we immediately reissue the query:

```
Table 'accounts'. Scan count 1, logical reads 24306,
physical reads 0, read-ahead reads 0.
```

In this case the pages are already in data cache. The read-ahead mechanism is never initiated.

The System Monitor can also be used to monitor read ahead. The Buffer Manager object has an associated counter: Readahead pages/sec.

### Shrinking database files

One consideration to be made when scanning the pages of a table is the utilization of the pages. If we have many pages that are only partly filled because of row deletions, perhaps made by an archive program, we are scanning more pages than should be necessary to retrieve our data. We need some way of detecting the problem and then fixing it by compacting the file.

The DBCC SHOWCONTIG statement, which we discussed in Chapter 3, can show us how densely rows are stored on pages. For example:

```
DBCC SHOWCONTIG ('accounts')


     :
- Pages Scanned.............. : 1570
     :
- Avg. Page Density (full)... : 42.34%
     :
     :
```

To compact the file we can use DBCC SHRINKFILE. We also discussed this statement in Chapter 2, and we noted that in the default case data rows from the pages at the end of the table would migrate to the free space in pages at the beginning of the table. Let us issue a DBCC SHRINKFILE:

```
DBCC SHRINKFILE (BankingDB_Data,10)
```

Now let us execute DBCC SHOWCONTIG again:

```
DBCC SHOWCONTIG ('accounts')


     :
- Pages Scanned.............. : 782
     :
- Avg. Page Density (full)... : 84.70%
     :
     :
```

We can immediately see that the page density has increased by about a factor of two. This means we are storing twice as many rows per page and that we need half the pages to hold our data compared with what we needed previously. This is clear from the Pages Scanned value, which has changed from 1,570 to 782. So, although it may take a while to shrink a large file, you may find that subsequent scans take somewhat less time.

### 5.3.4  Investigating disk I/O bottlenecks

The tool used to observe disk I/O bottlenecks is typically the System Monitor. The Task Manager displays little useful information as far as disk I/O is concerned. There are also a number of tools in the Windows 2000 Resource Kit that are useful. We will focus on using the System Monitor, since it is the most comprehensive tool, and we will also introduce a useful system table-valued function, fn_virtualfilestats.

If you are using Windows 2000, the statistics collection for the Logicaldisk object is not active by default. However, the statistics collection for the Physicaldisk object is active by default.

**Note:** If you are using Windows NT, the statistics collection for both the disk objects is not active by default.

To activate statistics collection in Windows 2000 for the Logicaldisk object, run the diskperf command and reboot Windows 2000. To turn on statistics collection for the Logicaldisk object, type in:

```
diskperf -yv
```

To deactivate statistics collection, type in:

```
diskperf -nv
```

The Physicaldisk object uses the syntax –yd and –nd.

Once the diskperf command has been run, it will not have to be run again until you want to change the statistics collection.

For Windows NT the syntax is just –y and –n.

Let us look at some of the more useful counters associated with disk activity.

The Logical Disk, Physical Disk, and a number of SQL Server 2000 objects are a useful place to start, and it is worth a look at some of their counters. Again, note that it often is a memory bottleneck that manifests itself as a disk bottleneck, and therefore the counters associated with the Memory object, as described earlier, should also be monitored. Some of the most useful Logical Disk Physical Disk counters are shown in Table 5.5. Useful SQL Server counters are shown in Table 5.6.

Be aware that the % Disk Time, % Disk Read Time, % Disk Write Time, and % Idle Time counters can exaggerate. You may see values over 100 percent. It is a good idea to monitor % Idle Time with the other three counters to get an indication of whether this is happening.

In the System Monitor chart shown in Figure 5.25 we have added the PhysicalDisk: Avg. Disk Bytes/Read counter and the Buffer Manager: Page lookups/sec counter. We have executed a query that retrieves a row from the Accounts table using a nonclustered index. We can see a blip in the Buffer Manager: Page lookups/sec counter. However, note the value of the PhysicalDisk: Avg. Disk Bytes/Read counter. It is 8,192 bytes. This shows us that a single page read was performed.

In the System Monitor chart shown in Figure 5.26 we have added the PhysicalDisk counters, Avg. Disk Queue Length and %Disk write time,

**Table 5.5**    *Logical and Physical Disk Counters*

| Logical/Physical Disk Object Counter | Explanation |
| --- | --- |
| % Disk Time | How busy is the disk? This is the percentage of elapsed time that the selected disk is busy handling read and write requests. |
| % Disk Read Time | This is the percentage of elapsed time that the selected disk is busy handling read requests. |
| % Disk Write Time | This is the percentage of elapsed time that the selected disk is busy handling write requests. |
| % Idle Time | This is the percentage of elapsed time that the selected disk is not processing requests. |
| Disk Reads/sec | The rate of read operations on the disk |
| Disk Writes/sec | The rate of write operations on the disk |
| Avg. Disk Queue Length | This is the average number of read and write requests for the disk in the sample interval. If disk queue length is greater than two and the %Disk Time is high, this may indicate a disk bottleneck. |
| Current Disk Queue Length | This is an instantaneous value at the point of sample. It includes the requests being serviced. |
| Avg. Disk Bytes/Read | This is the average number of bytes transferred to disk during read operations. |
| Avg. Disk Bytes/Write | This is the average number of bytes transferred to disk during write operations. |

and the Buffer Manager counters, Page writes/sec and Checkpoint pages/ sec.

We have initiated an update of a large table, resulting in many rows being changed. The Avg. Disk Queue Length counter is labeled (1). This peaks at 14 and averages 2.7. The counter that closely tracks it is %Disk write time, which is 100 percent at peak. Clearly, a lot of write activity is being performed. The data file and log file are on one disk, so what is responsible for the activity? The clue is our highlighted counter, Checkpoint pages/sec. This averages 140 pages/sec with a peak of 904 pages/sec. This results in a Page writes/sec, labeled (2), averaging 140 and peaking at 904. This is the checkpoint that is flushing to disk.

**Table 5.6**    *Useful SQL Server Counters*

| SQLServer Object Counter | Explanation |
| --- | --- |
| Access Methods: Forwarded Records/sec | Number of records per second fetched through forwarded record pointers |
| Access Methods: Full Scans/sec | Number of unrestricted table or index scans per second |
| Access Methods: Page Splits/sec | Number of page splits per second that occur as the result of over-flowing index pages (data pages in a clustered index) |
| Buffer Manager: Buffer cache hit ratio | The percentage of time that a page was found in the data cache. Usually 95% plus on a server in steady state with a large cache. |
| Buffer Manager: Checkpoint pages/sec | Number of pages written to disk per second by a checkpoint |
| Buffer Manager: Database pages | Number of database pages in the buffer pool |
| Buffer Manager: Free list stall/sec | Number of requests per second that had to wait for a free page |
| Buffer Manager: Free pages | Total number of pages on all free lists |
| Buffer Manager: Lazy Writes/sec | The number of pages written out to disk per second by the lazy-writer. This cleans buffers and returns them to the free buffer pool. |
| Buffer Manager: Page life expectancy | Number of seconds a page will stay in the buffer pool without any references to it |
| Buffer Manager: Page lookups/sec | Number of requests per second to find a page in the buffer pool |
| Buffer Manager: Page Reads/sec | The number of physical page reads per second. This is what we try to minimize with indexes and data cache. |
| Buffer Manager: Page Writes/sec | The number of physical page writes per second |
| Buffer Manager: Procedure cache pages | Number of pages used to store compiled queries |
| Buffer Manager: Readahead Pages/sec | Number of pages read in by the read-ahead mechanism |
| Buffer Manager: Reserved Pages | Pages reserved in the buffer pool |
| Buffer Manager: Stolen Pages | Number of pages used for miscellaneous server purposes |
| Buffer Manager: Target Pages | Ideal number of pages in the buffer pool |
| Buffer Manager: Total Pages | Number of pages in the buffer pool—includes database, free, and stolen pages |
| Databases: Data File(s) Size (KB) | Total size of all data files in a database |
| Databases: Log File(s) Size (KB) | Total size of all log files in a database |

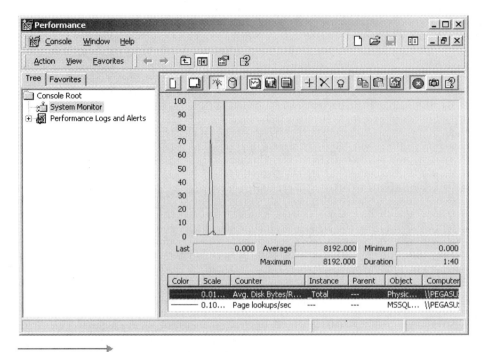

**Figure 5.25**   *Investigating disk activity—looking at read size*

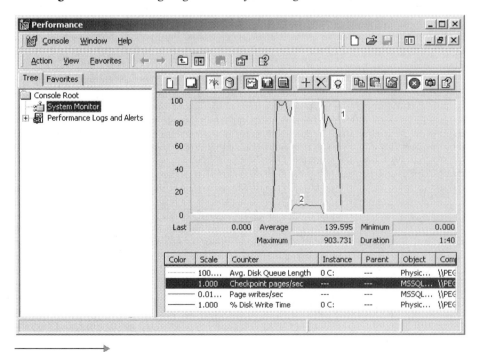

**Figure 5.26**   *Investigating disk activity—looking at a large update*

Finally, let us have a look at fn_virtualfilestats—a system table-valued function. This gives us very useful information about I/O statistics for individual data and log files. It is very easy to use.

```
SELECT * FROM :: fn_virtualfilestats(11, 1)
```

The first parameter is the database ID, and the second parameter is the file ID. Personally, I find the best way to obtain these values is with sp_helpdb and sp_helpfile. If you prefer, use the system functions DB_ID() and FILE_ID() to find these values. Example output is as follows:

```
DbId   FileId   TimeStamp   NumberReads   NumberWrites   BytesRead   BytesWritten   IoStallMS
----   ------   ---------   -----------   ------------   ---------   ------------   ---------
11     1        9293172     1579          572            398663680   73203712       11810
```

## 5.3.5   Solving problems with disk I/O

Having determined that there is indeed a disk I/O bottleneck and that there is a sustained queue of requests, the next step is to eliminate causes other than SQL Server 2000, such as a memory bottleneck causing high levels of paging to disk.

If the disk bottleneck proves to be SQL Server 2000, it could be a specific set of queries—in which case it is possible that these queries could be made more efficient by rewriting or by a change in index design. This often cures the problem. However, if the workload on the SQL Server 2000 as a whole is generating more disk I/O than the I/O subsystem can handle, it may be time to invest in a RAID approach.

There are a number of RAID topologies that can be used; the fastest implementation of RAID, however, is usually hardware based. We have already discussed RAID configurations in this chapter.

If RAID configurations are not available, using multiple data files and filegroups on multiple disk spindles may be another option.

Also, remember that Windows 2000 can defragment disk drives. It is possible that a database file is fragmented because of the way it was created. This may have happened if many automatic extensions took place and the disk was shared with other applications that create files.

Ensure that the hardware components can theoretically handle the load. Apart from the disk drives, the disk controllers and I/O bus have a finite bandwidth.

# 6

# *Transactions and Locking*

## 6.1    Introduction

I once visited a customer to sanity check the physical design for a new database. In the course of checking the design I happened to notice that there were some people in an adjoining room entering data into forms on their PCs. Every so often one of these people would raise their hands in the air for a few seconds. After a while my curiosity got the better of me, and I asked the person who had invited me to do the sanity check what was happening.

It transpired that the people in the next room were entering trades into a financial system, but the lock conflict caused by the action of entering two trades simultaneously was so bad that they found it easier to raise their hands just before they pressed Enter on the keyboard to signal to their colleagues not to do the same. Ironically, what they were doing was implementing a locking protocol, which single-threaded the insertion of a trade. This is an example of a multiuser system where two users are one user too many!

Unfortunately, there are many multiuser systems out there that suffer from locking problems. Whether you design a system with locking in mind tends, like most things in life, to depend on your previous experiences. While I was working for Digital Equipment Corporation I was involved in the design of many multiuser online transaction processing systems (OLTPs). I came to learn very quickly that if I did not constantly ask the question, "Is this transaction likely to be the cause of a locking bottleneck?" I would run into trouble. If your background is single-user systems or read only databases, this question might not be the first one on your mind.

This chapter introduces the concepts of transactions and locking, perhaps two of the most important features provided by a modern database management system and, perhaps, two of the features whose correct implementation by a database designer is most critical to database performance. The default SQL Server locking protocol provided by SQL Server 2000 is sophisticated; however, for those developers who need it, the default locking protocol provided by SQL Server can easily be changed to behave in a number of different ways. These capabilities will be covered in this chapter.

# 6.2    Why a locking protocol?

Single-user access to a database does not require a locking protocol nor does single or multiuser access to a read only database. Database management systems in reality must support more than one user concurrently accessing information, and it is this multiuser access that requires the database management system to provide a protocol to ensure that the changes being made to the database data by one user are not corrupted by another. Locking is not a luxury in a multiuser environment—it is a necessity.

Locking protocols are not all or nothing. Some protocols are more stringent than others with different database management systems adopting their own unique approaches. Locking is the natural enemy of performance, and so a more stringent locking protocol is more likely to adversely affect performance than a less stringent one. However, a more stringent locking protocol is also likely to provide a more consistent view of the data.

To provide an idea as to why a locking protocol is necessary let us consider some multiuser scenarios.

## 6.2.1    Scenario 1

In this scenario Mike modifies a stock level by subtracting 1,000 from it, leaving 100 items. Katy reads the stock level and sees that there are only 100 items in stock. Immediately after Katy has read this value and acted upon it, Mike's transaction fails and is rolled back, returning the stock level to its original value of 1,100.

This scenario highlights a classic problem. Katy has been allowed to read changes made by Mike before Mike has committed the changes—in other words, before Mike has irrevocably changed the data by ending the transaction with a commit. Until the transaction ends, Mike can choose to roll back the transaction, change the value again, or commit the transaction. In our example, Mike's transaction actually fails before it completes, causing the database management system to roll back the change. Katy is said to have read uncommitted, or dirty data. This is shown in Figure 6.1.

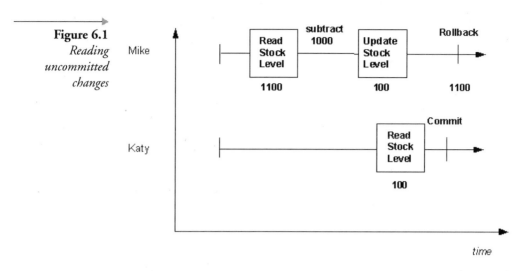

**Figure 6.1**
*Reading uncommitted changes*

## 6.2.2   Scenario 2

In this scenario Mike's transaction sums a list of debts in a table and checks the result against a total debt value held elsewhere in the database. While Mike's transaction is summing the values in the list, Katy's transaction inserts a new row into the debt table after Mike's transaction has passed by and updates the total debt value. When Mike finishes summing the list and compares the calculated sum with the total debt value, it reports a discrepancy, where, in fact, there is no discrepancy at all. This is called the phantom insert phenomenon. This is shown in Figure 6.2.

These are only two examples of a number of possibilities that can occur if locking protocols are not used or the locking protocol used is not stringent enough. We will revisit some of these scenarios later. We have said that SQL Server uses a locking protocol, so let us now investigate how this works.

**Figure 6.2**
*The phantom insert phenomenon*

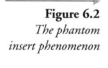
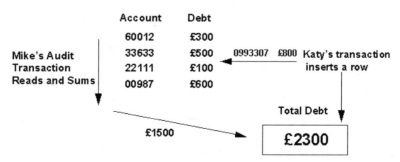

# 6.3   The SQL server locking protocol

The locking protocol adopted by SQL Server consists of placing different types of locks on different database objects. In SQL Server 2000 these objects include a table, a database page, a row and an index entry. As we have seen, a database page is 8 KB in size, and any object resident within this 8 KB is locked implicitly when the database page is locked. Therefore, if a database page is locked, every row held on that page is effectively locked. Similarly, if a table is locked, every row in that table is locked.

We will now look in detail at the types of locks used, what objects can be locked, and the duration of these locks.

## 6.3.1   Shared and exclusive locks

To generalize, SQL Server applies a write lock when it writes information or a read lock when it reads information. Writing information usually refers to inserting, updating, or deleting rows, whereas reading information usually refers to retrieving rows with, for example, a SELECT statement. There are some simple rules that we can make at this point.

- If a user has placed a read lock on an object such as a row, another user can also place a read lock on that object. In other words, both users can read the same object simultaneously. In fact, any number of users can place a read lock on an object at the same time.

- If a user has placed a write lock on an object, another user cannot also place a write lock on that object. Also, another user cannot place a read lock on that object. In other words, once a user has placed a write lock on an object, other users cannot place read or write locks on the same object simultaneously.

Because many users can place read locks on the same table, page, or row concurrently these read locks are usually referred to as shared locks. Write locks, on the other hand, are normally referred to as exclusive locks. Table 6.1 shows the compatibility between shared and exclusive locks. As can be seen, only shared locks are compatible.

Once a lock has been placed on an object, it has a lifetime. Suppose a Transact-SQL statement that causes a row lock to be taken out is executed inside a user-defined transaction. In the default case, shared locks live for the time it takes the SQL statement to read the row, whereas exclusive locks live for the length of the user-defined transaction. This is shown in Figure 6.3. This behavior can be overridden with the use of the REPEATABLE

**Table 6.1**     *Compatibility between Shared and Exclusive Locks*

| Mode of Currently Granted Lock | Mode of Requested Lock | |
|---|---|---|
| | exclusive | shared |
| exclusive | ✗ | ✗ |
| shared | ✗ | ✓ |

READ keyword or transaction isolation levels, as we will see later in this chapter.

**Note:** Beware of the SET IMPLICIT_TRANSACTIONS ON statement. It will automatically start a transaction when Transact-SQL statements such as SELECT, INSERT, UPDATE, and DELETE are used. The transaction will not be committed and its locks will not be released until an explicit COMMIT TRANSACTION statement is executed. To see if it is set, use DBCC USEROPTIONS (described later).

SQL Server also uses locks other than shared or exclusive. For example, it uses update locks as an optimization to avoid deadlocks. We will look at update locks when we investigate deadlocks later in the chapter.

**Figure 6.3**
*The default lifetime of SQL server locks*

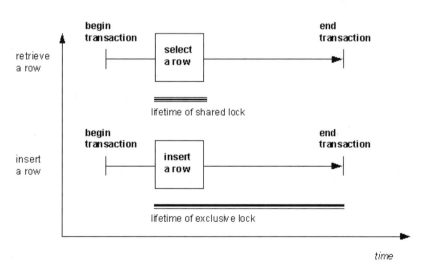

## 6.3.2   Row-, page-, and table-level locking

Is row-level locking better than page-level locking? It depends. Applications require different levels of locking granularity. One application may benefit from page-level locking while another application may benefit from row-level locking. Why is this? To investigate it is useful to consider the different granularity of lock that could be taken out by some theoretical database management system.

Figure 6.4 shows the database concurrency for different lock granularity. By lock granularity we mean the object that is locked from, on one side of the spectrum, an individual column in a row to the other side of the spectrum, a whole database. As can be observed from Figure 6.4, locking individual columns provides the highest level of concurrency. By this we mean that multiple users could be updating different columns in the same row simultaneously. They would not be involved in lock conflict.

If the lock granularity is implemented at the database level, the lowest level of concurrency is achieved. Multiple users could not simultaneously change anything at all in the database. If they tried, they would be involved in lock conflict.

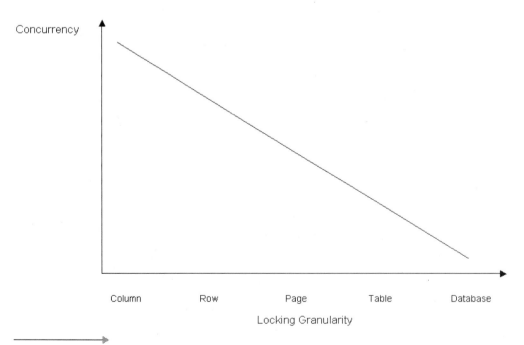

**Figure 6.4**   *Concurrency versus locking granularity*

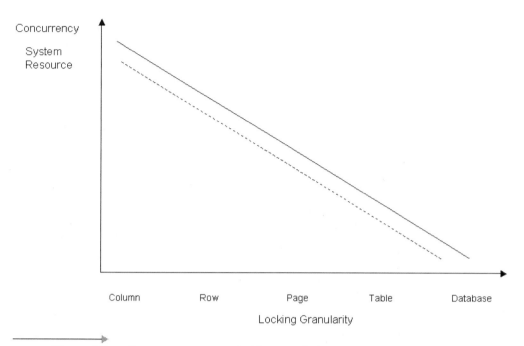

**Figure 6.5**   *System resource versus locking granularity*

So, if locking individual columns provides the highest level of concurrency, why do SQL Server and databases in general not lock at the column level? To explain this we need to add some more information to our graph.

In Figure 6.5, we have added system resource use to our graph. It can be seen that an increase in system resource use parallels an increase in lock granularity. The finer the granularity, the more system resource used.

This is why SQL Server and databases in general do not lock at the column level. The system resource use in terms of the number of locks required and their management would be too great. Locks are approximately 100 bytes each in SQL Server 2000. Using 100 bytes of memory to lock a ten-byte column seems a little over the top. To lock at the column level would probably use tens of thousands of locks in a medium-sized database, which could equate to many megabytes of memory. The CPU resource needed to manage these locks would be massive.

Consequently, SQL Server 2000 locks rows, pages, and tables, which, depending on the application, is a reasonable approach. The database itself can, of course, be set to single-user mode, which effectively provides locking at the database level.

### When are row-level locks used?

Locking at the row level can be considered to be the default situation. Usually, unless you have changed the default behavior, SQL Server will take shared and exclusive locks out on rows. When we refer to rows, we are referring to data rows in the data pages of a table. However, within an index, index pages contain index entries. These can also be locked with a lock equivalent to a row lock, known as a key lock.

Conventionally, the data pages in a table on which there is a clustered index present are considered to be the leaf level of the clustered index—that is, part of the clustered index. For this reason, the row locks on the data rows in a table with a clustered index are managed as key locks. Figure 6.6 shows individual rows being locked within the pages of a table.

Figure 6.7 shows page locks being used to lock the individual pages within a table. In this case one lock will effectively lock all the rows in the page.

### When are table-level locks used?

One of the reasons that SQL Server tends to lock at the row level is that it has the capability to escalate locks but not to deescalate locks. Therefore, if SQL Server decides that a SQL statement is likely to lock the majority of rows in a table, it may lock at the table level. The same logic is used if SQL Server determines that most of the rows in a page are likely to be locked—it may take out a page lock instead of multiple row locks.

The advantage to holding a single table lock is due to system resource. Managing a single table lock is less resource intensive than managing multiple row locks, and saving locks will save memory. However, locking at the table level may reduce concurrency—for example, an exclusive lock held at

**row locking in a table**

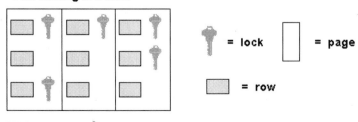

**Figure 6.6**   *Row-level locking*

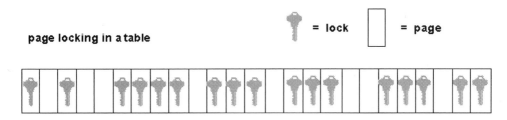

**Figure 6.7**    *Page-level locking*

the table level will block all other users from accessing rows within that table, whether they wish to acquire shared or exclusive locks. Figure 6.8 shows table-level locking.

SQL Server controls when escalation occurs. The database administrator has no control over this, since there is no relevant server configuration option.

**Note:** If a table scan is being used to read data, row locks will be taken out and released in a sequential fashion. If we choose to use certain lock hints— for example, REPEATABLEREAD, discussed later—we are requesting not to release the row lock when we have finished with the row. In this circumstance, when performing a table scan, SQL Server may well take out a table lock if the number of row locks exceeds an internal threshold.

So, we have introduced shared and exclusive locks, as well as page-, table-, and row-level locking. We need to introduce more types of locks before we can give examples of the SQL Server locking protocol in action; but first let us look at lock timeouts and then a phenomenon known as a deadlock or deadly embrace.

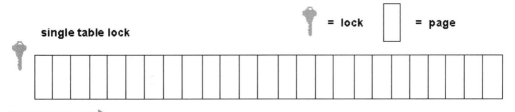

**Figure 6.8**    *Table-level locking*

### 6.3.3   Lock timeouts

If a user's lock is blocked by another lock, the user must wait until the blocking lock is released before he or she can acquire the lock. If the blocking lock is not released for a long time, the user will have to wait for a long time. An application design flaw may mean that the blocking lock is not released at all, and then the database administrator must intervene.

It is possible in SQL Server to set a lock timeout value for a connection so that it will only wait to be granted its lock for a predefined period of time, after which it will receive an error message informing it that the timeout period has been exceeded. This approach assumes that if a lock is kept waiting for a period of time there must be a problem, and it is better that the connection gives up and releases its locks rather than wait indefinitely, perhaps blocking other users. The connection can always try again or log the problem and gracefully inform the user that it cannot proceed.

What constitutes a realistic timeout value? Too long and the user will become impatient, too short and the connection will give up when it would have acquired the lock had it waited a little longer. Personally, I think around ten seconds is not unreasonable.

A lock timeout value is set per connection as follows:

```
SET LOCK_TIMEOUT 10000
```

The timeout value is specified in milliseconds. A value of −1 means wait indefinitely (the default), whereas a value of 0 means do not wait at all. I do not recommend using this value. You could timeout as soon as you attempt to execute a statement, whereas if you had waited a fraction of a second you would have acquired the lock.

If a timeout occurs, an error, 1222, is returned and the connection is rolled back.

To test the value of lock timeout set for a connection the function @@LOCK_TIMEOUT can be used.

### 6.3.4   Deadlocks

A deadlock situation can occur in SQL Server when a user holds a lock on a resource needed by a fellow user who holds a lock on a resource needed by the first user. This is a deadly embrace, and the users would wait forever if SQL Server did not intervene. (See Figure 6.9.)

**Figure 6.9**

*A deadlock between*

*two users*

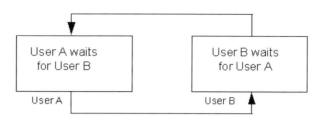

SQL Server chooses one of the deadlocked users as a victim and issues a rollback for its transaction. It will receive an error message similar to the following:

```
Server: Msg 1205, Level 13, State 1, Line 1

Your transaction (Process ID 52) was deadlocked on {lock}
resources with another process and has been chosen as the
deadlock victim. Rerun your transaction.
```

In the application code, this error should be trapped and dealt with cleanly. The application might retry a number of times before giving up and informing the user that there is a problem.

A connection can set its deadlock priority such that, in the event of it being involved in a deadlock, it will be chosen as the victim, as follows:

```
SET DEADLOCK_PRIORITY LOW
```

To return to the default deadlock handling mechanism, use the following code:

```
SET DEADLOCK_PRIORITY NORMAL
```

Generally, the transaction involved in the deadlock that has accumulated the least amount of CPU time is usually chosen as the victim.

## 6.3.5   Update locks

As well as placing shared and exclusive locks on database rows, SQL Server also makes use of a type of lock known as an update lock. These locks are associated with SQL statements that perform update and delete operations, which need to initially read rows before changing or deleting them. These rows have update locks placed on them that are compatible with shared read locks but are not compatible with other update locks or exclusive locks. If the rows must subsequently be updated or deleted, SQL Server attempts to promote the update locks to exclusive locks. If any other shared locks are associated with the rows, SQL Server will not be able to promote the update locks until these are released. In reality the update lock is not promoted, but a second lock is taken out, which is, in fact, an exclusive lock.

Why bother with update locks? Update locks are really an optimization to minimize the possibility of deadlocks. Consider two users, Mike and Katy, who are about to update the same row. Without update locks, each user will take out a shared lock on the row. Shared locks are compatible, so both users will acquire the lock successfully. Mike's UPDATE statement, finding that the row that meets the criteria in its WHERE clause, attempts to take out an exclusive lock on it. Mike's UPDATE statement will now have to wait, since it is blocked by Katy's shared lock.

Katy's UPDATE statement, finding that the row meets the criteria in its WHERE clause, attempts to take out an exclusive lock on the row. Katy's UPDATE statement cannot take out the exclusive lock, since it is blocked by Mike's shared lock. Her update statement would also be forced to wait, except that this is clearly a deadlock. SQL Server will choose a victim and its transaction will be rolled back. This is shown in Figure 6.10.

Now let us take the same example, but this time we will make use of update locks. This is exactly what SQL Server does.

When Mike issues his UPDATE statement, he now takes out an update lock on the row instead of a shared lock. Katy's UPDATE statement also attempts to take out an update lock on the row, but update locks are not compatible so she will be forced to wait. Mike's UPDATE statement, find-

**Figure 6.10**
*A deadlock caused by two users updating the same page*

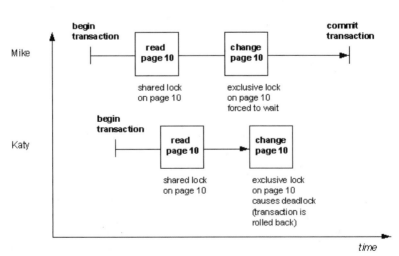

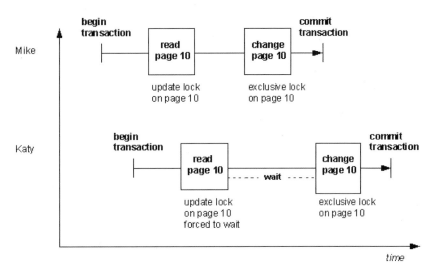

**Figure 6.11**
*A deadlock avoided*
*by using update*
*locks*

ing that the row meets the criteria in its WHERE clause, attempts to take out an exclusive lock on the row. Since Katy does not have any locks on the row, Mike's UPDATE statement successfully acquires the exclusive lock and completes. Mike now commits his transaction and releases his locks. Katy's UPDATE statement, which has been waiting, can now proceed. This is shown in Figure 6.11.

Clearly, this is a cleaner mechanism. No transactions are deadlock victims, which means no transactions are cancelled and rolled back. Transactions that are rolled back have their work effectively thrown away. Using update locks, Katy's UPDATE statement merely suffers a short delay.

### 6.3.6   Intent locks

As well as placing shared and exclusive locks on database tables, SQL Server also makes use of a type of lock known as an intent lock. Intent locks are placed on the table and pages in the table when a user locks rows in the table, and they stay in place for the life of the row locks. These locks are used primarily to ensure that a user cannot take out locks on a table or pages in the table that would conflict with another user's row locks. For example, if a user was holding an exclusive row lock and another user wished to take out an exclusive table lock on the table containing the row, the intent lock held on the table by the first user would ensure that its row lock would not be overlooked by the lock manager.

### 6.3.7  Modifying the default locking behavior

There are two ways in which SQL Server's default locking behavior can be modified. Individual SQL statements can be qualified with a keyword known as a lock hint to modify the locking behavior for that particular statement, or a default locking behavior for the connection can be set with the SET TRANSACTION ISOLATION LEVEL statement.

#### Transaction isolation levels

SQL Server allows the transaction isolation level to be set for a connection. This sets a default locking behavior.

Levels of transaction isolation are specified by the ANSI standard, with each one defining the type of phenomenon not permitted while concurrent transactions are running. The higher the isolation level, the more stringent the locking protocol—with the higher levels being a superset of the lower levels. The transaction isolation levels are as follows:

- Read uncommitted

- Read committed

- Repeatable read

- Serializable

The locking behavior that corresponds with read uncommitted provides the least integrity but potentially the best performance. The read committed isolation level provides more integrity than read uncommitted, and the repeatable read isolation level provides even more integrity. The greatest integrity is provided by the serializable isolation level. We have already met dirty reads and the phantom phenomena. Table 6.2 shows whether the

**Table 6.2**   *Isolation Levels and Allowed Locking Phenomena*

| Isolation Level | Dirty Reads | Nonrepeatable Reads Allowed | Phantoms Allowed |
|---|---|---|---|
| Serializable | No | No | No |
| Repeatable Read | No | No | Yes |
| Read Committed | No | Yes | Yes |
| Read Uncommitted | Yes | Yes | Yes |

dirty read and the phantom phenomena are allowed by the various isolation levels.

It can be seen that only the serializable isolation level prevents all these phenomena from occurring.

By default, SQL Server runs at transaction isolation level read committed.

The transaction isolation level is set for the connection with the following syntax:

```
SET TRANSACTION ISOLATION LEVEL READ UNCOMMITTED

SET TRANSACTION ISOLATION LEVEL READ COMMITTED

SET TRANSACTION ISOLATION LEVEL REPEATABLE READ

SET TRANSACTION ISOLATION LEVEL SERIALIZABLE
```

The DBCC utility with the USEROPTIONS parameter can be used to check the current isolation level of the connection, as follows:

```
DBCC USEROPTIONS
```

| Set Option | Value |
| --- | --- |
| textsize | 64,512 |
| language | us_english |
| dateformat | mdy |
| datefirst | 7 |
| quoted_identifier | SET |
| arithabort | SET |
| ansi_null_dflt_on | SET |
| ansi_defaults | SET |
| ansi_warnings | SET |
| ansi_padding | SET |
| ansi_nulls | SET |
| concat_null_yields_null | SET |
| isolation level | repeatable read |

We will study how transaction isolation levels modify locking behavior between users later in this chapter.

### Lock hints

The keywords available as lock hints for modifying locking behavior are as follows:

- HOLDLOCK
- NOLOCK
- PAGLOCK
- READCOMMITTED
- READPAST
- READUNCOMMITTED
- REPEATABLEREAD
- ROWLOCK
- SERIALIZABLE
- TABLOCK
- TABLOCKX
- UPDLOCK
- XLOCK

Some of these hints are supported for backward compatibility such as:

- HOLDLOCK
- NOLOCK

The recommended hints to use instead are as follows:

- SERIALIZABLE
- READUNCOMMITTED

Some hints enable the developer to specify the lock granularity, such as:

- PAGLOCK
- ROWLOCK
- TABLOCK
- TABLOCKX

Other hints enable the developer to specify the transaction isolation level behavior at the statement level, such as:

- READUNCOMMITTED
- READCOMMITTED

- REPEATABLEREAD

- SERIALIZABLE

  Lock hints are used, for example, on a SELECT statement, as follows:

```
SELECT * FROM branches WITH (SERIALIZABLE)
```

```
SELECT balance FROM accounts WITH (READUNCOMMITTED)
   WHERE account_no = 1000
```

The effect of these lock hints is described in the following text.

### HOLDLOCK

The HOLDLOCK hint forces a shared lock on a table to remain until the transaction completes. Key range locking will also be used to prevent phantom inserts. Nonrepeatable reads are also prevented This is equivalent to the SERIALIZABLE hint. Data consistency will be provided to the level experienced by transactions running at transaction isolation level SERIALIZABLE.

Using the HOLDLOCK keyword may, and usually will, degrade performance, since lock contention may increase.

### NOLOCK

The NOLOCK hint allows a dirty read to take place—that is, a transaction can read the uncommitted changes made by another transaction. The exclusive locks of other transactions are not honoured, and the statement using this hint will not take out shared locks. This is equivalent to the READUNCOMMITTED hint. Data consistency will be provided to the level experienced by transactions running at transaction isolation level READ UNCOMMITTED.

Using the NOLOCK keyword may increase performance, since lock contention may decrease, but this will be at the risk of lower consistency.

### PAGLOCK

The PAGLOCK hint forces shared page locks to be taken where otherwise SQL Server may have used a table or row lock. For example, consider the following statement:

```
SELECT balance FROM accounts WITH (REPEATABLEREAD,
PAGLOCK)
```

If there is no appropriate index, the query optimizer will choose a table scan as the strategy used to execute the query. Depending on the number of rows that may be locked, the lock manager will take out row locks or perhaps a table lock because the REPEATABLE READ lock hint will force the shared row locks to be held until the end of the transaction, and therefore a single table lock is far more efficient. The PAGLOCK hint will ensure that the lock manager will use page locking instead of table locking or row locking. This hint does not only apply to shared locks. Exclusive page locks will also be forced if, say, an UPDATE statement rather than a SELECT statement was using the hint.

### READCOMMITTED

The READCOMMITTED hint ensures that the statement behaves in the same way as if the connection were set to transaction isolation level READ COMMITTED. This is the default behavior for SQL Server. Shared locks will be used when data is read, which prevents dirty reads, but the shared locks are released at the end of the read and are not kept until the end of the transaction. This means that nonrepeatable reads or phantom inserts are not prevented.

### READPAST

This lock hint enables a statement to skip rows that are locked by other statements. The READPAST lock hint applies only to transactions operating at READ COMMITTED isolation level and will read only past row-level locks. This is only valid on a SELECT statement. This is useful when, for example, multiple transactions are reading items from a queue implemented as a table and a transaction wants to skip a locked queue item and read another item to process.

### READUNCOMMITTED

This lock hint is equivalent to the NOLOCK lock hint.

### REPEATABLEREAD

The REPEATABLEREAD hint ensures that the statement behaves in the same way as if the connection were set to transaction isolation level REPEATABLE READ. This is not the default behavior for SQL Server. Shared locks will be used when data is read, and these will not be released until the end of the transaction. This means that nonrepeatable reads are prevented. However, phantom inserts are not prevented. This lock hint may reduce concurrency, since shared locks are held for longer periods of time than if the default read committed behavior is used.

## ROWLOCK

This hint forces the use of rowlocks and is similar in use to PAGLOCK.

## SERIALIZABLE

The SERIALIZABLE hint forces shared locks to stay until the transaction completes. This is equivalent to specifying the HOLDLOCK hint. Key range locking will be used to prevent phantom inserts if indexes are present. Nonrepeatable reads are also prevented. Data consistency will be provided to the level experienced by transactions running at transaction isolation level SERIALIZABLE.

Using the SERIALIZABLE keyword may, and usually will, degrade performance, since lock contention may increase.

## TABLOCK

The TABLOCK hint forces a shared table lock to be taken where otherwise SQL Server may have used row locks. It will not be held until the end of the transaction unless hints such as REPEATABLEREAD are also used.

## TABLOCKX

The TABLOCKX hint forces an exclusive table lock to be taken. It will be held until the end of the transaction

## UPDLOCK

The UPDLOCK hint forces SQL Server to take update locks where otherwise SQL Server would have used shared locks. The update locks are held until the end of the transaction. Update locks are compatible with shared locks but not exclusive locks or other update locks.

## XLOCK

This hints forces exclusive locks to be taken out. It is typically used with TABLOCK and PAGLOCK.

## 6.3.8   Locking in system tables

Transact-SQL statements such as CREATE TABLE manipulate system tables. For example, when a table is created, rows are inserted into the sysobjects, sysindexes, and syscolumns system tables. Data definition language (DDL) statements can appear in explicit transactions, and, therefore, any locks taken out as a result of actions to the system tables can be held for a period of time—blocking other users if the developer is not careful. Here are some examples of DDL statements that can appear in an explicit transaction.

| | |
|---|---|
| ALTER TABLE | DROP PROCEDURE |
| CREATE DEFAULT | DROP RULE |
| CREATE INDEX | DROP TABLE |
| CREATE PROCEDURE | DROP TRIGGER |
| CREATE RULE | DROP VIEW |
| CREATE TABLE | GRANT |
| CREATE TRIGGER | REVOKE |
| CREATE VIEW | SELECT INTO |
| DROP DEFAULT | TRUNCATE TABLE |
| DROP INDEX | |

As an example of this behavior, suppose a table is created in an explicit transaction. SQL Server takes out exclusive locks in the sysobjects, sysindexes, and syscolumns system tables. These locks are key locks, since each of these system tables has a clustered index present. If the transaction does not complete, a query issued in another connection against these system tables will be blocked. For example, a CREATE TABLE statement issued within an explicit transaction will block an sp_help issued on another connection. It is important, therefore, that these transactions are committed quickly.

Note that Sch-M locks are taken when a table data definition language (DDL) operation is being executed. This is incompatible with all other lock types.

## 6.3.9  Monitoring locks

Finally, we need to introduce the means by which we can observe SQL Server lock management in action, and then we can look at some examples of the SQL Server locking protocol. There are a number of ways to find information about the locking that is happening within SQL Server. These include the following:

- Use the sp_lock system stored procedure.
- Use the SQL Enterprise Manager.

- Use the Performance Monitor.

- Interrogate the system table syslockinfo directly.

- Use the SQL Profiler.

Additionally, the sp_who system stored procedure is useful in finding blocked and blocking processes, and the DBCC utility can be used to set trace flags to record lock and deadlock information.

### Using the sp_lock system stored procedure

The sp_lock system stored procedure displays information about the locks held by processes using the server. It can be entered as a standalone statement, in which case it will display all locks managed by the server, or it can take up to two SQL Server process identifiers (SPIDs) as a parameter. Some example output from the sp_lock system stored procedure is as follows:

```
EXEC sp_lock
```

| spid | dbid | ObjId | IndId | Type | Resource | Mode | Status |
|------|------|-------|-------|------|----------|------|--------|
| 51 | 7 | 0 | 0 | DB | | S | GRANT |
| 51 | 7 | 965578478 | 2 | PAG | 1:113 | IS | GRANT |
| 51 | 7 | 965578478 | 2 | KEY | (4501518d90d1) | S | GRANT |
| 51 | 7 | 965578478 | 0 | RID | 1:348:14 | S | GRANT |
| 51 | 7 | 965578478 | 0 | PAG | 1:348 | IS | GRANT |
| 51 | 7 | 965578478 | 0 | TAB | | IS | GRANT |
| 52 | 7 | 965578478 | 0 | TAB | | IX | GRANT |
| 52 | 7 | 965578478 | 0 | PAG | 1:348 | IX | GRANT |
| 52 | 7 | 965578478 | 0 | RID | 1:348:14 | X | CNVT |
| 52 | 7 | 965578478 | 0 | RID | 1:348:14 | U | GRANT |
| 52 | 7 | 965578478 | 2 | KEY | (4501518d90d1) | U | GRANT |
| 52 | 7 | 965578478 | 2 | PAG | 1:113 | IU | GRANT |
| 52 | 7 | 0 | 0 | DB | | S | GRANT |

**Hint:** To translate the ObjId to a table name, use the built-in system function OBJECT_NAME. For example:

```
SELECT OBJECT_NAME (965578478)
--------
accounts
```

The above output from sp_lock shows a number of locks held on various objects. Let us discuss the meaning of the columns in the output before we investigate the rows.

The first column contains the SPID value. A client connection to SQL Server is allocated an SPID value, and each row in the output represents a lock requested by the SPID that has not been released at the time sp_lock was executed. A typical server will be managing many locks at a given instance in time, so it is often more practical to limit the output to a particular SPID or pair of SPIDs by supplying these values as parameters.

The next five columns, dbid, ObjId, IndId, Type, and Resource, help to define the resource that is locked. We know already that SQL Server locks objects such as rows and tables, and these columns let us know what type of resource is locked as well as which instance of this resource type. The dbid column contains the database ID, the ObjId column contains the object ID, and the IndId contains the index ID. This column can contain the values 0, to represent the table itself; 1, the clustered index, if one is present; > 1 for a nonclustered index; and 255 for TEXT/IMAGE data. The Type column tells us the type of resource locked, such as a row or page, and, finally, the Resource column provides information to completely identify the resource instance. Whether these columns contain data depends on the type of resource being locked. For example, in the case of a database, the Resource column is empty.

The Mode column tells us whether we have a shared lock or exclusive lock or one of a myriad of other modes of lock on our resource. Finally, the Status column shows us whether the lock has been granted (GRANT), is waiting to be granted (WAIT), or is waiting to be converted to another mode (CNVT). When investigating lock problems, I often hunt first for locks that have not been granted. They normally relate to the blocked user and represent a small number of locks on the system. Let us now look at the connections in our example.

All the connections—that is, SPIDs—have been granted a shared lock on the database with ID value 7.

```
51   7   0      0   DB        S   GRANT
52   7   0      0   DB        S   GRANT
```

An easy way to translate the dbid to a database name is to execute the system stored procedure sp_helpdb, which returns this information in its display. Alternatively, use the function DB_NAME(). The reason the connections have been granted a shared lock is that any connection that has selected a database with a USE statement explicitly or implicitly via the drop-down list in the query analyzer is granted such a lock. This is used to manage such operations as a connection attempting to set the database to single-user mode.

Let us investigate the locks held by SPID 51. Apart from the database lock, it has requested and been granted shared (S) locks on two resources: a KEY and a RID.

```
51    7    965578478    2    KEY    (4501518d90d1)    S    GRANT
51    7    965578478    0    RID    1:348:14          S    GRANT
```

A RID is a row lock on a data row on a data page. A KEY lock is a row lock on an index entry (key plus pointer) on an index page.

---

**Note:** Conventionally, the data pages in a table with a clustered index are considered to be part of the clustered index. For that reason a row lock on a data row on a data page in such a table is considered to be a KEY lock, not a RID lock.

---

If we take the row lock first, we can see that the resource information shows us that we have a dbid value of 7, which represents the database BankingDB, and an ObjId value of 965578478, which, when translated with the OBJECT_NAME function, represents the table, Accounts, in this database. The IndId column contains a value of 0, which represents the table rather than an index on the table. The Resource column value is 1:348:14, which specifies that the resource in the table is identified as file ID 1, page 348, slot 14. This uniquely identifies a row on the page. The file ID must be present, since page numbers are only unique with a database file.

---

**Hint:** To convert a file ID to a filename, use the FILE_NAME() function.

---

If we look at the KEY lock, we can see the same values in the dbid and ObjId columns, but there is a value of 2 in the IndId column.

The following Transact-SQL will translate this index ID to an index name.

```
SELECT name FROM SYSINDEXES
    WHERE
    id = OBJECT_ID('Accounts') AND
    indid = 2
```

Of course, since we already know the object ID value, we could have just used this instead of translating the object name.

So we now know the index in which our KEY lock is held. The Resource column value is (4501518d90d1). This is of little use to us, since it is a hexadecimal number, which is the result of some hash function used internally, presumably used on the key value and other inputs.

The other locks held by SPID 51 are intent locks.

```
51    7    965578478    2    PAG    1:113         IS    GRANT
51    7    965578478    0    PAG    1:348         IS    GRANT
51    7    965578478    0    TAB                  IS    GRANT
```

We discussed intent locks earlier in the chapter. We stated that intent locks are placed on the table and pages in the table when a user locks rows in the table, and they stay in place for the life of the row locks. We can see that a shared intent (IS) lock has been taken out on page 1:348 and page 1:113. This is expected behavior, since we have a row lock held in data page 1:348. Page 1:113 will be the index page containing the locked index entry. Both of these pages are subordinate to the table, and so we see an intent lock on the table. These intent locks will prevent, for example, another connection from taking out an exclusive (X) lock on the table while our connection has shared (S) locks on rows in the table.

Those were the locks held by SPID 51. Let us now investigate the locks held by SPID 52. They are repeated here for clarity.

```
52    7    965578478    0    TAB                  IX    GRANT
52    7    965578478    0    PAG    1:348         IX    GRANT
52    7    965578478    0    RID    1:348:14      X     CNVT
52    7    965578478    0    RID    1:348:14      U     GRANT
52    7    965578478    2    KEY    (4501518d90d1)  U   GRANT
52    7    965578478    2    PAG    1:113         IU    GRANT
52    7    0            0    DB                   S     GRANT
```

We can see that SPID 52 has been granted two update (U) locks. These are compatible with shared (S) locks, as we described earlier in the chapter, and are used in UPDATE and DELETE statements during the search phase, when target rows are being identified. In fact, SPID 52 has issued an UPDATE statement, which is attempting to change a row on which SPID 51 has shared (S) locks. Both update (U) locks have been granted, and the columns in the display contain values that are the same as the shared (S) locks on the KEY and RID for SPID 51. However, we can see that SPID 52 also has a lock that has not been granted.

```
52    7    965578478    0    RID    1:348:14      X     CNVT
```

The lock manager has attempted to convert an update (U) lock to an exclusive (X) lock in order to change the row. It cannot do this, since SPID

51 has a shared (S) lock on this row and we know that these locks are incompatible. For this reason the lock is now waiting to be converted, at which point it will have a status of GRANT. If the blocked lock were a new lock that the connection had tried to acquire, rather than the conversion of an existing lock, we would have seen a status of WAIT.

The intent locks behave in a fashion similar to those for SPID 51.

```
52    7    965578478    0    TAB              IX    GRANT
52    7    965578478    0    PAG    1:348     IX    GRANT
52    7    965578478    2    PAG    1:113     IU    GRANT
```

Exclusive intent (IX) locks have been granted on the data page and table, since these are compatible with the shared intent (IS) locks of SPID 51. An update intent (IU) lock has also been granted on the index page, since an update lock (U) has been granted on the index entry. The lock manager is not going to take out an exclusive (X) lock on the index entry, since the index column was not being updated.

### Using the SQL Server Enterprise Manager

The SQL Server Enterprise Manager allows the database administrator to monitor current locking activity in a graphical manner. The server should be expanded and the Management folder followed by Current Activity. The console tree is shown in Figure 6.12.

If we expand Process Info and hide the console tree, we find the display shown in Figure 6.13.

SQL Server Enterprise Manager allows us to move columns and sort by a particular column. I have moved the columns in the display and sorted by the Database column to make the display more useful. We now see the display shown in Figure 6.14.

The display is mainly formed from the information obtained by executing the system stored procedures sp_lock and sp_who (described later).

Notice that we can easily see the blocking and blocked SPID and the resource involved.

This blocking can often be seen more clearly if the Locks/Process ID folder is expanded, as shown in Figure 6.15.

We can clearly see the blocked connection and the blocker. By selecting the blocked connection in the console tree, we can find information about the locks involved.

**Figure 6.12**
*The Current
Activity folder*

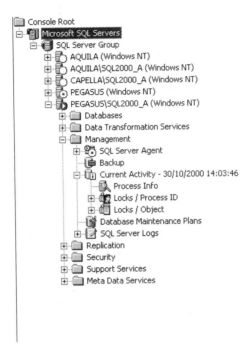

The Locks/Object folder displays lock information for a particular object. This is shown in Figure 6.16.

The Accounts table object in the console tree has been selected, and the locks pertaining to this object are displayed.

Note that for any of the three Current Activity folders an item in the detail pane can be double-clicked to display more information about the connection. This is shown in Figure 6.17.

As can be seen, the last Transact-SQL statement executed is displayed. This window also allows the database administrator to terminate a connection (Kill Process) or send a message to the user.

### Using the System Monitor

The System Monitor is a Windows 2000 utility that enables system managers and database administrators to monitor the many objects within a Windows 2000 system. There are many counters that can be monitored for many objects, but here we are interested in those counters specific to the SQL Server:Locks object. These counters are shown in Table 6.3.

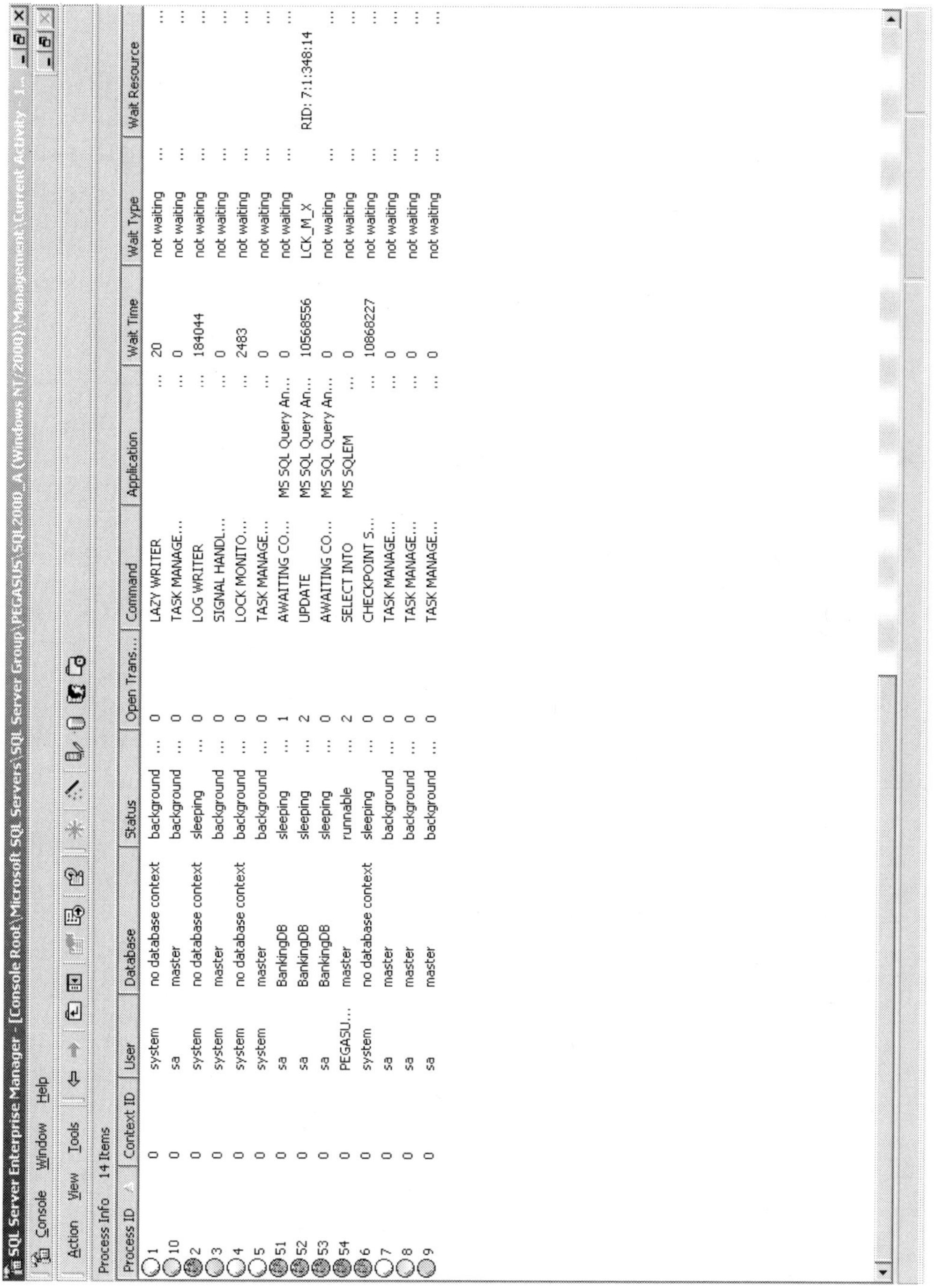

**Figure 6.13** *The Process Info folder*

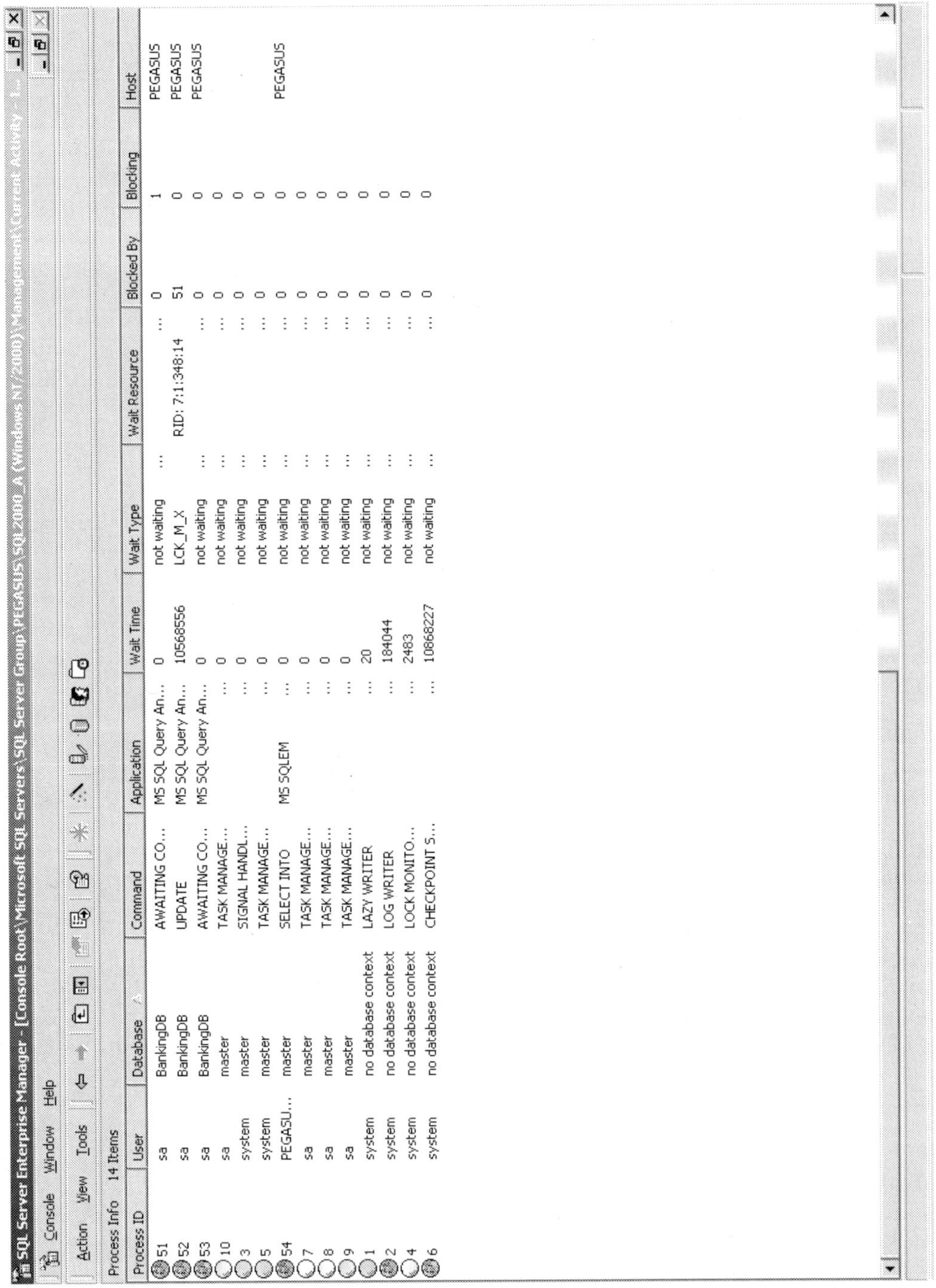

**Figure 6.14**    *The Process Info folder after customizing*

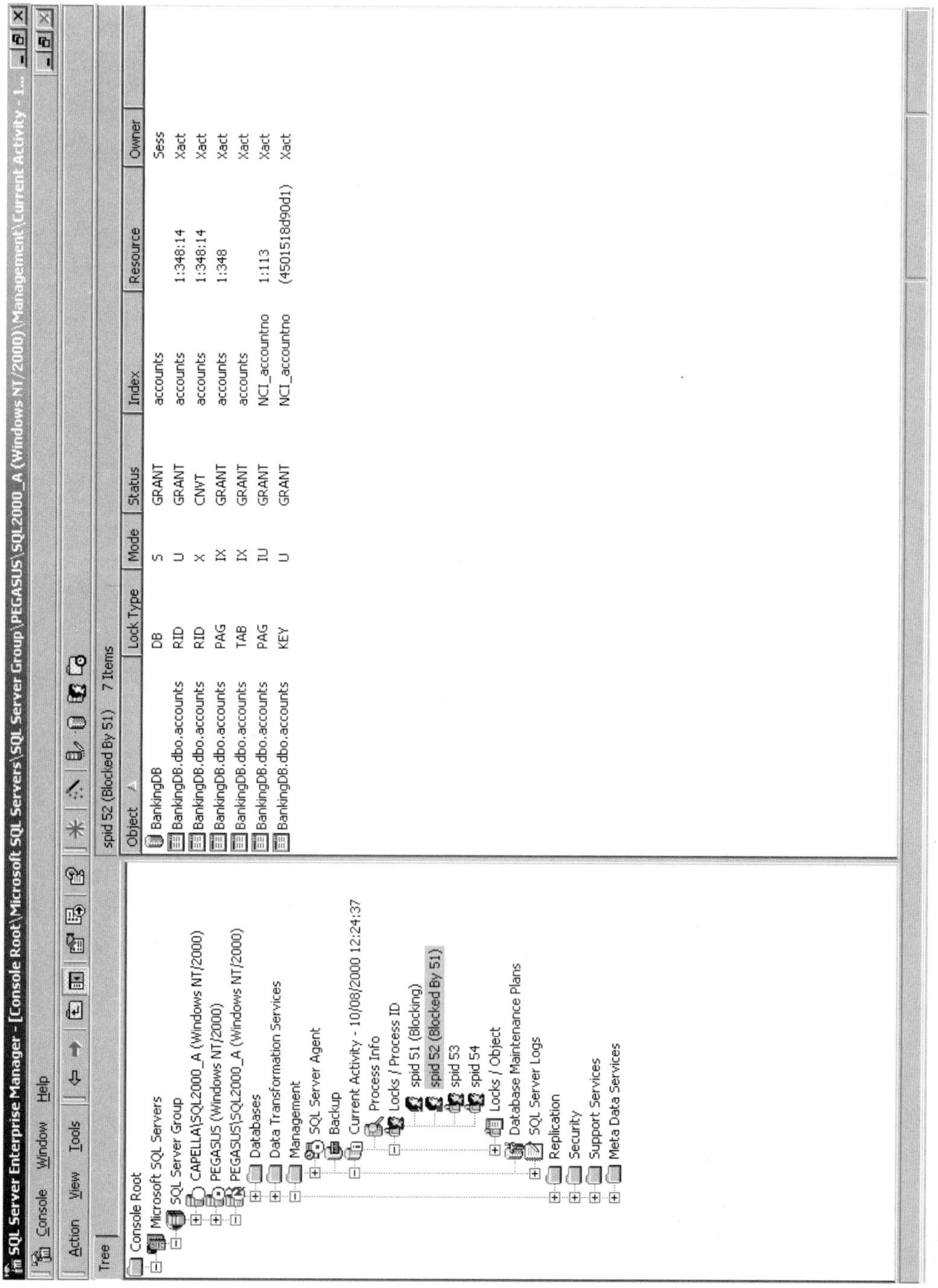

**Figure 6.15**   *The Locks/Process ID folder*

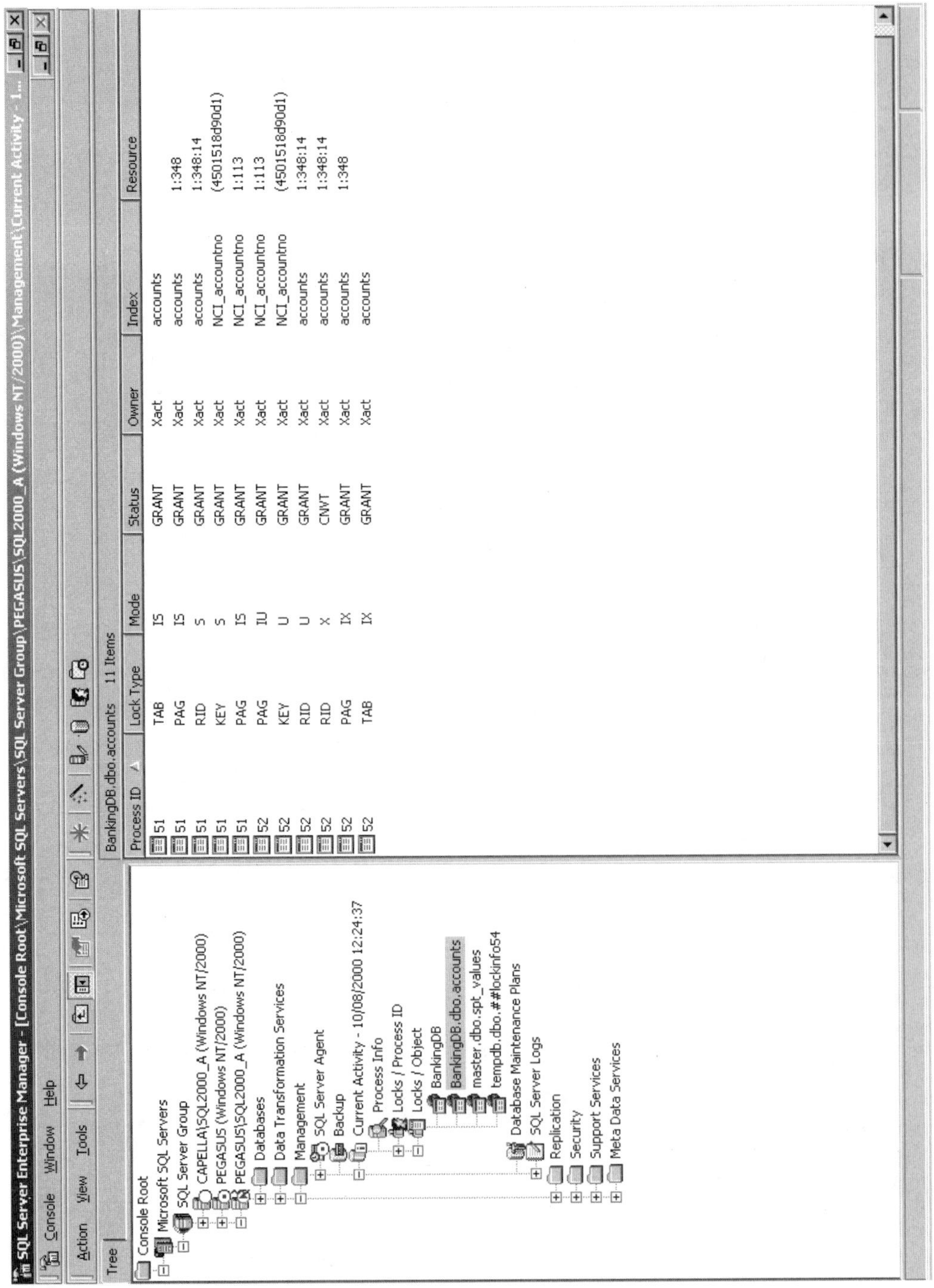

**Figure 6.16**   *The Locks/Object Folder*

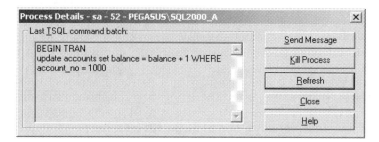

**Figure 6.17**
*The Process Details window*

The counters shown in Table 6.3 are for a particular instance of locked object. The instances that can be monitored are as follows:

- RID

- Key

- Page

- Extent

- Table

- Database

- Total

This allows us to monitor counters for a particular type of lock or for all locks (Total).

**Table 6.3**   *Counters Monitored for the SQL Server Lock Object*

| SQL Server: Locks Object Counters | Explanation |
| --- | --- |
| Average Wait Time (ms) | Average amount of wait time (in milliseconds) for each lock request that resulted in a wait |
| Lock Requests/sec | Number of new locks and lock conversions per second requested from the lock manager |
| Lock Timeouts/sec | Number of lock requests per second that timed out, including internal requests for NOWAIT locks |
| Lock Wait Time (ms) | Total wait time (in milliseconds) for locks in the last second |
| Lock Waits/sec | Number of lock requests per second that could not be satisfied immediately and required the caller to wait before being granted the lock |
| Number of Deadlocks/sec | Number of lock requests per second that resulted in a deadlock |

**Note:** The System Monitor differentiates between SQL Server 2000 instances. An instance named PEGASUS\SQL2000_A running on server PEGASUS will have a locks object named MSSQL$SQL2000_A:Locks. The System Monitor is described in Chapter 7.

### Interrogating the SYSLOCKINFO Table

The syslockinfo system table can be interrogated in the same way that any other system table can be interrogated. It is only found in the master database, where it holds information concerning the locks held in SQL Server. Unlike most other system tables, it is materialized when a query is executed that accesses it; otherwise, it does not exist physically. A query issued against the syslockinfo table produces the following output:

```
SELECT rsc_text, rsc_dbid, rsc_indid, rsc_objid, rsc_type, req_mode, req_status,
req_spid
   FROM syslockinfo
```

| rsc_text | rsc_dbid | rsc_indid | rsc_objid | rsc_type | req_mode | req_status | req_spid |
|----------|----------|-----------|-----------|----------|----------|------------|----------|
|  | 7 | 0 | 0 | 2 | 3 | 1 | 52 |
|  | 7 | 0 | 0 | 2 | 3 | 1 | 51 |
| 1:113 | 7 | 2 | 965578478 | 6 | 7 | 1 | 52 |
| 1:113 | 7 | 2 | 965578478 | 6 | 6 | 1 | 51 |
| (4501518d90d1) | 7 | 2 | 965578478 | 7 | 4 | 1 | 52 |
| (4501518d90d1) | 7 | 2 | 965578478 | 7 | 3 | 1 | 51 |
| 1:348:14 | 7 | 0 | 965578478 | 9 | 4 | 1 | 52 |
| : | | | | | | | |
| : | | | | | | | |

Not all the columns from syslockinfo have been displayed, since some are a binary representation of the ones shown and some are for Microsoft internal use. The displayed columns have the definitions shown in Table 6.4.

Examples of common values for rsc_type are shown in Table 6.5.

Apart from the locks we have already discussed, there are several other types of locks. File locks tend to be acquired when a file is being added to a database, or a file is being shrunk, or similar file-related activities. Extent locks are used by SQL Server to internally manage the allocation and deallocation of extents. Extents, as discussed in Chapter 2, are of type mixed and uniform and are 64 KB (eight pages) in size. These locks can often be seen while you are inserting rows into a table. Index locks can be seen when an index is being created on a table.

**Table 6.4**   *Column Definitions for the syslockinfo System Table*

| Column | Definition |
| --- | --- |
| rsc_text | Textual description of a lock resource |
| rsc_dbid | The database ID of the resource |
| rsc_indid | The index ID of the resource if an index |
| rsc_objid | The object ID of the resource if an object |
| rsc_type | The type of resource—e.g., page |
| req_mode | The mode of the lock—e.g., shared(S) |
| req_status | The status of the lock—e.g., granted |
| req_spid | The SPID owning the lock |

The column req_mode represents the mode of the lock requested. We have discussed most of the common ones. There are, however, a number of more obscure modes, and we will list these here for completeness. Numbers greater than 12 are used for key range locks, discussed later. The req_mode values are listed in Table 6.6.

The schema stability locks are used to control access to schema objects such as tables to avoid problems where multiple connections are referencing an object that a connection wishes to modify or drop. The SIX, SIU, and

**Table 6.5**   *Values for the rsc_type Column in syslockinfo*

| Value | Type |
| --- | --- |
| 1 | NULL Resource |
| 2 | Database |
| 3 | File |
| 4 | Index |
| 5 | Table |
| 6 | Page |
| 7 | Key |
| 8 | Extent |
| 9 | RID |

**Table 6.6**   *Values for the req_mode Column in syslockinfo*

| Value | Lock Mode Code | Lock Mode Name |
|---|---|---|
| 0 | NULL | Used as a placeholder only |
| 1 | Sch-S | Schema stability |
| 2 | Sch-M | Schema modification |
| 3 | S | Shared |
| 4 | U | Update |
| 5 | X | Exclusive |
| 6 | IS | Intent Shared |
| 7 | IU | Intent Update |
| 8 | IX | Intent Exclusive |
| 9 | SIU | Shared Intent Update |
| 10 | SIX | Shared Intent Exclusive |
| 11 | UIX | Update Intent Exclusive |
| 12 | BU | Bulk |

UIX locks are special kinds of intent locks. The bulk lock is used when bulk loads are being performed into a table—for example, when the data transformation services BULK INSERT task is used to load data into a table and the option Table Lock has been set on the task. There are also some other lock modes used for serializable transactions, which we will discuss later.

Finally, the req_status column contains just three values, as shown in Table 6.7.

**Table 6.7**   *Values for the req_status Column in syslockinfo*

| Value | Status |
|---|---|
| 1 | Granted |
| 2 | Converting |
| 3 | Waiting |

### Using the system procedure sp_who

The system procedure sp_who can be used to obtain information on the processes active within SQL Server. It can be entered as a standalone statement, in which case it will display information about all users and processes. It can take a SQL Server process identifier (spid) or alternatively a SQL Server login name as a parameter. Also, the parameter value ACTIVE can be used, which eliminates user connections that are waiting for input from the user—that is, with AWAITING COMMAND in the cmd column. Some example output from the sp_who system stored procedure is as follows:

| SPID | ecid | status | loginame | hostname | blk | dbname | cmd |
|------|------|--------|----------|----------|-----|--------|-----|
| 1 | 0 | background | sa | | 0 | NULL | LAZY WRITER |
| 2 | 0 | sleeping | sa | | 0 | NULL | LOG WRITER |
| 3 | 0 | background | sa | | 0 | master | SIGNAL HANDLER |
| 4 | 0 | background | sa | | 0 | NULL | LOCK MONITOR |
| 5 | 0 | background | sa | | 0 | master | TASK MANAGER |
| 6 | 0 | sleeping | sa | | 0 | NULL | CHECKPOINT SLEEP |
| 7 | 0 | background | sa | | 0 | master | TASK MANAGER |
| 8 | 0 | background | sa | | 0 | master | TASK MANAGER |
| 9 | 0 | background | sa | | 0 | master | TASK MANAGER |
| 10 | 0 | background | sa | | 0 | master | TASK MANAGER |
| 51 | 0 | runnable | sa | PEGASUS | 0 | master | SELECT |
| 52 | 0 | sleeping | dave | PEGASUS | 0 | BankingDB | AWAITING COMMAND |
| 53 | 0 | sleeping | sue | PEGASUS | 52 | BankingDB | UPDATE |
| 54 | 0 | sleeping | tony | PEGASUS | 0 | BankingDB | AWAITING COMMAND |

Note that the process with SPID 53 has a value of 52 in the blk column, whereas other processes have 0. This is because the process with SPID 53 is being blocked by another user—in fact, the user with SPID 52.

**Note:** Microsoft also ships a stored procedure, called sp_who2. This outputs more information and in a slightly more readable form than sp_who.

### The SQL Server Profiler

The SQL Server Profiler will be discussed in detail in Chapter 7. However, we need to mention it here, since it has capabilities that help us investigate lock problems. The SQL Server Profiler allows us to trace events graphically into a table and/or into a file. If the events are captured into a file or table, they can be analyzed later.

**Table 6.8**    *Lock Event Classes in the SQL Server Profiler*

| Event Class | Description |
|---|---|
| Lock:Acquired | A lock has been taken out on a row, page, etc. |
| Lock:Cancel | A held lock has been cancelled—e.g., by a deadlock. |
| Lock:Deadlock | A deadlock has occurred. |
| Lock:Deadlock Chain | The events preceding a deadlock. |
| Lock:Escalation | Lock escalation has occurred—e.g., a row escalated to a table. |
| Lock:Released | A lock has been taken off on a row, page, etc. |
| Lock:Timeout | A lock has timed out. |

The Locks Event Category contains a number of Locks Event Classes, and these are shown in Table 6.8.

When an event is traced, the SQL Server Profiler captures various pieces of information about the event. These pieces of information are specified as Data Columns in the trace definition. Many data columns always contain the same information, regardless of the event class being traced. For example, the CPU column is the amount of CPU in milliseconds used by the event. However, some data columns contain values that are specific to a particular event class. For the Lock Event Class there are some very useful data columns.

Generally, the Binary Data column contains the resource ID for a lock event class and the Object ID contains the ID of the object participating in the lock. Duration tends to represent wait time and the Mode represents the lock mode.

With a little practice some elements of the resource ID can be recognized and decoded as the lock type. If the SQL Server Profiler is being used interactively, this is done for you. Selecting the lock event with the mouse pointer will display the lock type.

### Using Trace Flags with DBCC

The SQL Server documentation states that trace flag behavior may or may not be supported in future releases. It is worth mentioning this here, though, since trace flags can be used to provide some lock trace information. The database consistency checker, more usually referred to as DBCC, can be used to set trace flags, or they can be set if SQL Server is started at the command line or via the Startup Parameters in the General tab of Server Properties in the SQL Server Enterprise Manager. Trace information can be sent to destinations such as the errorlog (using trace flag 3605) or the client (using trace flag 3604). Locking information can be generated by setting the trace flags to 1200 or, for deadlock information, 1204 and 1205. An example trace output is as follows:

### Trace Flag 1204

```
DBCC TRACEON (3604,1200)

SELECT SUM(balance) FROM accounts

Process 51 acquiring S lock on KEY: 7:1:2 (9c0206b5c98d) (class bit0 ref1) result: OK
Process 51 acquiring S lock on KEY: 7:1:1 (ee006c4e98d2) (class bit0 ref1) result: OK
Process 51 acquiring Schema lock on TAB: 7:965578478 [] (class bit0 ref1) result: OK
Process 51 acquiring S lock on KEY: 7:3:2 (9302d58cf78b) (class bit0 ref1) result: OK

:
Process 51 acquiring S lock on PAG: 7:1:41 (class bit0 ref1) result: OK
Process 51 releasing lock on PAG: 7:1:41
Process 51 acquiring S lock on PAG: 7:1:42 (class bit0 ref1) result: OK
Process 51 releasing lock on PAG: 7:1:42
Process 51 acquiring S lock on PAG: 7:1:50 (class bit0 ref1) result: OK
Process 51 releasing lock on PAG: 7:1:50
Process 51 acquiring S lock on PAG: 7:1:91 (class bit0 ref1) result: OK
Process 51 releasing lock on PAG: 7:1:91
Process 51 acquiring S lock on PAG: 7:1:160 (class bit0 ref1) result: OK
Process 51 releasing lock on PAG: 7:1:160
:
Process 51 releasing lock on TAB: 7:965578478 []
```

The output can be somewhat cryptic, but with a little effort a database administrator can follow what is happening. In this example, SPID 51 is performing a table scan and, after some initial reading of the system tables, is sequentially reading pages. When it wants to read a page, it requests and acquires a page lock; when it has read a page, it releases the page lock. Note that page locks refer to page numbers, whereas table locks (we will have taken out an intent table lock) refer to the object ID of the table. As we have seen, the OBJECT_NAME() function can be used to find the table name, as follows:

```
SELECT OBJECT_NAME (965578478)
-----------------------------
accounts
```

Whether tables or pages are being referenced, the number preceding the object ID or page number is the database ID. The DB_NAME() function can be used to find the database name, as follows:

```
SELECT DB_NAME(7)
-----------------
BankingDB
```

To find which object a page belongs, use the DBCC PAGE statement, as follows:

```
DBCC TRACEON (3604)
DBCC PAGE (7,1,50,0)


PAGE: (1:50)
------------

BUFFER:
-------

BUF @0x10EB7FC0
---------------
bpage = 0x1BA2E000      bhash = 0x00000000      bpageno = (1:50)
bdbid = 7               breferences = 1         bstat = 0x9
bspin = 0               bnext = 0x00000000

PAGE HEADER:
------------

Page @0x1BA2E000
----------------
m_pageId = (1:50)       m_headerVersion = 1     m_type = 1
m_typeFlagBits = 0x0    m_level = 0             m_flagBits = 0x8000
m_objId = 965578478     m_indexId = 0           m_prevPage = (0:0)
m_nextPage = (0:0)      pminlen = 424           m_slotCnt = 16
m_freeCnt = 1232        m_freeData = 6928       m_reservedCnt = 0
m_lsn = (1274:16:151)   m_xactReserved = 0      m_xdesId = (0:0)
m_ghostRecCnt = 0       m_tornBits = 805306369

Allocation Status
-----------------
GAM (1:2) = ALLOCATED      SGAM (1:3) = NOT ALLOCATED
PFS (1:1) = 0x63 MIXED_EXT ALLOCATED  95_PCT_FULL   DIFF (1:6) = CHANGED
ML (1:7) = NOT MIN_LOGGED
```

The field containing the object ID is in bold type. Note also that to the right of that field is the index ID of the index to which the page belongs, if it is an index page.

The DBCC PAGE statement is specifying, in order, the database ID of 7, the file ID of 1, the page number 50, and 0 to indicate that we only need to see the header, not the data.

### Trace Flag 1204

This trace flag returns the type of locks participating in a deadlock and the current commands involved. I usually set this trace flag with trace flag 3605 (log to errorlog) via the Startup Parameters in the General tab of Server Properties in the SQL Server Enterprise Manager. Here is some example output when a deadlock occurred.

```
10:39:49.10 spid4      Deadlock encountered .... Printing deadlock information
10:39:49.10 spid4
10:39:49.10 spid4      Wait-for graph
10:39:49.10 spid4
10:39:49.10 spid4      Node:1
10:39:49.10 spid4      RID: 7:1:537:14               CleanCnt:1 Mode: X Flags: 0x2
10:39:49.10 spid4       Grant List::
10:39:49.10 spid4        Owner:0x1b69f380 Mode: X Flg:0x0 Ref:0 Life:02000000 SPID:55
ECID:0
10:39:49.10 spid4        SPID: 55 ECID: 0 Statement Type: UPDATE Line #: 1
10:39:49.11 spid4        Input Buf: UPDATE CUSTOMERS SET customer_lname = 'Phillips'
                                 WHERE customer_no = 1000
10:39:49.11 spid4       Requested By:
10:39:49.11 spid4         ResType:LockOwner Stype:'OR' Mode: U SPID:53 ECID:0
Ec:(0x1b9e13e0)
                          Value:0x1b6a3300 Cost:(0/A0)
10:39:49.11 spid4
10:39:49.11 spid4      Node:2
10:39:49.11 spid4      RID: 7:1:338:9                CleanCnt:1 Mode: X Flags: 0x2
10:39:49.11 spid4       Grant List::
10:39:49.11 spid4        Owner:0x1b69f2e0 Mode: X        Flg:0x0 Ref:0 Life:02000000
SPID:53 ECID:0
10:39:49.11 spid4        SPID: 53 ECID: 0 Statement Type: UPDATE Line #: 1
10:39:49.11 spid4        Input Buf: UPDATE ACCOUNTS SET balance = 99
                                 WHERE account_no = 2000
10:39:49.11 spid4       Requested By:
10:39:49.11 spid4         ResType:LockOwner Stype:'OR' Mode: U SPID:55 ECID:0
Ec:(0x1c1cd3e0)
                          Value:0x1b6a33c0 Cost:(0/98)
10:39:49.11 spid4      Victim Resource Owner:
10:39:49.11 spid4        ResType:LockOwner Stype:'OR' Mode: U SPID:55 ECID:0
Ec:(0x1c1cd3e0) Value:0x1b6a33c0 Cost:(0/98)
```

I have removed the data from the date/time to fit more information onto the page. We can see that a deadlock was encountered, and by examining the output we can see the following:

- SPID 53 and SPID 55 are involved in a deadlock.

- Resources involved are RID: 7:1:537:14 and RID: 7:1:338:9.

- The last statements sent by the participating connections were:

```
'UPDATE CUSTOMERS SET customer_lname = 'Phillips'
   WHERE customer_no = 1000 '
'UPDATE ACCOUNTS SET balance = 99 WHERE account_no =
2000'
```

- SPID 55 was chosen as the deadlock victim.

- The locks involved were update (U) locks.

### Trace Flag 1205

This trace flag returns more detailed information about the deadlock. You will need to set trace flag 1204 to get information out of trace flag 1205, but, to be honest, the extra information is probably only likely to be useful (and understandable) by Microsoft Support.

## 6.4    SQL Server locking in action

Now that we understand how SQL Server uses its locking protocol, we can look at some examples. Our examples will all follow the same format, that of the T graph. Some people believe it is called a T graph because it looks like a T; others believe it is because the vertical axis represents time! Whatever the reason, it is a useful method for representing the interaction of locks in a multiuser scenario. In order to keep the output as clear as possible, the actual results of the SELECT statements are not shown.

Our examples will use the Accounts table in the BankingDB database. In these examples, all indexes have been removed from this table unless otherwise specified. Also, until we change it, the default locking protocol will be used—that is, transaction isolation level read committed.

| Mike | Katy |
|------|------|
| `SELECT * FROM accounts`<br>`    WHERE account_no = 1000` | `SELECT * FROM accounts`<br>`    WHERE account_no = 2000` |
| `*** OK ***` | `*** OK ***` |

In the above example, Mike retrieves all the rows in the Accounts table. Katy attempts to concurrently retrieve all the rows in the Accounts table and is successful. This is because Mike places and releases shared locks on the rows in the Accounts table as he scans through it. Katy also attempts to place shared locks on the rows in the Accounts table, and, since shared locks are compatible, her attempt is successful.

In the following example, Mike updates all the rows in the Accounts table. He performs this operation within a transaction, which he does not end. Katy attempts to retrieve rows from the Accounts table.

**Mike**                                          **Katy**

```
BEGIN TRANSACTION

UPDATE accounts SET balance = 0
    WHERE account_no = 1000
```

```
                                      SELECT * FROM accounts
                                          WHERE account_no = 2000
```

```
*** OK ***
```

```
                                      *** wait ***
```

In this example, Mike is updating a row in the Accounts table, and so SQL Server takes out an exclusive (X) row lock. Katy's SELECT statement needs to search the table looking for rows that match her criteria (account_no = 2000). SQL Server decides that it is efficient to search using page locks. This is not unreasonable, since it knows it will be retrieving every row on every page. This is because, with no indexes present, a table scan is performed, and every page must be retrieved from the Accounts table.

As Katy scans through the table acquiring and releasing shared (S) page locks, she reaches the page on which Mike as taken an exclusive (X) lock on his row. As SQL Server will have also placed an Exclusive Intent (IX) lock on the page in which his row resides, Katy's shared (S) page lock will be blocked. A shared (S) lock is not compatible with an exclusive intent (IX) lock.

This example serves to illustrate a very important point: Transactions should be kept as short as possible. If they are not, then they could block another transaction for an unacceptable length of time.

If we were to issue an sp_lock at this point, we would see the following fragment of output relating to Mike and Katy's connections.

| SPID | dbid | ObjId | IndId | Type | Resource | Mode | Status |
|------|------|-------|-------|------|----------|------|--------|
| 53 | 7 | 965578478 | 0 | TAB | | IS | GRANT |
| 53 | 7 | 965578478 | 0 | PAG | 1:348 | S | WAIT |
| 54 | 7 | 965578478 | 0 | RID | 1:348:14 | X | GRANT |
| 54 | 7 | 965578478 | 0 | PAG | 1:348 | IX | GRANT |
| 54 | 7 | 965578478 | 0 | TAB | | IX | GRANT |

Her shared lock is blocked on the page. An sp_who issued at this point would show the following columns (with some deleted).

```
SPID    status    loginame    hostname      blk    dbname
----    ------    --------    --------      ---    ------
54      sleeping  mike        PEGASUS       0      BankingDB
53      sleeping  katy        PEGASUS       54     BankingDB
```

In the following example, Mike again updates all the rows in the Accounts table. Again, he performs this operation within a transaction, which he does not end. This time Katy attempts to delete the rows in the Accounts table.

**Mike**                                          **Katy**

```
BEGIN TRANSACTION

UPDATE accounts SET balance = 0   BEGIN TRANSACTION
    WHERE account_no = 1000

                                  DELETE FROM accounts
                                      WHERE account_no = 2000

*** OK ***

                                  *** wait ***
```

In this example, Katy attempts to place an update (U) lock on the rows in the Accounts table while searching for a row that meets her criteria for deletion. Since there are no indexes on the table, every row must be checked. Eventually Katy attempts to place an update (U) lock on the row Mike has just updated, which holds an exclusive (X) lock. An exclusive (X) lock is incompatible with all other locks, so Katy is blocked. If we were to issue an sp_lock at this point, we would see the following fragment of output relating to Mike and Katy's connections.

```
Spid    dbid    ObjId        IndId    Type    Resource    Mode    Status
----    ----    -----        -----    ----    --------    ----    ------
53      7       965578478    0        RID     1:348:14    U       WAIT
53      7       965578478    0        PAG     1:348       IU      GRANT
53      7       965578478    0        TAB                 IX      GRANT
54      7       965578478    0        TAB                 IX      GRANT
54      7       965578478    0        RID     1:348:14    X       GRANT
54      7       965578478    0        PAG     1:348       IX      GRANT
```

We can see Katy's blocked update (U) lock on row 1:348:14. This example is similar to the previous example with the exception that Katy is searching with update (U) locks on rows rather than shared (S) locks on pages.

In the following example Mike will again update rows in the Accounts table and Katy will retrieve them. This is the same as the second example except that now Katy will issue her SELECT statement first. We will use BEGIN TRANSACTION for both users.

**Mike**                                       **Katy**

```
                                               BEGIN TRANSACTION

                                               SELECT * FROM accounts
                                                   WHERE account_no = 2000
BEGIN TRANSACTION

UPDATE accounts SET balance = 0
    WHERE account_no = 1000

                                               *** OK ***

*** OK ***
```

In this example, Katy attempts to place shared locks in the Accounts table. She is successful, since Mike has not issued his update yet. Mike then issues his update, which is also successful. Mike's exclusive lock is not blocked by Katy's shared locks, because SQL Server will have released the shared locks when the SELECT statement completed. Katy's locks were gone before Mike issued his update. The fact that Katy issues her SELECT statement within a transaction is irrelevant.

Because SQL Server runs at the default transaction isolation level of READ COMMITTED, shared locks are not held until the end of the transaction but are released as soon as the row or page is read. This increases concurrency (and therefore performance), but this does mean that the read is not guaranteed to be repeatable, as we shall see shortly.

Let us now create some indexes on the Accounts table.

```
CREATE UNIQUE NONCLUSTERED INDEX NCI_AccountNo
    ON accounts (account_no)
```

Mike will now update rows in the Accounts table while Katy attempts to delete them. We will use a WHERE clause in order to choose different rows.

**Mike**                                       **Katy**

```
BEGIN TRANSACTION

UPDATE accounts SET balance = 0
    WHERE account_no = 1000
                                               BEGIN TRANSACTION

                                               DELETE FROM accounts
                                                   WHERE account_no = 2000

*** OK ***

                                               *** OK ***
```

Both users succeeded. This is because indexed access can now be used, and, consequently, row-level locks can be taken out just on the resources required. If we were to issue an sp_lock at this point, we would see the following fragment of output.

| Spid | dbid | ObjId | IndId | Type | Resource | Mode | Status |
|------|------|-------|-------|------|----------|------|--------|
| 53 | 7 | 965578478 | 0 | RID | 1:537:14 | X | GRANT |
| 53 | 7 | 965578478 | 2 | KEY | (ea003d68f923) | X | GRANT |
| 53 | 7 | 965578478 | 0 | PAG | 1:537 | IX | GRANT |
| 53 | 7 | 965578478 | 2 | PAG | 1:2612 | IX | GRANT |
| 53 | 7 | 965578478 | 0 | TAB | | IX | GRANT |
| 54 | 7 | 965578478 | 0 | TAB | | IX | GRANT |
| 54 | 7 | 965578478 | 0 | RID | 1:348:14 | X | GRANT |
| 54 | 7 | 965578478 | 0 | PAG | 1:348 | IX | GRANT |

We can see that all locks have been granted. Katy (SPID 53) holds exclusive locks on a row and an index entry. This is because her delete will not only remove the row but will also remove the index entry. Mike holds an exclusive lock on the row only, since he will not change the index entry in any way—he is updating the balance column, not the account_no column.

Suppose Mike and Katy insert rows into the Accounts table. Let us assume that there are no indexes on the Accounts table.

**Mike**                                    **Katy**

```
BEGIN TRANSACTION

INSERT INTO accounts VALUES
    (112501, 2000, 1000, 156.77,
'some notes')
```
```
                                            BEGIN TRANSACTION

                                            INSERT INTO accounts VALUES
                                                (112502, 2012, 987, 123.78,
                                            'some notes')
```

```
*** OK ***
```
```
                                            *** OK ***
```

There is no problem. Because SQL Server supports row-level locking, there is generally no blocking on insert. The same is true if indexes are present on the table, since the individual index entries will be locked with KEY locks.

# 6.5   Uncommitted data, repeatable reads, phantoms, and more

With our knowledge of locking protocols we can now investigate how SQL Server deals with the reading of uncommitted data, nonrepeatable reads, and phantoms.

## 6.5.1   Reading uncommitted data

Figure 6.1 illustrated the problems with reading uncommitted data. As should already be clear, SQL Server forbids this by virtue of the fact that any row that has been changed cannot be read by another user, since an exclusive lock will prevent the row from being retrieved until the write transaction ends.

SQL Server, however, allows the default behavior to be overridden. A query is allowed to read uncommitted data with the use of the READUNCOMMITTED keyword, introduced earlier in this chapter. For example, the following SELECT statement would read the row from the Accounts table regardless of whether another transaction had a row locked with an exclusive lock.

```
SELECT balance FROM accounts WITH (READUNCOMMITTED)
   WHERE account_no = 15000
```

The lock hint is recommended rather than NOLOCK, which is retained for backward compatibility.

Suppose Mike updates a row in the Accounts table. He performs this operation within a transaction, which he does not end. Katy attempts to retrieve rows from the titles table.

**Mike**                                        **Katy**

```
BEGIN TRANSACTION

UPDATE accounts SET balance = 500
   WHERE account_no = 5000
```

```
                                  SELECT balance FROM accounts
                                  WITH (READUNCOMMITTED)
                                     WHERE account_no = 5000
```

```
*** OK ***
```

```
                                  *** OK ***
```

In this example, Katy does not attempt to place a shared lock and she can read the row that Mike has updated. She will read a balance of 500. Mike may well ultimately choose to roll back his change, leaving Katy with incorrect balance information.

This behavior is the same as if the connection had set the transaction isolation level to READ UNCOMMITTED. However, the behavior would apply to all the transactions executed on that connection until another SET TRANSACTION changed the isolation level, or the statement overrode the isolation level for itself with a lock hint.

## 6.5.2    Nonrepeatable reads

In the case of a nonrepeatable read, a transaction is allowed to read a data item on more than one occasion and retrieve different values each time. This is shown in Figure 6.18. By default, SQL Server allows nonrepeatable reads. It is sometimes desirable, however, to guarantee repeatable reads—that is, each read of the same data item while in the same transaction returns the same value. The means of guaranteeing repeatable reads in SQL Server is by the use of the REPEATABLEREAD keyword.

If the REPEATABLEREAD keyword is used, when the page is read the first time a shared lock is taken out as usual. This then remains until the end of the transaction. This blocks any other transaction from changing the data item.

Mike                                      Katy

```
                                          BEGIN TRANSACTION

                                          SELECT balance FROM accounts
                                             WITH (REPEATABLEREAD)

                                                WHERE account_no  = 5000

                                          *** OK ***


BEGIN TRANSACTION

UPDATE accounts SET balance =
50.00
   WHERE account_no  = 5000

*** wait ***

                                          SELECT balance FROM accounts
                                             WITH (REPEATABLEREAD)

                                                WHERE account_no  = 5000

                                          *** OK ***
```

**Figure 6.18**
*Nonrepeatable*
*reads*

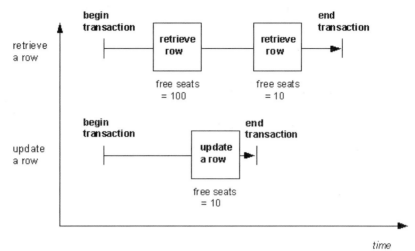

Now Mike is forced to wait. Katy's shared locks block Mike's exclusive lock, and when Katy repeats her read she will receive the same value—hence, the use of the REPEATABLEREAD keyword has provided repeatable reads. Again, this is at the expense of concurrency.

Setting the isolation level to REPEATABLE READ (or SERIALIZABLE) will also provide repeatable reads.

| **Mike** | **Katy** |
|---|---|
| | ```
SET TRANSACTION
    ISOLATION LEVEL REPEATABLE
READ

BEGIN TRANSACTION

SELECT balance FROM accounts

    WHERE account_no  = 5000

*** OK ***
``` |
| ```
BEGIN TRANSACTION

UPDATE accounts SET balance =
50.00
   WHERE account_no  = 5000

*** wait ***
``` | |
| | ```
SELECT balance FROM accounts

    WHERE account_no  = 5000

*** OK ***
``` |
```

Again, Mike is forced to wait. Katy's shared locks block Mike's exclusive lock, and when Katy repeats her read she will receive the same value. The use of the REPEATABLEREAD lock hint is not required, since the set transaction isolation level repeatable read statement has provided repeatable reads.

### 6.5.3   Phantoms

The phantom problem was illustrated in Figure 6.2. By default, SQL Server does not forbid phantoms, but the use of the SERIALIZABLE hint will prevent them, as the following examples show.

| Mike | Katy |
|------|------|
| BEGIN TRANSACTION | |
| SELECT SUM(balance) FROM accounts<br>   124961532.6600 | |
| *** OK *** | |
| | INSERT INTO accounts VALUES<br>   (112502, 2012, 987, 123.78,<br>'some notes') |
| | *** OK *** |
| SELECT SUM(balance) FROM accounts<br>   124961656.4400 | |
| *** OK *** | |

In the previous example, phantoms are allowed to occur. The two sums of the same list of values give different results. In the following example, Katy's transaction is blocked, and the phantom phenomenon is not allowed to occur.

| Mike | Katy |
|------|------|
| BEGIN TRANSACTION | |
| SELECT SUM(balance)<br>   FROM accounts WITH<br>(SERIALIZABLE)<br>     124961532.6600 | |
| *** OK *** | |
| | INSERT INTO accounts VALUES<br>   (112502, 2012, 987, 123.78,<br>'some notes') |
| | *** wait *** |

| Mike | Katy |
|------|------|

```
SELECT SUM(balance)
   FROM accounts WITH
(SERIALIZABLE)
      124961532.6600
```

```
*** OK ***
```

The use of the SERIALIZABLE keyword is not required if the set transaction isolation level serializable is used.

| Mike | Katy |
|------|------|

```
SET TRANSACTION
   ISOLATION LEVEL SERIALIZABLE
```

```
BEGIN TRANSACTION
```

```
SELECT SUM(balance) FROM accounts
   124961532.6600
```

```
*** OK ***
```

```
                              INSERT INTO accounts VALUES
                                 (112502, 2012, 987, 123.78,
                              'some notes')
```

```
                              *** wait ***
```

```
SELECT SUM(balance) FROM accounts
   124961532.6600
```

```
*** OK ***
```

Note that the SERIALIZABLE lock hint is recommended rather than HOLDLOCK, which is retained for backward compatibility.

To enforce serializability the lock manager must use some special techniques. In a sense, if we consider our previous example, the lock manager must lock something that does not exist! It cannot lock the row that Katy inserts, because it does not exist at the time of the first SELECT operation. Now SQL Server could lock the whole table if it wanted to, and, if there were no relevant indexes on the table, this is possibly what it might do. This would certainly stop phantoms.

However, if there are indexes on the table, then the SQL Server lock manager uses a technique known as key-range locking. A key-range lock works by covering the index rows and the ranges between those index rows. Any row insertion, update, or deletion within the range by another connection that requires a modification to the index causes the second connection to wait.

For example, suppose we execute the following query against the Branches table.

```
SELECT branch_no, branch_name FROM branches
    WHERE branch_name BETWEEN 'Ealing' AND 'Exton'
```

We find the following branch names.

```
branch_no      branch_name
---------      -----------
1081           Ealing
1021           Eden
1031           Edmonton
1051           Elton
1061           Epsom
1071           Eton
1041           Exton
```

We may want to ensure that we cannot insert a new branch between executions of this query. To do this we run the statement with the SERIALIZABLE lock hint.

```
BEGIN TRANSACTION

SELECT branch_no, branch_name FROM branches WITH
(SERIALIZABLE)
    WHERE branch_name BETWEEN 'Ealing' AND 'Exton'
    :
    :
```

If we investigate the locks acquired during this transaction, we find the following (simplified) output from sp_lock.

| SPID | dbid | ObjId | IndId | Type | Resource | Mode | Status |
|------|------|-------|-------|------|----------|------|--------|
| 57 | 7 | 0 | 0 | DB | S | GRANT | |
| 57 | 7 | 981578535 | 2 | KEY | (680236ce107b) | RangeS-S | GRANT |
| 57 | 7 | 981578535 | 0 | PAG | 1:102 | IS | GRANT |
| 57 | 7 | 981578535 | 0 | PAG | 1:103 | IS | GRANT |
| 57 | 7 | 981578535 | 0 | PAG | 1:100 | IS | GRANT |
| 57 | 7 | 981578535 | 2 | KEY | (b8020849fa4b) | RangeS-S | GRANT |
| 57 | 7 | 981578535 | 2 | KEY | (b802f9924eb9) | RangeS-S | GRANT |
| 57 | 7 | 981578535 | 2 | KEY | (b702b7e93c9b) | RangeS-S | GRANT |
| 57 | 7 | 981578535 | 2 | KEY | (b002a45d0732) | RangeS-S | GRANT |
| 57 | 7 | 981578535 | 2 | KEY | (b802194c7ac6) | RangeS-S | GRANT |
| 57 | 7 | 981578535 | 2 | KEY | (bb025ab1833d) | RangeS-S | GRANT |
| 57 | 7 | 981578535 | 2 | KEY | (6c028abdf769) | RangeS-S | GRANT |

There are eight key locks acquired, but if we look at the mode we can see RangeS-S. This tells us that these are key-range locks. Basically, a key-range lock covers a range of values starting with the key before the key that is locked.

In our example, the first branch name in our range is Ealing. The branch name preceding the start of our range is Ducklington. The key-range lock on the index entry Ealing would cover Ducklington to Ealing and this would then prevent a branch being inserted with the name Eaglesfield or Duddington, because those key values lie in between Ducklington and Ealing. In theory this is too restrictive, since these are not in our range. This said, key-range locking is pretty good and a lot better than locking the whole page or table; after all, we can successfully insert the local branch in Duchally!

Similarly, the branch name following the end of our range is Fairford. We would not be able to insert branches named Eyam or Failsworth, but we would be able to insert Fairlight.

---

**Note:** In fact, we would be able to insert branches named Ducklington or Fairford but, of course, only if the index on branch_name was not unique.

---

The number of RangeS-S locks held is $N + 1$, where $N$ is the number of rows that satisfy the query. In our case, seven rows satisfy the query, so eight RangeS-S locks are held.

The name of the key-range mode is in two parts. The RangeS part represents the lock mode protecting the range between two consecutive index entries, and the part after the "-" represents the lock mode protecting the index entry itself. So, RangeS-S means the range is locked in shared mode and the index entry itself is locked in shared mode. Another key range mode is RangeS-U. The difference between RangeS-S and RangeS-U is similar to the difference between shared (S) and update (U) locks, which has been discussed previously. RangeX-X is used when a key in a range is updated. Finally, RangeI-N is used as a probe to test ranges before inserting a key into an index.

## 6.5.4    More modified locking behavior

While showing examples of how the lock hints and transaction isolation levels can modify the default locking behavior, it is also worth looking at examples of some of the other lock hints introduced earlier in this chapter.

Let us look at TABLOCKX, for example. The TABLOCKX keyword forces an exclusive table lock to be taken on a table, which means that no other user, regardless of his or her Transact-SQL statement, can access rows in the table.

| Mike | Katy |
|------|------|
| `BEGIN TRANSACTION` | |
| `SELECT SUM(balance) FROM`<br>`   accounts WITH (TABLOCKX)` | |
| `*** OK ***` | `BEGIN TRANSACTION` |
| | `SELECT SUM(balance) FROM accounts` |
| | `*** wait ***` |

Even though the two transactions are only reading the table, Katy is forced to wait.

Another interesting lock hint is READPAST. Consider the case when we have no index on the Accounts table.

| Mike | Katy |
|------|------|
| `BEGIN TRANSACTION` | |
| `UPDATE accounts SET balance = 0`<br>`   WHERE account_no = 1000` | |
| | `SELECT * FROM accounts`<br>`   WHERE account_no = 2000` |
| `*** OK ***` | |
| | `*** wait ***` |

This was our second example. Katy is forced to wait because her sequential table scan hits Mike's locked row and cannot get past it With the READPAST lock hint Katy will skip the locked row and continue searching.

| Mike | Katy |
|------|------|
| `BEGIN TRANSACTION` | |
| `UPDATE accounts SET balance = 0`<br>`   WHERE account_no = 1000` | |
| | `SELECT * FROM accounts WITH`<br>`(READPAST)`<br>`   WHERE account_no = 2000` |
| `*** OK ***` | |
| | `*** OK ***` |

# 6.6   Application resource locks

SQL Server 2000 exposes an interface to its lock manager with the system stored procedure sp_getapplock and sp_releaseapplock. Suppose we execute sp_getapplock, as follows:

```
DECLARE @resultcode int
EXEC @resultcode = sp_getapplock @Resource = 'Store 5',
                                 @LockMode = 'Exclusive',
                                 @LockOwner = 'Session'
```

We are taking out an exclusive lock on a resource named Store 5. Although this resource may have no relationship to objects in the SQL Server database, we are able to use the SQL Server 2000 lock manager to manage our application lock protocol. Any other connection attempting to take out a lock on a resource named Store 5 will be forced to wait.

An application resource lock may be acquired with an owner of Transaction (the default) or Session. If the owner is Transaction the application resource lock behaves like any other lock acquired in an explicit transaction—it will disappear when the transaction completes with a commit or rollback. However, if the owner is Session, the application resource lock will be held until it is explicitly released with the system stored procedure sp_releaseapplock. For example:

```
DECLARE @resultcode int
EXEC @resultcode = sp_releaseapplock @Resource = 'Store 5',
                                     @LockOwner = 'Session'
```

This is very useful, since it means that an application resource lock may be acquired for a period of time that is independent of the individual SQL Server transactions that are being performed on the underlying data. In our example, we can take out an application resource lock on a resource known as Store 5. This stops any other user from working on Store 5. However, our inserts, updates, and deletes against the database data that represent Store 5 can be performed in very short transactions, so normal SQL Server resource locks do not become bottlenecks.

# 6.7   A summary of lock compatibility

We have seen a number of scenarios involving locks and it is worth now summarizing the compatibility between different locks. Locks can be shared (S), exclusive (X), or update (U). They can also be intent shared (IS), intent exclusive (IX), or intent update (IU). These interact as shown in Table 6.9.

**Table 6.9**   *Lock Compatibility*

| Mode of Requested Lock | Mode of Currently Granted Lock | | | | | |
|---|---|---|---|---|---|---|
|  | IS | S | U | IX | SIX | X |
| intent shared (IS) | ✓ | ✓ | ✓ | ✓ | ✓ | ✗ |
| shared (S) | ✓ | ✓ | ✓ | ✗ | ✗ | ✗ |
| update (U) | ✓ | ✓ | ✗ | ✗ | ✗ | ✗ |
| intent exclusive (IX) | ✓ | ✗ | ✗ | ✓ | ✗ | ✗ |
| shared with intent exclusive (SIX) | ✓ | ✗ | ✗ | ✗ | ✗ | ✗ |
| exclusive (X) | ✗ | ✗ | ✗ | ✗ | ✗ | ✗ |

We mentioned schema stability locks earlier in this chapter. They too have a compatibility. The schema stability lock (Sch-S) is compatible with all lock modes except the schema modification lock (Sch-M). The schema modification lock (Sch-M) is incompatible with all lock modes. The bulk update (BU) lock is compatible only with schema stability and other bulk update locks. This is how parallel BCP loads are possible.

This chapter has discussed locking. In a multiuser system that has not been designed with concurrency in mind, lock conflict is often the cause of performance degradation, and the effects of this are second only to the effects of bad query/index design.

# *Monitoring Performance*

## 7.1    Introduction

As we have mentioned on a number of occasions, physical database design is not a static, one-off process. Once the database has gone into production, the user requirements are likely to change. Even if they do not, the database data is likely to be volatile, and tables are likely to grow. Figure 7.1 shows a typical monitoring and tuning cycle.

In the previous chapters, we have seen a number of tools that can be used to monitor performance. There are also other tools that have hardly been mentioned. This chapter will look at the array of tools the database administrator can use to monitor SQL Server performance. These tools include the following:

- System stored procedures
- Windows 2000 System Monitor, Performance Logs, and Alerts
- SQL Profiler
- Index Tuning wizard
- Query Analyzer

## 7.2    System stored procedures

There are a number of system stored procedures that can assist in performance monitoring, including:

- `sp_lock`
- `sp_who`
- `sp_monitor`

**Figure 7.1**
*The monitoring
and tuning cycle*

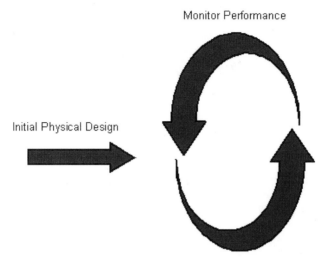

The system stored procedures sp_lock and sp_who provide information on locks, blocked connections, and much more. Both these system stored procedures were described in Chapter 6, so we will concentrate on sp_monitor here.

SQL Server keeps resource use information available through system statistical functions and sp_monitor then formats and displays this information. In fact, it displays the current values of resource use and the difference between these current values and the values last time sp_monitor was run.

```
EXEC sp_monitor

last_run                        current_run                    seconds
----------------------          ----------------------         -------
2000-08-17 18:33:25.263         2000-08-17 18:36:43.500        198

cpu_busy                io_busy         idle
--------------          -------         -----------
62(61)-30%              1(0)-0%         651(130)-65%

packets_received        packets_sent    packet_errors
----------------        ------------    -------------
110(66)                 109(66)         0(0)

total_read              total_write     total_errors    connections
-------------           -----------     ------------    -----------
432(217)                69(6)           0(0)            18(2)
```

The cpu_busy, io_busy, and idle values are measured in seconds. The value 62(61)-30% is decoded as 62 seconds of CPU use since SQL Server was started, and (61) is decoded as 61 seconds of CPU use since sp_monitor was last executed. The CPU has been busy 30 percent of the time since sp_monitor was last executed. Similarly, for total_write the value 69(6) can be decoded as 69 writes since SQL Server was started and (6) is decoded as six writes since sp_monitor was last executed.

These functions are available to be executed by Transact-SQL statements if the database administrator prefers his or her own format. The sp_monitor Transact-SQL definition can easily be examined using the SQL Enterprise Manager.

Many database administrators use their own home-grown stored procedures to interrogate the system tables. Taking this approach means that the output is customized to individual preference and is fine-tuned for the application.

# 7.3 System monitor, performance logs, and alerts

The System Monitor and Performance Logs and Alerts are provided with Windows 2000 to facilitate performance monitoring through a graphical interface. They can be accessed by selecting Administrative Tools from Start Menu/Programs and then Performance.

There are many objects that can be monitored for Windows 2000, such as the processor object and the memory object, and for each object various counters can be monitored. The processor object has counters such as %Processor Time.

There are special objects for SQL Server, including the following:

- SQLServer: Access Methods
- SQLServer: Backup Device
- SQLServer: Buffer Manager
- SQLServer: Buffer Partition
- SQLServer: Cache Manager
- SQLServer: Databases
- SQLServer: General Statistics
- SQLServer: Latches
- SQLServer: Locks

- SQLServer: Memory Manager

- SQLServer: Replication Agents

- SQLServer: Replication Dist.

- SQLServer: Replication Logreader

- SQLServer: Replication Merge

- SQLServer: Replication Snapshot

- SQLServer: SQL Statistics

- SQLServer: Use Settable Object

If multiple instances of SQL Server are being used, the object name is formed from the instance name. For example, the SQL Server instance named SQL2000_A will use object names such as MSSQL$SQL2000_A: Locks.

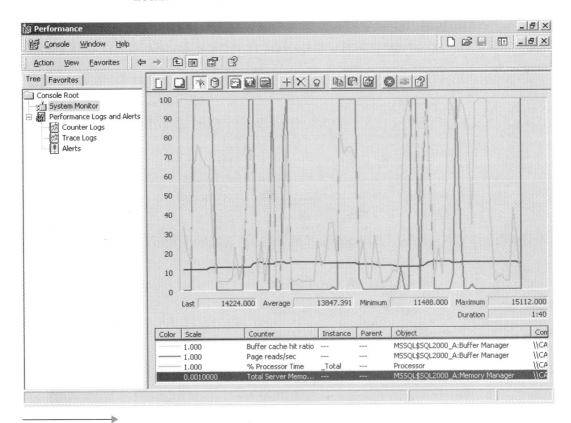

**Figure 7.2**   *The System Monitor chart display*

Ensuring that System Monitor is selected in the console pane, click the Add (+) button. This will display drop-down lists of objects and counters and the computers that can be monitored. Monitoring performance will affect performance, so running the System Monitor on a computer other than the server being monitored will reduce its impact on that server.

The SQLServer: Access Methods object has associated counters such as Page Splits/sec, the SQLServer: Buffer Manager object has associated counters such as Buffer cache hit ratio, the SQLServer: Databases object has associated counters such as Percentage Log Used, and the SQLServer: Locks object has associated counters such as Lock Requests/sec. A typical display, showing Buffer cache hit ratio and three other counters, is shown in Figure 7.2.

Many counters can be displayed simultaneously, and the display can be changed to a histogram or a report. A report display using SQLServer: Databases counters is shown in Figure 7.3.

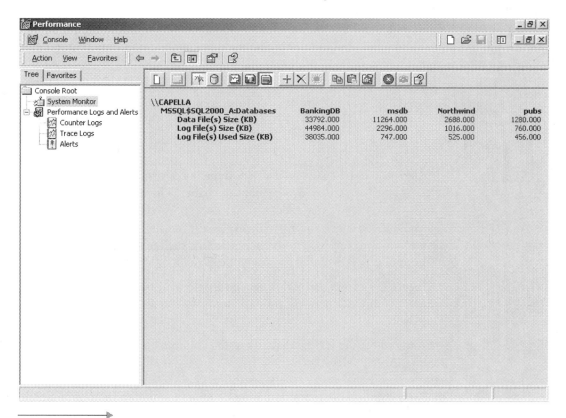

**Figure 7.3**   *The System Monitor report display*

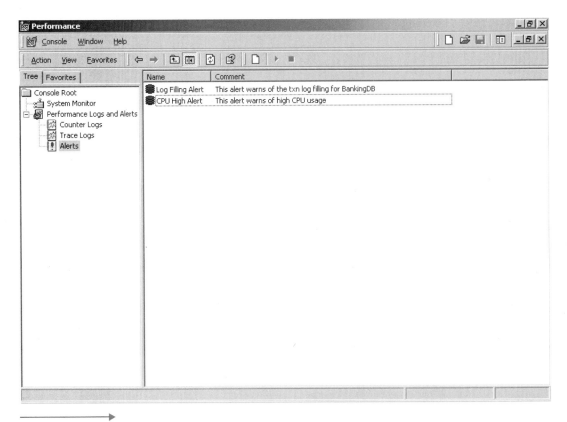

**Figure 7.4**    *The alert display*

Alerts can also be defined via Performance Logs and Alerts. This must be selected and expanded in the console pane. The Alerts folder is right mouse–clicked and New Alert Settings chosen. A counter is selected and a threshold value chosen over (or under) which the alert is signaled. When an alert is signaled, various actions can be taken, such as an entry being logged in the application event log, a program executed, or a network message sent.

Figure 7.4 shows the performance console with two alerts running, and Figure 7.5 shows a network message sent when one of the alerts has been exceeded.

A useful feature is the capability to log counters to a file and then monitor the logged values later. This facility is very useful, since it means that samples can be taken, say every few minutes, over a period of days. Performance monitoring over a long period of time makes it easier to spot trends and sustained bottlenecks. A log is set up via Performance Logs and Alerts.

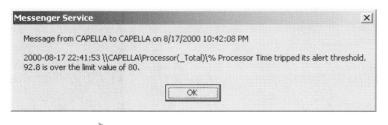

**Figure 7.5**   *A network message resulting from an alert*

This must be selected and expanded in the console pane. The Counter Logs folder is right mouse–clicked and New Log Settings chosen.

The System Monitor and Performance Logs and Alerts are key tools for monitoring SQL Server performance, and any SQL Server database administrator should familiarize himself or herself with these tools.

## 7.4   The SQL Profiler

The SQL Profiler is probably one of the most useful tools for performance investigation. It allows the database administrator to trace the events that are happening on a SQL Server. One or more traces are defined that are designed to capture a set of events. The trace definition will also specify what information is to be captured concerning the events and what filtering criteria are to be used. It may be that you only wish to capture events for a particular database or that exceed a minimum duration.

The information captured by the trace can be displayed graphically and can also be written to a file and/or a database table. This allows the traced data to be analyzed later.

### 7.4.1   What events can be traced?

There are many events that can be traced. These are known as event classes, and event classes that are related are grouped into event categories. For example, the Lock:Acquired and Lock:Timeout event classes are grouped together in the Locks event category. Some event classes are very useful and are often traced, while some event classes are more obscure. You will often find that the traces you wish to create will involve the same event classes. For this reason, as we shall see, templates can be created containing your common event classes that can then form the basis of your traces.

Table 7.1 lists the SQL Profiler event categories.

**Table 7.1**   *SQL Profiler Event Categories*

| Event Category | Definition |
|---|---|
| Cursors | Event classes concerned with cursors |
| Database | Event classes concerned with data and log file growth and shrinkage |
| Errors and Warnings | Event classes concerned with errors, warnings, and writes to error logs |
| Locks | Event classes concerned with locks |
| Objects | Event classes concerned with an object being opened, closed, created and deleted, as well as the execution of autostats |
| Performance | Event classes concerned with query plans and parallelism |
| Scans | Event classes concerned with table and index scans |
| Security Audit | Event classes concerned with security operations; logins/logouts; and server starts, stops, and pauses |
| Server | Event classes concerned with server memory changes |
| Sessions | Event classes concerned with connects and disconnects |
| Stored procedures | Event classes concerned with stored procedures |
| Transactions | Event classes concerned with transactions starting and stopping—includes MS DTC transactions and writes to the transaction log |
| TSQL | Event classes concerned with SQL statements and batches |
| User Configurable | Event classes concerned with user-defined events created with the stored procedure sp_trace_generateevent |

## 7.4.2   What information is collected?

Before looking at specific event classes, let us look at the information that can be collected about them and how they are filtered. The elements of information that can be collected are known as Data Columns and there are over 40 of them. Some data columns are not relevant for an event class. For example, the Reads data column is not relevant for the Lock:Aquired event class. Generally speaking, though, many data columns are relevant for most event classes.

Some data columns contain information whose definition remains the same regardless of the event class being traced. A data column such as CPU, which holds the amount of CPU time (in milliseconds) used by the event, always holds this value for any event that CPU is relevant for. On the other hand, data columns such as Binary Data, Integer Data, and TextData hold values that are dependent on the event class captured in the trace. For example, the Errorlog event class, which occurs when error events have been logged in the SQL Server error log, causes the Text data column to hold the text of the error message. On the other hand, the Missing Column Statistics event class, which occurs when column statistics that could be used by the query optimizer are not available, causes the Text data column to hold the list of the columns with missing statistics.

When defining a trace, the data columns can be grouped. Grouping overrides the default behavior in the graphical interface of the SQL Profiler by displaying events in the order that they occur. For example, grouping the events by Application Name groups together all the events for an application.

### 7.4.3   Filtering information

In order to reduce the volume of information traced, it can be filtered. Filtering can also reduce the impact of the trace on the server. You will need to take care, however, that what you choose to filter out of the trace is not a participant in the situation you are trying to observe. It may be that filtering out events whose duration is less than one second will help you see the wood for the trees, but if a SQL:StmtCompleted event takes just less than a second but is being executed thousands of times, it may be the culprit behind a performance problem.

Most, but not all, data columns can have filters defined for them. We can create a filter that includes applications with a filter that specifies LIKE MyProc% or NOT LIKE MS EM%. The % symbol represents a wildcard character, which can substitute for zero or more characters (just the same as LIKE in Transact-SQL). We might specify that we only wish to trace events with Duration greater than or equal to 1,000 or DatabaseID = 7.

### 7.4.4   Creating a SQL profiler trace

Now that we have introduced the basic concepts behind a SQL Profiler trace, we can create one. Let us start by creating a trace to capture events whose duration is greater than or equal to one-hundredth of a second. This will filter out very short-lived events. Let us assume we are interested in looking for rogue Transact-SQL statements.

Having launched the SQL Profiler from the Start menu, we will be faced with a fairly blank window, as shown in Figure 7.6.

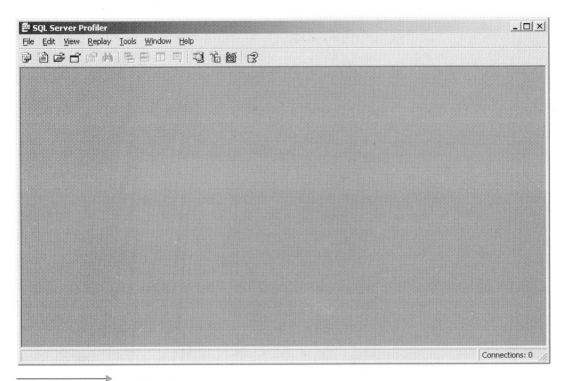

**Figure 7.6**    *The SQL Profiler initial window*

We can then select File → New → Trace, click on the New Trace button, or type CTRL+N. Having responded to the connection prompt with appropriate security credentials, the SQL Profiler displays the Trace Properties window, as shown in Figure 7.7.

First of all, the trace is named and the SQL Server or SQL Server instance that is to be traced selected. A trace template is then selected. A trace template contains a predefined set of event classes and data columns. These are used as a convenience when creating new traces. Their event classes and data columns can be added to or removed, and the resulting template can be saved under a new name if desired. Apart from Blank, there are 16 template names to choose from. We will choose the SQLServerProfilerStandard template, since this fits our needs quite well.

Next, we must specify where we are going to save trace information, if at all. The information will always be displayed in the SQL Profiler graphical interface, but we also have the choice of saving the information in a file or database table, or both. Microsoft suggests that saving data to a file is faster than saving data to a database table. Analyzing data in a table, though, is

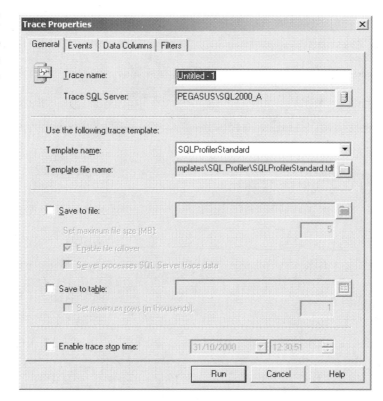

**Figure 7.7**
*The SQL Profiler*
*Trace Properties*
*window*

much easier. To have the best of both worlds save the trace information to a file and then afterwards open the trace file and save it as a trace table.

If Save to file is checked, the SQL Profiler will prompt for a location and filename. This SQL Profiler trace file will have an extension of .trc. A maximum file size (MB) may be optionally specified. A trace whose maximum file size has been specified, finishes saving trace information to the file after the maximum file size has been reached. Another option, Enable file rollover, may be checked if the Set maximum file size (MB) is checked. With this option set, when the original file reaches the maximum size, a second file is opened and trace data is written to it. When the second file reaches the maximum size, a third file is opened and so on. The SQL Profiler adopts a simple strategy for the filenames. It merely appends an integer to the original filename. The filename MyTrace.trc becomes MyTrace_1.trc, then MyTrace_2.trc, and so on.

The Server processes SQL Server trace data option may be checked if the server running the trace is to process the trace data rather than the client. Selecting this option may adversely affect the performance of the server

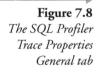

**Figure 7.8**
*The SQL Profiler*
*Trace Properties*
*General tab*

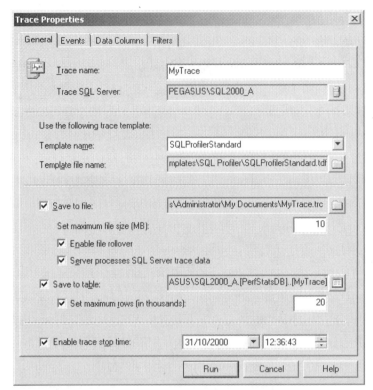

being traced, since it ensures that no events are skipped—even when the server is overloaded.

As well as, or instead of, capturing trace information to a file, it can also be captured in a table. The table can be present on any SQL Server, and, by default, it takes the name of the trace. The maximum number of rows to capture can be set, after which no more trace information is stored in the table.

Finally, a stop time can be set. Once this time is reached, the trace will stop and close itself. Figure 7.8 shows an example of the General tab of the SQL Profiler Trace Properties window.

Next, the event classes that are to be traced must be specified. The event classes are chosen in the Events tab of the SQL Profiler Trace Properties window. An example of this is shown in Figure 7.9.

The tab is split into two lists—Available event classes and Selected event classes. The event classes can be moved between the two lists with the Add >> and << Remove buttons. Depending on the template chosen in the Gen-

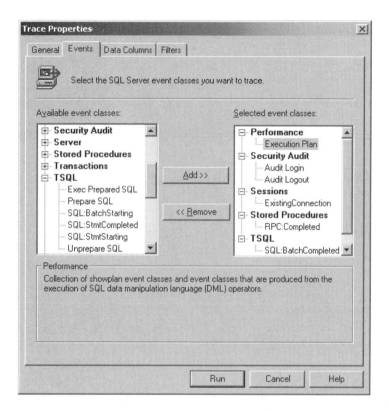

**Figure 7.9**
*The SQL Profiler Trace Properties Events tab*

eral tab, an assortment of event classes will already be present in the Selected event classes list. We will add another event class. We will select Execution Plan from the Performance event category so we can see the query execution plan for a traced query.

Now we will choose the information we need to capture about our event classes. The Data Columns tab of the SQL Profiler Trace Properties window is now selected. Again, as shown in Figure 7.10, we find two lists—Unselected Data and Selected Data. There are a number of selected data columns based on our template. Apart from changing the data column order with the Up and Down buttons, we have not changed the list of selected data columns.

Finally, we must specify our filter. Filters are specified using the Filters tab of the SQL Profiler Trace Properties window. An example of this is shown in Figure 7.11.

We have decided only to include events of duration greater or equal to one-hundredth of a second. Now all we have to do is click the run button and our trace will start.

**Figure 7.10**
*The SQL Profiler
trace properties
Data Columns tab*

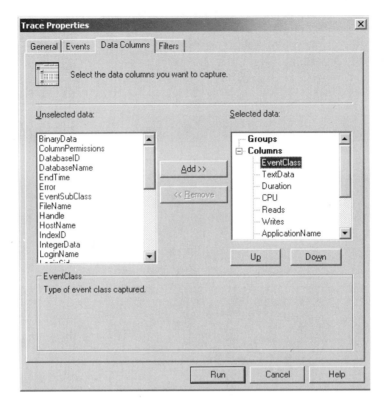

Our trace window is shown in Figure 7.12.

We can see the data columns arranged across the top of the window, and the traced events are displayed one after the other in time sequence. We can see a SQL:BatchCompleted event, and, when we highlight it, the TextData column is displayed in the lower pane, showing us the SQL statement that was executed. We can also see other columns, such as the duration of the statement and the amount of CPU it took (both in milliseconds). The number of logical reads can also be seen.

We also added the Execution Plan event class to this trace, and, if we select that event, we can see the execution plan simply described in the lower pane. This is shown in Figure 7.13.

In reality, as a database administrator, you will probably be so busy that sitting and watching a SQL Profiler trace graphically will not be the best use of your time. It is often more convenient and productive to analyze the trace output that you have captured into a table. For example, the trace we have just run was captured in the database table MyTrace in database Perf-StatsDB.

**Figure 7.11**
*The SQL Profiler*
*Trace Properties*
*Filters tab*

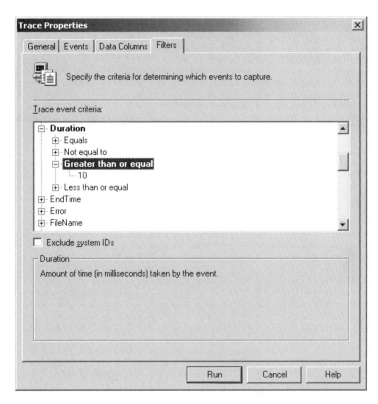

Suppose we execute the following query:

```
SELECT TextData, Duration, CPU FROM MyTrace where Duration >
1000
```

Sample output would be as follows:

```
TextData                                        Duration   CPU
------------                                    --------   -------
SELECT * FROM accounts WHERE balance = 100        1693       40
SELECT * FROM customers WHERE customer_no = 1000  1540       40
```

By using familiar Transact-SQL statements, the trace data can be analyzed to look for problem statements. As well as responding to problems, traces can be run on a regular basis and the trace data analyzed to monitor trends. The Transact-SQL functions AVG, MIN, and MAX are useful, and the data can be grouped by the first few characters of the TextData column so that the statements are distinguished.

```
Statement         AverageDuration  MaxDuration  AverageCPU  MaxCPU
---------         ---------------  -----------  ----------  ------
exec USP_CustBal  33.333333        40           33.333333   40
```

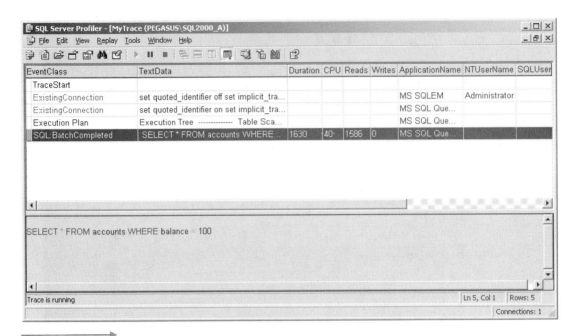

**Figure 7.12**    *SQL Profiler trace output*

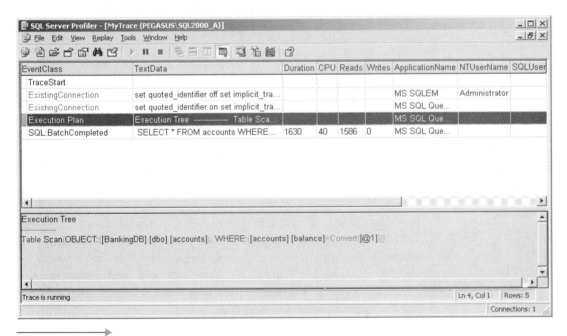

**Figure 7.13**    *SQL Profiler trace output with the execution plan event*

This line of output was generated by the following Transact-SQL statement.

```
SELECT
CAST(TextData AS CHAR(16)) AS Statement,
    AVG(Duration) AS AverageDuration,
    MAX(Duration) AS MaxDuration,
    AVG(CPU) AS AverageCPU,
    MAX(CPU) AS MaxCPU
    FROM MyTrace4
    WHERE Duration > 10
    GROUP BY CAST(TextData AS CHAR(16))
```

The GROUP BY uses as CAST of CHAR(16) to group only by the stored procedure name and not include any parameters. Of course, the other aggregate functions, such as COUNT, can be used. It is also useful to filter out the stored procedures and statements you are interested in with a LIKE operator in the WHERE clause.

## 7.4.5   Creating traces with stored procedures

As well as using the SQL Profiler graphical interface to create, modify, start, and stop traces, various system stored procedures can also be used. These are all documented, but the easiest way to create a script that utilizes them is to create a trace using the SQL Profiler graphical interface and then from the File menu in the graphical interface choose Script Trace. The trace can be scripted using the SQL Server 2000 system stored procedures or using the SQL Server 7.0 extended stored procedures for backward compatibility. The script produced can then be edited and executed using the query analyzer.

There are only a few system stored procedures that need to be used when creating and managing a trace. The ones we will use are as follows:

- ■ sp_trace_create
- ■ sp_trace_setevent
- ■ sp_trace_setfilter
- ■ sp_trace_setstatus

The system stored procedure sp_trace_create is typically run first to create the trace. Information such as the stop time, trace file name, maximum file size, and whether file rollover is performed can be specified. This system stored procedure returns an integer trace ID, which is subsequently used to identify the trace.

The system stored procedure sp_trace_setevent is used to add or remove an event or event column to a trace. The event ID and column ID pair is specified and is either turned on or off. The trace that is to be modified is identified through the trace ID.

The system stored procedure sp_trace_setfilter is used to specify filters. The trace that is to be modified is identified through the trace ID. A column is specified together with a value specifying whether it will be ANDed or ORed with other filter conditions. A value to represent a comparison operator, such as Greater Than, is specified for the column together with the value to be compared. Finally, the system stored procedure sp_trace_setstatus is used to stop and start the event. Again, the trace that is to be started or stopped is identified through the trace ID.

Here is a trace script generated by the SQL Profiler.

```
-- Create a Queue
DECLARE @rc int
DECLARE @TraceID INT
DECLARE @maxfilesize BIGINT
SET @maxfilesize = 5344176266805258
EXEC @rc = sp_trace_create @TraceID OUTPUT, 2, N'C:\
MyTrace.trc', @maxfilesize, NULL
IF (@rc != 0) GOTO error

-- Client side File and Table cannot be scripted

-- Set the events
DECLARE @on BIT
SET @on = 1
EXEC sp_trace_setevent @TraceID, 10, 1, @on
EXEC sp_trace_setevent @TraceID, 10, 6, @on
EXEC sp_trace_setevent @TraceID, 10, 9, @on
EXEC sp_trace_setevent @TraceID, 10, 10, @on
EXEC sp_trace_setevent @TraceID, 10, 11, @on
EXEC sp_trace_setevent @TraceID, 10, 12, @on
EXEC sp_trace_setevent @TraceID, 10, 13, @on
EXEC sp_trace_setevent @TraceID, 10, 14, @on
EXEC sp_trace_setevent @TraceID, 10, 16, @on
EXEC sp_trace_setevent @TraceID, 10, 17, @on
EXEC sp_trace_setevent @TraceID, 10, 18, @on
EXEC sp_trace_setevent @TraceID, 12, 1, @on
EXEC sp_trace_setevent @TraceID, 12, 6, @on
EXEC sp_trace_setevent @TraceID, 12, 9, @on
EXEC sp_trace_setevent @TraceID, 12, 10, @on
EXEC sp_trace_setevent @TraceID, 12, 11, @on
EXEC sp_trace_setevent @TraceID, 12, 12, @on
EXEC sp_trace_setevent @TraceID, 12, 13, @on
EXEC sp_trace_setevent @TraceID, 12, 14, @on
EXEC sp_trace_setevent @TraceID, 12, 16, @on
```

```
EXEC sp_trace_setevent @TraceID, 12, 17, @on
EXEC sp_trace_setevent @TraceID, 12, 18, @on
EXEC sp_trace_setevent @TraceID, 14, 1, @on
EXEC sp_trace_setevent @TraceID, 14, 6, @on
EXEC sp_trace_setevent @TraceID, 14, 9, @on
EXEC sp_trace_setevent @TraceID, 14, 10, @on
EXEC sp_trace_setevent @TraceID, 14, 11, @on
EXEC sp_trace_setevent @TraceID, 14, 12, @on
EXEC sp_trace_setevent @TraceID, 14, 13, @on
EXEC sp_trace_setevent @TraceID, 14, 14, @on
EXEC sp_trace_setevent @TraceID, 14, 16, @on
EXEC sp_trace_setevent @TraceID, 14, 17, @on
EXEC sp_trace_setevent @TraceID, 14, 18, @on
EXEC sp_trace_setevent @TraceID, 15, 1, @on
EXEC sp_trace_setevent @TraceID, 15, 6, @on
EXEC sp_trace_setevent @TraceID, 15, 9, @on
EXEC sp_trace_setevent @TraceID, 15, 10, @on
EXEC sp_trace_setevent @TraceID, 15, 11, @on
EXEC sp_trace_setevent @TraceID, 15, 12, @on
EXEC sp_trace_setevent @TraceID, 15, 13, @on
EXEC sp_trace_setevent @TraceID, 15, 14, @on
EXEC sp_trace_setevent @TraceID, 15, 16, @on
EXEC sp_trace_setevent @TraceID, 15, 17, @on
EXEC sp_trace_setevent @TraceID, 15, 18, @on
EXEC sp_trace_setevent @TraceID, 17, 1, @on
EXEC sp_trace_setevent @TraceID, 17, 6, @on
EXEC sp_trace_setevent @TraceID, 17, 9, @on
EXEC sp_trace_setevent @TraceID, 17, 10, @on
EXEC sp_trace_setevent @TraceID, 17, 11, @on
EXEC sp_trace_setevent @TraceID, 17, 12, @on
EXEC sp_trace_setevent @TraceID, 17, 13, @on
EXEC sp_trace_setevent @TraceID, 17, 14, @on
EXEC sp_trace_setevent @TraceID, 17, 16, @on
EXEC sp_trace_setevent @TraceID, 17, 17, @on
EXEC sp_trace_setevent @TraceID, 17, 18, @on


-- Set the Filters
DECLARE @intfilter INT
DECLARE @bigintfilter BIGINT

EXEC sp_trace_setfilter @TraceID, 10, 0, 7, N'SQL Server
Profiler%'
SET @intfilter = 100
EXEC sp_trace_setfilter @TraceID, 13, 0, 4, @intfilter

EXEC sp_trace_setfilter @TraceID, 35, 1, 6, N'BankingDB'
```

```
-- Set the trace status to start
EXEC sp_trace_setstatus @TraceID, 1

error:
GO
```

This trace creates a trace file, C:\MyTrace.trc, with file rollover (option value 2). There is no stop time (NULL) and the maximum file size possible is set.

Event IDs 10, 12, 14, 15, and 17 are set. These are RPC:Completed, SQL:BatchCompleted, Login, Logout, and ExistingConnection, respectively. The sp_trace_setevent stored procedure sets each required event ID and column ID pair. Therefore, we see examples such as the following:

```
EXEC sp_trace_setevent @TraceID, 12, 13, @on
```

This sets event ID 12 (SQL:BatchCompleted) with column ID 13 (Duration) on.

Filters are set to specify that the database must be BankingDB, the duration is greater than 100 milliseconds, and the application is not the SQL Profiler itself.

Finally, the trace is set to status value 1, which means start. A status value of 0 means stop. To subsequently view the trace file with the profiler, it is necessary to first stop the trace with status value 0 and then close it with status value 2.

To view information about current traces a useful function is ::fn_trace_getinfo. This takes a trace ID as an argument. Specifying NULL returns information for all existing traces. For example:

```
SELECT * FROM ::fn_trace_getinfo(NULL)
```

| traceid | property | value |
| --- | --- | --- |
| 1 | 1 | 2 |
| 1 | 2 | C:\DocumentsandSettings\Administrator\MyDocuments\MyTrace11.trc |
| 1 | 3 | 5344176266805258 |
| 1 | 4 | NULL |
| 1 | 5 | 1 |

The property value 1 is the trace option value to sp_trace_create. In our example, 2 means file rollover is enabled. The property value 2 is the trace file name, and 3 is the maximum file size. The property value 4 is the stop time, and 5 is the current trace status, as set in sp_trace_setstatus. In our example, no stop time is specified. The trace status 1 means the trace is started.

The SQL Profiler is a very powerful tool, and I would urge database administrators to familiarize themselves with it. It has many other capabilities, which we will not cover here, but it can, for example, replay a trace file, which is useful for regression and stress testing. It is also able to single step through a trace file, similar to a debugger. Also, a workload saved by the SQL Profiler can be used in the Index Tuning wizard, described next.

# 7.5   Index Tuning wizard

The Index Tuning wizard can make suggestions about the most effective indexes that could be created on a table (or view) based on a workload previously captured by the SQL Profiler. The Index Tuning wizard assumes that the workload is representative, and so the onus is on the database administrator to ensure that this is the case. I personally use the Index Tuning wizard to get a second opinion on my index design rather than as a tool that produces a definitive index design.

The Index Tuning wizard can be launched from the SQL Server Enterprise Manager, the SQL Profiler, or the Query Analyzer. It then presents the database administrator with a dialog, which enables him or her to specify information to it and to check an analysis of its design. It also enables the database administrator to implement the design immediately, later, or not at all.

Following the initial information window and the login window, the Index Tuning wizard displays a Select Server and Database window. This is shown in Figure 7.14.

As its name suggests, this allows the server and database that are to participate in the tuning to be selected. The Index Tuning wizard may be very resource intensive, so executing it on a server different from the production server is recommended.

The Select Server and Database window also allows other options to be specified. The option Keep all existing indexes is checked by default. The Index Tuning wizard will not suggest that any indexes should be removed if this option is selected. It will only suggest new indexes.

The Tuning Mode options Fast, Medium, and Thorough specify whether the Index Tuning wizard performs a more thorough analysis. This can often result in a more accurate index design but is at the expense of the time taken for the Index Tuning wizard to perform its analysis.

Finally, this window allows the database administrator to specify that the suggested design may incorporate indexed views.

**Figure 7.14**

*The Index Tuning wizard Select Server and Database window*

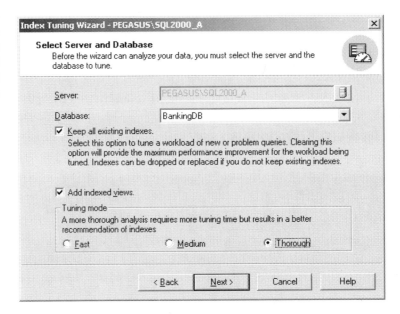

The next window to be displayed is the Specify Workload window. This is shown in Figure 7.15.

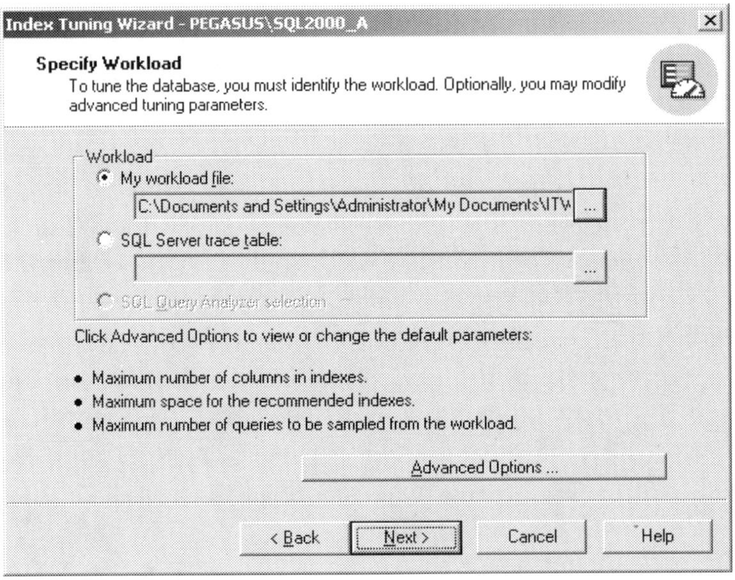

**Figure 7.15**

*The Index Tuning wizard Specify Workload window*

**Figure 7.16**

*The Index Tuning wizard Select Tables to Tune window*

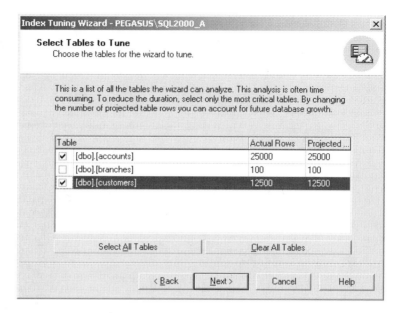

The database administrator can specify the location of a file or table that holds workload information previously traced by the SQL Profiler. The Query Analyzer option will be highlighted if the Index Tuning wizard was launched from the Query Analyzer.

The Advanced Options button can be mouse clicked. This then allows the database administrator to specify restrictions in terms of the space available for new indexes, the maximum columns per index, and the maximum number of queries to tune. Current space utilization is also reported.

The next window, shown in Figure 7.16, is the Select Tables to Tune window.

This enables the specification of the tables to tune. The fewer tables selected in this window, the less analysis the Index Tuning wizard will have to perform. The database administrator can also input a value for the projected number of rows for a table to allow for future growth.

Once you proceed past this window, the Index Tuning wizard starts to analyze the workload. After a period of time, it will display an Index Recommendations window similar to the one shown in Figure 7.17.

In our example, the Index Tuning wizard has recommended that three indexes, if created, should improve performance based on the workload. In fact, it predicts an 83 percent improvement.

**Figure 7.17**

*The Index Tuning wizard Index Recommendations window*

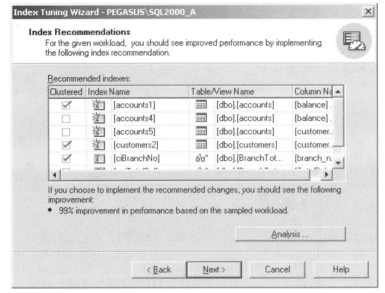

The indexes recommended are as follows:

- A clustered index on the Accounts table on columns balance (accounts1)

- A nonclustered index on the Accounts table on columns balance, account_no (accounts4)

- A nonclustered index on the Accounts table on column customer_no (accounts5)

- A clustered index on the Customers table on column customer_no (customers2)

To investigate this further we can mouse click the Analysis… button. This displays a set of reports. The first report is an Index Usage report based on the recommended configuration—that is, with the new indexes. This is shown in Figure 7.18.

This report shows the percentage of queries in the workload that would make use of the new index and the estimated size of the new index.

The next report shows index use based on the current configuration. We have no indexes at present on our base tables, so this is not a meaningful report for us. Next is the Table Analysis report. This is shown in Figure 7.19.

**Figure 7.18**
*The Index Tuning
wizard Index
Usage report*

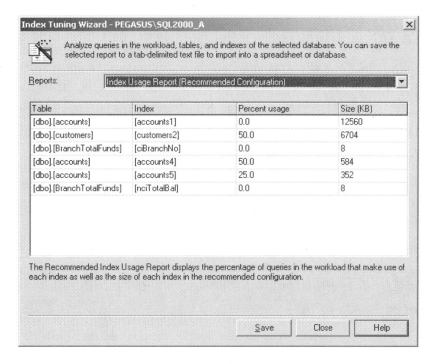

**Figure 7.19**
*The Index Tuning
wizard Table
Analysis report*

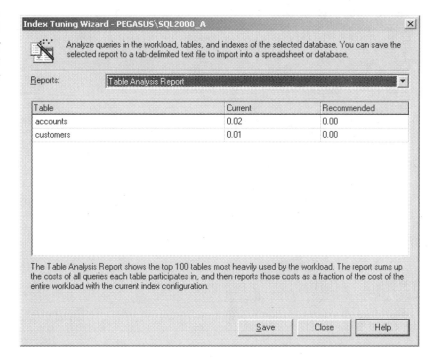

This report shows the top 100 tables most heavily used by the workload. In our example we only have two tables used by our workload. The report sums up the costs of all queries each table participates in, and then reports those costs as a fraction of the cost of the entire workload for the current and recommended index configuration.

The next report is the View – Table Relations report. This shows which tables are involved in building a particular indexed view. We have no new indexed views in the recommendation, so this is not a meaningful report.

The next report, perhaps the most useful, is the Query – Index Relations report for the recommended configuration. This shows us the queries in the workload and the indexes that the query is predicted to use. This is shown in Figure 7.20.

In our example, the queries in the workload are as listed in Table 7.2.

The first query, an inner join of the Accounts table and the Customers table on the customer_no column uses the indexes accounts5 and customers2. These are the indexes on the customer_no column in the Accounts table and the Customers table, respectively. This is reasonable, since this column is used in the join and the WHERE clause of the query.

**Figure 7.20**
*The Index Tuning wizard Table Analysis report*

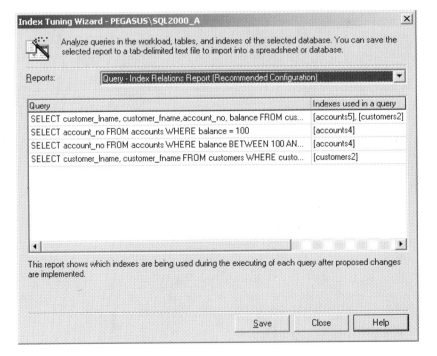

**Table 7.2**     *Workload Queries*

| Query | Indexes |
| --- | --- |
| SELECT customer_lname, customer_fname,account_no, balance FROM customers C INNER JOIN accounts A ON C.customer_no = A.customer_no WHERE C.customer_no = 1100 | [accounts5], [customers2] |
| SELECT account_no FROM accounts WHERE balance = 100 | [accounts4] |
| SELECT account_no FROM accounts WHERE balance BETWEEN 100 AND 200 | [accounts4] |
| SELECT customer_lname, customer_fname FROM customers WHERE customer_no = 1100 | [customers2] |

The second query, a simple selection from the Accounts table, uses the index accounts4. This is a covering index, since it contains both the balance and account_no columns. We discussed covering indexes in Chapter 3, and we know that these can be very efficient.

The third query is similar to the second query but uses a BETWEEN operator. This also uses the index accounts4. Since this is a covering index, this makes sense.

The fourth query, a simple selection from the Customers table, uses the index customers2. This makes sense, since this index supports the WHERE clause of the query, which uses the customer_no column.

The next report is the Query Cost report. This shows us the most expensive 100 queries in the workload and the performance improvement predicted for the recommended configuration. This is shown in Figure 7.21.

The next report is the Workload Analysis report. This report groups the queries into ten cost groups based on the most expensive query for the current and recommended configuration. In other words, the most expensive query defines the most expensive cost group. The other queries are then placed in the appropriate cost group. The distinction is also made between the type of query—SELECT, INSERT, UPADTE, and DELETE. This is shown in Figure 7.22.

The final report is the Tuning Summary report. This gives an overview of the analysis performed by the Index Tuning wizard and is shown in Figure 7.23.

Any of the above reports can be saved in a textual format.

Once we have studied the reports, we can mouse-click Close and we will return to the Index Recommendations window. If we now mouse-click

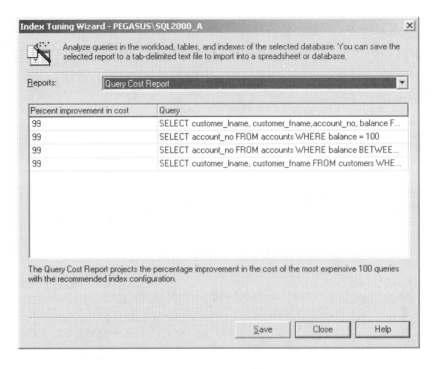

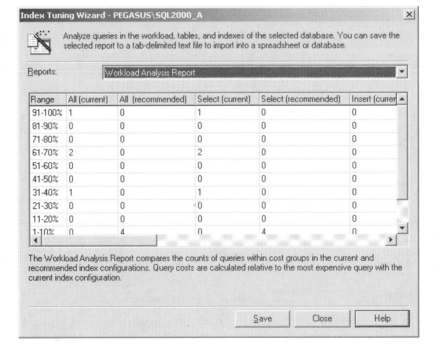

**Figure 7.23**

*The Index Tuning wizard Tuning Summary report*

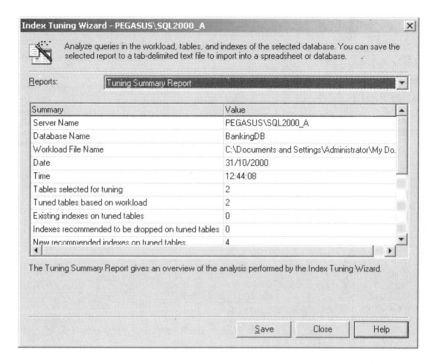

Next, the Schedule Index Update Job window is displayed. This gives the database administrator the opportunity to apply the recommended changes. This window is shown in Figure 7.24.

If we wish to apply the changes, they can be applied immediately or scheduled for a time and date in the future. Whether we apply the changes or not, a script file containing the changes may optionally be generated. In fact, after applying the recommendations, the queries used the indexes as predicted. Interestingly, the Index Tuning wizard created a clustered index on the Accounts table on the balance column. It predicted that it would not use this and it didn't!

It's worth a few words here regarding how the Index Tuning wizard approaches the problem of index analysis. It basically takes each query in the workload (unless the database administrator sets a limit on the number of queries to analyze) and designs single-column indexes. It then moves into a phase where it designs multicolumn indexes. All the time it is eliminating indexes that do not improve performance. As you can imagine, there are theoretically many indexes that could be defined for even a simple workload. Most importantly, the Index Tuning wizard works with the query optimizer. In fact, it creates pseudoindexes by defining an entry in the sysindexes system table but not actually creating the physical index structure.

**Figure 7.24**
*The Index Tuning
wizard Schedule
Index Update Job
window*

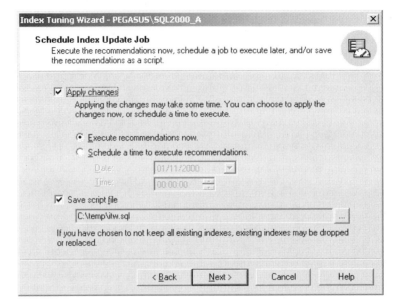

The query optimizer then may or may not use the index when the Index Tuning wizard asks it to optimize the workload. If you look at the indexes present on a table while using the Index Tuning wizard, you will see these indexes. They generally have names such as hind_965578478_2_1_4, where hind means hypothetical index.

To summarize, the Index Tuning wizard works with statistical information, just like the query optimizer, so it's not perfect—yet! It does a pretty good job though, and for many users of SQL Server with limited experience it will be a great asset. For database administrators with many years tuning experience it will be a useful assistant.

## 7.6   Query analyzer

We have already looked at the query analyzer extensively in previous chapters but in the context of viewing estimated query execution plans. There are other capabilities in the query analyzer that are worth a mention. These are Show Server Trace and Show Client Statistics.

These options can be selected from the Query menu or the Execute mode button.

The Show Server Trace option shows the impact on a query on the server. It displays the event classes with some data columns we are familiar

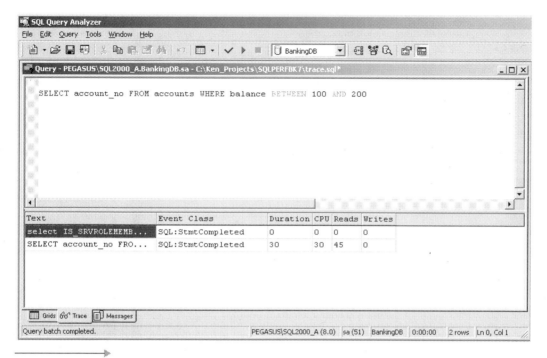

**Figure 7.25**    *The Query Analyzer Trace tab*

with from the SQL Profiler. An example of the Trace tab is shown in Figure 7.25.

At the time of writing, with a full release of SQL Server 2000, I still find that this server trace is giving me problems. Sometimes the query is not traced at all, and sometimes the statistics completely disagree with the SQL Profiler.

The Show Client Statistics option shows client-side information about the execution of the query. An example of the Statistics tab is shown in Figure 7.26.

The client statistics are grouped into three areas, as follows:

1.   Application Profile Statistics—containing information such as the number of SELECT statements

2.   Network Statistics—containing information such as the number of server roundtrips

3.   Time Statistics—containing information such as the cumulative client processing time

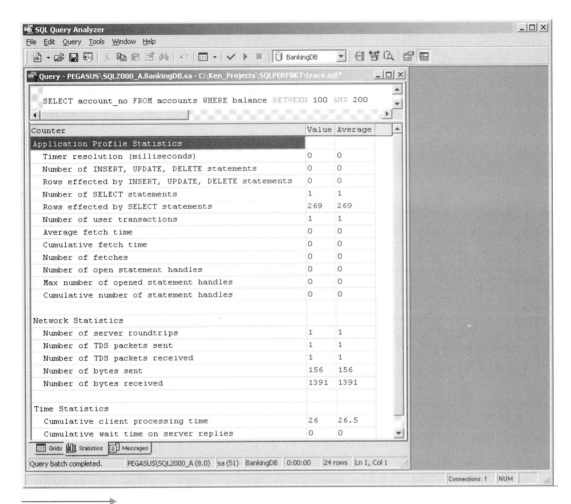

**Figure 7.26**   *The Query Analyzer Statistics tab*

We have looked at a number of monitoring tools in this chapter. I find the SQL Profiler particularly useful when hunting for poorly performing queries. The Query Analyzer is then really useful for analyzing the problem query to check on the query plan. As an initial step, the System Monitor is very useful for getting an overall feel for the system.

# *A Performance Tuning Checklist*

Here are a few thoughts that might be useful as an *aide-memoir* when you are considering performance issues.

## 8.1 System resource use

Establish trends. Use the System Monitor to monitor resources into a log file over a period of time. Get to know the normal ranges of the key counters.

When using the System Monitor interactively, run the graphical user interface on a machine other than the server being monitored to minimize the System Monitor impact.

Do not jump to conclusions. The performance problem may be caused by something you do not expect. It's easy to become convinced that something is causing a problem and to subconsciously twist the evidence to fit your theory.

Remember that system resource bottlenecks may be a symptom of something else. A classic is a disk I/O bottleneck caused by paging due to a memory shortage.

Ensure that you have sufficient page file space.

Remove services and protocols you are not using from the server. Do not run a screen saver on the server.

Try to run SQL Server on a dedicated server with no other applications running. It is much easier to optimize SQL Server in this situation. Try to avoid installing SQL Server on a Domain Controller (PDC).

Place tempdb on a fast device. Use the System Monitor or Alert subsystem to track it if it expands dynamically. By default it will be reset to its initial size on SQL Server restart. It may be beneficial to manually expand it to the size to which it frequently grows.

Use RAID for your database and transaction log. One approach would be to use a RAID 0 stripe set for the database and mirror it. Use a dedicated disk for the transaction log and mirror it. Hardware-based RAID is faster than software-based RAID.

Use a good quality network card. A 32-bit network card has better throughput that a 16-bit card.

# 8.2   Choosing efficient indexes

It is likely that for all but the smallest of tables the database designer will need to define indexes. These will probably consist of a clustered index with a number of nonclustered indexes. Queries benefit from lots of indexes, but too many indexes will degrade the performance of Transact-SQL statements that change data, such as INSERT, UPDATE, and DELETE, since all the indexes will need to be maintained, which requires CPU and disk I/O. Even worse, many indexes being updated are likely to increase lock contention.

Consider using a clustered index in the following situations.

- The physical ordering supports the range retrievals of important queries—that is, queries that use BETWEEN and LIKE.

- Few duplicate values mean that an equality test (=) returns few rows.

- Many duplicate values mean that an equality test (=) returns many rows.

- The clustered index key is used in the ORDER BY clause of critical queries.

- The clustered index supports the GROUP BY clause of critical queries.

- For a given row in the outer table of a join, there are few rows that match in the inner table. A clustered index on the join column in the inner table will be beneficial.

- For a given row in the outer table of a join, there are many rows that match in the inner table. A clustered index on the join column in the inner table will be beneficial.

Avoid using a clustered index on a volatile column—that is, a column that is updated frequently. This would result in the data row moving around the table repeatedly.

Consider using a nonclustered index in the following situations.

- Few duplicate values mean that an equality test (=) returns few rows.

- The nonclustered index key is used in the ORDER BY clause of critical queries.

- The nonclustered index supports the GROUP BY clause of critical queries.

- For a given row in the outer table of a join, there are few rows that match in the inner table. A clustered index on the join column in the inner table will be beneficial.

- A critical query can be efficiently covered.

Avoid using a nonclustered index when a query returns many rows, such as a range retrieval, or when there are many duplicate values returned by an equality test. Also, if, for a given row in the outer table of a join, there are many rows that match in the inner table, a nonclustered index on the join column in the inner table will not be beneficial.

Avoid using a nonclustered index on a volatile column. The result may not be as unfavorable as using a clustered index, since the data row will not move; however, the index will still have to be maintained.

Also, consider that many applications will require the selection of a row by the primary key. This is a single-row selection and therefore would normally benefit from the creation of an index containing the same columns as the primary key. Since it is not common to request ranges of primary keys, a nonclustered index is probably the best option. If a primary key constraint is created, the index will be automatically created; it is recommended that this be a nonclustered index.

Do not create an index on a column that is not very selective. An example of this would be a column that contained a status flag containing two or three values. It is unlikely that such an index would be used by the query optimizer.

Be careful when creating indexes with large keys. Fewer keys can be held in an index page, resulting in many index pages and deeper indexes. Take care with a large key in a clustered index. This will be used as the pointer in all the nonclustered indexes on the table.

Regularly check the levels of internal and external page fragmentation with DBCC SHOWCONTIG. Tidy up by rebuilding indexes. Make sure that there is enough free space in the database to rebuild clustered indexes. Another approach is to use the Database Maintenance Wizard.

Consider using DBCC INDEXDEFRAG on tables where there is little opportunity for maintenance—for example, a 24 × 7 system.

# 8.3   Helping the Query Optimizer

Ensure that the UPDATE STATISTICS statement (or sp_updatestats) is run regularly.

Set the database options to allow automatic statistics updating and creation.

Always test query performance on representative data. Data distributions that do not reflect live data in the production database and tables that are smaller than those in the production database could result in query plans different from those used when the application goes live.

Make sure that join conditions are not omitted. Always check in the case of joins involving many tables that $N$ tables must have a minimum of $N-1$ join conditions. Better still, use the ANSI SQL-92 join syntax.

Try to establish a standard so that program documentation includes an attached showplan output. This has a number of advantages. First, it forces the SQL developer to actually run the query and obtain a showplan output, which otherwise may not have happened. Second, it allows the person responsible for database performance to quickly scan the showplan output for obvious problems. Third, if the query performance suddenly degrades in the future, it is easy to check if the query optimizer has adopted a new query plan. Attaching statistics IO output is also recommended.

Use query optimizer hints only if it is absolutely necessary. Revisit them to check if the plan they force is still the most efficient.

Ensure that stored procedures are not being passed a range of parameters such that a highly inefficient query plan is being used for some values.

The use of order by, distinct, and union in a query results in SQL Server having to do more work. If they can be avoided, do so. It might be that you know there are no duplicates, or a sort may be performed elsewhere, perhaps on the client.

# 8.4   Avoiding lock contention

No matter how well the database is tuned to minimize disk I/O, all the database designer's efforts will be wasted if lock contention is prevalent in the database. SQL Server's locking mechanisms were described in Chapter

6, and we will now look at some general guidelines to follow when designing a database. Remember: In most multiuser systems that make changes to data some lock contention is unavoidable. The secret is to minimize both the locking hot spots and the length of time for which locks are held.

## 8.4.1   Rule 1: Keep transactions as short as possible

If a transaction has placed an exclusive lock on a row, page, or table, it will keep that lock until it ends with a commit or rollback. This is also true with shared locks if the REPEATABLE, SERIALIZABLE, or HOLDLOCK hints are used or the repeatable read or serializable isolation level is used. The longer the lock is held, the more chance there will be that the lock blocks another user. This has a cascade effect, with the blocked user blocking other users. Minimize the time the locks are held. Do not perform work inside a transaction that can be performed outside of it.

## 8.4.2   Rule 2: Do not hold locks across user interactions

This follows from Rule 1. Unless special considerations apply, you have a real need to, and you know what you are doing, this rule should be adhered to at all costs in a multiuser environment. What does this mean? It means that transactions should be completed before control is passed back to the user, and the transaction should not be active while the user is staring at the screen.

The reasons are obvious. The computer may process a transaction's workload in less than a second, and if that transaction then completes, another transaction will only have waited a fraction of a second before it acquired its locks. If, however, a transaction places locks on rows, pages, or tables, and the transaction is left active while the application returns to the user, it will keep its locks while the user stares at the screen, scratches his or her head, chats with a colleague, or, worse still, goes to lunch!

This could be, and usually is, disastrous for system throughput, and it is more commonplace that one might imagine! I know of instances where businesses have stopped trading for critical periods of time because a user went to lunch while a screen prompt sat on his or her workstation. This is not the user's fault. Blame resides with the application designer.

If it becomes necessary to retrieve data in the database for later modification, it is usually far better to choose an option where locks are not held on database objects and an optimistic locking approach is taken—that is, the retrieved rows are not locked and, when updates are eventually performed, a check is made in the application to see if another user has changed the data since the data was read. SQL Server provides the rowversion data type to assist the developer.

### 8.4.3   Rule 3: Try not to interleave updates and reads

If a transaction changes data when it starts, it will hold exclusive locks until it finishes. Try not to change data and then spend time reading data. If possible read the data, save all of the updates until the end of the transaction, and then issue them in one short burst. This minimizes the length of time that exclusive locks are held.

### 8.4.4   Rule 4: Help the query optimizer to choose indexed access

The query optimizer chooses whether a table scan or index is used to retrieve data. Judicious use of indexes and care when writing Transact-SQL statements will help the query optimizer to choose an indexed access. From a locking contention viewpoint this is preferable to a table scan, since a table scan may lock at the table or page level if shared locks are to be held.

### 8.4.5   Rule 5: Only lock as strictly as is necessary to meet your integrity requirements

Only hold shared locks if you require that the row you have read must not be changed by anyone else before your transaction ends.

### 8.4.6   Rule 6: Update tables in the same order throughout the application

If one program updates table A and then updates table B, and another program updates table B and then updates table A, there is potential for deadlock. It is better to settle on some simple application development standard, such as always updating tables in alphabetical order wherever possible.

In this case, the first program will cause the second program to wait cleanly and avoid the potential deadlock scenario.

### 8.4.7 Rule 7: Perform multiuser testing before the application goes live

This is often forgotten or left to the last minute. Whether you use sophisticated multiuser testing products or you persuade your users to stay late in the evening—do it!

We could add more rules but we have found that if the above seven are adhered to, lock contention should be minimized.

## 8.5 Database integrity

Integrity is the natural enemy of performance. The greater the data consistency requirements the more the impact on performance.

Do not implement your data integrity checks at the last minute before you go live. It does not matter whether you have used triggers or constraints, your performance is likely to suddenly drop.

Remember that if you do not index your foreign key column(s), you are likely to experience bad performance if you delete a row from the referenced table, since a table scan will probably be performed on the child table.

A table that has many foreign key constraints defined on it will have degraded insert performance, since many lookups will be performed against the referenced tables.

## 8.6 Database administration activities

Avoid running DBCC statements, UPDATE STATISTICS, and backups during periods of high user activity.

Consider creating a reporting database to off-load reporting and ad hoc querying. This could be kept up-to-date by replication or log shipping if required.

When loading a table using Data Transformation Services, the BULK INSERT statement, or BCP, be aware of the logging impact of the different SQL Server recovery models.

Put the file to be loaded on the same server as the database and data file to avoid network traffic.

Creating indexes will usually impact performance on the server, so it is better to perform index rebuilds during a quiet period.

Creating a nonclustered index has less impact than creating a clustered index. Clustered index creation uses an exclusive table lock, whereas nonclustered index creation uses a shared table lock.

Use the DROP_EXISTING clause of the CREATE INDEX statement when rebuilding a clustered index to minimize the impact on the nonclustered indexes on the table.

Consider using the SORT_IN_TEMPDB option on the CREATE INDEX statement to spread the I/O load across multiple disk drives.

When creating a database, try to set a realistic initial size to avoid multiple file extensions.

It might be better to switch variable-length datatypes to fixed-length datatypes in some cases to avoid the potential use of forwarding pointers.

Consider shrinking database files at periodic intervals.

## 8.7    Archiving data

This is a requirement that usually gets left until the last minute. The fact remains, however, that the larger a database gets, the more performance is likely to degrade. Many database administration tasks will also take longer: database backups, the update of statistics, DBCC checks, and index builds.

The reasons that performance degrades include the following.

- Larger tables mean longer table scans.

- Larger tables mean deeper indexes—hence, more I/O to reach the table row.

- Longer table scans and index traversals mean locks may be held longer.

Ensure that there is an archiving strategy in place before the database gets too large.

## 8.8    Read only report databases

If we consider a typical OLTP production system comprised of many users, we would probably expect to find that the system included many short transactions that updated the tables in the database in real time. In reality, we would also find that there was a requirement to run long and perhaps complex reports against portions of the database. The fast-response time requirements of the lightweight online transactions and the data-hungry requirements of the heavyweight report transactions often do not mix well. The report transactions can severely impact the response times of the online transactions in the production system and in the worst case may cause lock conflict.

One option is to separate these two different workloads into their own databases on their own server. This can never, in reality, be done completely, since there is usually no clear break between the requirements of the two systems. However, there is a case for off-loading as much reporting work as possible to another database. This also means that there will be a natural frozen cut-off point. If the report database is only updated overnight, then it will hold the close of day position all the following day, which can be a useful asset.

A separate report database can also have extra indexes added to it that would have been unacceptable in the production database for performance reasons.

Updating information in the report database could be a simple matter of restoring it from last night's backup of the OLTP database, or the replication capabilities present in SQL Server could be used. Whatever the method, consider the approach of separating the different workloads, since this can greatly help performance and increase flexibility.

If the report database is created from last night's backup, there are also two more added bonuses. First, the fact that you are restoring your backup means that you can feel confident that your backup/restore scripts work. Second, since the database is identical to the OLTP database, those lengthy DBCC integrity checks can be run on the report database instead of the OLTP database.

## 8.9 Denormalization

Before considering denormalization, a fully normalized database design should be your starting point. A fully normalized database design helps to avoid data redundancy and possible update anomalies, but it usually results in a design that requires tables to be joined frequently.

Possible approaches to denormalization include the duplication of columns from one or more tables into another to avoid the join in a critical query. For columns that are volatile, this can make updates more complex.

Another denormalization technique is to store derived data in the database. Transactions that change data can, usually by means of triggers, modify the derived data column. This can save query time, since the work has already been done calculating the derived column. The downside is that the modifying transactions have additional work to do.

# Bibliography

At the time of writing there are few SQL Server 2000 books available. I mention a couple of SQL Server 7.0 books that you may find useful.

*The SQL Server 7.0 Handbook*, Ken England and Nigel Stanley, Digital Press (1999), ISBN: 1-55558-201-X. (That's a self-plug!)

A great book that should grace any SQL Server database administrators/designers bookshelf is:

*Inside Microsoft SQL Server 7.0*, Ron Soukup and Kalen Delaney, Microsoft Press (1999), ISBN: 0-7356-0517-3.

I highly recommend that you check out Microsoft TechNet for performance articles on SQL Server. There is an excellent white paper on the query processor by Hal Berenson and Kalen Delaney.

Also check out the Microsoft Official Course—Optimizing Microsoft SQL Server 7.0 (course 2013). I do not know of any SQL Server 2000 performance course at the time of writing.

# Index

 Database

Technologies

---

## SQL Server 2000 Consulting and Training

### Consulting Services

⇒ Microsoft SQL Server Database Design

⇒ Microsoft SQL Server Performance and Tuning

⇒ Microsoft SQL Server Database Health Check

### Training Courses

⇒ Microsoft SQL Server 2000 Overview and Concepts (1 day)

⇒ Microsoft SQL Server 2000 Performance and Tuning (3 days)

⇒ Microsoft SQL Server 2000 Fast Track (Administration and Implementation) (5 days)

---

Database Technologies Limited
Nortons Farm
Kent Street,
Sedlescombe, Battle
East Sussex, United Kingdom
TN33 0SG

Voice: (44) 1424 870077
Fax:    (44) 1424 870101

Email: sales@database-tech.co.uk

www.database-tech.co.uk